This book offers a new approach to the study of the political history of the Renaissance: its analysis of government is embedded in the context of geography and social conflict. Instead of the usual institutional history, it examines the Florentine state from the mountainous periphery – a periphery both of geography and class – where Florence met its most strenuous opposition to territorial incorporation.

Yet, far from being acted upon, Florence's highlanders were instrumental in changing the attitudes of the Florentine ruling class. From a tributary state, which treated its surrounding as little more than a tax reservoir and buffer against foreign invaders, Florence began to see its own self-interest as intertwined with that of its region and the welfare of its rural subjects at the beginning of the fifteenth century. Contemporaries either remained silent or purposely obscured the reasons for this change, which related to widespread and successful peasant uprisings across the mountainous periphery of the Florentine state. This book therefore presents a crucial but hitherto unrecorded chapter of Renaissance history.

SAMUEL K. COHN JR is Professor of Medieval History, University of Glasgow. His many publications include *The Laboring Classes in Renaissance Florence* (1980), *Death and Property in Siena* (1988), which won the Marraro Prize of the American Historical Association, *The Cult of Remembrance and the Black Death* (1992), *Women in the Streets* (1996), and *The Black Death and the Transformation of the West* (1997, with David Herlihy).

CREATING THE FLORENTINE STATE

Peasants and Rebellion, 1348–1434

SAMUEL K. COHN, JR.

CAMBRIDGE
UNIVERSITY PRESS

PUBLISHED BY THE PRESS SYNDICATE OF THE UNIVERSITY OF CAMBRIDGE
The Pitt Building, Trumpington Street, Cambridge, United Kingdom

CAMBRIDGE UNIVERSITY PRESS
The Edinburgh Building, Cambridge CB2 2RU, UK http://www.cup.cam.ac.uk
40 West 20th Street, New York, NY 10011-4211, USA http://www.cup.org
10 Stamford Road, Oakleigh, Melbourne 3166, Australia

© Samuel K. Cohn Jr 1999

First published 1999

Printed in the United Kingdom at the University Press, Cambridge

Typeset in Monotype Baskerville 11/12½ [SE]

A catalogue record for this book is available from the British Library

Library of Congress cataloguing in publication data

Cohn, Samuel Kline.
Creating the Florentine State: Peasants and Rebellion, 1348-1434
Samuel K. Cohn Jr.
p. cm.
Includes bibliographical references and index.
ISBN 0 521 66337 7 (hardbound)
1. Peasant uprisings – Italy – Florence Region – History.   2. Social
conflict – Italy – Florence Region – History.   3. Social change – Italy –
Florence Region – History.   4. Florence (Italy) – Politics and
government – To 1421.   5. Florence (Italy) – Politics and
government – 1421-1737.   I. Title.
HD1536.I8C576   1999
945'.5105'08863 – dc21   99-20440   CIP

ISBN 0 521 66337 7 hardback

To the memory of Ralph Miliband,
colleague and friend

The best kind of fortress, however, is not to be hated by the people. Because even though you have fortresses, if the people hate you they will not save you, for there is never a shortage of outsiders ready to help the people when they take up arms.

Niccolò Machiavelli, *The Prince*, bk 20, pp. 111–12

Contents

Illustrations

Tables

Acknowledgments

A book long in the making incurs numerous debts to institutions, librarians and archivists, friends, and colleagues. Without their support this book from conception to press would have been impossible to write. Over the period of its gestation I have been a part of several institutions. It began while I was teaching at Brandeis University and a pilot study was funded with a summer grant from Brandeis's Mazer Foundation. I carried out the major portion of research as a Fellow of the Villa I Tatti in Florence in 1993–4, and wish to thank the staff and fellows for their assistance and intellectual exchange. During that twelve-month period I also belonged to another community – a group of archivists and researchers who normally assembled at 9 A.M. at the Archivio di Stato, Florence. I remember fondly discussions, lunches, and coffee breaks that year with Giovanni Ciappelli, Carlo Corsini, Lorenzo Fabbri, Richard Goldthwaite, Henry Knox, Lynn Laufenberg, Andrea Osanno, John Padgett, Sara Sensoli, Franek Sznura, Raffaella Zaccharia, and many others.

I spent the following academic year as a John Simon Guggenheim Fellow in London, where I put the mountains book on the back burner to write another on women in the Renaissance. I was not able to return to the mountains until January 1997, while commuting between London and Glasgow. Much of the first draft of this mountains book was written at 29 Edis Street, London, where I enjoyed hospitality and intellectual stimulation from Marion Kozak and her household.

I wrote the book's second, third . . . nth drafts within the walls of the Department of Medieval History at the University of Glasgow. Here I benefited from the assistance of colleagues, especially from Graeme Small, Michael Kennedy, Stuart Airlie, and Martin MacGregor, who read parts of the manuscript. I also gained insights from discussions with friends in Renaissance studies – Chris Black, Alison Brown, John Larner, Amanda Lillie, Lauro Martines, Nicolai Rubinstein, and others. I wish to thank the University of Glasgow for study leave to finish this book and to "a small research grant" from the British Academy to return to the Florentine archives for several short trips in 1997 and 1998. I was also assisted by Kylie Seretis in the production of maps.

Finally, I thank Rudolph Binion, William Bowsky, Anthony Molho, Lauro Martines, and Genevieve Warwick. All went well beyond the call of any duty in their patient, careful, and critical readings of various versions of this text.

Note on citations, dates, and measures

I have translated all names in the text into Italian but have left them in the original Latin or Italian in the notes. I used the modern calendar in the text but have left the dates of documents in the notes as in the originals. The year in Florence began on March 25. The measures *stiori, staii,* and *braccia* appear in the text. A *stioro* was equivalent to about 0.313 acres; a *staio* to 0.73 bushels; and a *braccio* to 0.613 meters or about 2.1 feet. See Herlihy, *Medieval and Renaissance Pistoia,* p. xix. Further, s = *soldi* or shillings and d = *denari* or pennies. There 12 *denari* per *soldo* and 20 *soldi* per *lira* or pound.

REFERENCES TO NOTARIES IN THE ARCHIVIO DI STATO, FLORENCE (ASF) CITED IN THE TEXT

Old archival references	New numbers
A 779	792
A 845	858
A 849	862
B 302	1316
B 178	1502
F 30	6599
G 507	9844
G 606	10136
G 685	10423
I 18	11059
M 352–M360	13521–13534
P 91	16091
P 146	16255
P 375	16870

Introduction

The transition from the late-medieval to the Renaissance state[1] in Florence has had a long and venerable historiography, spanning the fields of political thought and consciousness to public finance. For Francesco Guicciardini (1483–1540), after a brief mention of the revolt of the Ciompi, it was Cosimo de' Medici's return from exile and rise to power in 1434 that began the "rivoluzione dello stato"[2] and where his *Storia fiorentina* truly begins. The Medici's importance in the rise of a new Florentine state held sway until the Second World War,[3] when historians began to push its critical moment earlier, even as far back as the creation of its funded state debt, the *Monte*, in 1345.[4] Most historians now mark the rise of a new state sometime between the government of the Albizzi's rise to power in 1393 and 1411.[5] More than Cosimo il Vecchio, Maso

---

[1] For a useful transhistorical definition of the state, see Charles Tilly, *Coercion, Capital, and European States, AD 990–1992* (Cambridge, Mass., 1990), pp. 1–2: "Let us define states as coercion-wielding organizations that are distinct from households and kinship groups and exercise clear priority in some respects over all other organizations within substantial territories. The term therefore includes city-states, empires, theocracies, and many other forms of government, but excludes tribes, lineages, firms, and churches as such." Also, see Ralph Miliband, *The State in Capitalist Society* (London, 1969), esp. pp. 46–51.

[2] Francesco Guicciardini, *Opere inedite di Francesco Guicciardini: Storia Fiorentina*, ed. by Piero and Luigi Guicciardini (Florence, 1859), p. 6.

[3] See François Tommy Perrens' monumental three volumes, *Histoire de Florence depuis la domination des Médicis jusqu'à la chute de la république (1434–1531)* (Paris, 1888), I, p. 17: "A Florence, sous Cosimo, comme à Rome, sous Auguste, la République a bel et bien cessé d'exister, quoique ces deux patients ambitieux affectent d'en respecter les formes, en briguent et en obtiennent les charges." For a work expressing much the same sentiment written on the eve of the Second World War, see Kurt S. Gutkind, *Cosimo de' Medici, il Vecchio* (Florence, 1940).

[4] See Marvin Becker, *Florence in Transition*, I: *The Decline of the Commune*; II: *Studies in the Rise of the Territorial State* (Baltimore, 1967–68); "The Florentine Territorial State and Civic Humanism in the early Renaissance," in *Florentine Studies*, ed. by Nicolai Rubinstein (London, 1968), pp. 109–39; Philip J. Jones, *The Italian City-State: From Commune to Signoria* (Oxford, 1997), ch. 4; and Anthony Molho, *Marriage Alliance in Late Medieval Florence* (Cambridge, Mass., 1994), pp. 237–50, in which a new sense of the ruling class as a social caste originates with the Black Death.

[5] See Hans Baron, *The Crisis of the Early Renaissance*, 2 vols. (Princeton, 1955; revised edn., 1966); Molho, "The Florentine Oligarchy and the *Balìa* of the Late Trecento," *Speculum*, 43 (1968):

degli Albizzi is seen as the innovator of what historians have called the Renaissance, territorial, regional, or even the modern state.[6] Recent historians of the Medici also now see this dynasty's rise to power more as continuity than change, whether the subject is the mechanisms of the Florentine constitution[7] or the social networks of political patron-

---

Footnote 5 (*cont.*)
23–51; "Politics and the Ruling Class in Early Renaissance Florence," *Nuova Rivista Storica*, 52 (1968): 401–20; Gene Brucker, *The Civic World of Early Renaissance Florence* (Princeton, 1977), pp. 3–13; "Humanism, Politics and the Social Order in Early Renaissance Florence," in *Florence and Venice: Comparisons and Relations*, I: *Quattrocento*, ed. by Sergio Bertelli, Rubinstein, and Craig Hugh Smyth (Florence, 1979), p. 11; Riccardo Fubini, "Italia quattrocentesca: un'introduzione," in *Italia Quattrocentesca: Politica e diplomazia nell'età di Lorenzo il Magnifico* (Milan, 1994), pp. 19–39; "Il regime di Cosimo de' Medici al suo avvento al potere," in *Italia Quattrocentesca*, pp. 62–86; "From Social to Political Representation in Renaissance Florence," in *City States in Classical Antiquity and Medieval Italy*, ed. by A. Molho, K. Raaflaub, and J. Emlen (Stuttgart, 1991), p. 233; Giorgio Chittolini, "Ricerche sull'ordinamento territoriale del dominio fiorentino agli inizi del secolo XV," in *La formazione dello stato regionale e le istituzioni del contado: secoli XIV e XV* (Turin, 1978); Andrea Zorzi, *L'Amministrazione della giustizia penale nella Repubblica fiorentina: Aspetti e problemi* (Florence, 1988). Still others have marked the change with the return of the oligarchy in 1382: Lauro Martines, *Lawyers and Statecraft in Renaissance Florence* (Princeton, 1968), esp. pp. 464–76; John Najemy, *Corporatism and Consensus in Florentine Electoral Politics, 1280–1400* (Chapel Hill, N.C., 1982), ch. 8 and epilogue; "Guild Republicanism in Trecento Florence: The Successes and Ultimate Failure of Corporate Politics," *American Historical Review*, 84 (1979): 53–71; however, in "The Dialogue of Power in Florentine Politics," in *City States*, pp. 269–88, his critical divide is 1400.

[6] See especially Fubini, "Italia quattrocentesca," p. 3; "Il regime di Cosimo de' Medici," pp. 67 and 74; and "Diplomazia e governo in Firenze all'avvento dei reggimenti oligarchici," in *Quattrocento fiorentino: Politica, diplomazia, cultura* (Pisa, 1996), p. 13. Looking across Florence's bureaucratic history from the fifteenth through the eighteenth century, R. Burr Litchfield, *Emergence of a Bureaucracy: The Florentine Patricians 1530–1790* (Princeton, 1986), p. 4, has claimed that the changes in Florentine bureaucracy of the fourteenth and fifteenth centuries pale by comparison with those wrought by the less-studied Medici princes. But others, like Antonio Anzilotti, "Il tramonto dello stato cittadino," *Archivio Storico Italiano* [hereafter *ASI*], 82 (1924): 72–105, have been less convinced about Medicean absolutism and modernity in the early-modern period. Marino Berengo, "Il Cinquecento," in *La storiografia italiana negli ultimi vent'anni* (Milan, 1970), pp. 485–518 has argued that the particularist nodes of power in subject cities and rural provinces resisted the centrifugal forces of the princes. And Elena Fasano Guarini, "Gli Stati dell'Italia centro-settentrionale tra Quattro e Cinquecento: continuità e trasformazioni," *Società e Storia*, 6 (1983): 617–39 and "Centro e periferia accentramento particolarismi: dicotomia o sostanza degli Stati in età moderna?" in *Origini dello Stato: Processi di formazione statale in Italia fra medioevo ed età moderna*, ed. by Chittolini, Molho, and Pierangelo Schiera (Bologna, 1994), pp. 147–76, has stressed the "dualism" between central and local power.

Finally, Jones, "Communes and Despots: The City-State in Late-Medieval Italy," *Transactions of the Royal Historical Society*, 5th ser. 15 (1965), pp. 92 and 95, has gone a step further, claiming that "the 'Renaissance state' is a fiction to be banned from books." Yet he acknowledges the change in Italian political geography, from a myriad of small city-states of the early fourteenth century to five or six regional power blocks of the fifteenth century, dating this change even earlier than do others. For Jones ("Communes and Despots," p. 71, and especially *The Italian City-State*, ch. 4) it occurred in the late Middle Ages with the "political revolution" from Commune to *Signoria*.

[7] See, most importantly, Rubinstein, *The Government of Florence under the Medici (1434 to 1494)* (Oxford, 1966); and more recently Rubinstein, "Cosimo *optimus civis*," in *Cosimo "il Vecchio" de' Medici, 1389–1464. Essays in Commemoration of the 600th Anniversary of Cosimo de' Medici's Birth*, ed. by Francis Ames-Lewis (Oxford, 1992), pp. 5–20 esp. pp. 13–14.

age.[8] This shift in the timing and meaning of the Florentine territorial state derives from a wide array of sources bearing on the institutions and ideology of early Renaissance Florence – fiscality and the funded debt, law and the legal profession, diplomacy, electoral procedures, bureaucracy, the Florentine constitution, historiography, and the language of ruling-class debate.

This book, too, analyzes changes in Florence's governance of its region but approaches the subject differently from traditional or more recent political histories. Instead of political tracts, historiography, diplomacy, foreign wars, statutes, or constitutional reforms, my research began with the demography of the countryside. Because of the political decisions of the Florentine elite not to tax themselves but to lay the burden on their rural communities, it is possible to know more about certain aspects of society and economy of Florence's surrounding countryside (its traditional *contado*[9]) than of the city itself, at least until the famous tax reform and survey, the *catasto* of 1427.

Second, I have not studied the development of the Florentine regional state from the usual perspective of institutional history and, in particular, of those institutions at the center, the city of Florence. My view

[8] D. V. Kent, *The Rise of the Medici: Faction in Florence 1426–1434* (Oxford, 1978). Although Kent and Rubinstein emphasize continuity, Fubini, "Il regime di Cosimo de' Medici," pp. 63–5, has claimed that they have seen too much innovation in the Medicean techniques of rule and reforms of republican government.

[9] As Guidubaldo Guidi, *Il Governo della città-repubblica di Firenze del primo Quattrocento*, I. *Politica e diritto pubblico* (Florence, 1981), p. 24, has said: "The distinction of the territorial state into its *contado* and district was never clearly defined and varied over time," but a working definition needs to be offered. Although the *contado* corresponds mostly with the Carolingian county, the *contado*/district distinction begins largely with Florence's post-Black Death territorial expansion and the incorporation of previously independent city-states into its dominion. For the most part, these new acquisitions formed the *districtus* and were able to preserve many of their ancient prerogatives of administration, justice, and fiscality. Like the city of Florence, they did not owe direct taxes and were not surveyed by the *estimo*, but instead had to pay a fixed yearly military tax called the *taxa lancearum*, or tax on lances.

However, not all these acquisitions were incorporated into the district. In 1351 Florence acquired both Prato and Pistoia; Pistoia's administrative and fiscal structures were left largely intact, while Prato and its forty-five rural *ville* were absorbed into Florence's *contado* and were immediately surveyed in Florence's first *estimo* after the Black Death. Other new areas were brought into the Florentine *contado* instead of the district, as with the nineteen mountain communes rebaptized as the vicariate of the Alpi Fiorentine after Florence's defeat of the Ubaldini lords in 1373. The basic distinction between the *contado* and district was fiscal – whether a subject community was charged direct taxes by the *estimo* or subject to a fixed sum called the *taxa lancearum*. There were, however, exceptions such as the territories of the Valdinievole and Ariane, hived off from Lucca's territory and which formed Florence's first administrative *vicariatus* in the 1330s. The documents continue to describe these zones as part of the *districtus*, but they were subject to the Florentine *estimo*; see Provvisione registri [hereafter Provv. reg.], 40, 156v–7r, 1353.x.16: "Extimum comunium vallisnebule." Also see Giovanni Francesco Paganini dal Ventura, *Della Decima e di varie altre gravezze imposte dal comune di Firenze* (Lisbon, 1765), I, pp. 1–2.

comes from the mountainous periphery of the Florentine state – a periphery both of geography and class – where Florence met its most strenuous opposition to territorial incorporation. Yet, far from being merely acted upon, these highlanders, I argue, were instrumental in changing the fiscal and administrative strategies of the Florentine oligarchy in the opening years of the fifteenth century. These changes are revealed in an analysis of Florence's fiscal records as well as in its concrete policies that redefined welfare toward its rural subjects. From viewing the *contado* merely as a reservoir of tax revenue and a buffer against foreign invaders, Florence's elites by the turn of the fifteenth century began to see their own fate as more deeply intertwined with the demographic and economic health of the hinterland. One consequence of this change of heart and purse strings was an increase in the wealth of the surrounding countryside by more than three times and that of Florence's previously most taxed and impoverished subjects, its highlanders, by sevenfold from 1402 to 1460.

Why did the ruling class change its mind? Despite the vast literature on the origins of civic humanism in Florence and the corresponding rise of a new regional state, historians have missed one key element effecting this change – tax revolts that spread across the mountains of Florence's periphery from the Montagna di Pistoia in the northwest to the Valdambra in the southeasternmost tip of the Florentine state. Perhaps these facts and their consequences for Florentine rule and mentality have eluded historians because of their obfuscation and failure to appear with any clarity in contemporary narrative sources of Florence, from chronicles to poetry. As a result, Florentine historians have continued to propagate the myth of Florence embedded in these contemporary writings, which saw lone republican Florence – united without class or factional rifts – defending the values of liberty against a rising tide of feudal Milanese tyranny. But, as we will see, the archival sources shed a wholly different light on events at the beginning of the fifteenth century.

Thus, this book does not see the development of the regional state as a Weberian one-way street, the relentless consolidation of power in the hands of an elitist Florentine executive at the expense of corporatist identities, whether they were the guilds, the church, the *parte guelfa* within the city walls, or feudal powers and peasant communes on the periphery. In the critical years at the start of the fifteenth century, the periphery led the center's actions and changed fundamentally Florence's strategy of governance. Negotiations favorable to Florence's peasant communes proved as important for Florence's state-building and the consolidation of its region as the naked aggression triumphantly celebrated by its chroniclers and later by historians as the fount of its *virtù*.[10] While the centralization and bureaucratization of Florence during the early fifteenth century may have eroded the privileges of formerly independent city-states – Pistoia, Arezzo, Cortona, and Pisa – those within Florence's rural communities and especially along the mountainous periphery benefited politically and economically from this centralization and standardization of power.

In this respect, this book has implications that reach beyond the domain of Florentine historiography or even the vast literature on state-building in late-medieval and early-modern Italy.[11] The historical and theoretical literatures on the formation of the modern state in Western Europe have emphasized peasant uprisings but almost exclusively in the negative, as resistance and temporary setbacks to the long and relatively steady march of centralization and absolutism, especially in "Latin Europe" during the early-modern period.[12]

Such has been the case even with Charles Tilly, who has studied the resistance of "ordinary people of Europe" over the long term perhaps more intensely and sensitively than any historian or social scientist. Certainly, Tilly and other scholars of European state formation have shown that "for all their reputed docility, the ordinary people of Europe fought the claims of central states for centuries."[13] Nonetheless, by these accounts, artisans and peasants ultimately were dragged, shoved, or enticed "into a world of centralized communications, extensive markets, and a large span of control."[14] Further, it was merchants and officials at the center who called the shots, dictating the multifarious patterns of

---

[10] As Najemy says, "The civic humanists were notoriously reluctant to acknowledge the dialogue of power in Florentine politics" ("The Dialogue of Power," p. 287). Although Machiavelli may have been explicit about such a dialogue between the great families and the *Popolo* in Florentine politics, he remained silent about any such negotiations between Florence and the communities of its subject territory.   [11] For a recent assessment of this literature, see *Origini dello Stato*.

[12] For an excellent recent summary of this literature, see Thomas Ertman, *Birth of the Leviathan: Building States and Regimes in Medieval and Early Modern Europe* (Cambridge, 1997), pp. 1–34.

[13] Tilly, "Reflections on the History of European State-Making," in *The Formation of National States in Western Europe* (Princeton, 1975), p. 22.

[14] *Ibid.*, pp. 22 and 61. Also, see Immanuel Wallerstein, *The Modern World-System: Capitalist Agriculture and the Origins of the European World-Economy in the Sixteenth Century* (New York, 1974), p. 354: "The European world-economy of the sixteenth century tended overall to be a one-class system. It was the dynamic forces profiting from economic expansion and the capitalist system, especially those of the core-areas, who tended to be class-conscious, that is to operate within the political arena as a group defined primarily by their common role in the economy." Recently, historians of early-modern and modern Europe have begun to challenge these more or less one-sided views of the formation of European states and their historical diversities; see Wayne Te Brake, *Shaping History: Ordinary People in European Politics, 1500–1700* (Berkeley, 1998); and Michael Hanagan, Leslie Moch, and Te Brake, eds., *Challenging Authority: The Historical Study of Contentious Politics* (Minneapolis, 1998), although the latter concentrates on the nineteenth and twentieth centuries. I wish to thank Charles Tilly for these references.

state control that would develop from the Renaissance to the twentieth century. According to these models, only by 1800 did "wider circles of the population" become involved in the "struggle for influence over the state."[15] Before, those on the periphery of Europe's state systems and the peasantry in particular lacked any vital or creative role and suffered as a consequence of state development.[16]

In the hands of Perry Anderson and from a perspective further to the left, the peasantry assumes an even smaller role in the history of state formation. Even in peasant revolts themselves, the peasantry disappears almost altogether from sight. Thus Anderson defined the peasant revolts of seventeenth-century France as "a nobilitary revolt against the consolidation of Absolutism."[17]

The evidence from Florence suggests another pattern to state formation and regional consolidation of power. Instead of blocking the juggernaut of the centralizing state's inexorable progress, resistance from those on the periphery of the state (in Florence's case, peasants in the mountains) stimulated state development and, in doing so, molded it to their own advantage. With the peasant revolts of the opening years of the fifteenth century, taxes on the peasantry began to fall even in the face of Florence's greater need for military outlays. Ultimately, the protests and petitions of the peasantry convinced city elites to revolutionize the Florentine tax system from an old mosaic of unequal taxation based on the rural community to a "universal tax" based on individual wealth, which ended the vast inequalities of the late fourteenth century between privileged peasants in the plains and distant highlanders. Second, the Florentine state became increasingly involved in shoring up the welfare of its rural subjects. As citizens feared the demographic emptying of their rural hinterland and as its military, fiscal, and economic realities

---

[15] Tilly, "Entanglements of European Cities and States," in *Cities and the Rise of States in Europe, A.D. 1000 to 1800*, ed. by Tilly and Wim Blockmans (Boulder, Colo., 1994), p. 26: "This means they [the wider circles of the population] also became objects of struggle for influence over the state, unprecedented before 1800. The unparalleled post-1800 interventionism of states and hence the increasing incentives for popular struggle to influence state personnel and policy rested on an expanded capacity to monitor, contain, seize, and redistribute resources within national territories."

[16] See, for instance, Tilly, "Reflections," p. 81: "All the builders of European states occupied themselves, one way or another, in wresting their wherewithal from largely self-sustaining agrarian populations." In his later *Coercion, Capital, and European States*, p. 27, Tilly hints that the peasantry may have possibly taken a more active role in influencing state formation in Sweden as compared with Prussia or Russia. For a more complex and positive view of the peasants' role in the formation of the Russian state from the end of the seventeenth century to 1861, see D. Moon, "Reassessing Russian Serfdom," *European History Quarterly*, 26, no. 4 (1996): 481–526.

[17] Perry Anderson, *Lineages of the Absolutist State* (London, 1974), p. 54.

began to dawn on them, they began to associate their own well-being as interlocked with that of their peasants. While the great historian of the modern state, Otto Hintze, concluded long ago that "conflict between nations has been more important" than "class conflict" as "the driving force in history" and in particular for understanding the formation of the modern state in Europe, perhaps it is now time to reevaluate "class conflict" as a creative and not only as a negative force in the formation of centralized states before the nineteenth century.[18] As sociologists have recently called for the state to be brought back into the study of class and society,[19] the story of state-building in the Renaissance suggests that notions of class, the periphery, and the peasantry need to be brought back into the study of state formation before the birth of working-class movements in the nineteenth century. They need to be brought back not simply as the temporary obstacles that occasionally punctuated the modern state's evolution but as positive "driving forces" that shaped the multifarious outcomes charted by Perry Anderson, Stein Rokkan,[20] Charles Tilly, Thomas Ertman, and other social scientists.[21]

This book is divided into three parts. The first investigates the relationship between city and *contado* and compares the social world of highlanders with lowlanders, most of whom lived close to the city of Florence. It argues that the city/*contado* distinction presents a false dichotomy for understanding political, social, and fiscal relations after the Black Death through the early fifteenth century. Instead, the *contado* was a mosaic of fiscal communities whose connections with the city differed drastically

[18] See Ertman, *Birth of the Leviathan*, p. 11; and Otto Hintze, "Military Organization and the Organization of the State," in *The Historical Essays of Otto Hintze*, ed. by Felix Gilbert (New York, 1975), p. 183.
[19] Theda Skocpol, "Bringing the State Back In: Strategies of Analysis in Current Research," in *Bringing the State Back In*, ed. by Peter Evans, Dietrich Rueschemeyer, and Skocpol (Cambridge, 1994), pp. 72–95. Long before, when such a call would have been more apropos, Miliband drew the following paradox: "While the vast inflation of the state's power and activity in advanced capitalist societies with which this book is concerned has become one of the merest commonplaces of political analysis, the remarkable paradox is that the state itself, as a subject of political study, has long been very unfashionable" (*The State in Capitalist Society*, pp. 3–4).
[20] Stein Rokkan, "Dimensions of State Formation and Nation-Building: A Possible Paradigm for Research on Variations within Europe," in *Formation of National States*, pp. 562–600.
[21] On the work of Otto Hintze, Charles Tilly, Michael Mann, Perry Anderson, and Brian Downing, see Ertman, *Birth of the Leviathan*, pp. 10–19. Of these Ertman is the only one to consider the positive and creative roles of local governments in the shaping of state formation in the early-modern and modern periods, but these local elites are limited to parliamentary representatives and dignitaries such as the English Justices of the Peace and do not extend to the peasantry.

from the privileged suburbs of Florence to the mountainous extremities. Yet, despite these fiscal and political differences, the society and culture of the mountains did not differ so dramatically from the plains as historians have supposed. Instead of "backward" peasants who sought every opportunity to escape brutal lives in mountain hollows, the archival records show that these peasants more often moved upward to other mountain villages than downward to supposedly greener pastures in the plains or to the city. Moreover, the highlanders were as numerate as peasants lower down the hills and in valleys, and by 1427 their percentages of given Christian names equaled those in the lowlands and subject towns. The sources fail to show a world where Christ stopped at Borgo San Lorenzo (as the slopes of the Mugello begin to climb); the highlanders' last wills and testaments even suggest that they were more pious than those in the lowlands.

Further, instead of being wedged within the glacial structures of geological or geographic time, "mountain civilization" was dynamic; its social structure could change over the short term of a single generation and its fate was tied more to the history of events – war, fiscality, and social unrest – than to deep-seated geographical structures. While peasants in the mountains had been wealthier than those in the plains after the Black Death (and perhaps before), the tables turned in the last decade of the fourteenth century. As a direct consequence of heavy taxation and war, the Florentine Alps quickly assumed those economic and social characteristics that Braudel and others have seen as inherent in the long-term structures of these geographical zones.[22]

This *histoire immobile* or "geographical time" proved, however, to be of short duration. At the turn of the century, political events of another sort – peasant rebellion against the Florentine state – intervened and, largely as a consequence, the Florentine oligarchy changed its stance toward those on its mountainous periphery. The highlanders prospered throughout much of the fifteenth century, both absolutely and relative to lowland peasants, and by 1460 possessed twice the wealth of those in the plains.

From chronicles, criminal records, and the daily activity of Florentine legislative bodies left in volumes of decrees, laws, and petitions called the

---

[22] On Braudel's models of geographical and historical time, see *Ecrits sur l'histoire* (Paris, 1969); "History and the Social Sciences, The Long Term," in *Society and Economy: Articles from Annales*, ed. by P. Burke (New York, 1972), pp. 11–40; Emmanuel Le Roy Ladurie, "L'histoire immobile," *Annales, E.S.C.*, 29 (1974): 673–92. Also see Le Roy Ladurie's about-face in "The 'Event' and the 'Long Term' in Social History: the Case of the Chouan Uprising," in *The Territory of the Historian* (Chicago, 1979 [Paris, 1973]), pp. 111–32.

provvisioni, part II of the book investigates the events that were to change Florence's governance of its region as well as the ecology of its mountains. These were peasant uprisings that spread through the mountainous districts from the Montagna di Pistoia in the northwest to the Chianti in the south. The sources portray three views of the same political realities. The chroniclers distorted and disguised them but, more importantly, mostly ignored them altogether. The judicial records' version shows that these movements did not arise solely or even more significantly from the leadership of Florence's rival feudal families, as the chroniclers relate. Rather, mountain peasants formed the rank and file and were often the leaders who planned military operations and devised tactics. Further, unbearable and unequal taxes were more at the heart of the opposition's bitterness than noblemen's desires to recapture ancient castles.

These records, however, show only one side of the story – the heavy hand of state oppression – and, like those few literary accounts that mention the revolts in passing, leave the impression that they were quickly crushed, the insurgents rounded up, led to Florence, and executed with new forms of torture and humiliation. On the other hand, the Florentine decrees (*provvisioni*) show a less heroic side to Florentine state policy – the need to negotiate with peasant insurgents. From 1403 to 1405 the insurgents' ringleaders were singled out for special privileges, and thousands of mountain villagers in hundreds of parishes from the Alpi Fiorentine to the Chianti won tax exemptions and cancellations of public debts.

Part III argues that these peasant victories were neither short-lived nor without significance for Florentine dominion over the formation of a new regional state. First, tax rates and tax inequalities in the countryside reached their apex on the eve of the peasant uprisings, 1401, and declined progressively until the *catasto* of 1427, when Florence replaced a medieval mosaic of unequal taxation with a "universal" tax that charged individuals according to the same principles regardless of residence within the *contado*. Second, an analysis of over a thousand peasant petitions found in the *provvisioni* registers from 1347 to 1434 reflects a long-term change in the rhetoric of peasant petitions as well as in the mentality of the Florentine ruling class. Again, 1402 was the watershed of an unstated policy as Florence voted more generous outcomes to more peasant communities across a wider array of peasant discontents. Unlike those approved before 1402, afterwards successful pleas from the countryside were not pinned narrowly on shoring up Florence's military defenses. Clemency toward the countryside changed from a rationale focused on Florence's desire to protect its citizens from foreign invasion to a new sensitivity to the politics of demography and the weakening of the countryside through peasant discontent and mass migration. As becomes evident in its handling of new waves of peasant unrest in 1426 and 1427, when war and fiscal crisis once again struck the Florentine state, Florence had learnt its lessons of 1402. The second time around, Florence intervened with tax immunities and slashed administrative charges before insurgent mountain peasant communes in the Aretino even had time to petition the government in Florence. Furthermore, the reforms of the more equitable *catasto* of 1427 were founded in the experiences of 1402, as our charts on taxation and the debates in Florence's highest councils make clear.

This book began as a short project to utilize the under-studied *Capi di famiglia* tax surveys and resulted in an essay on rural migration to honor the late David Herlihy.[23] After its completion, one question left unresolved led to another and one source to another, producing five more essays in various volumes.[24] Parts of the present book intersect with data, analyses, and formulations presented in these earlier essays.

[23] Samuel K. Cohn Jr., "Inventing Braudel's Mountains: The Florentine Alps after the Black Death," in *Portraits of Medieval and Renaissance Living. Essays in Honor of David Herlihy*, ed. by Cohn and Steven A. Epstein (Ann Arbor, 1996), pp. 383–416.

[24] *Women in the Streets: Essays on Sex and Power in the Italian Renaissance* (Baltimore, 1996), chs. 6 and 7; "Insurrezioni contadine e demografia: il mito della povertà nelle montagne toscane (1348–1460)," *Studi Storici*, 36, no. 4 (1995): 1023–49; "Marriage in the Mountains: The Florentine Territorial State, 1348–1500," in *Marriage in Italy, 1300–1650*, ed. by Trevor Dean and K. J. P. Lowe (Cambridge, 1997), pp. 174–96; and "Fiscal Policy and Demography in the Florentine Contado, 1355–1487," in *Florentine Tuscany: Structures and Practices of Power*, ed. by William Connell and Andrea Zorzi (Cambridge, forthcoming).

PART I

Culture, demography, and fiscality

Networks of culture and the mountains

This book explores two central and interconnected questions well established within Florentine historiography – the rise of a regional state, charted above, and the relationship between city and countryside.[1] Both have roots going back to Niccolò Machiavelli and Francesco Guicciardini and both have been enlivened since World War II with new archival research and international discussion. For the second debate, argument has centered on whether Florence viciously exploited its countryside, taxing it to the extreme and thus draining it of its talent, manpower, and material resources, or whether taxation was light and even preferential to the surrounding countryside.

In the early years of the twentieth century, Romolo Caggese argued that the relationship between city and *contado* was wholly exploitative whereby the city drained the countryside of its resources through oppressive taxation.[2] Fifty years later, Enrico Fiumi contested Caggese's arguments with more archival rigor. In place of oppression and conflict, Fiumi saw Florence's fiscal policy towards its *contado* as benign, maintaining that it taxed its own citizens more severely. But,

---

[1] On the particularity of city-states in central and northern Italy during the later Middle Ages, see Chittolini, "The Italian City-State and its Territory," in *City States*, pp. 589–602. For a recent review of the literature, see Jean-Claude Maire Vigueur, "Les rapports ville–campagne dans l'Italie communale: pour une révision des problèmes," in *La ville, la bourgeoisie et la genèse de l'état moderne (XIIe–XVIIIe siècles)*, ed. by Neithard Bulst and J.-Ph. Genet (Bielefeld, 1985), pp. 21–34. It is interesting to note the centrality of Florence in this literature even for a historian of Umbria and the Marche.

[2] Romolo Caggese, *Classi e comuni rurali nel Medio Evo italiano*, 2 vols. (Florence, 1908). On the "classics" of the city–*contado* literature (Salvemini, Volpe, Caggese, De Vergottini, Ottokar, Plesner, Fiumi), see Giuliano Pinto, *Città e spazi economici nell'Italia comunale* (Bologna, 1996), p. 48; and Antonio Ivan Pini, "Un aspetto dei rapporti tra città e territorio nel Medioevo: la politica demografica 'ad elastico' di Bologna fra il XII e il XIV secolo," in *Studi in Memoria di Federigo Melis* (Naples, 1978), I, pp. 368–70.

although Fiumi's argument extended to the fifteenth century, his evidence focused on the period before the Black Death.[3]

From evidence on taxation, the growth of Florence's funded debt, and the concentration of wealth in the hands of an oligarchy centered in Florence at the expense of the territory, Marvin Becker,[4] Anthony Molho,[5] David Herlihy, and Christiane Klapisch-Zuber[6] attacked this picture of Florentine city–country relations, one describing it "as being little short of idyllic."[7] But with Judith Brown the pendulum swung back to the other side. By viewing in detail one place within the hinterland – Pescia – she argued that the relationship between the dominant city, Florence, and its region was symbiotic, benefiting both center and periphery.[8] Her most compelling evidence came, however, from the much later period of the Florentine Grand Duchy and not from the late Trecento and early Quattrocento. More recently, historians have again stressed Florence's exploitation of its territory, such that its efforts proved counterproductive both economically[9] and politically.[10] But these works, like most that preceded them, have failed to draw conclusions about this exploitative relationship over time.

The one striking exception to this historiography is Becker's work on the rise of the "Florentine territorial state," which largely accepted Fiumi's thesis for the pre-Black Death period but saw in the formation of the funded debt (*Monte*) in 1345 a new departure in Florence's taxes

---

[3] Enrico Fiumi, "Sui rapporti economici tra città e contado nell'età comunale," *ASI*, 114 (1956): 18–68; "Fioritura e decadenza dell'economia fiorentina," part 1, *ASI*, 115 (1957): 385–439; part 2, 116 (1958): 443–510; part 3, 117 (1959): 427–502, esp. part 3, pp. 440–66; and *Storia economica e sociale di San Gimignano* (Florence, 1961). Also see, Emilio Cristiani, "Città e campagna nell'età comunale in alcune pubblicazioni dell'ultimo decennio," *Rivista Storica Italiana*, 75 (1963): 829–45.

[4] Becker, *Florence in Transition*; and "Problemi della finanza pubblica fiorentina della seconda metà del Trecento e dei primi anni del Quattrocento," *ASI*, 123 (1965): 433–66.

[5] Molho, *Florentine Public Finances in the Early Renaissance, 1400–1433* (Cambridge, Mass., 1971).

[6] David Herlihy, "Direct and Indirect Taxation in Tuscan Urban Finances, ca. 1200–1400," in *Finances et comptabilité urbaines du XIIIe au XIVe siècle* (Brussels, 1964), pp. 385–405; and Herlihy and Christiane Klapisch-Zuber, *Les Toscans et leurs familles. Une étude du Catasto florentin de 1427* (Paris, 1978), pp. 18–19.

[7] Becker, "Economic Change and the Emerging Florentine Territorial State," *Studies in the Renaissance*, 13 (1966), p. 32.

[8] J. Brown, *In the Shadow of Florence: Provincial Society in Renaissance Pescia* (Oxford, 1982), pp. 126–76 and 199–202.

[9] Stephan Epstein, *An Island for Itself: Economic Development and Social Change in Late Medieval Sicily* (Cambridge, 1993); "Cities, Regions and the Late Medieval Crisis: Sicily and Tuscany Compared," *Past and Present*, 130 (1991): pp. 3–50; and "Regional Fairs, Institutional Innovation and Economic Growth in Late Medieval Europe," *Economic History Review*, 2nd ser. 47 (1994): 459–82.

[10] Giuseppe Petralia, "Fiscality, Politics and Dominion in Florentine Tuscany at the End of the Middle Ages," in *Florentine Tuscany*.

and relations with its *contado*.[11] Before this cardinal date, Florentine governance both in the city and the territory was marked by a "gentle paedeia" or style of rule; afterwards its policy turned increasingly towards bureaucratic control and governmental severity. But for the long period from 1345 to perhaps the end of the Florentine Republic, Becker does not mark any further changes. Neither the Milanese wars, the Florentine *catasto* of 1427, the rise of the Medici, nor shifts with the Laurentian oligarchy registered a shift in the fundamental paths of political strategy set in motion and necessitated by Florence's state debt that began its inexorable rise on the eve of the Black Death.

This book will contribute to this historiography on taxation and the relationship between city and countryside in two ways. First, it will propose a fundamental break in Florentine tax policy and the attitudes of the ruling elites towards its hinterland that occurred towards the end of the "third war" with Milan at the beginning of the fifteenth century. According to Hans Baron, these same years brought the "early Renaissance" to Florence, registering a fundamental change in Florentine political thought and consciousness, which he named "civic humanism." But far from studying this change in mentality in social or fiscal terms, Baron hotly denied that it had any relation whatsoever to internal conflicts. The politics fundamental to Baron's argument were diplomacy and foreign affairs. Baron and later historians such as Antonio Lanzi have read this history as the Florentine humanist and literary propagandists presented it: circa 1400 Florentine patriotism was undivided and stood as the last bastion of liberty against Milan's encircling threat of "tyranny."[12]

In addition to proposing a new chronology, the opening chapters of this book argue that the city/countryside dichotomy must be refined, even beyond the formal distinction made clear in legislation and tax policy between the obligations of the *districtus* and the *contado* of Florence. While historians have recently shown that Florence did not devise a consistent policy regulating either the fiscal or juridical obligations of its

---

[11] See especially his *Florence in Transition*, I.
[12] Hans Baron, *The Crisis of the Early Renaissance*; Antonio Lanza, *Firenze contro Milano: Gli intellettuali fiorentini nelle guerre con i Visconti (1390–1440)* (Rome, 1991). Among the many reviews of Baron, see Jones, "Review of Baron," *History*, 53, no. 179 (Oct., 1968): 410–13; Fubini, "La rivendicazione di Firenze della sovranità e il contributo delle 'Historiae' di Leonardo Bruni," in *Leonardo Bruni cancelliere della repubblica di Firenze (Convegno di studi [Firenze, 27–29 ottobre 1987])*, ed. by Paolo Viti (Florence, 1990), p. 35; "Renaissance Historian: The Career of Hans Baron," *Journal of Modern History*, 64 (1992): 541–74; James Hankins, "The 'Baron Thesis' after Forty Years and Some Recent Studies of Leonardo Bruni," *Journal of the History of Ideas*, 56 (1995): 309–38; and Ronald Witt, "The *Crisis* after Forty Years," *American Historical Review*, 101, no. 1 (1996): 110–18.

subject towns – Arezzo, Cortona, Pisa, Pistoia, and Volterra[13] – less work has been done on Florence's traditional *contado*. To date, historians have framed this city/countryside relationship, whether exploitative or symbiotic, as though the countryside (*contado*) were a single unit without broad geographic differences bearing different social, economic, and political relationships with the city of Florence. Although recent studies have considered political patronage beyond the ambit of urban politics and urban elites, historians have yet to distinguish these Florentine networks over the contrasting zones of the hinterland.[14]

The parishes, *ville*, communes, and towns within the Florentine *contado* varied enormously in economy, terrain, and military importance for the city of Florence. The *contado*'s Quarter of Santa Maria Novella contained towns as commercially important as Prato, which housed perhaps the richest merchant of the early fifteenth century within the city or territory of Florence – Francesco di Marco Datini.[15] Further, suburban parishes whose churches lay within the city walls housed agricultural laborers, but also comprised numbers of artisans and workers, who commuted to the city and were directly involved in its urban economy. Such was the listing in 1487 of a certain twenty-eight-year-old Giovanni di Romolo di Tommaso, a stone-cutter (*scarpellino*) who lived alone in the section of San Lorenzo outside the walls just beyond the gate of San Gallo and worked for Lorenzo de' Medici as the assistant to "Bertoldo the sculptor" at the

---

[13] Chittolini, "Ricerche sull'ordinamento"; Robert Black, "Arezzo and the Florentine Territorial State, 1384–1515," in *Florentine Tuscany*; Petralia, "Fiscality, Politics and Dominion"; and "Imposizione diretta e dominio territoriale nella repubblica fiorentina del Quattrocento," in *Società, istituzioni, spiritualità: Studi in onore di Cinzio Violante*. (Spoleto, 1994), II, pp. 639–52; W. J. Connell, *City of Sorrows: Clientage and Faction in the Republican State* (forthcoming); Herlihy, *Medieval and Renaissance Pistoia: The Social History of an Italian Town, 1200–1430* (New Haven, 1967), pp. 214–31; Zorzi, "Lo Stato territoriale fiorentino (secoli XIV–XV): aspetti giurisdizionali," *Società e storia*, no. 50 (1990): 799–825; Lorenzo Fabbri, "La sottomissione di Volterra allo stato fiorentino: Controllo istituzionale e strategie di governo (1361–1435)," Ph.D. diss. Università degli Studi di Firenze, 1994.

[14] For the Medici and church appointments, see Roberto Bizzocchi, *Chiesa e potere nella Toscana del Quattrocento* (Bologna, 1987). From the letters of Lorenzo de' Medici, see Connell, "Changing Patterns of Medicean Patronage: The Florentine Dominion during the Fifteenth Century," in *Lorenzo il Magnifico e il suo mondo*, ed. by G. C. Garfagnini (Florence, 1994), pp. 87–107; "Clientelismo e Stato territoriale: Il Potere fiorentino a Pistoia nel XV secolo," *Società e Storia*, no. 53 (1991): 523–43; and Patrizia Salvadori, "Rapporti personali, rapporti di potere nella corrispondenza di Lorenzo de' Medici," in *Lorenzo il Magnifico e il suo tempo*, ed. by Garfagnini (Florence, 1992), pp. 125–46. For relations between the Guidi and their *fideles*, see Charles M. de la Roncière, "Fidélités, patronages, clientèles dans le contado florentin au XIVe siècle," *Ricerche Storiche* 15, no. 1 (1985): 35–60. But as la Roncière admits, the relations between these peasants and the Commune of Florence have yet to be written, p. 57.

[15] See Federigo Melis, *Aspetti della vita economica medievale: Studi nell'archivio Datini di Prato* (Siena, 1962); and Giovanni Ciappelli, "Il cittadino fiorentino e il fisco alla fine del Trecento e nel corso del Quattrocento: uno studio di due casi," *Società e Storia*, no. 46 (1989): 823–72.

Medici palace. Lorenzo intervened in Giovanni's tax assessment as well as that of his brother, another stone-cutter also living alone in the same part of San Lorenzo "outside the walls." Both were exempted from paying an *estimo* on their property and were charged a mere shilling (*soldo*) head tax apiece – an amount usually charged to elderly widows or handicapped men without taxable property and called "miserabili."[16]

In addition, legislation concerned with the evasion of the gate gabelle shows the mixed status of those who lived "near the walls" (*prope le mura*). In 1371 the councils passed a law that insisted that those living within 1,000 *braccia* of the city walls (which corresponded roughly to the "fuori le mura" districts of the urban churches) would have to pay the gate gabelle "as though they were Florentine citizens living within the city of Florence." Apparently, some in this zone had managed to obtain a mixed fiscal status that gave them the best of both worlds: as "citizens" they paid no direct taxes and as *comitatini* they paid no gate taxes on their consumption of rural produce.[17]

The distinctiveness of this 1,000–*braccia* ring around Florence is perhaps best illustrated by the occupations held by those residing within the "outside the walls" districts of urban parishes. The tax officials of 1487 identified two-thirds of household heads from San Lorenzo and Santa Lucia Ognissanti "outside the walls" by profession (81 of 122) – a proportion exceeding even that of city household heads in the *catasto* of 1427. Of these most were artisans involved in commercial tasks associated with the city. They practiced at least twenty different professions ranging from various skills in the textile industry – wool, silk, and linen – to running shops within the city walls; only one-sixth of them were agricultural workers.[18] By contrast, all of those identified by profession in adjacent parishes to the west, Santa Maria a Novoli and Santa Maria a Quarto, tilled the soil as sharecroppers (*mezzadri*) or tenants.[19]

Beyond this innermost ring of rural population, other rural parishes still lay within the urban "pieve" of San Giovanni, whose parishioners

---

[16] Catasto 1123, 452r and 416r for his brother. William Wallace, *Michelangelo at San Lorenzo. The Genius as Entrepreneur* (Cambridge, 1994), pp. 99–100, finds that Michelangelo as well as 94 percent of his sculptors and stone-cutters resided in Settignano and Fiesole (both about 7 kilometers from Florence's center) and must have commuted regularly to Florence to work at San Lorenzo and on the Laurentian library.

[17] Provv. reg., 59, 262v, 1371.iii.23. Also, see la Roncière, "Indirect Taxes or 'Gabelles' at Florence in the Fourteenth Century: The Evolution of Tariffs and Problems of Collection," in *Florentine Studies*, p. 189. In 1373 the ban was extended to 3,000 paces. Unlike Siena and Lucca, Florence did not make a juridical distinction between its nearby rural parishes – the *Masse* or *Sei Miglia* – and the rest of the *contado*. [18] Catasto 1123, 244r–335r, 400r–81r, and 648r–89r.

[19] Catasto 1124, nos. 12 and 17.

brought their babies to the font of San Giovanni in the city's center as did citizens of Florence. The lure and prestige of Florence's San Giovanni extended even beyond its already extensive baptismal district. Peasants as far away as Impruneta carted their neonates to be baptized at San Giovanni (about 15 kilometers from the city's baptistery), even though Impruneta had its own font.[20]

Another ring of peasant villages stretched outward for 10–15 kilometers, depending on the roads and terrain. Fourteenth- and fifteenth-century notarial contracts show that the majority of these peasants were tied to the city through dependent relations with citizen landlords as wealthy as the Strozzi[21] and Brunelleschi[22] or as common as doublet-makers.[23] Even disenfranchised workers in the wool industry, such as the shearer (*cimatore*) Nero called Trica and the comber (*pettignangnolo*) Giovanni called Malanta invested in rural real estate within walking distance of the city walls farmed by dependent peasants.[24]

The myriad rental contracts and land sales redacted by the Mazzetti family within the alluvial plains and hills extending from the city walls through the *pievi* of Santo Stefano in Pane, Sesto, Campi, Signa, and partially up the hillsides of Monte Morello show these peasants interlocked in the contractual life of the city. This family's notarial business, comprising well over five thousand contracts contained in fifteen surviving protocols from 1348 to 1426, are filled with *mezzadria* or sharecropping contracts as well as other short-term, non-feudal rents of property. The contracts show a peasantry under the economic and social rule of absentee urban landlords and their agents.

The oppressive side to this relationship is well attested in the number

---

[20] At least four babies from Impruneta were baptised at San Giovanni during the first recorded year: on January 31, 1450/1, February 28, April 4, and May 26; Archivio dell'Opera del Duomo: Registro delle fedi di battesimo, I (1450–1).

[21] Notarile antecosimiano [hereafter Not. antecos.], 13533, no pagination [hereafter np], 1364.ix.11; np, 1365.ix.4. Later, for Palla Strozzi's properties in this area, see Amanda Lillie, "Lorenzo de' Medici's Rural Investments and Territorial Expansion," *Rinascimento*, 36 (1993), pp. 54 and 65.

[22] See, for instance, Not. antecos., 13533; np, 1364.ii.7; and 13521, 124v, 1384.i.14; 143r, 1386.vi.21; 164r, 1388.x.23.

[23] See the many acts of land sales, rent and *mezzadria* contracts initiated in the 1360s and 1370s by the doublet-maker (*farsettarius*) Pierus f.q. Neri with peasants in Sesto and Campi; Not. antecos., 13533, np, 1364.viii.3; np, 1364.xi.16; np, 1364.i.18; np, 1364.i.24; np, 1365.v.14; np, 1370.ix.30; and 13521, 61v, 1374.i.1; 69v, 1376.ix.13; 70v, 1376.x.22; also those of the doublet-maker, Baldus f.q. Domenci Dante and his mother, a *pinzochera*, np, 1373.x.30; np, 1371.iv.25.

[24] Not. antecos., 13521 130r, 1385.xi.24; and 13533, np, 1364.xi.14. For other examples of disenfranchised workers in the wool industry with holdings in the nearby villages, see *ibid.*, np, 1369.xi.13; np, 1366.ii.13; and np, 1371.v.8.

of criminal prosecutions against peasants who "neglected" their work, cut trees for their own use, and violated their contracts in other ways. They were subject to punitive action and fines from 200 to 500 *lire* – well beyond their capacity to pay.[25] But there was a softer, paternalistic side to these relations as well, illustrated in numerous diaries (*ricordanze* and *zibaldoni*) that advised sons to take minute care in the management of their rural estates and to provide for the welfare of their peasants.[26]

In addition, the contracts themselves show the close and near-feudal relations between the landlord (*oste*) and the *mezzadro*. Periodically *mezzadri* were required to ride or walk into the city and at the "gate" (*gabella*) of their landlord's house present their share of the produce at least twice a year along with honorific gifts, such as a pair of capons and five to ten eggs.[27] It was from within this ring that the peasants came every morning to sell their produce "that filled every kitchen" and may have led to other social relations as Antonio Pucci's morning description of the Mercato Vecchio and his pun on "cocina" suggest.[28]

Moreover, villages such as Peretola and Varlunga and other neighboring villages in the Arno basin just beyond Florence's suburbs supplied apprentices who worked in the city's wool and silk industries.[29] From these villages, peasants also regularly walked to town to sell or pawn their goods, as did Boccaccio's protagonist of Varlunga in story 2, day 8, when she needed spending money.[30]

By contrast, the *contado* encompassed distant mountain communes, such as those in the Alpi and Podere Fiorentino north of the Mugello. These villages lay across several mountain passes from the city of Florence, ultimately leading to the borders of Bologna and the lands of the Romagna lords. Throughout much of the fourteenth century these northernmost lands faded in and out of Florentine control. Even after Florence's successful war in 1373 to "exterminate" the Ubaldini (the Mugello's and Alpi's dominant feudal clan) to outlaw their feudal

---

[25] See Cohn, *Women in the Streets*, p. 25; and Atti del Podestà [hereafter AP], 2208, 1369.vi.21–ix.6.
[26] Giovanni di Pagolo Morelli, *Ricordi*, ed. by Vittore Branca (Florence, 1956); Bernardo Machiavelli, *Libro di ricordi*, ed. by Cesare Olschki (Florence, 1954); Giovanni Rucellai, *Giovanni Rucellai ed il suo Zibaldone*, I: *Il Zibaldone quaresimale. Pagine scelte*, ed. by Alessandro Perosa (London, 1960).   [27] Hundreds of such contracts survive in the Mazzetti notarial books.
[28] Antonio Pucci, "Proprietà di Mercato Vecchio," in *Poeti Minori del Trecento*, ed. by Natalino Sapegno (Milan, 1952), p. 405: "E contadin vi vengon la mattina / e rinnovar le cose alle fantesche; / ciascuna rifornisce sua cocina."
[29] Franco Franceschi, *Oltre il "Tumulto": I fiorentini dell'Arte della Lana fra Tre e Quattrocento* (Florence, 1993), p. 130.
[30] Giovanni Boccaccio, *Decameron*, ed. by Vittore Branca (Milan, 1976), pp. 674–80.

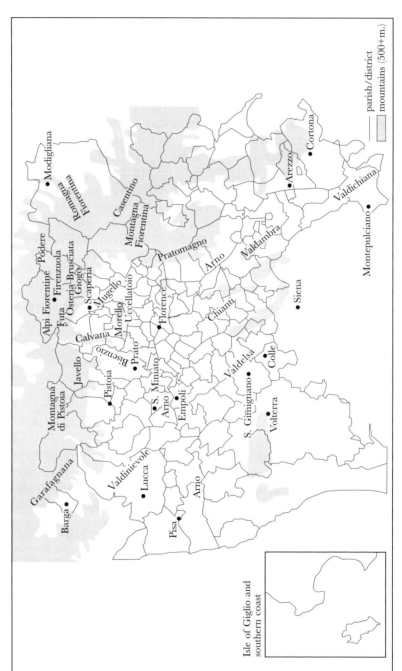

Map 1 Florentine Tuscany: physical characteristics

parish/district
mountains (500+ m.)

Modigliana
Romagna Fiorentina
Casentino
Montagna Fiorentina
Podere
Alpi Fiorentine
Firenzuola
Futa
Osteria-Brusciata
Giogo
Scaperia
Mugello
Uccellatoio
Morello
Florence
Pratomagno
Arno
Valdambra
Cortona
Arezzo
Valdichiana
Montepulciano
Chianti
Siena
Calvana
Bisenzio
Prato
Valdelsa
Colle
Javello
Pistoia
S. Miniato
Arno
Empoli
S. Gimignano
Volterra
Montagna di Pistoia
Garfagnana
Valdinievole
Lucca
Arno
Barga
Pisa

Isle of Giglio and
southern coast

rents,[31] these and other lords such as the Alidosi della Massa and the Lords of Imola[32] continued to hold feudal contracts with peasant "fideli" and "vassali" from whom they collected perpetual rents in kind.[33]

These places, still within Florence's *contado*, were as far removed in distance and social-economic ties from the city as places in the territorial *districtus*. A border village such as Santa Maria a Bordignano was over 70 kilometers from Florence as the crow flies. But with the treacherous roads, tortuous mountainous trails and passes blocked throughout much of the winter, travel time would have made these places further removed than the centers of other city-states such as Pisa, Siena, and Arezzo. Even for those as privileged and well equipped as the early fifteenth-century ambassador Rinaldo degli Albizzi, travel through the Alpi Fiorentine across either the Giogo di Scarperia or the older pass of the Osteria Brusciata was hazardous and time-consuming and mostly limited to the good months of May and October.[34]

The roads that passed through the upper Mugello and Alpi to Bologna and points further north remained among the most difficult to traverse in Italy until the "road revolution" of the Lorenian Habsburgs during the mid-eighteenth century, when the new Grand Duke,

---

[31] On the eleventh-century origins of the Ubaldini and their early conflicts with Florence, see George Dameron, *Episcopal Power and Florentine Society 1000–1320* (Cambridge, Mass., 1991), pp. 44, 65, 100–1, and 159–61. For the later period, see Laura Magna, "Gli Ubaldini del Mugello: Una signoria feudale nel contado fiorentino," in *I ceti dirigenti dell'età comunale nei secoli XII e XIII. Atti del II Convegno, Firenze, 14–15 dicembre 1979* (Pisa, 1982), pp. 13–66; and Giovanni Cherubini, "Appunti sul brigantaggio in Italia alla fine del medioevo," *Studi di storia medievale e moderna per Enesto Sestan*, I: *Medioevo* (Florence, 1980), pp. 103–33, esp. p. 120. On an early fifteenth-century view of the Ubaldini as the tyrants and enemies of Florence, see Morelli, *Ricordi*, pp. 96–8; and *I Capitoli del Comune di Firenze*, ed. by Cesare Guasti (Florence, 1866), I, pp. 88 and 96.

[32] See John Larner, *The Lords of Romagna: Romagnol Society and the Origins of the Signorie* (New York, 1965).

[33] See the complaints from the men of Santa Maria di Bordignano, who claimed they paid heavy rents to the Ubaldini of Galliano and to "gli Alidogi dalla Massa e chi del Signor d'Imola." Estimo 218 (1393), 235v. Also, the tax entries of Castro di San Martino lists the amounts they owed to their feudal lords in perpetual grain rents; *ibid.*, 279r–87v.

[34] Daniele Sterpos, "Evoluzione delle comunicazioni transappenniniche attraverso tre passi del Mugello," in *Percorsi e Valichi dell'Appennino fra storia e leggenda. Futa, Osteria Bruciata, Giogo. Manifestazione espositiva itinerante* (Florence, 1985), p. 21, based on Rinaldo degli Albizzi, *Commissioni di Rinaldo degli Albizzi per il comune di Firenze dal MCCCXCIX al MCCCCXXXIII*, ed. by Cesare Guasti, 3 vols. (Florence, 1867–73). The route through the Giogo was opened in 1361 (Johan Plesner, *Una rivoluzione stradale del dugento* [Copenhagen, 1938], p. 33) and was the most treacherous of the three major arteries over the Tuscan–Emilian Apennines, see J. Larner, "Crossing the Romagnol Appennines in the Renaissance," in *City and Countryside in Late Medieval and Renaissance Italy: Essays presented to Philip Jones*, ed. by Trevor Dean and Chris Wickham (London, 1990), pp. 147–70. In early June 1433, Ambrogio Traversari, (*Hodoeporicon*, ed. by Vittorio Tamburini [Florence, 1985], p. 114), traveled from Florence to Cavrenno in a day and reached Bologna the next. He was able to repeat this journey again in two days in early September, 1433 (p. 157), but even in good weather he needed a guide to negotiate the mountain passes.

Francesco di Stefano, began construction on a western route over the Futa.[35] In the sixteenth century, even after the Medici Grand Dukes improved Florentine roads and invented one of the earliest postal systems of house addresses, Venetian ambassadors still viewed the network of mountain roads across the Alpi and Mugello Apennines "as almost inaccessible for artillery and armies."[36] In mid-century, Montaigne found his crossing over the Florentine Alps from the Bolognese village of Loiano (probably over the Giogo) to Scarperia more difficult and fierce than any he had previously made over the northern Alps in France, Switzerland, or Italy.[37]

In the fourteenth and early fifteenth centuries these roads were made even more treacherous by banditry and brigandage. Numerous Ubaldini attacks and robberies of international merchant caravans can be found in the criminal court records and some were so notorious as to be described in the chronicles of Giovanni and Matteo Villani and Marchionne di Coppo Stefani, in the poetry of Franco Sacchetti, and in the letters of Francesco Petrarch. Further, the normal economy of the highwaymen (*malandrini*) who lay in wait for merchants crossing the Giogo led to military operations and fortifications on a scale usually reserved for defense against foreign invasion.[38]

Here, in the highlands, few if any Florentines possessed land from the mid-fourteenth century, when magnate citizens such as the Bardi sold their titles to feudal castles at Mangona and Vernio,[39] until the period of

[35] Sterpos, "Evoluzione delle comunicazioni," pp. 15–17; and Leonardo Rombai and Marco Sorelli, "La viabilità del Mugello occidentale intorno alla metà del Settecento: Dall'assetto *ancien régime* alla 'rivoluzione stradale' lorenese," in *Percorsi e Valichi*, pp. 35–49.

[36] See Rombai, "Prefazione: Strade e politica in Toscana tra medioevo ed età moderna," in *Il Libro Vecchio di Strade della Repubblica fiorentina*, ed. by Gabriele Ciampi (Florence, 1987), p. 19; and Sterpos, "Evoluzione delle comunicazioni."

[37] Michel Montaigne, *Journal de voyage*, ed. by Louis Lautrey (Paris, 1906), pp. 184–5: "un chemin qui, à la verité, est le premier de notre voïage qui se peut nommer incommode et farouche, et parmy les montaignes plus difficiles qu'en nulle autre part de ce voïage."

[38] For Florence's thirteenth- and fourteenth-century incursions into Ubaldini lands, see Giovanni Villani, *Nuova Cronica*, ed. by Giuseppe Porta, 3 vols. (Parma, 1990), I, bk. 7, rubrica or capitolo [hereafter r.] 47, p. 341; III, bk. 13, r. 8, p. 307; r. 36, p. 383; Matteo Villani, *Cronica di Matteo Villani*, ed. by Ignazio Moutier, 5 vols. (Florence, 1825), I, bk. 1, r. 25, pp. 48–9; r. 27, pp. 50–3; r. 79, p. 152; bk. 2, r. 4, p. 198; r. 15, pp. 217–18; r. 23, p. 234; r. 33, pp. 251–2; r. 54, pp. 286–7; r. 55, pp. 287–90; r. 69, pp. 310–11; r. 79, p. 323; bk. 3, r. 41, pp. 374–5; Sterpos, "Evoluzione delle comunicazioni," p. 13. For special fortifications, see Provv. reg. 88, 86r–7r, 1399.vi.17: "Pro hedifitiis supra Jugo Alpium Florentinorum." The councils allocated "no less than 1,200 *lire*" to build elaborate fortifications at the Giogo pass between Scarperia and Firenzuola to defend this road "against the murders and bandits" of the upper Mugello.

[39] See *I Capitoli*, I, pp. 107–8. Bardi e Mangona (Vendita di Mangona) on January 15, 1340 (Florentine style); and Emmanuele Repetti, *Dizionario storico della Toscana*, 6 vols. (Florence, 1833–45) [hereafter Repetti, *Diz.*], III, pp. 42–7.

Lorenzo, when the Florentine elites began to consider building estates and hunting lodges in the forests and mountains on the Florentine periphery.[40] The survival of notarial acts from the upper Mugello and Alpi is scanty before the sixteenth century, but we are blessed with the survival of one protocol that concentrated on the villages of the Alpi Fiorentine.

From 1428 to 1435 Ser Antonio di Giusto, who was usually stationed in Barberino di Mugello, redacted 540 acts in his lone surviving protocol. His business covered much of the western Mugello and Alpi from Sant'Agata in the south into mountain villages such as Baragazza across the border in the state of Bologna. In Ser Antonio's business the urban presence in land sales, rents, and other contracts was minuscule. A Bardi, but one of the Vernio branch and apparently not living in Florence, sold a strip of arable land to a villager in Mangona for 15 florins.[41] A man from the Florentine Guasconi family sold a strip of arable land to a nobleman from Migneto in the *Podesteria* of Barberina for 14 *lire*;[42] another Guasconi sold a house in the center of Scarperia (*in loco dicitur al Mercatale*) to a spice dealer from the town for 30 florins. But these were the only instances in which a Florentine is found among the hundreds of sales contracted by Ser Antonio.

Further, short-term land rents and *mezzadria* contracts in his records are negligible in number, and a Florentine (in this case, landlady) appears in only one of these contracts. She was a widow from the urban parish of San Simone, but her tenant, another widow, as well as the house and attached properties she let, were not in the highlands; instead they lay in the town of Barberino (270 meters in altitude), south of the Alpi Fiorentine.[43] This absence of urban landlords, patrons, and land speculators is in striking contrast to the business redacted by Ser Antonio's colleagues who worked parishes in the plains near Florence.

The Florentines most prominent in Ser Antonio's business were members of the Cattani family. Pellegrino, the son of the deceased Ubaldo and his brother possessed the *ius patronatus* to the parish church

---

[40] See, for instance, Lorenzo's abortive attempts to buy land from Vallombrosa at Pitiana; Caroline Elam and Ernst Gombrich, "Lorenzo de' Medici and a Frustrated Villa Project at Vallombrosa," in *Florence and Italy: Renaissance Studies in Honour of Nicolai Rubinstein*, ed. by Peter Denley and Elam (London, 1988), pp. 481–92 and for the diversification of Lorenzo's land purchases in the 1470s, Lillie, "Lorenzo's Rural Investments."   [41] Not. antecos., 792, 157v, 1433.iv.11.
[42] *Ibid.*, 174v, 1433.viii.21.
[43] *Ibid.*, 163r–v, 1433.v.24. The one agricultural rent found in Ser Antonio's business was in Le Valle (Alpi Fiorentine). Although by birth a Florentine, the landlady was a widow of the Ubaldini who resided also in the Alpi village of Monte; *ibid.*, 166v, 1433.vi.4.

of San Silvestro at Barberino and "elected" a new priest at the beginning of 1433.[44] But rather than as land speculators or landlords these
brothers appeared as witnesses to marriages in Barberino and as owners
of the "palazzo" in the town's parish of San Silvestro where Ser Antonio
often conducted business.[45] Moreover, despite their citizenship, these
brothers were identified as residents of Barberino. As Pucci's poem suggests, the mountainous periphery of the Florentine state was beyond the
pale of citizens' daily contacts and horizons. From the hustle-bustle of
Florence's central market the furthest places seen by Pucci in his panoramic view of the Florentine countryside were in the hills (Poggibonsi),
where peasants brought "so many things he could not bother naming
them."[46]

Through tax records, criminal sentences, and notarial contracts, historians such as Elio Conti, Giovanni Cherubini, and Guiliano Pinto have
described the diversity of the Tuscan countryside during the later
Middle Ages, the differences in terrain, animal husbandry, crops, work,
diet, and to a lesser extent the culture of peasants from the plains near
urban centers to the distant mountains.[47] In surveying the rich diversity
of the Tuscan countryside, historians, however, have yet to enter the
political realm, to show whether a similar diversity was reflected in the
fiscal and social relations with the dominant power, Florence. By investigating ten tax surveys from 1356 to 1487 and variations in rates of taxation before the *catasto* of 1427, this book explores the social, economic,
and political diversity within the traditional *contado* of Florence. In so
doing, it enters yet another historiography, that of the Mediterranean
mountains and the plains: was there a separate mountain civilization
and, if so, what were its structures, characteristics, and cultural hall-
marks?
   The historical analysis of "mountain civilization" must begin with
Fernand Braudel, for whom altitude more than nationality distinguished
social traits in premodern Europe.[48] For Braudel, mountain commu-

---

[44] *Ibid.*, 150r, 1432.i.21.   [45] *Ibid.*, 70r, 1430.vii.2.
[46] Pucci, "Proprietà di Mercato Vecchio," p. 407: "Ricavi, quand'è 'l tempo, i contadini / di mele
   calamagne molte some / da Poggibonsi e d'altri confini; / e di più cose ch'io non dico il nome."
[47] Elio Conti, *La formazione della struttura agraria moderna nel contado fiorentino*, I: *Le campagne nell'età comunale*; II, part 2: *Monografie e Tavole Statistiche (secoli XV-XIX)* (Rome, 1965); Pinto, *La Toscana nel tardo
   medio evo: Ambiente, economia rurale, società* (Florence, 1982), esp. ch. 1, and *Città e spazi*, ch. 1;
   Cherubini, *Una comunità dell'Appennino dal XIII al XV secolo: Montecoronaro dalla signoria dell'abbazia
   del Trivio al Dominio di Firenze* (Florence, 1972) and "La 'civiltà' del castagno in Italia alla fine del
   Medioevo," *Archeologia Medievale*, 8 (1981): 247–80.
[48] Braudel, *The Mediterranean and the Mediterranean World in the Age of Philip II*, transl. by Sîan Reynolds,

nities were poor, self-sufficient, and egalitarian without sharp contrasts in the distribution of wealth. They were the backward and patriarchal refuge of outlaws, harboring "rough men, clumsy, stocky, and close-fisted."[49] Along with other niceties of urban culture, religion was here slow to penetrate. "Sorcerers, witchcraft, primitive magic, and black masses were the flowerings of an ancient cultural subconscious."[50]

Braudel supported these static characterizations with testimony taken from the late Middle Ages through the nineteenth century. Although he called for a historical analysis, claiming that "the contrast between plain and mountain is also a question of historical period,"[51] his own historical analysis was limited to a single paragraph, speculating that the earliest pre-Biblical, even prehistoric, civilizations may have arisen in the mountains and then spread irreversibly to the plains.[52]

In evaluating the differences between mountains, hills, and plains, the historian is faced straightaway with a thorny problem of classification: what constitutes a mountain village? While geographers and historians usually take 500 meters in altitude and above to demarcate a mountain settlement and 200 for "the hills," Braudel has rightly questioned this arbitrary standard. In zones such as Colorado or the Alto Adige, 500 meters would constitute the lowlands, while in Scotland, no village in the highlands or elsewhere qualifies as a mountain village by these measures.[53] However, to avoid the relativity of geographical location, Braudel falls into the trap of tautology: rejecting a quantitative threshold, he instead defines mountain communities by those very characteristics he wishes to use to argue for a distinctive "mountain civilization."

Defining the "mountains" north of Florence is less problematic than a global definition. The near sea-level cities of the Arno basin – Florence and Prato (50 and 61 meters respectively) – are the points of departure, and thus 500 meters can readily be adopted to demarcate the mountains.[54] Nonetheless, how do we classify villages whose parish churches

---

2 vols. (New York, 1966 [Paris, 1949]). For a survey of trends in the historiography of mountains from Vidal de la Blache's "possibilisme" to Braudel, see Pier Paolo Viazzo, *Upland Communities: Environment, Population and Social Structure in the Alps since the Sixteenth Century* (Cambridge, 1989), introduction. [49] Braudel, *The Mediterranean*, I, p. 46. [50] *Ibid.*, p. 37. [51] *Ibid.*, p. 53.
[52] *Ibid.*, pp. 51–3. Recent research, however, seriously contests these assumptions: in the prehistoric and ancient period the Mediterranean mountains were less populated relative to the plains than they were after the year 1000. See J. R. McNeill, *The Mountains of the Mediterranean World: An Environmental History* (Cambridge, 1992), ch. 3; and Brent Shaw, "Bandit Highlands and Lowland Peace: The Mountains of Isauria-Cilicia," *Journal of the Social and Economic History of the Orient*, 33 (1990): 199–233 and 237–70.
[53] Ironically, the highest village in Scotland is in the lowlands: Wanlockhead at 421 meters.
[54] McNeill, *The Mountains*, p. 31, uses 500 meters as the demarcation of mountains throughout the Mediterranean area.

may lie below this critical divide but whose lands extended up mountain slopes to peaks as high as 1,000 meters?[55] One way around the problem of definition is to rely on what contemporaries called the mountains or "le alpi." For the most part, this approach has been taken here. Five of the ten mountain villages included in this study are drawn from a zone which had been called the "Alpe degli Ubaldini" and, after Florence's reconstitution of the *vicariatus* of Firenzuola in 1373, was rebaptized as the Alpi Fiorentine;[56] three more are from the area just to the south called the *prope Alpes* but whose villages were all above 500 meters and among the highest within the territory of Florence. The other two lay closer to the cities of Florence and Prato and perhaps are more problematic. The parish church of Schignano in the district of Prato at 460 meters lay just under the critical threshold of 500 meters, but its lands climbed the slopes of the Poggio di Javello to 984 meters. In addition, notarial descriptions of land conveyances and the *estimi* of 1401/2 – the first Florentine tax records to itemize the property holdings of villagers – describe Schignano's property boundaries as "alpi," and its properties of arable land mixed with woodlands, chestnuts, and highland pastures resemble peasant plots found on the other side of the Calvana mountains in the highlands of Montecuccoli and Montecarelli.[57] Hence, I classified the village among the mountain communes. Similarly the parish of Santa Maria Morello lay below the critical level, but its fields, pastures, and woodlands extended up the slopes of Monte Morello which peaked at 934 meters, and like Schignano contemporary notarial transactions described its property borders as "alpes."

Since Braudel's *Mediterranean*, others have been more historically-minded in their treatment of Tuscan highlands. From archival sources, Elio Conti updated Braudel's shift of civilization to the plains, finding the

---

[55] I have taken the altitudes of villages from *Annuario Generale dei comuni e delle frazione d'Italia: Edizione 1980/1985* (Milan, 1980) [hereafter *AG*]; its measures are calculated at the parish church or market square, usually the lowest spot in a mountain village. Cherubini, "San Godenzo nei suoi statuti quattrocenteschi," in *Fra Tevere, Arno e Appennino: Valli, communità, signori* (Florence, 1992), pp. 145–65, and others have recognized as mountain villages places such as San Godenzio at 404 meters but with lands that climb the slopes of the Alpi di San Benedetto to peaks at over 1,000 meters.

[56] See Zorzi, *L'Amministrazione della giustizia*, p. 24; Guidi, *Il Governo*, I, pp. 179–213. According to Stefano Casini, *Dizionario biografico, geografico storico del Comune di Firenzuola*, 3 vols. (Florence, 1914), I, p. 5, this district covered an area that was 38,500 *braccia* wide (east to west) and 45,500 *braccia* long (23.6 kilometers by 27.9).

[57] On these mountains, see Giuseppe Barbieri, "Il Mugello. Studio de geografia umana," *Rivista Geografica Italiana*, 60 (1953), p. 102; and for their castles, Riccardo Francovich, *I Castelli del contado fiorentino nei secoli XII e XIII* (Florence, 1976), pp. 152–3. For Schignano's properties, see Estimo 222, village 59.

plains still "scarcely populated" from the tenth through the twelfth century, while "in the hills life flourished at a pace that it would never again realize."[58] More recently, Chris Wickham underscored Conti's chronology, adding that "economic integration [between the city and mountains] was far less in earlier periods [the ninth through the twelfth century] and, as a consequence, the economic contrasts between mountains and plains were less as well."[59] Yet Wickham argued that "the major difference demonstrated by a study of references in charters, area by area in the Lucchesia and Pisano, is between the plain and the mountains."[60] Furthermore, for the territory just east of Wickham's Garfagnana, David Herlihy has shown the mountains' historical malleability. After the Black Death and through the fifteenth century, the mountains of Pistoia again flourished economically and demographically relative to the lower hills, which earlier had been the cradle of rural wealth and population.[61]

Yet the historian most conversant with medieval and early-modern mountain communities in Tuscany, Giovanni Cherubini, has largely upheld Braudel's view of the mountains of the Mediterranean. Cherubini's panoramic surveys of mountain ecology and society extend from Monte Amiata in the southernmost corner of Tuscany to the mountains of Romagna on the southern watershed of the Po valley. While attempting to preserve Braudel's paradigm,[62] Cherubini's descriptions betray the strains and contradictions inherent in these generalizations. His analysis of the *catasto* of 1428–9 shows wide discrepancies in the social structure across the Florentine Apennines from the "dry mountains" of the Casentino in the southeast, where the poor[63] constituted 88.4 percent of taxpayers, to the Pistoiese mountains in the northwest, where its percentage fell by nearly half (46.2 percent). Here, those of middling wealth – the "mediani" – approached the poor in number (40.8 percent). He

---

[58] Conti, *La formazione*, I, p. 211.

[59] Chris Wickham, *The Mountains and the City: The Tuscan Appennines in the Early Middle Ages* (Oxford, 1988), p. 6.

[60] Wickham, "Economic and Social Institutions in Northern Tuscany in the Eighth Century," in *Istituzioni ecclesiastiche della Toscana medievale*, ed. by Wickham, M. Ronzani, Y. Milo, and A. Spicciani (Galatina, 1980), pp. 7–34.

[61] Herlihy, *Medieval and Renaissance Pistoia*, pp. 50–1. For a similar transformation in the Maritime Alps of Piedmont, see Rinaldo Comba, "Il problema della mobilità geografica delle popolazioni montane alla fine del medioevo attraverso un sondaggio sulle Alpi Marittime," in *Medioevo rurale*, ed. by V. Fumagalli and G. Rossetti (Bologna, 1980), pp. 309–10.

[62] See his *Una comunità*, p. 170: "Una cosa pare comunque sicura: l'equalitarismo' sociale che distingue la montagna rispetto alle pianure dominate dalle città pare anche qui provato."

[63] Cherubini utilizes the categories of property holding devised by Conti from the 1427 *catasto* (*La formazione*, II, part 2, pp. 243–5), which defines "the poor" as property holders with taxable wealth between 1 and 50 florins as opposed to the *miserabili* without any taxable property.

dismisses these variations, however, to argue that "the presence of a few conspicuously wealthy individuals does not change the overall picture in which mountain egalitarianism is distinguished from the proletariatized peasants of the hills and plains." Yet he never supplied figures to compare this "mountain egalitarianism" with holdings lower down.[64]

When Cherubini later turned south to the mountains of Monte Amiata and the alluvial plains of the Maremma, his data further weakened Braudel's paradigm. Because of problems of drainage, marshlands, and malaria, the plains remained as the depressed periphery well into the seventeenth century, while villages on the high slopes of Amiata possessed the highest population densities and greatest sources of wealth. Despite the rich commentary of contemporaries such as Pope Pius II and the figures supplied by the survey of 1640, Cherubini did not question his earlier conclusions of mountain poverty, equality, and backwardness.[65]

True, none of the historians of Tuscany cited above have explored the full range of mountain traits on which Braudel generalized. No one has studied criminal records systematically to test whether mountain violence or its control differed in kind or quantity from violence in the plains.[66] Nor have historians explored the supposed "backwardness" of Italian highlanders' religious attitudes and practices before the Apostolic Visitations of the late sixteenth century.[67] The state archives of Florence and Bologna – the records of the *Capitano*, *Podestà*, and the *Notarile* – allow such an inquiry even if not to gainsay Braudel's generalizations definitively.

[64] Cherubini, "La società dell'Appennino settentrionale (secoli XIII–XV)," in *Signori, contadini, borghesi: ricerche sulla società italiana del basso medioevo* (Florence, 1974); Cherubini, "Qualche considerazione sulle campagne dell' Italia centro-settentrionale tra l'XI e il XV secolo," in *Signori, contadini, borghesi*; and Cherubini, *Una comunità dell'appennino*, pp. 127 and 170. At times Cherubini describes the mountain villagers as desperately impoverished; see, for instance, "Appunti sul brigantaggio," esp. p. 121. From the eighth to the thirteenth century, Wickham, "Economic and Social Institutions," p. 12, has found that while estates may have been smaller in the mountains, "no backward egalitarian pastoralists" filled the mountains of the Garfagnana.

[65] Cherubini, "Risorse, paesaggio ed utilizzazione agricola del territorio della Toscana sud-occidentale nei secoli XIV–XV," in *Civiltà ed economia agricola in Toscana nei secc. XIII–XV: Problemi della vita delle campagne nel tardo medioevo (Pistoia, 21–24 aprile 1977)* (Pistoia, 1981), pp. 91–115.

[66] Such was the objective behind Arturo Palmieri's *La montagna bolognese del Medio Evo* (Bologna, 1929), pp. 415–22. He claimed that the Bolognese Apennines possessed high levels of incest and brigandage, especially toward the end of the fifteenth century, and that the population was prone to insurrection against the magistrates. But the work offers no statistics, few citations of criminal sources, and no comparisons between mountains and plains.

[67] See Susanna Peyrouel Rambaldi, "Podestà e inquisitori nella montagna modenese: Riorganizzazione inquisitoriale e resistenze locali (1570–1590)," *Società e Storia*, no. 52 (1991): 297–328.

In regard to violence, I know of no effective way of measuring it in preindustrial societies. The usual means is through an analysis of criminal records, but before the nineteenth century and perhaps to a large extent even to the present day, these records track the state's strategies of prosecution and social control as much, if not more, than criminal behavior or violence.[68] Nonetheless, a comparison of the criminal sentences from the lowlands near the city of Florence, and highland zones near the Futa pass in communities such as Castro and Casaglia, do show marked differences in the character of violence, if not in its quantity.

From the surviving sentences of the *Podestà* and *Capitano del Popolo*, lowland villages such as Campi, Peretola, and Brozzi abounded in violent acts of armed robbery and assault and battery in the fourteenth and early fifteenth centuries. Indeed, the level of violence counted by fist fights and knifings for late-medieval Campi suggests that the proverb – "Peretola, Brozzi e Campi: the worst rabble god has given us!" – may have had deep-rooted historical origins.[69] Similarly, based on modern-day impressions of mountain violence and backwardness, we might wish to assume that acts of sexual violence and incest in particular were traits more common to highlanders than to others, but the vicariate courts of the early fifteenth century do not support such images; charges of incest clustered as much in the lowlands as in the mountains.[70]

On the other hand, the criminal acts in the mountains describe collective violence, often listing large numbers of perpetrators and victims, while crime in the lowlands tended to be of an individual character. In the lowlands assaults, house-breakings, or acts of slander rarely involved more than the assailant and the victim, and when they did, the partners in violence as well as those injured generally came from the same village or, if not, from within the same parish (*pieve*). While insurrection was spreading through the mountains of the Pistoiese and the Alpi Fiorentine in 1401 to 1403, the criminal acts for places like Brozzi in the plains described men from the same village "coming to words" which led to blows and sentences with relatively small monetary fines.[71] Such valley violence often touched the lives of women, both as perpetrators and targets of violence. In 1428, two married women, both from the village of San Martino a Sesto, were washing their clothes in the river called the Gravina. One called the other a whore ("Tu sy una puetana"); the other grabbed her by the hair and dragged her along the road also

[68] See Cohn, *Women in the Streets*, ch. 2.
[69] "Peretola, Brozzi e Campi: la peggio genìa che dio ci scampi!" I thank Giovanni Ciappelli for this proverb. [70] Cohn, *Women in the Streets*, ch. 6. [71] AP, 3886, 12r.

calling her a whore. Denounced by the village rector, they were both
fined small amounts.[72]

Most of the descriptions of these assaults are monotonous and tell us
little about the perpetrators' motivations, but some paint small cameos
of village life that cannot be seen from other sources. For instance, in
1403 while two men both from the same village of San Donnino were
fishing at the bridge on the Osmannoro road, a man from neighboring
San Martino (the same parish as Brozzi) approached them with an iron-
handled spade, charging that they had no business fishing in that pool
since it belonged to him, and threatened one of them with his spade.
The second fisherman rushed to his friend's defense with a lance that
just happened to be in his hands (while fishing!) and knocked their assailant into the stream. It is clear that these men all knew one another: while
the man claiming to own the fishing rights was now floating in his
stream, the fisherman with the lance asked with a certain satisfaction:
"So Luke, what'd you say you're going to do?"[73]

Although such cases of violence involving two or three men or women
can be easily multiplied, cases of collective violence, whether of a political sort or not, are much harder to spot in the lowlands near Florence
for the late Trecento and Quattrocento. The acts that come closest to
political violence were occasional attacks on the *Podestà*'s police (*berrovarri*
and *nuntii*) who came to arrest those who had not paid their taxes or,
more commonly, for debts owed to Florentine citizens. Such incidents
were usually staged by the wife of the debtor and rarely involved more
than family members; when they did, those who gave assistance were
neighbors. Yet, despite prior planning, as is often made clear, the courts
did not define these crimes as political (*conventiculum, conspiratio, rebellio*).

In the acts of the *Podestà* that I have surveyed from the 1340s to 1430 I
have seen only one case of collective political violence from the lowlands.
It is found in a case from the village of Gangalandi, in Valdarno
Inferiore[74] adjudicated in August, 1402. In December of the previous
year, the *Podestà* arrested six men, all from Gangalandi who had congregated over eighty people in the village piazza. The men of the village
had raised their banners and flags and with offensive and defensive arms
attacked the house of a certain Martin and carted off his goods.
Unfortunately, the court's description does not say what was on their
flags, who this Martin was, what he had done to offend his neighbors, or

---

[72] AP, 4392, np.
[73] Capitano del Popolo [hereafter CP], 2188, 81r–2r (Inquisition); and 2207, 28v–9r (sentence):
"Luca, che dì tu che farai?"   [74] AP, 3856, 48r–9r; see also p. 219.

why the case was described in political terms (*ad invicem compositum, posturam et tractatum et ordinationem* – words that formulaically accompanied descriptions of "rebellion" and occupations of castles taken from Florentine suzerainty). But the Gangalandi incident was the exception that proves the rule. Unlike collective action from the mountains, where social networks could extend over great distances and cross state borders, all the named participants at Gangalandi were from that commune, the place of their armed robbery.

To be sure, violence in the mountains also arose between neighbors and could be as spontaneous as that between the two washerwomen from Sesto. Such was a case from Mangona in 1411, when two men from the village "came to words" and one began hurling rocks at the other.[75] But, by contrast, the *Podestà* and *Capitano del Popolo* provide a rich array of collective acts of violence from the mountains that crossed parish and other wider neighborhood boundaries, linking highwaymen across the mountainous frontiers of Florence.[76] Often these bands comprised men who lived on both sides of the Florentine border, as did the cattle rustlers in 1402 who freely crossed the Florence–Siena border to invade various southern mountain communities.[77] Similarly, territorial boundaries seemed to make little difference to the scores of highwaymen, vagabonds, and insurgents who regularly captured men and animals during the period of insurgency in the Montagna di Pistoia, the Alpi Fiorentine, and the Romagna from 1401 to 1403. Such remained the case certainly through the Laurentian period, as is revealed in letters to Lorenzo when youths from Firenzuola assisted by their friends from across the border in Bologna attacked and injured the *vicarius*'s officers.[78]

In addition, the numerous acts of peace (*pax*) and treaties (*tregua*) among villagers in the notarial acts highlight these differences in social bonding and networks of friendship. In the highlands, such "compromises" over daily disputes could cross parish boundaries and even mountain ranges, as did a "peace" in 1432 whose social bonds criss-crossed the Calvana mountains from the *contado* of Prato (San Cresci de Pimonte) to various points in the Mugello (San Niccolò a Latera, Santa Reparata, and Camoggiano).[79] These disputes and agreements also drew parties

[75] AP, 4261, 67v.
[76] See for instance CP, 2107, np, 1399.xi.8, where highwaymen mostly from the Montagna Fiorentina (Garliano) were supported by a man from San Giovanni Valdarno far to the south and another from the Romagna miles to the north of Garliano. [77] AP, 3886, 59r–v.
[78] Salvadori, "Rapporti personali," p. 140. [79] Not. antecos., 792, 138v, 1432.vii.28.

together across the borders of Florence and Bologna. In 1431, against previous "injustices, injuries, and assaults," three brothers from Barberino in the Mugello along with their children and all their descendants down the male line in perpetuity "made peace, concord, and good will" with two brothers, their sons, and descendants in Baragazza in the *contado* of Bologna, across several Apennine passes from Barberino.[80] Another truce absolved fines and settled a long-term armed struggle between two kin groups (*consortii*) in the Bolognese Apennines, one from Castel d'Alpi, the other from Qualto. But many of those who stood surety for this "peace" came from the Alpi Fiorentine, and the act was drawn up by a Florentine notary.[81]

Other notarized acts show the fluidity of borders and, in contrast to those in the plains, the long distances over which mountain dwellers made friends, gave trust, and engaged in business. When a woman in Florence entered into contracts she first had to abide by Lombard law and select a male protector or *mundualdus* to represent her.[82] In the plains, such acts of trust usually bonded together men and women from the same parish. In other instances, these rural women chose patricians from Florence (most likely their landlords) to "protect" them.[83] But when a woman from Galliano in the heart of the Mugello[84] wished to sell her house and several strips of land, she contracted as her *mundualdus* a man from Santo Stefano a Rapezzo 18 kilometers north in the Alpi Fiorentine.[85] Similarly, such long-distance bonds also connected those of the mountain elites. In 1435 a woman from the Ubaldini clan, who lived in the parish of San Bartolomeo a Galliano, entrusted a nobleman from across the border as her *mundualdus* – Lodovico di fu messer Ricciardo Alidosi of Imola (de Alediogis).[86]

Property sales and the termination of agreements (*finis*), usually credit–debt contracts, also show the cross-parish and cross-border character of mountain relationships. A man from the parish of San Michele a Baragazza in the mountains of Bologna sold arable land with vineyards in the parish of San Piero a Cirignano (Barberino) to a peasant from Barberino.[87] And a man from Montecarelli had business dealings with a man from San Piero Agliana across the Calvana mountains and

---

[80] *Ibid.*, 124r, 1431.ii.17.   [81] *Ibid.*, 162v, 1433.v.17.

[82] On the *mundualdus*, see Thomas Kuehn, "'Cum Consensu Mundualdi': Legal Guardianship of Women in Quattrocento Florence," *Viator* 13 (1982): 309–33.

[83] Not. antecos., 858, 83r, 1371.xi.24; a woman from Sesto chose a Brunelleschi as her *mundualdus*.

[84] See Francovich, *I Castelli del contado*, p. 92.   [85] Not. antecos., 792, 200v, 1434.vii.18.

[86] *Ibid.*, 217v, 1435.iii.25.

[87] *Ibid.*, 156v, 1432.iii.4; this parish does not exist in the *catasto* of 1427; see Repetti, *Diz.*, III, p. 42.

the border of Pistoia.[88] Such relations could span across the whole of the Mugello's vast territory.[89] In 1366 a certain Piero di Mazze from Agliana in the Pistoiese loaned 10 florins to a peasant residing in the Mugello's far eastern Quarter of San Giovanni, the *pieve* of San Casciano in Padule. The same Piero also sold property across the Mugello and into the northernmost corner of the Florentine territory, to men living in San Martino a Vespignano.[90]

Indeed, the distances traveled to use a particular notary's services show again the more open world of the mountains as opposed to the enclosed circuits of social bondings in the plains. Many of the patrons of the Barberino notary Ser Antonio di Giusto came from mountain villages in the state of Bologna, despite differences in law and custom between the two states. Perhaps they had come from Florentine families which had earlier migrated over the Apennines.

But the most impressive witness to these widespread networks of association within the mountains comes in the lists of insurgents who rebelled against Florentine rule from 1401 to 1405. Indeed, the framework of social relations and communications was probably one of the elements which enabled these peasants to resist Florentine might. An uprising in Barga in 1401 mixed men mostly from this market town and the surrounding district of Garfagnana with allies as far afield as Poppi in the former *contado* of Arezzo. Further, these insurgents show Tuscanwide allegiances, holding secret meetings in the city of Lucca.[91]

Lord Ricciardo Cancellieri's raids through the *contado* of Pistoia gathered men from the villages of the Montagna di Pistoia[92] with other mountain dwellers across the border in Bologna. Finally, the place names found in the *Podestà*'s and *Capitano*'s condemnations of the mountain rebels who occupied castles, built bastions, and made war on Florentine possessions in the Alpi Fiorentine and Podere Fiorentino during the fall and winter of 1402 sweep across the mountain ridges of the Mugello, the Alpi Fiorentine, the Podere, the Montagna Fiorentine, the Bolognese Apennines, the county of Alidosio, the territory of Imola, and the Romagna.[93]

---

[88] Not. antecos., 792, 201v, 1434.viii.5.
[89] The Mugello is 570 square kilometers; Barbieri, "Il Mugello," p. 96.
[90] Not. antecos., 858, 2r–v, 1366.xii.23 and 1366.i.18.
[91] Giudice degli appelli e nullità [hereafter Giudice], 97, 114r–15v, 1401.xii.24.
[92] Florence divided the Pistoiese *contado*, creating the district of the Montagna di Pistoia in 1373; in the same year it established the new vicariate of the Alpi Fiorentine: see Chittolini, "Ricerche sull'ordinamento," p. 296.
[93] CP, 2199, 34r–8v, 1403.v.23. In addition, the courts held back the names of others to facilitate future arrests: "et plures alii quorum nomina ad presens pro meliori tacentur."

This wider array of criminal and political association in the mountains corresponds with patterns of association gleaned from notarized marriage records. While a third of peasants from the plains found their partners within the same parish, less than 17 percent from the mountain villages of the Upper Mugello and Alpi and only 8 percent within the mountain communities of the Casentino married within their own villages. In addition, only 14 percent of couples in which at least one spouse came from the plains married across districts that jumped contiguous *pieve* or vicariate borders or crossed political divides, such as from the *contado* into the city or across state lines. By contrast, 36 percent of couples crossed such boundaries in the mountain zones of the Mugello, Alpi, and the Casentino, even though the secular zones used by state officials to classify these mountain areas were considerably larger and more populous than the ecclesiastical boundaries of the traditional *pievi*, which continued to be used for fiscal and notarial demarcations within the plains.[94]

These contrasting patterns of association from criminal collusion to marriage reflect differences in livelihood and land tenure. The predominance of landholding in the plains and hills near Florence and Prato was comprised of *mezzadria* and short-term rental contracts. These were of short duration, lasting from as little as one to at most five years and show the frequent but short distances these peasant families moved from one contract and one landlord to the next. Usually their change in contract took them to farms within the same *pieve* and often within the same parish.[95] As Herlihy and Klapisch-Zuber have observed, "the mobility in the *mezzadria* zones was largely a 'circular' mobility."[96] To this, it should be added that these circuits covered tiny distances.

---

[94] These results are further expounded in my "Marriage in the Mountains." They contrast sharply with the highly endogamous marriages found for the Genoese Apennines during the sixteenth and early seventeenth centuries; Osvaldo Raggio, *Faide e parentele: Lo stato genovese visto dalla Fontanabuona* (Turin, 1990), pp. 120–4.

[95] In addition to the numerous contracts redacted by the Mazzetti, see *Il Contratto di mezzadria nella Toscana medievale*, I: *Il Contado di Siena, secolo XIII–1348*, ed. by Paolo Pirillo and Pinto (Florence, 1987); *Il Contratto di mezzadria*, II: *Il Contado di Firenze, secolo XIII*, ed. by Oretta Muzzi and Maria Nenci (Florence, 1988); *Il Contratto di mezzadria*, III: *Il Contado di Siena, 1349–1518*, ed. by Gabriella Piccinni (Florence, 1992); Muzzi, "Aspetti dell'evoluzione demografica della Valdelsa fiorentina nel tardo medioevo (1350–1427)," in *Strutture familiari, epidemie, migrazioni nell'Italia medievale*, ed. by Comba, Piccinni, and Pinto (Naples, 1984), p. 140; and la Roncière, *Un changeur florentin du Trecento: Lippo di Fede del Sega (1285 env. – 1363 env.)* (Paris, 1973), pp. 118 and 163, who finds that the average length of contract in 1315–59 was three years. Such frequent but short moves continued to characterize the *mezzadria* through the eighteenth century; see Emmanuel Todd, "Mobilité géographique et cycle de vie en Artois et en Toscane au XVIIIe siècle," *Annales, E.S.C.*, 30 (1974): 726–44.

[96] Herlihy and Klapisch-Zuber, *Les Toscans*, p. 315. Also, see Maria Serena Mazzi and Sergio Raveggi, *"Gli uomini e le cose" nelle campagne fiorentine del Quattrocento* (Florence, 1983), p. 68.

By contrast, those in the mountains owned small plots of land and animals or had perpetual leases from feudal lords such as the Guidi, the Ubaldini, and the Lords of Romagna. Many possessed cattle and crossed large expanses of Tuscany in seasonal migrations from summer to winter pastures, known as transhumance.[97] Indirect evidence, such as the criminal records, reflects the distances these peasants traveled following their flocks and the interregional associations they encountered. The vicariate courts record the rape of a six-and-a-half-year-old traveling with her flocks on the transhumance from Verghereto high in the Romagna Apennines (beyond the present borders of Tuscany)[98] to the parish of San Cristofano a Lucignano in the southern Chianti. (Given the circuitous route through the mountains, the journey was certainly no less than a hundred kilometers and no doubt required several days or weeks.) She was sodomized by a "vagabond" from Ischia in the Maremma Senese, most likely also a shepherd on the transhumance, several hundred kilometers from home.[99]

But seasonal movement was not the only force that pushed the mountain villagers of the upper Mugello and Alpi across mountain ranges and political boundaries. The damages caused by war and brigands coupled with Florentine tax policy was the prod towards more permanent moves and resettlement in the late fourteenth and early fifteenth centuries. Once these highlanders had left Florentine territory, however, their ties of friendship (and enmity) with their former villages did not end, as the lists of insurgents and the places of their secret meetings prove. Such ties can also be seen in the deals that peasants successfully negotiated with the Florentine state in the aftermath of the 1402–3 insurrections in the Alpi Fiorentine and Podere. The peasant ringleaders who had crossed the border fleeing the Florentine tax collectors in the 1390s secured the rights in 1403 of choosing who among their former ex-patriate villagers would be allowed to move back into the Florentine *contado* with long-term tax exemptions.[100]

Whether from the seasonal moves of work or from the pressures of war and heavy taxation, highland peasants made permanent moves, if not more frequently, then certainly over longer distances than peasants from the lowlands. Four tax surveys of Florence called *Capi di famiglia*

---

[97] See Cherubini, "Paesaggio agrario, insediamenti e attività silo-pastorali sulla montagna tosco-romagnola alla fine del medioevo," in Cherubini, *Fra Tevere*, pp. 48–53; *Una comunità*, pp. 50–3; and Wickham, *The Mountains*, pp. 24–5 and 164.

[98] On these mountain communities in the Trecento, see Cherubini, *Una comunità*.

[99] Giudice, 102, I, 47r–v, 1429.ix.9.   [100] See chapter 6.

from 1383 to 1412 are remarkable in that they list villagers according to whether they had stayed in the community since the previous tax survey – the "stanti"; emigrated into the village – "venuti" or "tornati"; or had left – "perduti," "partiti," or "usciti." From twenty-eight rural parishes sampled from the Quarter of Santa Maria Novella, half of the lowland migrants had arrived from or left for other villages within the same *pieve*, while for the highlands, the percentage fell to little more than a quarter, despite the fact that these mountain zones were larger units. (In cases such as the Alpi Fiorentine they encompassed territories that had previously been three separate *pievi*.[101]) On the other hand, only 12 percent of the lowlanders crossed the Florentine border or had disappeared from the taxkeepers' reckoning, which the village commissioner would jot down with phrases such has: "one doesn't know where he's gone"; "gone begging"; "has left because of debts"; "has gone to collect charity."[102] By contrast, such moves beyond the Florentine borders comprised 40 percent of the highland migrants.

The highlanders' movements, however, do not substantiate claims made as early as the fourteenth-century Bolognese agronomist Pietro de' Crescenzi to the present[103] that mountain people inexorably moved downward in search of work in the supposedly greener pastures of the plains or the more lucrative markets of the cities.[104] As table 1.1 shows, Florence was the least likely place mountain villagers wished to move. As Niccolò Rodolico and others have shown, the time for such a migratory attraction would certainly have been the period after the Black Death through the early Quattrocento, when labor shortages and lower guild matriculation fees opened new opportunities for immigrants from the countryside.[105]

---

[101] The Alpi Fiorentine comprised the *pievi* of "Cornaclarii et Camaioris et Bordignani."
[102] "Non si sa dove"; "va accattando"; se n'andò per debito"; "se n'è ito per le limosina."
[103] Braudel, *The Mediterranean*, I, pp. 44, 47; Cherubini, "Conclusione," in *Strutture familiari*, p. 539; Fiumi, "Sui rapporti," p. 68.
[104] The most systematic study of rural migration in late medieval Florence is La Roncière, *Prix et salaires à Florence au XIVe siècle (1280–1380)* (Rome, 1987), pp. 661–80, which also focuses on those who moved to the city of Florence. Similarly, Herlihy and Klapisch-Zuber, *Les Toscans*, pp. 301–26, assumed that "rural emigration played largely to the benefit of the big towns" (p. 315). Elsewhere historians have studied more closely the migratory flows between localities in the countryside, see Franca Leverotti, "La crisi demografica nella Toscana del trecento: l'esempio delle Sei Miglia lucchesi," in *La Toscana nel secolo XIV. Caratteri di una civiltà regionale* (Pisa, 1988), pp. 67–150; *Popolazione, famiglie, insediamento: Le Sei Miglia lucchesi nel XIV e XV secolo* (Pisa, 1992), pp. 86–103; and Francesco Panero, "Popolamento e movimenti migratori nel contado vercellese, nel Biellese e nella Valsesia (secoli X–XIII)," in *Strutture familiari*, pp. 350–1.
[105] Niccolò Rodolico, *La democrazia fiorentina nel suo tramonto, 1378–82* (Bologna, 1905), pp. 1–45; La Roncière, *Prix et salaires*, pp. 661–80.

Table 1.1 *Migration, 1383–1412*

District	Florence	*Pieve*	*Contado*	Beyond borders	Total
Plains: (*venuti* + *usciti*)	88	436	253	107	884
	9.95%	49.32%	28.62%	12.10%	100%
Hills	23	136	181	64	404
	5.69%	33.66%	44.80%	15.84%	100%
Highlands	32	164	163	237	596
	5.37%	27.52%	27.35%	39.77%	100%
Prato	9	22	9	30	70
	12.86%	31.43%	12.86%	42.86%	100%
Total	152	758	606	438	1954
	7.78%	38.79%	31.01%	22.42%	100%

Yet the evidence from the *estimi* does not bear out these assumptions, at least for the last two decades of the Trecento. Of those highlanders whose destinations the local syndics of the commune recorded, only 5 percent went to Florence. Moreover, these were neither the wealthy found by Johan Plesner for late thirteenth-century Passignano[106] nor the brawny ("il braccio più forte"), soon to become revolutionary Ciompi, as Rodolico supposed in his classic version of Florentine immigration after the Black Death.[107] As can be seen from the *estimi*'s listings, the city-bound, not only from the mountains, but across the *contado* at the end of the Trecento, did not migrate as nuclear or extended families at all, but, for the most part, were single women seeking urban employ-ment as domestic servants (*fante*) or assistance in charitable institutions. Evidence from private memoirs (*ricordanze*) on domestic servitude, more-over, suggests that these trends became accentuated through the first half of the Quattrocento.[108]

The largest proportion of highland migration was out of Florence's *contado* and into lands not subject to the *estimo*. Unfortunately, either

---

[106] Plesner, *L'émigration de la campagne à la ville libre de Florence au 13e siècle* (Copenhagen, 1934).

[107] Rodolico, *La democrazia fiorentina*, pp. 44–5.

[108] From the mountain commune of Mangona, four left for Florence to become domestic servants. All were women and appear to have migrated alone. One was an unmarried girl whose father had recently died; two were widows; the fourth was a married woman whose husband remained behind in the village. On country women who came to the city as domestic servants, see Klapisch-Zuber, "Women Servants in Florence during the Fourteenth and Fifteenth Centuries," in *Women and Work in Preindustrial Europe*, ed. by Barbara A. Hanawalt (Bloomington, 1986), pp. 56–80.

because they did not know or did not need to say, the officials often failed to specify foreign villages of destination; usually they merely signaled them by phrases such as "quello di Pistoia" or "nel contado di Bologna." But when they did specify the foreign destination, it was most often a mountain village and not a city or place in the plains. Of forty-three specifically listed destinations for mountain dwellers who left the *contado* of Florence, thirty-two were to mountain communes and only one was to the plains (Agliana). The others were Pistoia, Bologna, and Grosseto, but like the designations vaguely put as "quello di . . .", these may have indicated these cities' territories rather than the cities themselves.

As the altitudes of these foreign villages suggest – Belvedere (463m), Scanello (490m), Castel di Càsio (533m), Ripoli (560m), Sant'Andrea in the Val di Sambro (589m), Quinzano (622m), San Pellegrino (653m), Baragazza (675m), San Damiano (691m), Castel dell'Alpi (694m), Sambuca (726m), Qualto (762m), Bruscoli (765m), Piamaggio (787m), Scaricalasino (present-day Monghidoro, 841m) Pietramala (851m – then within the confines of the Bolognese state)[109] – most often the highlanders' movement was, instead of downward, upward from the Alpi Fiorentine and *prope Alpes* to the higher Bolognese or Pistoiese Alps.[110] Occasionally, the Florentine highlanders migrated to places further along the transhumance highways, to villages as far away as Gerifalco in the Maremma (774m), Acquapendente and Viterbo in Lazio, and others within the *contadi* of Grosseto and Siena. Some even went beyond these networks, to destinations such as Padua, Naples, and Hungary. But, as we shall see, such further-flung networks of association, work, and migration did not mean that the highlanders' communities were less cohesive than those in the valleys. Instead, evidence from last wills and local statutes suggests that the mountain dwellers' corporate identity around their parish churches for both religious and social life was at the same time as strong as, if not stronger than, that of the plainsmen.

Thus, the criminal, notarial, and fiscal records show qualitative and quantitative differences between the social worlds of the highlanders and plainsmen that may have stretched over long periods of time. Do

---

[109] I was unable to find the following villages in the Bolognese and Imolese Apennines: Amazona, Castro Giavenzi, Pinzano, Qualia, Rovina Rossa, Saffiglione, Santa Cristina.

[110] On the receiving end, Palmieri, *La Montagna bolognese*, p. 242, claims that the population of the Montagna Bolognese began to increase at the turn of the century. Perhaps Florentine mountain flight was the reason.

the archives allow us to peer into the cultural and religious worlds of these largely illiterate peasant societies? One insight into the culture of the mountains can be gleaned from the tax registers. The Florentine *estimi* of 1371 are the first records I know anywhere in Europe to list ages of all household members. In this survey the extent of age rounding was extreme, but over time rural numeracy appears to have improved. Here, if we assume the backwardness of the mountains, the differences from mountains to plains to towns is surprising. As measured by the reporting and rounding of ages to ten- or five-year clusters, no significant differences separated those from the mountains and the valleys. In 1371 mountain dwellers were even slightly more numerate than those nearer the city and in the plains, and by 1487, highlanders were as numerate as the urban population of Prato.[111] This stands to reason, since those in the mountains dealt directly and daily in market exchanges, selling their animals and produce within interregional networks. Thus they were forced to deal with numbers as part of their daily survival.[112]

Another indirect source that historians have recently employed to study the diffusion of religious and cultural leanings has been changes in given names.[113] But historians have yet to dissect the Florentine territory into different zones or even to compare the city with its hinterland. Did mountain villagers retain their German and good-luck names such as Bonaguido or Dietisalvi longer than those in the plains? Was the impact of the mendicants stronger in the plains with a rise in saints' names such as Francesco, Domenico, Antonio, and the like as well as a new vogue for older Christian names such as Giovanni?

Over the relatively short period 1365 to 1427, the naming practices do not suggest that the mountain dwellers of the Mugello or even distant places on the edge of Tuscany were isolated pockets cut off from or resistant to religious practices and piety emanating from the city. True,

---

[111] In 1371, 242 of 287 (84 percent) who reported their ages rounded them in the plains, while 175 of 215 (81 percent) did so in the mountains. In 1487 those from the city of Prato rounded their ages in 35 percent of the cases (37 of 106) and those in the mountains in 39 percent (142 of 363). Even if this reporting depended solely on the notary, it would nonetheless reflect changes in the local intelligentsia, which at least before 1427 depended on local notaries.

[112] Melis, "Momenti dell'economia del Casentino nei secoli XIV e XV," in Melis, *Industria e commercio nella Toscana medievale*, ed. by Bruno Dini (Florence, 1989), p. 192.

[113] See la Roncière, "L'influence des franciscains dans la campagne de Florence au XIVe siècle (1280–1360)," *Mélanges de l'Ecole française de Rome: Moyen âge-Temps moderns*, 87, no. 1 (1975): 27–103, esp. p. 28; "Orientations pastorales du clergé, fin du XIIIe–XIVe siècle: le témoignage de l'onomastism toscane," in *Académie des Inscriptions et Belles-lettres. Comptes-rendus des séances de l'année, 1983 janvier-mars* (Paris, 1983), pp. 43–65; Herlihy, *The Black Death and the Transformation of the West*, ed. by Cohn (Cambridge, Mass., 1997), pp. 75–8; and "The Josephine Waters Bennett Lecture: Tuscan Names, 1200–1530," *Renaissance Quarterly* 41, no. 4 (1988): 561–83.

the earliest surviving *estimi* show the spread of Christian names in the mountain communes lagging behind the towns and the plains. While in Prato and Sesto the proportion of Christian names hovered around half in 1365, only 40 percent of first names in the mountain communes of Mangona and Montecuccoli were Christian, and the percentage declined further north, towards the Futa pass. As late as 1394, the number of saints' names in San Martino a Castro was less than a third of all first names.

But by the *catasto* of 1427, a remarkable uniformity in naming practices had swept across much of the Florentine state. In Prato, Sesto, Mangona, Montecuccoli, and Castro, the number of Christian names now comprised two-thirds of the first names of household heads. The percentage of Christian names in Mangona now even exceeded that of the city of Prato, and a place as far removed and as high up as Verghereto (at over 800 m) attained roughly the same level of Christian first names as Sesto less than 10 kilometers from Florence. Yet as David Herlihy suggested in one of his last essays, these changes may have depended as much on changes in the Florentine state's efforts to standardize names as on the mentality of the individuals themselves or shifts in popular piety.[114]

Can we delve further into the religious and charitable choices peasants made during the fourteenth and fifteenth centuries? Sources that reflect more directly on the religious attitudes and practices of mountain dwellers are among the most difficult to uncover in the archives. The Episcopal Visitations of Florence, so useful for looking at cultural and religious differences for the late sixteenth century and on,[115] did not penetrate beyond Borgo San Lorenzo in the fourteenth and fifteenth centuries.[116] One source, however, that reveals the religious choices of citizens as well as rural subjects is last wills and testaments, despite the constraints of notarial formulae and the presence of clerics at the bedside.[117]

As with marriage records, the survival of notarial books has been low in the mountains compared with the plains near Florence, especially for the fourteenth century. Nonetheless, I have been able to collect sixty-four

---

[114] Herlihy, "The Josephine Waters Bennett Lecture," pp. 575–6. I am more convinced by la Roncière's arguments, which Herlihy fails to mention.

[115] Rambaldi, "Podestà e inquisitori nella montagna."

[116] See the *Visite pastorali* of 1383 and 1422.

[117] For a discussion of the pitfalls and possibilities of using testaments for assessing changes in mentality, see Le Roy Ladurie, "Chaunu, Lebrun, Vovelle: The New History of Death," in *The Territory of the Historian*, pp. 273–84; and Cohn, *The Cult of Remembrance: Six Renaissance Cities in Central Italy* (Baltimore, 1992), pp. 11–17.

testaments of mountain dwellers. They come largely from notaries who worked in the Alpi Fiorentine and extend from the Mugello village of Sant'Agata (341 m) to Bruscoli (765 m) on the border of Bologna. A second sample of mountain testaments comes from notaries who worked in the Aretine highlands around Caprese (653 m). To draw comparisons I again rely largely on samples taken from the massive records left by the Mazzetti family, who worked the parishes just west of the Florentine city walls from Quarto to Campi.

Because the mountain testaments are confined almost exclusively to the fifteenth century, an analysis of religious customs and attitudes over time is restricted. Nonetheless, in the fifteenth century, contrary to what we may have expected, the mountain villagers appear more pious than plainsmen in their last wills. Half of those from the plains (sixteen of thirty-two testators) left no pious bequests at all (after the requisite 5 to 20 *soldi* to the Cathedral of Santa Reparata and its sacristy).[118] By contrast, only five (of sixty-four) of those from the Florentine mountains refrained from giving something to the church or a pious cause.

Nor do these differences emerge from differences in wealth. With few exceptions rural tenants with little landed property or other goods drew up these testaments; rarely did their legacies exceed five itemized bequests to both pious and nonpious beneficiaries. In fact, those who left nothing to charitable causes were not necessarily the poorest testators. For instance, in 1417 after the statutory legacies of 10s for the Cathedral and 20s for the sacristy, a man from the suburban parish of Santa Maria a Novoli chose to be buried in his parish church but left no sums for the church or any other charitable or ecclesiastical institution. Yet he was hardly a *miserabile*. He restored his wife's dowry of 50 florins (a large dowry by rural standards) and left her the usufruct of his house and all his other possessions so long as she lived there with his children and his mother and did not ask for her dowry. He also granted his mother the usufruct of his goods and the rights to live in the house so long as she remained a widow. Further, if his wife, then pregnant, should bear daughters, they would receive dowries of 50 florins each. If no sons succeeded, his estate would go to his paternal uncle, and if his uncle predeceased him, the estate would be divided between two sets of cousins, the sons of two paternal uncles. He elected his wife, mother, paternal uncle,

---

[118] It should not be assumed that this seeming rural detachment from the church (in comparison to that seen in urban wills) was the norm in late-medieval Europe. In mostly rural Forez (southern France) only 3 percent of testators left nothing to the church; see Marguerite Gonon, *Les Institutions et la société en Forez au XIVe siècle d'après les testaments* (Mâcon, 1960), p. 60.

one of his cousins, and an apparently unrelated man from his parish as his executors.[119] Such testaments, grounded in the anxiety of property succession among relatives, were typical of lowland testaments that conveyed no property or sums to the church or religious causes.[120] They even chose persons with no obvious kinship as their universal heirs over the church.

Despite this difference between plains and mountains, the wills of both rural zones appear otherwise remarkably similar, especially in contrast to the pious practices shown in the wills of laborers, artisans, and shopkeepers in Tuscan and Umbrian cities.[121] Unlike those in the cities, testaments from the plains and mountains were dominated by concerns over the allocation of property to kin and friends and not to an array of charitable causes. First, rural testators rarely made more than two pious bequests as opposed to six or more from urban laborers and artisans. Second, while pious outnumbered nonpious legacies in the cities, the reverse was the case in the countryside. Third, testators without living sons were far more reluctant in the country than in the city to name the church or any charitable institution as even a contingent universal heir to their estates. Instead, as in the will of the man from Novoli, rural testators turned to their wives, daughters, uncles, cousins, and even aged mothers or neighbors' sons before naming the church as their heir of last resort. Of the ninety-six wills I have collected for the mountains and plains, only seven chose an ecclesiastical body or pious cause as residual heir, and in four of these the choice was contingent on the death before adulthood of the first-chosen.[122]

Again, wealth was not the critical variable in explaining the charitable differences. Not only the number of pious choices but those choices themselves differed between city and countryside. First, by the early years of the fifteenth century, the foundation of dowry funds to endow from one to twenty-five girls of good character had become a distinctive trait of early Renaissance city wills.[123] By contrast, only one rural testament bequeathed such a foundation; it came from a man from the Florentine Romagna in 1437.[124] Nor did these rural testators even leave dowries unspecified as charitable legacies (*pro salute anime*) to individually named girls from their village as in hundreds of bequests

[119] Not. antecos., 13527, np, document no. 44, 1417.ix.4.
[120] *Ibid.*, np, 12, 1409.v.21; np, 16, 1413.v.7; np, 16; np, 18, 1413.iii.4; np, 28, 1417.vii.3; np, 38, 1417.ix.4; np, 59, 1420.ii.1.   [121] See Cohn, *The Cult of Remembrance.*
[122] Not.antecos., 6599, 51r–v, 1441.iii.27; 792, 213r, 1434.ii.7; and 11059, np, 1397.ix.2; 792, 241v, 1435.xii.3.
[123] See Cohn, *Cult of Remembrance*, pp. 65–71; and Cohn, *Women in the Streets*, ch. 3.
[124] Not. antecos., 1316, 69v–70v, 1437.v.9.

seen from the wills of early Renaissance cities. Only one testator, again, a man from the mountains, the *prope Alpes* village of Mangona, left 10 *lire* apiece to augment the dowries of three girls from his village.[125]

Second, although the importance of bequests to nunneries and the old Benedictine, Carthusian, Camaldolese, or Vallombrosian monasteries had declined in city wills by the early fifteenth century from their pre-Black Death heights, they still continued to command 10 percent or more of all pious bequests in the city of Florence well into the fifteenth century.[126] Yet not a single testator in my samples of either the mountains or plains left a bequest to these pious neighbors, in marked contrast to the patterns of deference and patronage found for rural Tuscany in the central Middle Ages,[127] or to the idealized picture drawn by Giovanni di Pagnolo Morelli, who claimed that the monastic houses of the Mugello were built and maintained by the devout legacies of the peasantry.[128] As with other reminiscences about his ancestral homeland, Morelli was either rhapsodizing about a past that never existed or reflecting on one that had faded by the time of his chronicling.

Nor did such lack of devotion stem from the absence of monastic foundations through the Mugello, the Alpi, and the Casentino. Rather, hermits (*romiti*) of the central Middle Ages had seen the mountainous wastelands as particularly attractive refuges from urban temptation, and such organizations grew in number and in wealth through the later Middle Ages and into the early-modern period. Nunneries such as that of Rapezzo regularly appear as contiguous property holders of lands belonging to mountain peasants.[129] These and other ancient houses at Vaiano, Montepiano, Luco di Mugello, Crespino, and Razzuolo were probably the largest property holders in the hills and mountains of the Mugello[130] with the possible exception of the cathedral chapter of

---

[125] *Ibid.*, 792, 213r, 1434.ii.7. [126] Cohn, *The Cult of Remembrance*, p. 42.

[127] See Wickham, *The Mountains*; for France, Stephen White, *Custom, Kinship, and Gifts to Saints: The Laudatio Parentum in Western France, 1050–1150* (Chapel Hill, N.C., 1988); and Barbara Rosenwein, *To be the Neighbor of Saint Peter: The Social Meaning of Cluny's Property* (Ithaca, N.Y., 1989).

[128] Morelli, *Ricordi*, p. 96: "E prima, e' sono persone divote e caritative, secondo loro essere [condizione], verso Idio; e questo vedi perchè da loro più luoghi di gran divozione sono nel detto paese edificati e non sanza grande aiuto e limosine fatte pe' paesani, e così di continuo sono da loro mantenuti."

[129] See the testament of a widow from Ronta, Not. antecos., 858, 66r–v, 1370.ix.16.

[130] For evidence of the Badìa di Vaiano's property holdings, see Estimo 222, village no. 59; on Montepiano, see Renato Piattoli, ed., *Regesta chartarum Italiae: Le Carte del Monastero di S. Maria di Montepiano (1000–1200)* (Rome, 1942); on the monastery at Luco, see Casini, *Dizionario*, I, p. 81; on the monasteries at Razzuolo and Crespino, see Barberini, "Il Mugello," pp. 95 and 97; and Not. antecos., 10136, 42r.

Florence,[131] which received no pious bequests beyond the mandatory amount given to the sacristy.

The Casentino was also particularly rich in monastic life with even larger houses and ones which were better known in the history of religion – Vallombrosa, Camaldoli, Strumi, and Prataglia[132] – whose properties spread from the city of Florence to the most remote wilderness outposts of late-medieval Tuscany. They possessed satellite houses that extended into the Mugello, such as Vallombrosa's San Paolo di Razzuolo.[133] And Camaldoli's network of houses and hospitals had reached every nook and cranny of Tuscany by the time of Traversari's visitations in the 1430s.[134]

Similarly, older monastic settlements continued to dominate property holding in the plains. The Badia di Settimo near Sesto possessed numerous properties in the city of Florence and through the alluvial plains of Campi, Sesto, and Signa. It employed lowland peasants as *mezzadri* on its estates and held ties with others through short-term contracts.[135] This rich house possessed lands and hospitals even as far north as the Alpi Fiorentine.[136] In the plains, these institutions were often also the peasants' lords[137] or the overlords of their parish communities.[138] As la Roncière has suggested, these economic ties may have soured relations between these peasants and the old monastic institutions,[139] but as we will see this explanation is problematic.

Third, and even more surprising than the absence of the old monasteries, is the scant appearance in these documents of the mendicant orders.[140] While the minor orders dominated urban wills, usually gar-

---

[131]   Dameron, "Patrimony and Clientage in the Florentine Countryside: The Formation of the Estate of the Cathedral Chapter, 950–1200," in *Portraits of Medieval and Renaissance Living*, pp. 259–81.   [132] For the eleventh century, see Wickham, *The Mountains*, pt 2.

[133]   According to La Roncière, "Aspects de la religiosité populaire en Toscane: le contado florentine des années 1300," in *La Toscana nel secolo XV: Caratteri di una civiltà regionale*, ed. by S. Gensini (Pisa, 1988), p. 346, the Florentine *contado* possessed twelve male and four female Vallombrosian houses.   [134] Traversari, *Hodoeporicon*.

[135]   See the numerous rents notarized by the Mazzetti family from 1348 to 1426, Not. antecos. 13521–34; and la Roncière, "A Monastic Clientele? The Abbey of Settimo, its Neighbours and its Tenants (Tuscany, 1280–1340)," in *City and Countryside*, pp. 55–67.

[136]   See Casini, *Dizionario*, I, pp. 85–6. For the position of ancient monasteries in Tuscany, see *Carta della Toscana*, ed. by Italo Moretti and Pietro Ruschi and taken from Fedor Schneider, *L'ordinamento pubblico nella Toscana medievale* (Florence, 1975 [Rome, 1914]); and Wickham, *The Mountains*, map 8.

[137]   See Not. antecos., 13533, np, 1365.xii.3; np, 1365.iii.14; np, 1366.iii.26; np, 1368.i.27; and np, same date [hereafter sd].

[138]   According to a notarial act (Not. antecos., 858, 71r–v, 1369.i.9), San Lorenzo a Gabbiano in the northern Mugello was subject to both the temporal and spiritual rule of the Vallombrosian abbot of San Salvatore di Spongia in the diocese of Volterra, who "descended on" the parish to "correct and reform" its practices.   [139] la Roncière, "A Monastic Clientele?" p. 66.

[140]   This is surprising given the emphasis la Roncière has placed on the mendicants and the

nering at least a quarter of all pious bequests, only six of these rural wills left anything to a friar or a mendicant house, and of these benefactors four were widows from market towns as opposed to rural villages: two from Pieve Santo Stefano, a third from Scarperia, and a fourth from Borgo San Lorenzo.[141] Further, the legacy bequeathed by the widow from Borgo San Lorenzo was contingent on her heirs not bearing any offspring and was not actually bequeathed to the Franciscans of Borgo but to a religious confraternity which had its altar in their church.[142] Thus of the rural villagers only two of ninety-six left anything to the mendicants.

Again, such low levels of affection did not result from the absence of mendicants within the Florentine countryside or even within the mountain districts of the periphery. From their earliest history, mendicants and especially Franciscans had penetrated the territory with a major shrine and congregation at La Verna in the mountainous wilderness above Chiusi (then within Tarlati hands but by 1385 a part of the Florentine district). By the third quarter of the thirteenth century the Franciscans had established friaries in most of the market towns of the Florentine *contado*[143] and by the fourteenth century they had gone beyond Florence's second rung of towns (San Gimignano, Castelfiorentino, Colle Valdesa). Many small and little-known houses such as the Franciscan "Frati di Morello" in the tiny mountain parish of Santa Maria a Morello appear as the contiguous borders in land transactions.[144] To trumpet the piety of the Mugello peasants, the early fifteenth-century diarist Morelli singled out two religious foundations that he claimed had been built and maintained by native peasant generosity – the Servites of Monte Senario and the Franciscans at "Bosco

---

Franciscans in particular in the pastoral care, preaching, and instruction of the rural laity of the *contado* and their impact on Christian names and the formation of religious confraternities in the countryside; see "Dans la campagne florentine au XIVe siècle: les communautés chrétiennes et leurs curés," in *Histoire vécue du peuple chrétien*, ed. by Jean Delumeau (Toulouse, 1976), pp. 296 and 307; "Orientations pastorales du clergé," p. 57; "Aspects de la religiosité populaire," p. 384; and L'influence des franciscains." Perhaps, as he has suggested in at least one place ("L'influence des franciscains," p. 33), lay sympathy towards the Franciscans began to sour about the time of the Black Death.

[141] Not. antecos., 16870, 37r, 1387.ii.17 and 37r, 1387.ii.19 (both testaments made bequests to La Verna); 6599, 64v–5v, 1441.xi.16 (to the Augustinians of Scarperia to paint an image of the Virgin in front of the altar of its church); and 792, 227r–v, 1435.vii.10 (whose legacy was contingent on her daughter not giving birth to male or female children). Villagers who made bequests to friars include an unmarried woman from the Val di Marina – a legacy to "the minor friars of the Mugello", 11059, np, 1397.ix.10; and a man from the suburban parish of Santa Maria a Quarto, 13533, np, 1364.viii.26 (to the friars of San Donnino).

[142] Not. antecos., 792, 227r–v, 1435.vii.10.

[143] la Roncière, "L'influence des franciscains," pp. 47–50.

[144] See Not. antecos., 13521, 244v–45r, 1386.vii.31.

ai frati," near San Piero a Sieve.[145] But despite this propinquity and Morelli's claims, Florentine peasants across the *contado* showed these mendicants little affection and placed little faith in the efficacy of their spiritual powers at least as far as death-bed wishes go. As Charles de la Roncière has argued, perhaps the quarrel over poverty and the spiritualist rebellion "had grave consequences" for the mendicants and especially the Franciscans.[146] After all, according to la Roncière, Florence was perhaps the most active center of the spiritualists in Italy.[147] Yet the mendicants' ability to attract pious bequests from the urban laity did not decline after the Black Death and may have even risen.[148] Besides, as la Roncière has argued elsewhere,[149] the spiritualists hardly had any effect in the countryside; thus by this explanation the long-term decline of the mendicants should have been more pronounced in the city than in the countryside, but it was not.[150]

In addition to differences in pious choices between the cities and countryside, the wills emanating from these two religious realms also express differences in the mentality that lay behind their pious giving. By the last quarter of the fourteenth century it was common for artisans and shopkeepers in cities such as Florence and Arezzo to leave concrete memorials for the preservation of their names and the memory of their ancestors in the form of burial tombs, paintings, and chapel foundations.[151] Urban testators could express such desires with legacies of as little as 10 *lire*, well within the range of the expenditures found in these country wills. But those in the countryside seldom made any such concrete efforts to preserve their memories in works of art or even in contributions earmarked for specific building repairs to churches or hospitals. A mountain peasant from Pietramala on the Bolognese border gave 10 florins for his parish church to buy a new bell.[152] A man from Luco di Mugello, but who had moved to the parish of San Lorenzo in the city of Florence, left 25 *lire* to build a portico for his church of San Piero back in Luco.[153] In 1388, a woman from the mountain village of Collungo in Pieve Santo Stefano left 10 *lire* to assist in the rebuilding of the fabric of her confraternity's chapter house.[154] But these were the exceptions.

---

[145] Morelli, *Ricordi*, p. 96.   [146] la Roncière, "L'influence des franciscains," p. 82.
[147] *Ibid.*, pp. 72–82.   [148] Cohn, *The Cult of Remembrance*, p. 36.
[149] la Roncière, "Dans la campagne florentine," p. 310.
[150] la Roncière's explanation ("L'influence des franciscains," pp. 85 and 103) rests on the assumption that peasants became poorer in the fourteenth century and the Franciscans' appeal shifted to the well-off. But the poor in Florence continued to sponsor the order in their wills.
[151] See my *Cult of Remembrance*, chs. 6, 7, and 8; and "Piété et commande d'oeuvres d'art après la peste noire, *Annales, HSS*, 51 (1996): 553–71.   [152] Not. antecos., 6599, 22r–3r, 1439.iii.2.
[153] *Ibid.*, 862, np. 1363.vi.2.   [154] *Ibid.*, 16870, 37r, 1387.ii.19.

Again in contrast to the cities,[155] commissions of paintings from these rural testators were rarer still. Only one testator from the mountain notarial protocols left instructions for the "making of a picture." It was to be a Virgin Mary for an altar in the Augustinian church of Scarperia. But in addition to being from a town, the testator was the widow of a Florentine bearing a family name (de Aleis).[156] Similarly, only one commission for a painting is found in the sample of the notarial protocols taken from the plains; it too was exceptional. The testator, a widow from Santa Maria a Quarto, left 5 florins for an image of the Virgin and Saint Jacob for the altar of her parish confraternity. But while this woman and her deceased husband were from the countryside, her testament was the longest and wealthiest found in these samples. Consisting of twenty-three "items" or bequests, it showed close ties with the city of Florence. She drew up her will in the Florentine parish of Santa Maria Maggiore, and her last bequest left the extraordinary sum of 500 florins to the Florentine church and confraternity of Orsanmichele.[157] Such an amount clearly separated her from the mass of Florentine rural inhabitants of the late fourteenth and fifteenth centuries.

Finally, only one peasant – a mountain dweller from Cavrenno on the Florentine–Bologna border – left sums to build or maintain a chapel (*quandam chapellam*). However, this chapel was not to be found in an existing church but was to be built (perhaps as a roadside shrine) in the testator's commune of Cavrenno at a place called "alle fela."[158]

Such urban legacies for works of art and chapels were made not only for the preservation of testators' own names and memories but as importantly for the memory and exaltation of their ancestors and family lineages.[159] Recent medieval historians of France, from Douai to Avignon, have assumed that the veneration of ancestors had begun to vanish from urban wills in France and elsewhere in Western Europe by the thirteenth century or by the Black Death at the very latest, and afterwards crop up only in backward and marginal rural areas.[160] But in Florentine Tuscany no such transition is seen. Instead, urban testaments after 1348 and into the Quattrocento Renaissance turned in the

[155] See my "Piété et commande d'oeuvres."   [156] Not. antecos., 6599, 64v–5v, 1441.xi.16.
[157] *Ibid.*, 13533, np, 1364.viii.26.   [158] *Ibid.*, 9844, np., 1491.ii.10.
[159] See my discussion of these testamentary commissions in *The Cult of Remembrance*, pp. 242–3.
[160] See Jean-Pierre Deregnaucourt, "Autour de la mort à Douai: Attitudes, pratiques et croyances, 1250/1500," 2 vols. Thèse de troisième cycle, Université Charles de Gaulle, Lille, 1993; "L'élection de sépulture d'après les testaments douaisiens (1295–1500)," *Revue du Nord*, 65 (1983), esp. pp. 137–41; Jacques Chiffoleau, *La Comptabilité de l'au-delà: Les hommes, la mort et la religion dans la région d'Avignon à la fin du Moyen Age (vers 1320–vers 1480)* (Rome, 1980), esp. pp. 206–7; and, more generally, Michel Lauwers, *La mémoire des ancêtres, le souci des morts. Morts, rites et société au moyen age* (Paris, 1997), esp. pp. 498–9.

opposite direction: increasingly, their last gifts concentrated on building, decorating, and maintaining communal family vaults and chapels, where priests were left property to pray for the souls of these testators' ancestors with perpetual masses. At the same time, testators in the countryside shunned any such efforts to preserve their own memories or to recall those of their forebears.

This absence of "pious egoism"[161] and ancestral veneration from rural wills did not turn on a lack of funds or landed property. In place of demands for concrete works of art, improvements to church fabrics, and the foundation of family chapels, these peasants often left sizable gifts of property from several strips of land to entire farms (*poderi*) to sponsor masses for their souls at their funerals or soon afterwards. Several of these legacies employed more than one parish priest. A widow from Sant'Andrea a Camoggiano in the *pieve* of San Gavino Adimari *prope Alpes* instructed her son to pay for eight masses "to the honor of God" to be recited by eight priests in her parish church of Sant'Andrea on the anniversary of her death for five years running.[162]

More flamboyant was the testament of a rich mountain peasant from Valmorciano in the Florentine Romagna,[163] who obliged his universal heirs, his two daughters, to employ eighteen priests for his funeral, ten at the place of burial and another eight for masses afterwards. His heirs were given 900 *lire* each for these services, probably sufficient for such a grand finale.[164] But despite this command of what were by peasant standards large sums, these peasants, rich or poor, from plains or distant mountains, seldom asked for perpetual masses or ones that remembered the souls of their ancestors as had become deeply ingrained in the wills from Tuscan and Umbrian cities across social classes by the last quarter of the fourteenth century.[165]

Despite differences in mobility and social networks between highlanders and plainsmen, the parish church dominated the spiritual worlds of plainsmen and mountain dwellers alike in the *contadi* of Florence and Arezzo. Almost all these rural testators who specified a pious bequest gave something to their own parish church or priest. And second in importance came the parish lay confraternity. Fourteenth- and fifteenth-

[161] So labeled by Deregnaucourt, "Autour de la mort à Douai," p. 64.
[162] Not. antecos., 792, 226r–v, 1435.vii.3.   [163] Repetti, *Diz.*, V, p. 442.
[164] Not. antecos., 1316, 15r–17r (an. nat.) 1437.i.28.
[165] One exception was the testament of a widow from Sant'Agata, who gave her house with its gardens, well, and pergola to her parish church for an "anovale" to be celebrated every year by six priests for the health of her soul and the souls of her kin (*parentum*); Not. antecos., 858, 3v, 1366.iii.5.

century testaments show the spread of these societies throughout the Florentine territory from the plains near the city,[166] to market towns in the Mugello,[167] to distant and isolated mountain parishes. The latter included parish societies such as San Michele in Montecarelli in the Mugello's *prope Alpes*,[168] Sant'Andrea in Camoggiano[169] under the Futa pass, at Galliano[170] above Scarperia, Ronta in the Mugello below the pass of Colla di Casaglia,[171] Montecuccoli *prope Alpes*,[172] and Santa Sophia in the mountains of the Florentine Romagna, which in fact possessed two lay confraternities: one for flagellants called the *"sotietas frustatorum de sancta sophia"*[173] and a Marian cult called *"sotietas anunciate de sancta sophia."*[174] Several rural testators gave to more than one parish society and thus may have belonged to more than one.[175] Far from being "largely an urban phenomenon" or "unknown" to those in the countryside, the lay confraternity by the early fifteenth century appears to have been more prevalent and active in the *contado* than in the city of Florence, where, except for San Frediano, the parish confraternity was not known until the Counter Reformation.[176]

In his study of Settimo, la Roncière finds a similar pattern and concludes: "The picture most clearly presented by the evidence is one of a coherent parish community, receptive to the models of solidarity and

---

[166] The wills give evidence of parish confraternities at Santa Maria a Quarto (Not. antecos., 13521, 144v–5r, 1386.vii.31), Settimo (*ibid.*, 951, 27v–8v, 1314.xi.17), Brozzi (*ibid.*, 96r, 1315.x.19), Sesto (*ibid.*, 7876, 64r, 1351.viii.13), Careggi (*ibid.*, 13521, 28r, 1371.viii.25), and San Piero a Ema (*ibid.*, 28r, 1371.viii.30).

[167] For Borgo San Lorenzo, see *ibid.*, 792, 227r–v, 1435.vii.10; and 11059, np, 1397.ix.10.

[168] *Ibid.*, 153r, 1432.ii.12.   [169] *Ibid.*, 226r–v, 1435.vii.3.

[170] *Ibid.*, 165v, 1433.v.31; and 11059, np, 1397.ix.2.   [171] *Ibid.*, 10136, 50r–v, 1375.vii.1.

[172] *Ibid.*, 792, 181r, 1433.iii.21.   [173] *Ibid.*, 1316, 45v–6v, 1437.iv.4.

[174] *Ibid.*, 71r–2r, 1437.v.9. They may have been the same confraternity.

[175] See, for instance, *ibid.*, 16870, 37r, 1387.ii.17. A widow gave 20s to her parish confraternity of Santa Marta at Pieve Santo Stefano and another 20s to a society called Santa Croce. Earlier, a man gave 1 florin to his parish confraternity of Saint John at Sant'Appiano then in Bologna, and another 20s to the society of Saint Mary in the same parish; *ibid.*, 16255, 45r, 1340.iv.6.

[176] David Friedman, *Florentine New Towns: Urban Design in the Late Middle Ages* (Cambridge, 1988), p. 190: "The institution of the lay confraternity was largely an urban phenomenon. Its participatory and emotional form of devotion and its corporate and republican administrative structure were probably unknown to Scarperia's immigrants in the villages of their earlier lives." On parish confraternities in Florence, see John Henderson, *Piety and Charity in Late Medieval Florence* (Oxford, 1994), pp. 430–8; and Ronald Weissman, *Ritual Brotherhood in Renaissance Florence* (New York, 1982), pp. 198ff. For detailed analysis of confraternities in the Florentine countryside, see la Roncière, "Les confréries à Florence et dans son contado aux XIV–XVe siècles," in *Le mouvement confraternal au Moyen Age: France, Italie, Suisse: Actes de la table ronde organisée par l'Université de Lausanne, 9–11 mai 1985* (Rome, 1987), pp. 297–339. Between 1325 and 1340, 205 parishioners were enrolled in the confraternity at S. Lorenzo a Settimo (p. 302). Yet la Roncière does not mention any confraternities in the highlands and assumes that they must have been rare in these "isolated places" beyond the bishops' influence; see "Dans la campagne florentine," pp. 309–10.

devotion offered by the pastoral care practised by the friars (and by some priests)".[177] In contrast to this religious and social harmony, he finds that the new patterns of monastic estate management based on short-term rents "did not favour the establishment or maintenance of a real group of faithful" or "lasting links of patronage."[178] Although the introduction of the *mezzadria* system may explain the fragmentation of loyalty between peasants and monastic landlords in the plains, it cannot explain a similar change in the mountains, where *mezzadria* contracts were almost nonexistent. Moreover, la Roncière's argument is inconsistent. With lay landlords, the *mezzadria* system brought tighter-knit, even familial, relations between landlords and peasants and new ideals of protection and *noblesse oblige*.

Why then would not the same have developed on monastic estates in the plains with corresponding expressions of gifts and affection? In addition, parish priests during the fifteenth century increasingly managed their estates in the plains by short-term rents and sharecropping. Yet parishioners continued to favor these lords with pious gifts even if less than in the mountains.[179] The answer to these differences in social bonds of affection – the apparent coolness between peasants and their monastic lords as opposed to their warmth towards their parish communities – must be sought in the social character of these communities.

The parish as a focus of peasant life both in the highlands and lowlands was manifested in more than last gifts and funerals. From notarial records and village statutes it is clear that the parish had become the unit of peasants' lives across a wide range of political and social concerns in addition to their spiritual life. Yet parish solidarities appear even stronger in the mountains than in the plains. While the rights of election (*ius patronatus*) for churches in the plains had long ago become the property of Florentine patricians or religious corporations,[180] the men of the mountains still elected their own priests in convocations that enlisted the presence of all

---

[177] la Roncière, "A Monastic Clientele?," p. 64.   [178] *Ibid.*, p. 66.
[179] For parish priests and parish lay confraternities as landlords in *mezzadria* contracts, see Not. antecos., 13533, np, 1365.xi.26; and *ibid.*, np, 1365.xi.11. Also, see la Roncière, "Dans la campagne florentine," p. 292. In addition, urban parishes were the landlords of peasants in the nearby countryside, see Not. antecos., 13533, np, 1368.xii.24, np, 1369.x.21; np, 1370.vi.6; np, sd.
[180] la Roncière, "Dans la campagne florentine," p. 289, finds already before the Black Death that these rights had been fragmented and taken from the parish communities throughout the Mugello. He does not, however, show his evidence or consider differences across the vast territory of the Mugello – its plains, hills, and mountains.

the adult men of the parish well into the fifteenth century and perhaps beyond.

Did the closer bonds of affection seen in wills between parishioners and priests stem from facts of propinquity – that the parish priests came from communities and social backgrounds like their own,[181] – whereas nuns, monks, and friars represented a more cosmopolitan world that could stretch across Italy and even across the Alps? Did parish priests, especially in mountain districts, share the same customs and mentality as their parishioners? Were they so ignorant of the church calendar as to miss even the day of Easter as the Quattrocento humanist Poggio Bracciolini reports in his story about a "backward" (*zotico*) mountain community in the Apennine Pratomagno above his home town of Terranuova?[182] Or were the priests outsiders sent to officiate at services in the alien world of the mountains, as was Gentile Sermini's friend Ser Cecco da Perugia in Sermini's story about mountain life and customs in Monte Amiata during the plague of 1424?[183]

The notarized convocations that elected parish priests suggest two answers: in the mountains and hills of the Mugello and the Alpi, where the adult male parishioners still held the rights of presentation, their priests came from neighboring villages of similar altitudes to the parishes of their employment. Thus when the parishioners of Sant'Agata in the Mugello elected their priest in 1368, they chose a cleric whose place of origin was not specified but who had previously officiated at San Michele in the mountain village of Ronta.[184] In the same year the parishioners of San Michele a Montaceraia in the Mugello highland *pieve* of San Cresci a Valcava chose a priest from Santo Stefano within the same *pieve*.[185] Similarly, the eleven assembled adult male parishioners of the tiny parish of San Michele a Aglioni in the *pieve* of San Casciano in

---

[181] In his excellent study of the social background of the secular clergy in rural Florence, la Roncière, "Dans la campagne florentine," pp. 286–8, shows that this clergy, particularly the *piovani*, came from among the village notables; however, he does not investigate the social background of the clergy in highland parishes.

[182] Poggio Bracciolini, *Facezie di Poggio Fiorentino*, 2nd ed. (Rome, 1885), pp. 20–1, Facezia xi: "Di un prete che ignorava il giorno della solennità delle Palme." Also see p. 21, Facezia xii: "Di alcuni contadini ai quai venne chiesto dall'artefice se volessero il Cristo, che dovean per incarico comprare, o vivo o morto"; and p. 129, facezia cl: "Della moglie di un pastore che ebbe un figlio da un prete."

[183] Gentile Sermini, *Le Novelle di Gentile Sermini da Siena*, ed. by F. Vigo (Livorno, 1874), XII: "L'autore e ser Cecco da Perugia," pp. 169–81.   [184] Not. antecos., 858, 18v–19r, 1368.v.27.

[185] *Ibid.*, 19r–v, 1368.v.20.

Padule chose a priest who came from their own _pieve_ – in this case, the village of Molezzano.[186] And in 1435 the mountain parishioners of Montecarelli in the Mugello's _prope Alpes_ elected a priest from the neighboring mountain village of Santa Maria a Casaglia.[187]

On the other hand, in the plains and lower hills, where these rights lay within the hands of Florentine patricians, the newly appointed priests came from outside. They moved either from lesser positions within the city of Florence or from market towns in the _contado_.[188] When the rectorship of the church of San Giovanni Baptista in the curia of lowland Brozzi became vacant, its "patrona," a noble lady from the Florentine Manfredi family and widow of a man from the politically powerful Strozzi family, elected a priest who had previously officiated at a chapel in the Florentine church of San Bartolo del Corso.[189] When the small parish of San Bartolomeo in the Mugello hills of Galliano needed a new priest, its patrons, four Florentine citizens who resided in the parish of San Pier Maggiore, chose a priest from the town of Empoli "of good acquaintances, life, and reputation."[190] The one exception of such elections by outside patrons comes from the mountains, where a member of the Cattani family of Florence (but who resided in nearby Barberino) owned the _ius patronatus_ of the _plebis_ church of San Michele a Montecuccoli and chose a priest from the same _Podesteria_ of Barberino of which Montecuccoli was a part.[191] Yet, despite these differing patterns in personnel, religious loyalty as seen in the testaments both in the mountains and plains went first to the testators' parishes, where they were buried and relied on their priests' final rites.

Nonetheless, these ties appear stronger in the mountains and may reflect social facts of parochial solidarities that went beyond the parish's religious functions. More often than plainsmen, highlanders appear in notarial records, congregating in their parish churches "at the sound of their church bells" (as the notarial formula put it) to carry out a wide range of social and civic business. Such meetings are easier to spot in the few remaining mountain notarial protocols than in those for the plains. These collective actions included the settlement of disputes with other

---

[186] _Ibid._, 21v–2r, 1368.xi.28. On this village, see Francovich, _I Castelli del contado_, p. 100.
[187] Not. antecos., 792, 206v, 1434.i.2.
[188] By contrast, la Roncière, "Dans la campagne florentine," pp. 291–2, claims that during the late thirteenth and early fourteenth centuries parish priests in both the hills and plains came from villages either in or near the churches where they officiated.
[189] Not. antecos., 13521, 33v, 1373.ix.16.   [190] _Ibid._, 792, 48v–50v.
[191] _Ibid._, 129r, 1431.iii.12.

parishes,[192] revision of village statutes,[193] discussion of civic issues and the initiation of litigation,[194] the appointment of advisors to the parish or commune,[195] and most frequently the election of their own lay syndics,[196] who, among other things, negotiated with the city of Florence on matters such as tax relief and indebtedness and (at least until 1427) decided how their taxes were to be apportioned within the community.[197]

This corporate identity based on the commune or parish can also be detected in the local statutes and again was more marked in the mountains. Unlike the statutes of the city, which limited the number of neighbors allowed to take part in funerals, local statutes for the mountains required the opposite – a full turnout. On the death of any neighbor over the age of fourteen, at least one member of the household in the parish or commune had to "honor the body" of his neighbor, accompanying it from the home to the parish church, under the threat of a fine from 5s to 10s.[198] Similarly, it was in the mountains rather than the plains that the parish church appears in the statutes as the point of organization for raising the hue and cry and the meeting place for the commune and its councilors.[199]

From the specification of ages, evidence of names, and testimony from last wills and testaments, Florentine highlanders do not easily fit a model of a backward, non-Christian people, distinct from those further down the hills, as contemporaries from cities charged and historians ever since have assumed.[200] Instead, by the fifteenth century, highlanders appear as

---

[192] See, for instance, the case when twenty-four men of San Giovanni a Cornacchiaia met to settle a dispute and to initiate other matters not spelled out in the notary's rough draft; *ibid.*, 6599, 39r–40r, 1440.x.30.

[193] See the numerous acts of submission in the *provvisioni* registers and their transcriptions in *I Capitoli*.

[194] Not. antecos., 858, 16r–17r, 1368.v.5.   [195] *Ibid.*, 6r, 1366.v.4.

[196] For the commune of Montecuccoli, see *ibid.*, 792, 99r, 1431.viii.4, and 155r, 1432.iii.1; Montecarelli, *ibid.*, 124r, 1431.ii.14; Casaglia "a pie d'alpe" *ibid.*, 157r, 1432.iii.4; San Giovanni a Firenzuola, *ibid.*, 6599, 52v–3r; Caburaccio, *ibid.*, 66v–7r; San Martino a Castro, *ibid.*, 73r; San Biagio a Petriolo, *ibid.*, 1502, 31r–v. The election of village syndics also took place in the plains; see for instance *ibid.*, 13534, 130v–1r, for San Cresci a Campi; and 13533, np, 1365.v.25, np, 1366.v.3, and np, 1367.v.9 for Sesto.

[197] *Ibid.*, 13522, np, 1365.vii.27; np, 1365.viii.10; 1502, 31r–v; and 10423, np, 6, 1414.iii.5.

[198] Statuti della comunità, 420 Mangona (1416), c. 79, 42v; 7 Piancaldoli (1419), 2v; and 447 Montagna Fiorentina (1396), c. 29, 26r–v.

[199] *Ibid.*, 7, 2v; 447, c. 34, 19v. Mountain statutes required one member per household to attend these meetings under the threat of 3s fine. I have not found similar statutes for the plains.

[200] Even la Roncière, presently our best authority on the life, customs, and religion of those from the Florentine *contado*, assumes (without presenting any evidence) that "the quality of religious life was certainly inferior in the mountain zones of the Apennines and the Chianti" ("Dans la campagne florentine," pp. 309–10) and that it was more "ritualistic and magical" (p. 312).

numerate and Christian as *mezzadri* and tenants from the lowlands near the city.

Let us now turn to the bulk of surviving documents for comparing the worlds of highlanders and lowland peasants – tax records. Do geographical comparisons show Mediterranean mountain equality steeped in poverty? Was it a world fixed in geographic time, removed from the "surface history" of politics?

2

Mountain civilization and fiscality, 1393

Tax surveys for the Florentine *contado* known as *estimi* and from 1364 as *Capi di famiglia* (the heads of family) allow a regional investigation into demographic and fiscal differences of Florence's hinterland after the Black Death and into the fifteenth century. Collectively, they show that the dichotomy of city versus countryside needs revision and elaboration. Until 1427, such a division was false even within the traditional *contado* of Florence, without considering Florence's formerly independent city-states and their *contadi*, each of which received different privileges and obligations depending on the historic circumstances of its submission to Florentine rule.[1] The city of Florence did not treat all areas of the *contado* alike – suburban parishes, plains, mountains, and territories on the fringes of the Florentine state recently annexed into its traditional *contado*. Only part of this story, moreover, can be detected from these negotiations and initial treaties.

To see the mosaic of taxation carved into the political geography of the Florentine *contado*, the historian must go beyond a *prima facia* reading of the written records and reconstruct tax rates for individual villages and communes by linking names between two fiscal reports. The first of these were the village *estimi* collected by local syndics, rectors, or Florentine "commissioners," who assessed the worth of peasant possessions, principally land and animals. The second, the *libbra* or *lira*, was drawn up in the city often as much as a year later by city officials, who farmed out the work of calculation and recording to monastic scribes at Santa Maria degli Angeli.[2]

---

[1] Petralia, "Fiscality, politics and dominion"; "Imposizione diretta"; and Chittolini, "Ricerche sull'ordinamento."

[2] For the *estimo* of 1414 the councils spelled out the procedures in greater detail than in the past (Provv. reg., 103, 27r–8v, 1414.vi.12), giving each commune, parish, *villa*, or other collective (*universitas*) no more than two months to make its "distributions." They were required to hand over the sealed registers to the friars at Santa Maria degli Angeli (*fratribus angelorum*), who were charged with making the calculations so that Florence's target sums were distributed correctly and "justly" across its *contado* (27v–8r). The friars were then required to register the sums for each parish by Quarter in a single book of parchment to be kept in the archives of the Florentine treasury (28v).

By these means, the city set the final tax base (*lira*) on which numerous taxes would be calculated until the next survey took place, usually a decade later. These taxes included the bridge and road tax, the "taxa ordinaria" or land tax, the extraordinary tax, theoretically exacted only in times of emergency, usually for the expenditures of war, and the salt tax.

In addition, at certain times and places in the *contado*, even indirect taxes, gabelles on meat and wine (wholesale and retail, *a congio*, and *a minuto*) had become in effect direct taxes. For stability and predictability of income as well as for lessening the costs of control and calculation, Florence converted these gabelles into a single stable fee, the "gabella taxationis mercatorum" calculated on the basis of the *estimo* and which varied between 2s and 14s on the *lira*.[3]

The tax procedures for estimating this base tax developed rapidly after the Black Death from the traditional medieval hearth tax to a complex report that reckoned the labor power of all male household members aged between thirteen and seventy,[4] listed all family members and their ages, singled out physical or mental handicaps that might impair a household's labor power, detailed property holdings, both in land and moveables, and their values, and recorded debts and credits. Elio Conti has described the evolution of the *Capi di famiglia* as the preparatory studies for the *catasto* of 1427.[5] The Florentine government and the syndics of the rural parishes and communes progressively refined the information over the fifty-year period covered by these tax records.

The first records so labeled (1364) differed little from earlier hearth-tax surveys common to Florence and other Italian city-states dating back to the twelfth century. By its second redaction (1371) the *estimo* began in some villages to include information on peasant migration and to give ages of some family members, usually the household heads and unmarried children. By the third redaction (1383), all parishes reported the migration of their villagers and the ages of all family members who had remained in the village since the last survey. Further, the extent of age rounding declined significantly since the first experiment with ages in 1371.[6] In the *estimi* of 1401, village rectors were required to specify their

---

[3] See, for instance, Provv. reg., 47, 65r–v, 1359.x.25; and 65, 123r–4r, 1377.viii.18.

[4] These ages varied slightly over time. On the early development of taxes in Florence, see Bernardino Barbadoro, *Le finanze della repubblica: Imposte diretta e debito pubblico fino alla istituzione del Monte* (Florence, 1929).

[5] Conti, *I Catasti agrari della repubblica fiorentina e il Catasto particellare toscano (secoli XIV–XIX)* (Rome, 1966), p. 19.

[6] While in 1371 78 percent (601 of 773) rounded their ages, in 1487 it had declined to 36 percent (403 of 1,126).

property holdings, usually dividing them between land and animals, and by the last survey (1412–14) these descriptions had become more detailed; most aspects of the *catasto* of 1427 had appeared: all household members were listed, their ages given, and their property holdings, obligations, and debts individually described and estimated.[7]

Before 1427, the Florentine state did not assess the individual household directly but instead the rural community (the *popolo* or *comune*). It then became the duty of the local officials of the rural communities to distribute the imposed communal tax burden among their residents, subject to city refinements, corrections, and increases.[8] It was a zero-sum game. First, the *Signoria* and councils would decide a target figure or base on which the *contado* would be taxed for the next ten or so years; then with the village surveys they would decide the tax base on which each community and each household was to be assessed. This base depended on estimates of property values, labor power, and other considerations not mentioned in the official documents, which, as we shall see, had a powerful influence on village assessments. Afterwards, depending on Florence's needs for roads, fortifications, war, and to repay the funded debt, the commune would fix the amounts or coefficients to be multiplied on the tax base or *lira*. In one year the taxes might be 2s per *lira* for roads and bridges, 10s per *lira* for the ordinary tax, and 1 florin per *lira* for the extraordinary; in the next, they might be raised or lowered, but the base or *lira* would remain the same.

For this purpose, evidence of demographic change was as important as the evaluation of property holdings. As a result, by 1383 the city officials began consistently to divide the rural populations into three categories – "stanti" (those who remained since the last *estimo*), "venuti" and "tornati" (those who had immigrated or returned), and "usciti" (those who had left), which often included other subcategories such as "perduti" (the lost ones) and especially "morti" (the dead).[9] With the shift

---

[7] As far as the assessment of debts and itemization of landed and movable property goes, Florence lagged behind Bologna, Milan, and Perugia, whose *estimi* had become virtual *catasti* in 1235, 1240, and 1260, respectively; see Francesca Bocchi, "Le imposte dirette a Bologna nei secoli XII e XIII," *Nuova Rivista Storica*, 57 (1973), p. 291; Alberto Grohmann, *L'imposizione diretta nei comuni dell'Italia centrale nel XIII secolo: La libra di Perugia del 1285* (Rome, 1986), p. 4; G. Biscaro, "Gli estimi del Comune di Milano nel secolo XIII," *Archivio di Stato di Lombardia* (1928): 343–495; and Renato Zangheri, *Catasti e storia della proprietà terriera* (Turin, 1980), pp. 3–70.

[8] On the *estimi* as communally based assessments, see Barbadoro, *Le finanze*; and Fiumi, "Sui rapporti," pp. 25–8.

[9] In some communities, other categories are found: noblemen and those who held property in the community but who were neither village residents nor citizens of Florence were taxed separately and at different rates. On occasion, the "miserabili" were taxed as a separate category.

in assessment from the community to the individual in 1427, the importance of such information disappeared, and with it the opportunity for examining directly that most elusive of demographic parameters for any period – migration.

Because of the oligarchy's reluctance to tax itself directly and impose *estimo* surveys on its citizens, we know more about the demography of the *contado* than we do for the city of Florence before 1427.[10] However, because the city of Prato was part of the Florentine *contado* since 1351, it opens one window onto demographic changes in an urban center.[11] With the wars against Milan in the 1420s and the increasing burden of Florence's funded debt, the city finally decided to survey in detail its own wealth with the *catasto* in 1427, even if it still preferred to pay its way by forced loans (*prestanze*).[12]

The *estimi* have received less attention from historians than the *catasti* of the fifteenth century, perhaps because they concern for the most part rural instead of urban populations and thus include almost no information on figures of importance for cultural and art history.[13] Nonetheless, the earlier *estimi* fill a hundred volumes, some of which approach a thousand folios and span the later Trecento and the early Quattrocento – (1355–7), (1364–5), (1371–3), (1383–4), (1393–4), (1401–2), and (1412–14). To make inroads into these records I have sampled twenty-nine communities, all in the Quarter of Santa Maria Novella, spread over four geographical areas – mountains, hills, plains, and the city (the "porta" of Santa Trinita, Prato).[14]

The first of these samples (which I call the plains) runs from the city walls of Florence (the rural sectors, or "fuori di mura" [outside the walls] parts of the urban parishes of San Lorenzo and Santa Lucia Ognissanti) and continues through the rich plains of the Valdarno

---

[10] On three occasions between 1315 and 1427 Florence imposed direct taxes on its citizens and made surveys; records survive for 1351, 1355, and 1379.

[11] See Fiumi, *Demografia, movimento urbanistico e classi sociali in Prato dall'età comunale ai tempi moderni* (Florence, 1968).

[12] As Conti, *Ricordi fiscali di Matteo Palmieri (1427–1474)* (Rome, 1983), has shown, a proportion of these "forced loans" became direct taxes in the fifteenth century.

[13] Art historians were among the first to use *catasto* records for systematic searches of individuals and their holdings; see most importantly, Ugo Procacci, "Sulla cronologia delle opere di Masaccio e di Masolino tra il 1425 e il 1428," *Rivista d'Arte* (1953), xxviii, 3a ser.-vol. III (Florence, 1954): 3–55; "L'uso dei documenti negli studi di Storia dell'Arte e le vicende politiche ed economiche in Firenze durante il primo Quattrocento nei loro rapporti con gli artisti," in *Donatello e il suo tempo. Atti dell'VIII convegno internazionale di Studi sul Rinascimento Firenze–Padova 1966* (Florence, 1968), pp. 11–39; *Studio sul catasto fiorentino* (Florence, 1996).

[14] The *catasto* of 1427 contains 224 tax units (*popoli, comuni,* and *porti* of provincial towns), comprising 3,385 households and 16,553 individuals for this Quarter.

Inferiore and the Bisenzio into the city of Prato. It includes villages within the *pievi* of Santo Stefano in Pane, Sesto, Campi, and *ville* of the former *contado* of Prato. These places vary in altitude between 30 and 60 meters.

A second sample of hill communities, between 200 and 300 meters high, are scattered within the Valdarno Inferiore *pievi* of Sesto and Artimino; the lower Mugello *pieve* of Vaglia, Larciano, Leccio, and San Piero a Sieve; and *ville* of the former *contado* of Prato.

The third, the mountains – places whose districts rise above 500 meters – starts in the highlands north of the Mugello bordering the state of Bologna and crosses the Apennine communities of the Alpi Fiorentine, extends through the Mugello, northwest of Scarperia, and continues across the highlands of Prato near the border of Pistoia. It is difficult to find mountain communities near the city; yet one mountain village, Santa Maria a Morello, on the slopes of Monte Morello, was in the *pieve* of Sesto and no more than 15 kilometers (as the crow flies) from Florence's city walls. Finally, the Porta di Santa Trinita, one of the six districts of Prato, represents the fourth zone, that of an urban population within the Florentine *contado* (see maps 1 and 2).[15]

Chance survival is not the only reason why the records of certain villages at certain times do not appear within these tax records. Exemptions, foreign domination, and temporary independence from Florence also account for gaps. Some entire areas of the *contado* of Florence are completely missing from various redactions of the *estimi*. Such is the case of a central area studied in this book, the Alpi Fiorentine, which from 1341 until 1373 broke from Florentine rule and achieved independence under the Ubaldini lords.[16] Moreover, because of Florentine strategy to divide and conquer, these communities were given extensive exemptions and privileges to persuade villagers to break their allegiances to their lords and to accept Florentine domination. As a result, they were not surveyed and taxed until the registers of 1393/4. Further, after the successful peasant revolts of 1402, many villages of the Alpi, such as Castro, again won extensive privileges and fail to appear in

---

[15] Selection of these villages depended on their relative consistency of appearance within the *estimi* and later *catasti*.

[16] On the Florentine conquests of the Alpi from 1302 to 1373, see Casini, *Dizionario*, I, pp. 130–80. While he reports in detail Florence's successes, he has less to say about its failures to govern these mountains. The preamble to the *provvisione* that established the *vicariatus* of Firenzuola in 1373 states that "it had been thirty-two years or so since the nobles of the Ubaldini had occupied the Alps and had cruelly ripped the goods and property from their peasants by violent exploitation." Provv. reg., 61, 39v–42r.

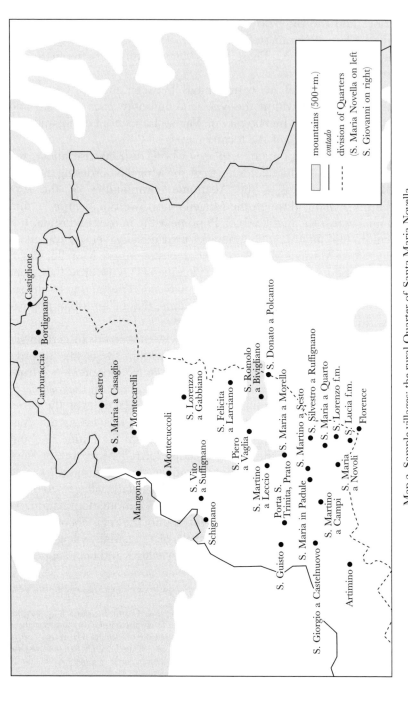

Map 2 Sample villages: the rural Quarter of Santa Maria Novella

mountains (500+m.)
contado
division of Quarters
(S. Maria Novella on left
S. Giovanni on right)

Castiglione
Bordignano
Carburaccia
Castro
S. Maria a Casaglio
Montecarelli
Montecuccoli
S. Lorenzo a Gabbiano
S. Felicita a Larciano
S. Romolo a Bivigliano
S. Donato a Polcanto
S. Vito a Suffignano
Mangona
S. Piero a Vaglia
S. Martino a Morello
S. Silvestro a Ruffignano
Schignano
S. Martino a Leccio
Porta S. Trinita, Prato
S. Martino a Sesto
S. Maria a Quarto
S;'Lorenzo f.m.
S; Lucia f.m.
Florence
S. Maria a Novoli
S. Maria in Padule
S. Martino a Campi
S. Guisto
S. Giorgio a Castelnuovo
Artimino

the *lire* assessments of that year, thus blocking any possibility of computing their tax rates through record linkage.

Until the *catasto* of 1427, the *estimo* and *lire* records of 1393/4 cover best the various geographical zones within the Quarter of Santa Maria Novella.[17] Because of the relative completeness of this tax survey and its subsequent *lira* assessments in 1394, I have chosen it as a point of departure for comparing the economic and social structure of the mountains, hills, and plains, before investigating change over time. It is well placed chronologically between 1355/7 – the first surviving tax survey for the *contado* that survives intact[18] – and the return of the Medici in 1434.

A glance at the most basic economic parameters laid bare by the tax of 1393/4 suggests that the Florentine *contado* northeast of the city does not support one of Braudel's generalizations later extended to late-medieval Tuscany – mountain poverty and egalitarianism. The wealthiest rural parish found in this study was the small mountain hamlet of Morello. The average family property value was over 241 *lire*, or 446 *lire* if only property holders are considered – a sum which would have purchased a well-furnished farm (*podere*) at the end of the Trecento.[19] The urban "porta" of Santa Trinita in Prato exceeded this average wealth but only by a slight margin, 283 and 576 *lire*, respectively. Morello's average wealth more than doubled that of the wealthiest parishes from the plains and the hills, the suburban San Lorenzo outside the walls (116 *lire*) and San Martino a Leccio (111 *lire*).

Further, once merchant residents of urban Prato are skimmed from the predominantly rural *contado*, the wealthiest "contadino" found in this study resided at Morello. This villager, Bartolo di Baroco di Bartolo, listed as 104 years old,[20] the head of a complex family comprising four married couples, and counting seventeen family members stretched over four generations, did not possess a family name. He was neither a nobleman (otherwise he would have been taxed as such) nor a Florentine citizen with a country residence who wished to be taxed in the *contado* (as

---

[17] For this year all the sample villages for the mountains, plains, and city appear, and only two communities from the hills are missing. For reasons which are not clear, the entire *pieve* of Vaglia is missing.
[18] On this *estimo*, see Abate, "Classi di imposta del contado fiorentino secondo l'estimo del 1357," tesi di laurea, Università degli Studi di Firenze, Facoltà di Magistero. Relatore Prof. Elio Conti, 1969–70.   [19] See for instance Not. antecos. 13521–32.
[20] Unfortunately, Bartolus's age was not stated in 1371 (Estimo 215, 69r), but between 1383 (Estimo 217, 877r) and 1393 he had aged twenty-four years.

Francesco di Marco Datini chose[21]). Nor was he among the handful of professionals left in the countryside. Instead, he was a rich peasant who owned a well-stocked family farm.[22]

Morello was not the only mountain village to house wealthy peasants. One of the highest communes of the upper Mugello, Montecuccoli (633 m), was home to three families each of whose taxable wealth exceeded 500 *lire* and among the fifteen wealthiest found in my country samples.[23] In fact, more of these wealthiest families came from Montecuccoli than any other village except Morello.[24] Thus not by chance did the late-fourteenth-century story-teller Franco Sacchetti choose a highlander as his victim, indeed one living in the Bolognese Alps (Scaricalasino, present-day Monghidoro) just across the border from the Alpi Fiorentine, when he wished to mock a peasant for having too much cash as opposed to the standard topos of peasant poverty. The hapless highland family of this story was stricken by goiter[25] and duped into squandering its money in payments for cures to the jester, il Gonnella, who posed as a university-trained doctor.[26]

Such a view of the wealth of the higher hills and mountains of the Mugello is also suggested by Morelli, who introduced his family diary by waxing rhapsodically over the beauty, nobility, and "grande abbondanza" of the Mugello highlands stretching from Uccellatoio beneath

---

[21] See Ciappelli, "Il cittadino fiorentino," pp. 838–41.

[22] Citizen-farmers did reside in the Florentine countryside, playing important roles in local politics, business, and society. In the notarial records of Ser Antonio di Giusto, who worked the Alpine villages north and east of Scarperia, the Florentine citizen Pellegrinus f.q. Ubaldini de Cattanis appears often as the patron of the local baptismal church of San Silvestro, a *mundualdus*, and a witness to village transactions. Despite his residence, Pellegrinus took advantage of his citizenship – the right to pay the less onerous forced loans (*prestanze*) to the city and thereby to avoid the direct taxes (*estimi*) imposed on the countryside. The largest category of individual petitions made to the officials of the *estimo* came from such alleged citizen-countrymen, who claimed to have paid or were entitled to pay the urban *prestanze* instead of the more onerous *estimo*. See Estimo 73, 74, and 79.   [23] *Ibid.*, 219, 848r–v.

[24] This tally does not include the urban population of Prato (the Porta di Santa Trinita).

[25] The illness was common among mountain people and results from a deficiency of vitamin C. By the fifteenth century Tuscan highlanders may have surmised the cause; a number of local statutes from the mountains alone required every household to have its own garden plot, to grow "cabbage, leeks, garlic, lettuce, parsley, and other things useful for the family." See Statuti, 624: Palazzuolo, Podere Fiorentino (1406), c. 49, 63v–4r; and 420 Mangona (1416), c. 57, 32v.

[26] Franco Sacchetti, *Il Trecentonovelle*, ed. by Lanza (Florence, 1984), CLXXIII, pp. 383–6. This story suggests that mountain villagers may have not been so cut off from city medicine and so reliant on their own folk remedies as is often assumed. Though duped by the "buffone" Gonnella, this mountain family had turned to the services of what they gathered was a university-trained doctor ("medico") to cure their goiter. Further, the patients at Florence's central hospital, Santa Maria Nuova, in John Henderson's tallies, shows that large numbers came from mountain outposts in the Alpi Fiorentine and the Casentino. I thank Dr. Henderson for showing me his tables before publication.

the peaks of Monte Morello to the "Giogo dell'Alpe degli Ubaldini" –
the treacherous pass that divided Scarperia and Firenzuola.[27]
Although this may have been a literary device to contrast Morelli's tra-
vails in coming of age in the harsher days of later Trecento Florence,[28]
it also may well signal some truth about the economic fortunes of the
hills and mountains of the Mugello during the fourteenth century.

Yet, mindful of Cherubini's caveat, we must ask whether individuals
such as the ancient *paterfamilias* Bartolo were not "conspicuous" exceptions "that fail to modify the overall pattern of mountain egalitarianism." When we move down the social ladder another rung to those who
possessed property assessed at between 50 and 100 florins – Conti's
"medianti" or middling sort – again the Alpine villages are well represented. The parish of Santa Maria Bordignano, north of Firenzuola
along the border of Bologna, here leads the list. However, in contrast to
rich peasants, these "middling" peasants were scattered equally through
the lowlands and the mountains; in both zones, they comprised 6
percent of the families.

As these statistics make clear, the majority of peasants found in the
samples from 1393 were either poor (with property values of between 1
and 50 florins) or propertyless. Thus, despite a handful of wealthy and
middling families, the mountain communities may still have been
peopled by peasants with small plots, in contrast to what Cherubini calls
"the proletariatized peasants" of the lower valleys.[29] On first impression,
the distribution of wealth found in the 1393 *estimo* appears to support this
generalization. Santa Maria in Padule,[30] as its name suggests, lay in the
marshlands of the Arno valley near Sesto and was by far the poorest community in this sample. All those who had remained since the previous tax
survey a decade earlier (1383) were propertyless. Moreover, the rate of
out-migration was higher there than anywhere else. Yet the propertyless
"nullatenenti" and "miserabili"[31] also filled the surveys of mountain parishes, constituting substantial portions of their populations. The wealthy

[27] Morelli, *Ricordi*, pp. 90–103.
[28] See Christian Bec, *Les marchands écrivains: affaires et humanisme à Florence 1375–1434* (Paris, 1967), pp. 72–5.
[29] Braudel and Cherubini stressed "mountain egalitarianism"; for Cherubini, however, it was the equality of poor but propertied peasants, while for Braudel, *The Mediterranean*, I, p. 30, the mountains harbored the most destitute and desperate elements of the Mediterranean.
[30] See Francovich, *I Castelli del contado*, p. 155.
[31] On occasion, the records distinguish between the "miserabili" and others without taxable possessions. The former were usually the truly wretched, not only lacking in taxable property, but whose labor power was impaired by physical handicaps or age. Their tax base was rarely more than 6 *soldi* and could be nothing at all.

village of Morello hardly displayed "mountain egalitarianism"; alongside Bartolo di Baroco, 46 percent of the population were propertyless. Further north and higher up, Montecarelli's propertyless exceeded 49 percent, and in the larger commune of nearby Mangona the portion reached 62 percent.

Indeed, whether they were located in the mountains, hills, or plains does not appear to have affected enormously the average household wealth; it varied insignificantly from 55.77 *lire* in the plains to 52.41 *lire* in the hills to 64.88 *lire* in the mountains.[32] To isolate further the importance of altitude in determining peasant household wealth, I have turned to a method used by economists – regression analysis. Better than the comparison of simple averages, a regression model distinguishes the interconnectedness of a cluster of variables and measures their impact on a dependent variable.

Thus I have regressed household taxable wealth against those independent variables that can be readily figured from the documents – distance of the village from Florence, whether the village lay in the newly annexed district of Prato (1351), whether it lay in the mountains, hills or plains, family size, family structure (the extent to which families were extended collaterally or generationally), whether its head was aged (over sixty), whether he or she was infirm or handicapped, and if a family had a woman as its head. Even though significant as a model, the adjusted R-squared of this regression is weak (0.06). Three factors, however, emerge as significant in their bearing on the wealth of rural households. The most important factor determining family wealth follows the Chayanov model of peasant wealth first generalized for early-twentieth-century Soviet farms. The larger and more complex the family, the wealthier it was.[33] To this model, another significant factor perhaps specific to the Mediterranean can be added: the age of the household head. Wealthy families like that of Morello's Bartolo tended to be lorded over by ancient patriarchs.[34] Third, and not surprisingly, physical

---

[32] A *t*-test of the most extreme difference, between the mountains and hills is insignificant: $t = -1.27$ with 780 degrees of freedom, probability $t = 0.20$.

[33] See A. V. Chayanov, *The Theory of the Peasant Economy*, ed. by D. Thorner, D. Kerblay, and R. Smith (Homewood, Ill., 1966 [1925]); and Herlihy and Klapisch-Zuber, *Les Toscans*, p. 429. On the complex and nonlinear relations between family size, family complexity, and wealth, see Klapisch-Zuber and Michel Demonet, "A Correspondence Analysis of a XVth Century Census: the Florentine Catasto of 1427," *Journal of European Economic History*, 4 (1975): 415–28; and " 'A uno pane e uno vino': La famille rurale toscane au début du XVe siècle," *Annales, E.S.C.*, 27 (1972): 873–901.

[34] North of the Alps, the elderly may have been held less in esteem; see Lutz Berkner, "The Stem Family and the Developmental Cycle of the Peasant Household: An Eighteenth-Century Austrian Example," *American Historical Review*, 77 (1972): 398–418.

impairments of a household head also handicapped the wealth of his or her household even after the other variables have been factored. On the other hand, residence in the mountains, hills, or plains played no role in determining wealth (see appendix 1, I). If the urban "gate" of Santa Trinita in Prato is added, the model changes and, not surprising, residence in the city emerges as the strongest variable determining wealth, but the other rural geographical zones remain insignificant.[35]

In addition, the distribution of wealth does not reflect any striking "mountain egalitarianism." The coefficient of relative variation (CRV, the standard deviation divided by the mean) for the plains is 245,[36] which does not depart radically from that of the mountains (198). Curiously, the most egalitarian areas were the hills (182).[37]

Do other characteristics distinguish the mountains from the plains at the end of the fourteenth century? For instance, were households larger or more complex in the highlands? Monte Morello's 104-year-old patriarch commanded not only the largest resources of any peasant found in this study; his seventeen-member family extended over four generations – a near impossibility for the preindustrial household according to Peter Laslett and his school.[38] Indeed, households of ten or more were extremely rare (forty-one representing 3 percent of all the families in which household members were individuated[39]). Fifteen of these are found in mountain communities. San Martino del Castro just under the Futa pass supplied the largest number (five), and the largest family surveyed as a single unit (twenty-one members) came from the mountain commune of Mangona.[40] The highest average household sizes also come from the mountains. Among "the stanti," Castro led the list with close to six members (5.76), while the impoverished marshlands of Padule sank to the bottom (2.83).

Yet, despite these extremes, household size does not invariably distinguish the mountains from the plains. In hosting large families of ten or more members, no significant differences arise between mountains, hills, and plains. In all these zones, such large families comprised only

---

[35] The *R*-squared of 0.15 is considerably higher than the previous models with Prato ("city") added. "City" is here by far the most significant and powerful variable; its coefficient is 296.68.

[36] The coefficient of relative variation is the standard deviation expressed as a percentage of the mean, $CRV = s/x \times 100$. The mean is 55.77; the standard deviation is 136.62.

[37] The mean is 52.41 and standard deviation is 95.56.

[38] *Household and Family in Past Time*, ed. by Peter Laslett and Richard Wall (Cambridge, 1972).

[39] By 1393, family members who were "stanti" or "venuti," were listed individually with their ages, but the "usciti" included only household heads or were indicated with vague phrases such as "the heirs of the former" or the head "with his wife and children." The one exception to this rule is Santa Maria a Novoli's listing of "usciti" in 1393.   [40] Estimo 219, 868v.

3 percent of families. Only the city of Prato possessed slightly higher proportions (4 percent). Moreover, two of the highest villages – Montecuccoli and Montecarelli – ranked next to Padule in possessing the lowest average household sizes in 1393 (3.32 and 3.31 respectively). On the other hand, the Arno valley parishes of Santa Maria Novoli and Santa Maria a Quarto in Florence's immediate hinterland as well as the "ville" di San Giorgio a Castelnuovo (40m) and San Giusto (47m) in the district of Prato (with high levels of *mezzadri* in 1427[41]) comprised average households of five members or more, among the largest found in these sample villages.

Nor did household complexity – generational and collateral extensions (married brothers or cousins and their families living in the same household or being taxed as a single family unit) – tend to cluster according to altitude. While impoverished Padule possessed no complex families, the greatest proportion came from the alluvial plains in Prato's Villa di San Giusto. Family structure varied widely across mountain communes, from Montecarelli, with a little over 5 percent of its households extended, to Castro, with a quarter. But on average little difference appears between plains and mountains; in both, about a third of families were extended either collaterally or generationally.[42] Instead, the proportion of extended families was highest for the city of Prato (40 percent) and lowest for the hills (19 percent).[43]

Finally, the notion that the mountains were patriarchal strongholds is tempered by the extent to which mountain women headed households. Although a comparison of patriarchy in the mountains and plains will have to await the study of other sources, these data are suggestive. By law, to count as a household head a woman had to be a widow or a spinster, but even these women did not invariably rule in the absence of other males; in some cases infant sons under five years old are listed as the official heads of families. On the other hand, several widows governed families with as many as five household members including adult males,[44] and in the small mountain hamlet of San Paolo di Castiglione the local officials violated an *estimo* statute by recognizing a married

---

[41] Herlihy and Klapisch-Zuber, *Les Toscans*, p. 285.
[42] For the plains 36 percent were extended (161 of 448 families, which were "stanti" or "venuti"); for the mountains, 32 percent (155 of 493).   [43] Forty of 206 and 67 of 167, respectively.
[44] A widow from Santa Maria Novoli, whose husband had recently died, headed a family of seven, which included her fifteen-year-old son (Estimo 219, 591r). In Quarto, a forty-year-old widow headed a household of five. (The eldest son, however, was only two; Estimo 219, 544v.) And a fifty-year-old widow from Bordignano headed a family of five; Estimo 218, 288v.

woman as the head of a household she shared with her husband, perhaps because she was identified as the owner of their 25 *lire* of taxable property, most likely her dowry.[45]

The mountain parishes of Bordignano and Santa Maria Casaglia, moreover, had the highest percentages of families with women household heads – 13 and 15 respectively. Next came the hill community of San Martino a Leccio with 11 percent. By contrast, households led by women are completely absent from Padule as well as the much larger and more prosperous baptismal parish of San Martino a Campi. In the alluvial San Giusto only one family out of eighty-seven was listed under a woman's name. Yet, on average, the differences for all three zones were insignificant, varying between 5 and 6 percent.

Prato possessed the largest proportion of female-headed households (9 percent), corroborating what Herlihy and Klapisch have found for the city of Florence in 1427: cities were the havens for widows, who on occasion controlled considerable material assets. Moreover, the preponderance of widows in the cities versus the countryside and the mountains in particular appears to have increased during the first half of the fifteenth century. By mid-century, the sex ratios found in the *catasti* show that mountain communities tended more often than the hills or plains to cast off their widows, who migrated to the cities to meet the growing demand for domestic servants and the growing supply of charitable institutions, while the widowers stayed behind, enjoying the fruits of the land.[46]

As we saw in the previous chapter, patterns of migration distinguished the mountains from the plains from 1383 to 1414. As Cherubini asserted, the mountains were "the great belchers of population" even if they did not rush downward to the cities and plains as historians have claimed.[47] With the exception of impoverished Padule, villages in the lowlands either remained stable or gained population at the end of the Trecento (1383–93), while the mountain districts spewed forth their human resources (see table 2.1). Only in Montecuccoli did newcomers balance out those who left in a mountain community. By contrast, nearby Montecarelli lost over one-third of its residents, and San Paolo

[45] Estimo 219, 298r. For the *estimo* law, see Estimo 73, 3r: "Quod nulla uxore alicuius viventis viro potuerit vel possit . . . referri vel allibrari in dicto nuovo extimo."
[46] See Cohn, *Women in the Streets*, ch. 7.
[47] Cherubini, "Conclusioni," p. 539: "il ruolo delle montagne come vomitatrici di uomini verso le colline e le pianure." Cherubini does not support his conclusions with any statistics.

Table 2.1 *Village migration in 1393*

Village	"Stanti"	"Venuti"	"Usciti"	Total
I Plains				
S Lucia Ognissanti fuori le mura	31 65.96%	8 17.02%	8 17.02%	47 100%
S. Lorenzo fuori le mura	31 54.39%	17 29.82%	9 15.79%	57 100%
Novoli	13 39.39%	12 36.36%	8 24.24%	33 100%
Quarto	21 42.86%	16 32.65%	12 24.49%	49 100%
Campi	42 57.53%	16 21.92%	15 20.55%	73 100%
Padule	6 21.43%	7 25.00%	15 53.57%	28 100%
Sesto	100 68.49%	19 13.01%	27 18.49%	146 100%
Castelnuovo-Prato	23 38.98%	17 28.81%	19 32.20%	59 100%
S. Giusto-Prato	37 42.53%	21 24.14%	29 33.33%	87 100%
II Hills				
Ruffignano	12 46.15%	5 19.23%	9 34.62%	26 100%
Artimino	81 69.23%	13 11.11%	23 19.66%	117 100%
Suffignano-Prato	26 66.67%	8 20.51%	5 12.82%	39 100%
Gabbiano	0 0%	10 47.62%	11 52.38%	21 100%
Polcanto	19 65.52%	6 20.69%	4 13.79%	29 100%
Leccio	23 58.97%	3 7.69%	13 33.33%	39 100%
III Mountains				
Schignano-Prato	12 66.67%	3 16.67%	3 16.67%	18 100%
Morello	18 48.65%	6 16.22%	13 35.14%	37 100%

Table 2.1 (*cont.*)

Village	"Stanti"	"Venuti"	"Usciti"	Total
Montecuccoli	82	9	9	100
	82.00%	9.00%	9.00%	100%
Mangona	107	8	47	162
	66.05%	4.94%	29.01%	100%
Montecarelli	42	13	30	85
	49.41%	15.29%	35.29%	100%
Casaglia	41	0	13	54
	75.93%	0%	24.07%	100%
Castro	60	0	17	77
	77.92%	0%	22.08%	100%
Bordignano	82	0	16	90
	83.67%	0%	16.33%	100%
Castiglione	7	0	6	13
	53.85%	0%	46.15%	100%
IV City				
Prato-S. Trinita	146	21	32	199
	73.37%	10.55%	16.08%	100%
Total	1062	238	393	1693
	62.73%	14.06%	23.21%	100%

Castiglione, near the Bolognese border,[48] lost as many families as remained there from the last *estimo* a decade earlier. Population change seen in the more reliable records of the *lire* show an even more devastating emptying of the mountains' population during the late fourteenth century (see figures 3.1–3.3).

How then can we account for the mountains' "vomiting" their human resources? In contrast to the celebrated thesis of Johan Plesner, which saw the wealthiest of "contadini" flow into the city of Florence,[49] the *estimi* of the post-Black Death Trecento reveal that

[48] This village is most likely the one Repetti, *Diz*, I, 590, identifies as Castiglioncello di Firenzuola, 12 kilometers northeast of Firenzuola, then on the border of the Grand Duchy of Tuscany and the Romagna Imolese; its parish in the eighteenth century was called SS. Giovanni e Paolo, and it appears on recent *carte militari* as Castiglioncello.

[49] The Plesner thesis lives on despite the devastating criticism marshaled against it early on by Gino Luzzato, "L'inurbamento delle popolazioni rurali in Italia nei secoli XII e XIII," in *Studi di storia e diritto in onore di Enrico Besta* (Milan, 1939), II, pp. 183–203; and later by Conti, *La formazione*, I,

poverty was the "motor" of peasant migration, as Herlihy and
Klapisch-Zuber have commented for the fifteenth century.[50]
Household wealth in 1393 shows that both the "venuti" as well as the
"usciti" were worse off than those who "stayed." Yet, if poverty were
the only explanation, mountains, hills, and plains should have shown
little difference in emigration. Indeed, since the mountain villagers
were slightly better off, it should have been less prevalent there than
for other areas, but it was not.

Nor were the propertyless the only ones "to go off begging" (*andarsene
acattando*) as the village scribes tersely put it. Later, in the survey of 1401/2,
when for the first time local officials were required to itemize villagers'
properties, abandoned *poderi* are found listed with their assessed taxes
alongside the names of mountain villagers who had left their farms for
foreign places to beg or wander far afield (*per lo mondo*). In one such case,
the rural rector from the Alpine village of Castro commented: "eviction;
abandoned farm; no one to work it, because no one wishes to pay the
estimo."[51]

In other instances, the mountain rectors and syndics ended their
reports to their "Lord officials" in passages beginning with *affarne ogni
chiarezza* to explain why their villagers needed the government's mercy
in setting the final tax base. At the end of their return, "the men" of
Mangona pleaded to the Florentine tax officials that their assessments
should be reduced because they had been levied for yearly expenses to
provide food and munitions and to repair Florentine fortifications, "*la
roccha di Manghone*."[52] The men of Castro claimed they were unable to
harvest their grain or draw "a drop of wine" because of the sterility of
their soil and the war "with the Count" (most probably the Count of
Alidosi della Massa).[53] The men of San Cristofano a Visignano as well
as those from San Michele da Monti (within the Alpi Fiorentine) complained of heavy feudal rents ("siamo tutti fedeli et affittati") owed to the
counts of Imola and the Alidosi.[54] Perhaps hoping to forestall Florentine
investigation into their returns, which even the villagers saw as suspi-
ciously low, the men of San Giovanni a Cornacchiaia added at the end
of their returns, "Lord officials, it is no wonder we have declared so little

Footnote 49 (*cont.*)
  p. 49. Other historians, such as Fiumi, "Fioritura e decadenza," part 1, pp. 429–34, criticized
  Plesner's definition of nobility, but continued to shore up his assumptions about the character of
  rural migration.   [50] Herlihy and Klapisch-Zuber, *Les Toscans*, p. 318.
[51] Estimo 225 (1412), 359r, the village of Castro.   [52] *Ibid.*, 219, 874r.
[53] *Ibid.*, 218, 285r.   [54] *Ibid.*, 218, 256v.

property, given that much of what we have belongs to the parish and three hospitals and many of us owe feudal rents to a certain Ubaldino of Galliano [one branch of the Ubaldini clan]."[55] Finally, the men of Caburaccio protested that most of their lands lay in the *contado* of Bologna where they were also taxed.[56] By contrast, not a single plea from a village in the hills or plains follows a tax return in the 1393 *estimo*.

Beyond these occasional marginal notes, the quantification of tax rates points to a characteristic which distinguishes the mountains from the low-lands in 1393/4 more than any other social fact gleaned from these records and helps to explain the differences in emigration. As Bernardino Barbadoro discovered against the claims of earlier historians, the late-medieval *estimi* of Florence did not fix a standard ratio of property values to the tax to be paid on them.[57] Instead, as we have seen, city officials set a communal tax for a rural district, which was then divided among the households within that community. Such community taxes could vary widely in relation to the property values possessed by those from the com-munity.

These tax bases set for the community as well as for the individual did not always meet with a community's approval, and the government set up a board to hear individual and community-wide grievances. The majority of individual grievances regarded household heads who claimed they had been taxed in more than one jurisdiction or those who claimed citizen status but had been charged (*allibratus*) a direct tax. Communities bickered over boundaries often caused by the changing courses of rivers and streams. On occasion, the petitions to the tax board even amounted to legalized tax revolts against their local officials.[58]

Such a dispute arose after the *estimo* of 1355, when the parish of Sant'Andrea a Legnaia in the southern suburbs of Florence claimed that its locally elected officials were corrupt and had used their positions to lower their personal shares of the tax burden. In response, the Florentine officials ordered a new election of the village syndics and a revised *estimo*, whereupon the assessments imposed on the previous officials (who proved to be the richest members of the parish) increased substantially. Yet the government seems not to have tolerated any disputes over the tax base assigned to a community, no matter how unfair. Despite wide dis-crepancies in the rates of taxation between one community and the next,

---

[55] *Ibid.*, 275r: "Signori uficiali non ve miravigliate perchè abbiamo posto si picchole somme, però che cio che noi abbiamo e della pieve e di tre spedali e siamo una grande partita di noi et affittati d'alchuno Ubaldino da Ghagliani. Di tutto questo e d'altro siamo presti affarne ogni chiarezza."
[56] *Ibid.*, 297r.   [57] Barbadoro, *Le finanze*, pp. 78–80.   [58] Estimo 73, 114r–15r.

not a single complaint made it before the tax board that protested against these inequalities.

So if not long-term geographical structures or endemic poverty, could the politics of patronage as seen in unequal tax burdens have been a factor determining the different rates of migration across the *contado* of Florence? By a method called probit analysis a dichotomous dependent variable, in this case out-migration (whether peasants stayed or left their village since the last *estimo*, that of 1383), can be regressed against various independent variables – distance from the city, household wealth, sex of household head, family size, and residence in the mountains, hills, or plains.[59] By these means, far more than any other factor including the geographic zones of residence, the tax rate emerges as the decisive cause of whether families stayed or left their homesteads for other places (see appendix 1, II).

Indeed, this model flies in the face of the assumption that poverty and the inclement conditions of mountain life were the factors forcing high-landers from their homesteads. Once these variables are interrelated, despite higher rates of migration from the mountains, Alpine residence in and of itself played no role in out-migration; instead mountain dwellers proved more intent on staying put on their farms than those further down the valleys, as accords with the general differences in land tenure – the prevalence of *mezzadria* and short-term rents in the plains and hills and independent farms in the mountains.[60]

As the above discussion should suggest, those in power in the city of Florence did not look upon the *contado* as an undifferentiated mass to be treated by a unified standard tax policy, as modern discussions of medieval Florentine fiscal policy and of the relationship between city and countryside sometimes assume. Table 2.2 shows the variation in tax base rates from one village to the next. Of course, fluctuations or differences in the tax rate could be offset by under- or overestimations of the property value. Thus, as the Kents have shown for the urban *gonfalone* of Leon Rosso during the fifteenth century, patronage, favoritism, and corrup-

---

[59] Because the tax officials rarely stated the family size or wealth of those who left, these variables along with the tax rate have been computed as the village average of those who "stayed" or "came."

[60] Both residence in the mountain villages and distance from the city were significant in determining out-migration, but these factors varied negatively despite what simple averages might suggest. Historians have pointed to the effects of taxation and war on peasant mobility elsewhere; see Comba, "Emigrare nel Medioevo: Aspetti economico-sociali della mobilità geografica nei secoli XI–XVI," in *Strutture familiari*, p. 63; "Il problema della mobilità"; Alfio Cortonosi, "Demografia e popolamento nel contado di Siena: la terra montalcinese nei secoli XIII–XV," in *Strutture familiari*, p. 173; Pini, "Un aspetto dei rapporti," pp. 399–400.

Table 2.2 *Summary of tax rates*

Village	Mean (%)
I Plains	
S. Lucia Ognissanti fuori le mura	0.36
S. Lorenzo fuori le mura	0.91
S. Maria a Novoli	0.68
S. Maria a Quarto	0.78
S. Martino a Campi	2.39
S. Maria in Padule	insufficient data
S. Martino a Sesto	2.04
Villa Castelnouvo (Prato)	0.95
Villa S.Guisto (Prato)	1.85
II Hills	
Ruffignano	1.62
Antimino	2.24
Suffignano	1.71
Polcanto	1.84
Leccio	1.16
III Mountains	
Villa Schignano (Prato)	6.58
S. Maria Morello	0.69
Comune di Montecuccoli	1.77
Comune di Mangona	10.51
Comune di Montecarelli	5.49
Comune di Casaglia	5.52
Comune di Castro	1.16
Comune di Bordignano	0.63
S. Paolo a Castiglione	1.02
Comune di Caburaccio	0.58
IV City	
City of Prato (Porta di S. Trinita)	1.44
Total	2.36

tion continued to play a decisive role in property assessments at least for the city even after the *catasto* reforms of 1427 established standardized rules for assessments.[61]

[61] D. V. Kent and F. W. Kent, *Neighbours and Neighbourhood in Renaissance Florence: The District of the Red Lion in the Fifteenth Century* (Locust Valley, N.Y., 1982), pp. 24–36; also see Paula Clarke, *The Soderini and the Medici: Power and Patronage in Fifteenth-Century Florence* (Oxford, 1991), pp. 35ff.; Nicolas Eckstein, *The District of the Green Dragon: Neighbourhood Life and Social Change in Renaissance Florence* (Florence, 1995), ch. 6; Conti, *L'imposta diretta a Firenze nel Quattrocento (1427–1494)* (Rome, 1984);

Table 2.3 *Summary of tax*
rates (based on 721 propertied
households)

Location	Mean (%)
Plains	1.60
Hills	1.99
Mountains	3.06
City	1.44
Total	2.36

Nonetheless, the discrepancies in tax rates of villages sampled for this study are extraordinary. The suburban parishes adjacent to Florence's city walls, which housed artisans and workers as well as peasants, and whose social composition was similar to those peripheral parishes within Florence's city walls, paid the lowest rates. The average tax base of those with property from Santa Lucia Ognissanti "outside the walls" amounted to only 0.37 percent of their assessed worth. Those further away in the Alpi Fiorentine invariably paid more. Highlanders from Montecarelli and Santa Maria Casaglia were required to hand over fifteen times more than Santa Lucia (5 percent of their property value). For the mountain village of Schignano in the district of Prato, the rate increased to 7.5 percent – eight times the rate imposed on peasants from Prato's lowland village of San Giorgio a Castelnuovo and twenty times the suburban rate of Santa Lucia "outside the walls."

In the *prope Alpes*, the rates climbed even higher. The peasants from the large commune of Mangona were assessed 10.50 percent, not of their yearly income, but of their property value.[62] Such a rate constituted a

Footnote 61 (*cont.*)

and *Ricordi fiscali*; Martines, "Forced Loans: Political and Social Strain in Quattrocento Florence," *Journal of Modern History*, 60, no. 2 (1988), p. 304; and Molho, "Fisco e società a Firenze nel Quattrocento (a proposito di una ricerca di Elio Conti)," *Società e Storia*, no. 30 (1985): 929–36. For patronage politics and taxation before the Medici from a contemporary account, see Morelli, *Ricordi*, pp. 252–3, 338, 499–500: "Appresso, sia cortese: ingegnati d'acquistare uno amico o più nel tuo gonfalone e per lui fa ciò che tu puoi di buono" (p. 253); and Giovanni Cavalcanti, *Istorie fiorentine*, ed. by F.-L. Polidori (Florence, 1838), p. 1: "La perversa condizione, la insaziabile avarizia, e la fastidiosa audacia de' malvagi cittadini, i quali erano eletti della fiorentina moltitudine a compartire le comuni gravezze, m'avevano sì ingiustamente prestanziato con gli altri miei simili, che, con assai antichi cittadini, eravamo fatti nuovi bifolchi, e la città abitare non potevamo."

[62] The actual tax charged in any given year depended on the tax coefficient, which varied from 10s to 1.5 florins, see appendix 2.

drastic inequality vis-à-vis the lowlands – 12.7 times that owed by peasants in the parish of Quarto, where sharecropping and urban investment in land had become widespread,[63] and a staggering 29.4 times that owed by the privileged *contadini* residing in Florence's suburbs. In 1395, when the emergency or "extraordinary tax" (*imposta straordinaria*) was levied at a rate of 1 florin on the *lira*, it meant that Mangona had to hand over 44 percent of its landed wealth to the Florentine state in that year alone and from that single tax. Matters only worsened with Florence's war with Milan and deepening fiscal crises at the end of the century, when the extraordinary tax rose to 1.5 florins on the *lira*.[64] Thus, even if 80 percent of communal receipts overall came from indirect as opposed to direct taxes (which I would question),[65] the impact of direct taxes could nonetheless be devastating for certain areas within the Florentine *contado*.

Did distance from Florence count for more than altitude? It appears that it did not, especially within the mountains themselves. Two of the most northern and distant villages in this sample – Santa Maria Bordignano and Caburaccio, nestled high in the valleys separating the territories of Florence and Bologna – paid less than Morello, in fact less than every other village found in this sample except for Santa Lucia Ognissanti. Perhaps the tax officials listened with compassion to the pleas, contained in these villages' returns, that they possessed the major part of their lands in the territory of Bologna, where they were also "allibrati."[66]

The tax officials may also have been sensitive to the military importance of these border villages, especially given the growing threats from the Bolognese, the incursions of the feudal forces of the Ubaldini, and the invading troops from Milan. Finally, Bordignano and Morello were the two wealthiest communities according to their property assessments, and wealth and the tax rate were negatively correlated across the villages sampled in this study. Even apart from the enormous tax advantages granted to Florentine citizens, the Florentine *estimo* was steeply regressive; the richer the peasant household, the lower its tax rate.

---

[63] For 1427, see Herlihy and Klapisch-Zuber, *Les Toscans*, pp. 268–72 and chapter 3 below.
[64] On tax coefficients, see Ciappelli, "Il cittadino fiorentino."
[65] See la Roncière, "Indirect Taxes," pp. 144–5; but as Herlihy, "Direct and Indirect Taxation," p. 393 cautions, many taxes that historians have considered as "indirect levies" such as the salt tax, repairs of roads and bridges, salaries of local officials, loans and military taxes were in effect direct taxes paid on the basis of the *estimo*. In addition to these so-called indirect levies even various wine and meat gabelles were often indirect only in name. Instead of calculating them on actual sales or consumption, Florence levied fixed charges for them (*taxa mercatorum*) based on the *estimo*. [66] Estimo 219, 296r.

Castro, near the Futa pass, was another mountain village not burdened as heavily as others in the Florentine Alps. The residents of this
village were mostly *fictaiuoli* or lease holders of the feudal Ubaldini
family, who had waged open warfare against the Florentine state periodically through the fourteenth and early fifteenth centuries.[67] Were
Castro's lower *estimi* a ploy on the part of the Florentine state to divide
these peasants' loyalties from their feudal lords? Or could they have
resulted from Florentine mercy on this village, which pleaded vigorously
in its returns that it had been badly hit by invading troops and crop failures?[68] Unfortunately, the tax records here remain silent. But Florentine
policy seen in the hundreds of tax exemptions, cancellations of debts,
and negotiations with peasant communes from the Black Death to the
return of the Medici demonstrates that Florence did pursue its tax policy
in close connection with its politics of dominion over the feudal powers
in the mountains.

Could the number of able-bodied men – an assessment of a family's
potential labor power – have affected tax rates and thereby help to
explain the discrepancies? The *estimo* was more than a property tax; it
was also a head tax on adult males.[69] For the *estimi* as for the later *catasti*,
tax officials mindful of the labor potential of the household took note of
handicaps, old age, and infirmities that might reduce a family's earnings.
These matters can readily be detected in inequalities in the rates among
those who possessed no property – the "nullatenenti." The average tax
burden varied from one village to the next, following roughly the
inequalities of the tax rates for those with assessed property. But the
amount of the tax could also vary radically from one "nullatenente" to
the next within the same parish, ranging from no tax at all for those
deemed the truly *miserabili*[70] to more than 1 *lira* – a tax usually charged
to those with substantial furnishings, animals, and land.[71]

---

[67] On the Ubaldini rebellions, see Stefani, *Cronaca fiorentina di Marchionne di Coppo Stefani*, ed. by N.
Rodolico. In *Rerum Italicarum Scriptores* [hereafter *RIS*], XXX, part 1 (Città di Castello, 1903),
r. 256, p. 97; r. 351, p. 130; r. 490, p. 172; rr. 548 and 549, p. 192; r. 611, p. 221; r. 639, p. 233; r. 641,
p. 234; r. 739, p. 286; and ch. 1, note 38 above.

[68] The local officials of Castro attached a note to their returns telling the Florentine authorities
that they did not know how to distribute the *estimo* given their poverty and the crop failures that
resulted from war with the "conte"; Estimo 218, 285r.

[69] Later, these two components of the *contado* tax would be separated.

[70] Total exemption from the *estimo* was extremely rare. Those called "miserabili", even elderly
widows who lived alone, possessed no property, and appeared to be on their deathbeds were
usually assessed at 4 or 5s.

[71] In one case, a family of six from Villa San Giusto sold all their lands, becoming propertyless by
the next *estimo*; yet they continued to be assessed by their earlier "imposte" – indeed one of the
highest in the village of 4 lire, 17s; Estimo 218, 976r.

Still other factors certainly affected tax rates, which are difficult to isolate from the records such as levels of corruption, patron–client relations, previous relations between a rural commune and Florence, and the favors to be granted and scores to be settled on the individual as well as community level. But the records do allow us to isolate a number of variables and from these regression analysis might lead us to more informed speculation about the factors underlying the wide discrepancies in village tax rates and what remains undisclosed.

When tax rates are regressed against the variables that can readily be extracted from the documents, the resulting model proves highly significant in explaining the variation of tax rates from village to village; the R-squared of 0.2439 (adjusted R-squared 0.2319) is strikingly high for preindustrial data, indicating that a quarter of the variation in the tax rates were determined by the listed factors (see appendix 1, III). Not all of these factors are significant (below the conventional 0.05 confidence level). Neither family structure nor any variable that concerned the personal characteristics of the household heads – age, sex, physical deficiencies – have any meaningful bearing on the tax rates. It might be assumed that these factors would come more into play with those who possessed no taxable property. But a regression of the taxes the *nullatenenti* paid shows that such matters, even though carefully recorded by the village tax officials, had no significant impact on these families' tax-base assessments. Only household size affected the amounts those without property paid (see appendix 1, IV).

One the other hand, other factors were highly significant. As speculated earlier, Florence's tax on its countryside was regressive; the wealthier the rural property holder, the higher the tax but the lower the tax rate as a proportion of the taxable holdings. Family size was also significant; as one might expect with a tax that evaluated potential agricultural labor power, the larger the family, the more the household was taxed. As surmised earlier, distance played a significant role in Florentine tax policy, but not in the way envisioned from the simple tally of tax rates and distances. Once all the factors are brought together and regressed, distance does not appear to have disadvantaged the taxpayer. Instead, it was negatively correlated with the tax rate, once the geographic zones – mountain, hills, and plains – have been factored in. This can be seen best in the mountains, where Florence taxed much more heavily communities in the *prope Alpes* than those on the sensitive military borders with Bologna. But the variable that weighed heaviest by far in determining the tax rate was altitude – whether a peasant happened to live in the highlands.[72]

As we have said, unlike the later *catasti*, the *estimi* fused together the head tax with property assessments. Could a higher percentage of males, particularly able-bodied ones between the ages of thirteen and seventy,[73] have contributed to the drastic tax imbalance? After all, the harsh conditions of mountain life and patterns of migration may well have sent women down the slopes in search of employment as domestics, as is suggested at least during the fifteenth century by sex ratios and by testimony left in family *ricordanze*?[74] Such sex-specific migration would have left higher percentages of able-bodied men with higher head taxes in the mountains. Northern mountain girls can even be found on rural estates that lay south of the city of Florence as was the case of Bernardo Machiavelli's farm near San Casciano, which employed an eight-year-old girl from the commune of Mangona.[75]

For the late Trecento, however, the statistics do not confirm that the observed tax discrepancies arose from such possibilities in migration. When the estimated head taxes are subtracted from the total assessment, the differential in tax rates instead widens; Mangona's rate jumps to 35.3 times that required of Santa Lucia's more privileged suburbanites. Further, if the final tax (*lira*), instead of the tax rate, is regressed as the dependent variable, the model becomes much stronger (R-squared = 0.5232): more than any other factor, residence in the mountains determined a higher tax (see appendix 1, V). The regression of taxes charged to those without taxable wealth – the *nullatenenti* and *miserabili* – also shows the same bias against the mountain villagers.

This chapter has analyzed the geographic characteristics of villages spread through four geographical zones of the Florentine *contado* for the *estimo* and *lira* assessments of 1393/4. These two years marked a critical moment in Florentine political history: the Albizzi regime restored elitist politics, bringing a new integration of magnates into the Florentine *Signoria* and councils eleven years after the defeat of the government of the Minor Guilds. As Antonio Rado concluded long ago, the Albizzi

---

[72] The coefficient for the mountains = +0.050, which was eight times the weight of the next significant variable, the hills at +0.006.

[73] Whereas the *catasto* assessed able-bodied males between the ages of eighteen and sixty, a head tax (Otto Karmin, *La Legge del Catasto Fiorentino del 1427* [Florence, 1906], pp. 28–9), the *capi*, charged males between thirteen and seventy if they were not servants, blind, or mad (Estimo 79, Deliberation of 1414, np).

[74] See Klapisch-Zuber, "Women servants"; and Cohn, *Women in the Streets*, ch. 7.

[75] Machiavelli, *Libro di ricordi*, p. 167.

balìa of 1393 marked the final victory of the Arti Maggiori.[76] The years 1393/4 also renewed conflict with the Milanese state, which would lead to the fiscal and social crises of the early fifteenth century.

From this analysis, many aspects assumed to have been part of a Mediterranean mountain civilization fail to characterize the mountains of Florence's northern *contado*. These mountains did not harbor the most wretched of peasants: instead individual highlanders were among the wealthiest in Florence's rural *contado* and on average were better off than those from the hills or plains. Nor was the distribution of resources significantly more egalitarian in the mountains than in communities lower down, despite the large proportions of landless *mezzadri* in the hills and plains and their absence in the mountains.

Moreover, while the mountains did "belch out" its population, these peasants did not scamper down the slopes to the plains or cities as historians have assumed, but moved upward and across the border. The push of this migratory stream had less to do with long-term structural causes tied to geography than with politics and in particular the heavily unequal tax rates Florence charged to its mountain dwellers. The one characteristic that most distinguished mountain communities from others was the tax policy Florence imposed on them, draining them of more than twice the resources demanded from the hills, plains, or city of Prato. By setting these conclusions in the larger context of Florentine history from the Black Death to Lorenzo il Magnifico, the next chapter will ask just how fixed was this picture drawn from the *estimo* and *lira* of 1393/4.

[76] Antonio Rado, *Dalla Repubblica fiorentina alla Signoria medicea Maso degli Albizi, il partitio oligarchico in Firenze dal 1382 al 1393* (Florence, 1926), pp. 149; also see Molho, "The Florentine Oligarchy and the *Balìa* of the Late Trecento," *Speculum*, 43 (1968): 23–51; "Politics and the Ruling Class in Early Renaissance Florence," *Nuova Rivista Storica*, 52 (1968): 401–20; and Fubini, "Diplomazia e governo," p. 72.

3

Fiscality and change, 1355–1487

A long-term examination of Florentine tax registers from the late fourteenth through the fifteenth centuries is fraught with dangers. Not only do tax assessments for single years show the pitfalls of most tax records – evasion, deceit, and missing records – but changes in the rules and even the culture of taxation compound the difficulties of assessing change over time. From 1355 to 1427, these tax surveys progressed in the quantity and quality of information rural syndics and city officials demanded from each household. The most important change in the principles of rural taxation came with the *catasto* of 1427, which eradicated the medieval system of community taxation to assess individuals according to the same principles regardless of residence. This transformation in rural taxation, moreover, was not one the Medici would brush aside after their return from exile in 1434, when patronage politics returned to normal. A standard rate for the *contado* endured even into the sixteenth century with the new tax system of the *decima*.[1] However, before 1427, the mosaic of different tax rates shows that the community inequalities in fiscality between mountains and plains in 1393/4 were not an aberration of that year (see table 2.2 above and figure 3.4 below).

Taxes had been more unequal at the time of the *estimo* of 1371. In 1393/4 the rates for communities of the plains and hills were nearly the same (1.63 and 1.99 percent, respectively), while those imposed on mountain dwellers (3.72 percent) doubled those on plainsmen (see table 2.3). But in 1371/2 highlanders had been taxed almost three times more than those in the plains (5.08 vs. 1.72 percent) with hill peasants equidistant between the two at 3.80 percent. In addition to these higher inequalities, the amounts attached to the tax base (the coefficients) increased during the 1370s. Curiously, it was not the wars with Pisa (1362–4) or the revolt of San Miniato (1369–70) that brought higher demands; rather

[1] Paganini, *Della Decima*, I, p. 2.

they increased in peacetime (1371). In that year for the first time that I have spotted Florence imposed an emergency tax (*straordinaria*) of 10s on the *lira* to be added to other taxes based on the *estimo*[2] (see appendix 2).

The 1371 tax increases and inequalities may have arisen as the Florentine state sharpened its weapons against the Ubaldini and their peasant "fideles" – who resided not only in the Alpi Fiorentine but also in the neighboring areas of the Mugello's *prope Alpes*, which the judicial registers show still bore Ubaldini allegiances.[3] Rebellion and criminal excesses against merchants, pilgrims, and others who traversed the mountain passes between Florence and Bologna after the Black Death provided the justifications for Florentine military reprisals through the 1370s.[4] In 1371 Florence endeavored to reassert its authority in the north by rebuilding fortifications at Firenzuola, then surrounded by a sea of Ubaldini opposition.[5] Two years later its plans escalated with a declaration of war against the Ubaldini, appropriating 30,000 florins (about double the annual *estimo* tax base for the entire *contado* of Florence in the 1370s and 1380s[6]) to "exterminate" this feudal family and to break its allegiances with peasant followers.[7] According to the chronicler Marchionne di Coppo Stefani, the Florentine military operation was a resounding success,[8] and the anonymous chronicler of the years 1358 to 1389 sang the praises of Florence's war captain Obizzo di Cortesia da

---

[2] These included the "gabella taxationis mercatorum comunis Florentie" (which from at least 1359 was charged at 2s on the lira (Provv. reg., 47, 65r–v, 1359.x.25.), the tax for maintaining roads, bridges, and make-shift crossings (*pro viis pontibus et ponticellis*) usually charged at 2s on the *lira*, and the ordinary, formerly called the tax to fund five soldiers per hundred in the population (*ad rationem quinque peditum pro centenario que appeallatur tassatio quinque famulorum seu peditum pro centenario*), which fluctuated between 10s and 20s.

[3] See chapter 5. On the obligations of *fideles* (also called *vassalli*, *residentes*, and *adscriptitii*), see la Roncière, "Fidélités."

[4] On famous assaults on merchants and pilgrims who crossed the Alpi degli Ubaldini from 1302 to the 1370s, see the chronicles of Matteo Villani, *Cronica*, I, bk. 1, r. 25, pp. 48–9; bk. 2, r. 6, pp. 203–3; r. 55, pp. 287–90; III, bk. 7, r. 76, pp. 308–9; IV, bk. 9, r. 81, pp. 279–80; r. 88, pp. 289–90; bk. 10, r. 26, pp. 37–8; r. 57, pp. 72–3; and r. 81, pp. 106–7; Stefani, *Cronica*, r. 639, p. 233; r. 641, 234; Casini, *Dizionario*, I, pp. 130–80; and Sterpos, "Evoluzione delle comunicazioni," p. 13. Also, see Sacchetti, *Il libro delle rime*, ed. by Franca Ageno (Florence, 1990), p. 225, lamenting the past suffering of priests, abbots, pilgrims, and merchants who traversed the perilous passes controlled by the Ubaldini before the Florentine victory of 1373: "non riguardando frate / né prete né abate / né pellegrin né alcun mercatante."

[5] Casini, *Dizionario*, I, p. 143: "Arx Terrae Florentiolae rehedificetur," 1371.x.22.

[6] The actual amounts the *contado* was charged varied yearly depending on the coefficients and whether an "extraordinary" *estimo* was levied. I have not found the amount of the *estimo*'s "distribution" in 1371, but for the latest survey in 1383, it was set at 40,000 *lire*, Provv. reg., 72, 186r–7r, 1383.xi.24. In 1373 – the year of the Florentine war against the Ubaldini – the "ordinary" *estimo* was 12 *soldi* per *lira* and the "extraordinary" 10 *soldi* per *lira*; Provv. reg., 61, 121r. Thus the total expected return from these taxes would have been 44,000 *lire* or about 15,000 florins.

[7] Provv. reg., 61, 64r–6r, 1373.v.30.   [8] See Stefani, *Cronica*, pp. 286–7.

Montegarulli, who finally "destroyed the perverse house of the Ubaldini" and afterwards was showered with "honors and gifts" in the city of Florence.[9] This Florentine victory had further ramifications in verse with Sacchetti's praise of the triumph of liberty over tyranny in his poem "Fiorenza mia, poi che disfatt'hai," which gloried in that "haughty and cruel family" finally reaping their just deserts.[10]

As with previous attempts to placate and incorporate the mountain peasants on Florence's northernmost borders, the immediate aftermath of the war showed a strategy of divide and conquer. First, Florence granted the Ubaldini branch from Pagnole considerable sums to betray their clan allegiance, to become "original" citizens of Florence, and to assume "popolani" status.[11] But Florence's major efforts at coaptation were directed toward the peasantry. Its 1373 declaration of war against the Ubaldini expressed Florence's urban republican ideology against what it scorned as feudal tyranny. This appeal of liberty, however, was not directed toward foreign enemies, as has been well studied by historians, but toward the peasantry of its own *contado*.

Florence asserted that the Ubaldini had "most cruelly" stripped their peasants of their properties through "tyrannical exploitation." To combat such alleged injustices and to break these peasants' loyalties to their lords, Florence widened the peasant commune of the Alpi Fiorentine centered round the "new town" of Firenzuola to include districts lost to the Ubaldini in the 1340s.[12] For this recolonization, the councils granted these mountain dwellers three-year exemptions on most taxes (the *estimi* and the gabelles) and pardoned all (except members of the Ubaldini family) from any previously committed crimes including homicide.[13]

Further, Florence promised protection if these peasants refused to

[9] *Diario d'Anonimo fiorentino dall'anno 1358 al 1389*, ed. by Alessandro Gherardi, in *Cronache dei secoli XIII e XIV: Documenti di storia italiana*, VI (Florence, 1876), pp. 301–3; and 491–2: Consulte e Pratiche, reg. 47, 147; and Provv. reg., 62, 156, 1373.x.13.

[10] Sacchetti, *Libro delle rime*, 168, pp. 224–6: "punendo loro del passato tempo/ Festa dée far chi vive in questo tempo, / rubati inquesti passi, / ed ancor morti antichi di ciascuno" (p. 225).

[11] Provv. reg., 61, 101r–2r, 1373.viii.26: "Pro parte Andree, Guidonis, et Ugolini filiorum olim Actaviani de Ubaldinis qui vocantur dale Pignuole."

[12] On the Florentine "new towns," see Paolo Pirillo, "Uno caso di pianificazione territoriale nel contado di Firenze (secc. XIII–XIV)," in *Studi e Ricerche: Istituto di Storia* (Florence, 1981), I: pp. 179–200; Friedman, *Florentine New Towns*; and Charles Higounet, "Les 'terre nuove' florentines du XIV siècle," in *Studi in onore di Amintore Fanfani* (Milan, 1962), III, pp. 3–17. On the expansion of the commune of the Alpi Fiorentini, see Provv. reg., 61, 39r–42r, 1373.iv.28; and Casini, *Dizionario*, I, pp. 133–80.

[13] Provv., 61, 39r–42r, 1373.iv.28: "Plebatium Cornaclarii et Camaioris et Bordignani Alpium Florentinorum."

honor their feudal and rental obligations to the Ubaldini or even to repay loans owed to them. On the other hand, if the peasants did not accept Florence's "liberty," Florence would hunt them down as rebels. Finally, as in other documents of submission, the city gave (and imposed on) these peasants the "liberty" of writing their own statutes (subject of course to Florentine approval).

Perhaps as a result of this double-sided policy of territorial domination, the differentials in tax inequalities narrowed between the mountains, hills, and plains with the next redaction of the *estimo* in 1383. They may have also resulted from the Florentine efforts at fiscal reform in the aftermath of the defeat of the government of the Minor Guilds and from the attempts of Lionardo di Niccolò Beccanugi ("provveditore" of the Florentine treasury in 1383) to replace tax inequalities and corruption with a more systematic and careful accounting.[14] While the tax base within the plains and hills nudged slightly upward (1.82 and 3.85 percent), the rates for the mountains fell by almost half (to 2.79 percent), and for a rare moment the base rate of the Mugello hills exceeded that of the mountain districts to the north.[15]

These measures, however, were short-lived. With the rise of the Albizzi and the return to a more narrowly based oligarchic regime in 1393, the old tax inequalities resurfaced in the countryside. While the tax rates for the plains stayed at low levels, those for the hills tumbled, and those for the mountains increased by three-quarters to 3.73 percent. Two years later, the Albizzi regime, moreover, multiplied these inequalities by increasing sharply the coefficients attached to these base rates. They introduced the highest increases in taxes to date, jacking up the charge on the "extraordinary tax" from 20s on the *lira* to four times that amount, one gold florin or 80s on the *lira*.[16] Again, this second substantial increase came in a year of peace.

As tensions with Milan heated up, so did the pressures on the Florentine fisc,[17] and increasingly the Commune turned to its peasants to meet the costs with emergency payments based on the *estimo*. In 1398 (again, a year of peace on the eve of the "third war" with Milan) the

[14] See Molho, "Lo stato e la finanza pubblica. Un'ipotesi basata sulla storia tardomedioevale di Firenze." In *Origini dello Stato*, pp. 225–80.
[15] At the same time, the tax coefficients remained stable through the 1380s with the ordinary fluctuating between 10s and 12s and the extraordinary between 10s and 20s.
[16] Provv. reg., 84, 28v–30r, 1395.iv.23: "Pro imposta comitatinorum."
[17] On the military crisis, see Baron, *The Crisis*, I, pp. 11–37; on the fiscal consequences, see Becker, "Economic Change"; Becker, *Florence in Transition*, II, pp. 234–6; and Becker, "Problemi della finanza," p. 435.

extraordinary tax was raised to the highest levels seen in the history of the *estimo*, reaching one and a half gold florins on the *lira* or 120s – twelve times what the ordinary tax had been in the 1370s. Not even during the fiscal crisis brought on by the wars with Milan in the 1420s did the coefficients return to this turn-of-the-century peak.[18] Because the upper Mugello and Alpi were also the principal theaters of Milanese incursions into the territory of Florence, these same peasants bore the increased costs of warfare – the provisioning of castles, guard duty, conscription, plus enemy raids, ransoms, village burnings, and brigandage from both sides – all of which are described with horrific detail in hundreds of peasant pleas to the Florentine state.[19]

By the summer of 1401, the suffering of Florentine peasantry and the mountain dwellers in particular may have begun to dawn on the *Signoria* and councils; the preamble of a new *estimo* began:

For the good and practical governance of our subjects and especially for an equal and just distribution of taxes . . . and seeing that it has now been many years since the last distribution, it seems necessary and just that a new distribution be made. And among other reasons [for drawing up the new distribution], two stand out; the first is war and the second, plague, which have greatly changed the population and the resources of the *contado*.[20]

In addition to war and pestilence, the preamble to the tax reform of 1401 might have included a third reason for changes in the population of the Florentine countryside – emigration – signaled in a myriad peasant pleas to Florence's highest councils in the opening years of the fifteenth century.[21] From the *estimo*'s listings of "venuti" and "usciti," out-migration exceeded in-migration by 1.45 to 1 in the plains in the years from 1393 to 1401; by 1.172 to 1 in the hills; but by a staggering 3.88 to 1 in the mountains; nearly four left for every newcomer.

The household population figures taken from the more authoritative "lira" registers of 1402 are even more telling of the disasters that beset the mountains. During these nine years since the last *lira* (1384), the plains declined by nearly a fifth (from 542 to 441 households), the hills by

---

[18] Despite the conclusions of historians and what common sense might suggest, the highest jumps in taxes imposed on the *contado* came not in wartime but in peace. Before the introduction of the *catasto*, the only time tax coefficients would again climb above 1 florin on the *lira* was during the years of peace in 1414 and 1415 (see appendix 2). High taxes appear to have been spurred more by the anticipation of and preparation for war than by war itself.

[19] On these petitions see part III, below.

[20] Provv. reg., 90, 133r–7r, 1401.vii.23: "Supra bono et utili regimine subditorum et maxime supra equa et justa distributione extimi . . . et attendentes quam jam multis annis ordinata et facta fuit ultima distributio videbitur necessarium et justum quod de novo fiat distributio extimi antedicti. Et inter alia duo, videlicet quia prius fuit guerra et secundo fuit pestis que duo multa mutaverunt tam in substantiis quam personis."   [21] See part III below.

a tenth (from 300 to 270), and the mountains by over one-third (from 816 to 527) (see figures 3.1–3.3). Places in the Alpi Fiorentine and *prope Alpes* were even harder hit. From the ensemble of plague, war, brigandage, and flight, the populations of Caburaccio, Mangona, and Montecarello were halved in these nine years alone.

Despite the good intentions of the Florentine councils to adjust the *estimo* to a more "just and useful" distribution and further legislation that year to curb tax collectors' corruption and harassment,[22] the councilors' words seem to have fallen on deaf ears by the time the new Ten of the Tax Board drafted the Commune's plans into actions. Instead of lessening the tax inequalities and the burden on those who had suffered most severely from war and plague – those from the mountains of the upper Mugello – the taxes at the opening of the fifteenth century sent these inequalities to new heights. While the ratio of the tax base or *lira* to estimated wealth in the plains remained roughly the same (1.57 percent), it soared from 3.73 to 6.65 percent in the mountain communes in 1401 (see figure 3.4). Moreover, this spread in tax rates most likely was even more accentuated than it appears, because the *estimo* returns do not survive from Florence's most favored rural taxpayers – those from the suburban parishes "outside the walls."

We might well ask what difference such seemingly small percentages made to the daily lives of Florence's peasantry. The ratios for the plains and the city of Prato of a tax base of less than 2 percent might even evoke the idyllic city–country relations and low taxes Enrico Fiumi imagined before the Black Death.[23] But given the mounting coefficients the government attached to these tax bases, this was not the case. Just how devastating such a tax would have been at its extremes can be seen for the commune of Mangona. The 1393 *estimo* set a tax base of just under 11 percent of the villagers' assessed wealth. In the years 1398 to August, 1401, the coefficient of the "extraordinary" was 1.5 florins or 6 *lira* or six times the "lira" calculated in 1393, plus the ordinary tax at 20s on the *lira*. In addition, these peasants continued to pay at 2s, if not more, for the repair of bridges and roads.[24] Thereby, for these years, Florence demanded that this highland village "prope Alpes" hand over 79.2 percent of its landed wealth per annum in direct taxes alone.

This heavy sum did not include other taxes such as the salt tax based on the *estimo*, as well as indirect taxes (gabelles) or other charges such as

---

[22] Provv. reg., 90, 429v–31r, 1401.iii.21: "Pro taxatione comitatus": "et qualiter et quomodo tam pro utilitate comunis quam etiam pro tollendo molestias et vexationes quas fiunt comitatinis maxime per exactores."   [23] Fiumi, "Sui rapporti."

[24] Such payments do not appear as separate listings within the Camera del Comune, but their rates become clear in the *provvisioni*, when the government granted extensions on the payments of these taxes.

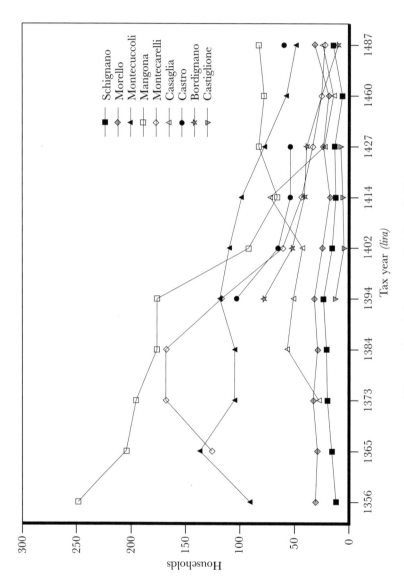

Figure 3.1 Population: mountains (households)

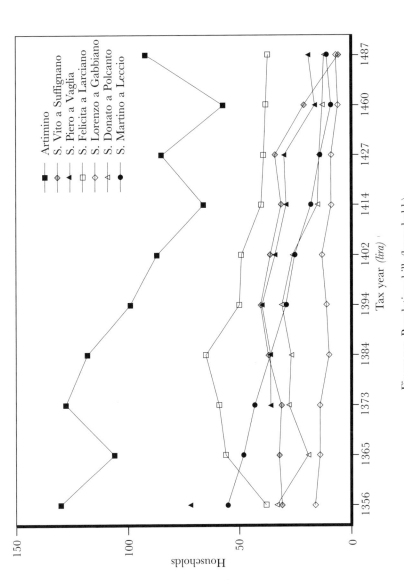

Figure 3.2 Population: hills (households)

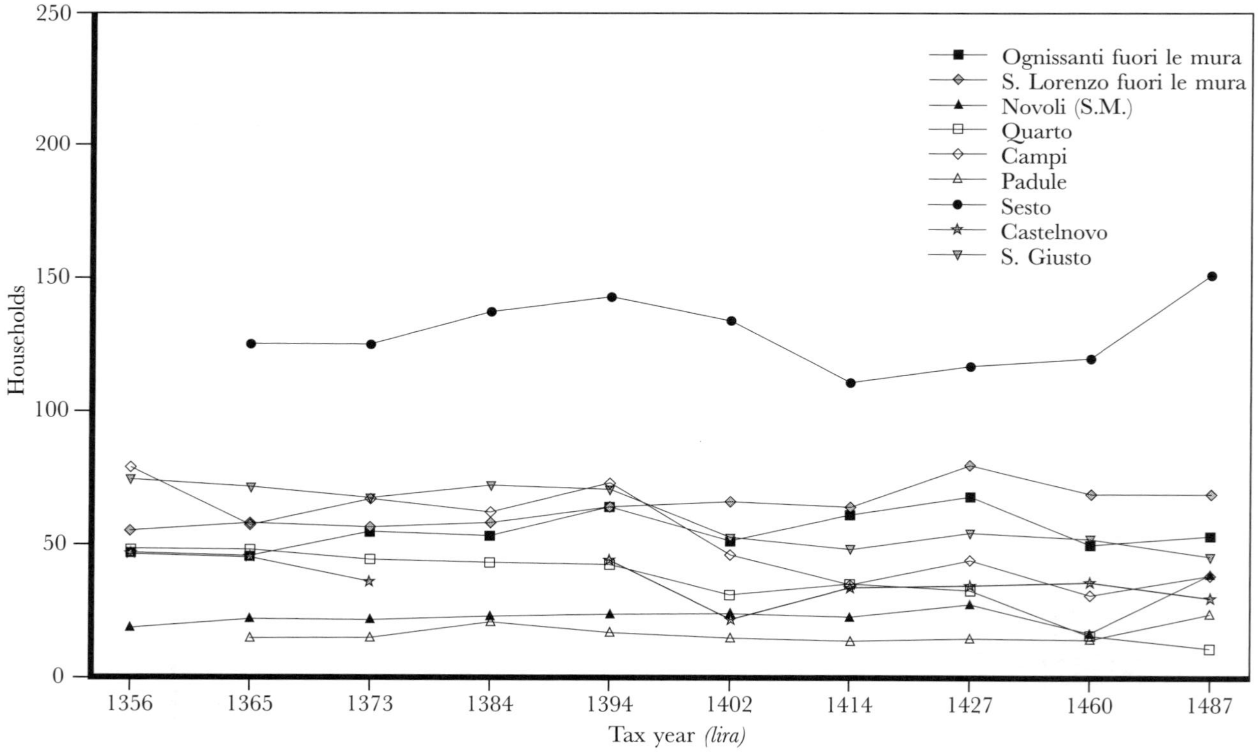
250
200
150
100
50
0
Households
1356
1365
1373
1384
1394
1402
1414
1427
1460
1487
Tax year (lira)
Ognissanti fuori le mura
S. Lorenzo fuori le mura
Novoli (S.M.)
Quarto
Campi
Padule
Sesto
Castelnovo
S. Giusto

Figure 3.3 Population: plains (households)

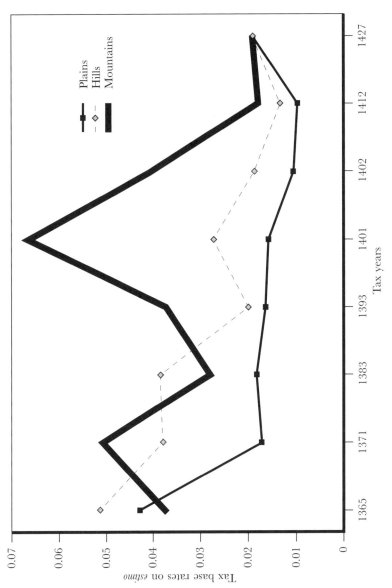

Figure 3.4 Tax rates: mountains, hills, and plains

the *Podestà*'s salary, castle duty and munitions, or wax for the feast of San Giovanni.[25] Thus, had these peasants paid only their direct taxes in these years, they would have been stripped of all their landed possessions within two years.

Although Mangona was the extreme case, the government demanded that the mountain villagers on average turn over 28 percent of their wealth during these years, which in a few years would have also wrecked their economies, forcing them off the land if the taxes had been collected. Yet, with the new distribution of 1401, their rates increased and the coefficients stayed at their highest point (see appendix 2).[26]

The devastation of these taxes is etched into the population histories of these mountain villages. For a village such as Mangona, taxation was more critical to its late medieval demographic history than even the Black Death of 1348. This supertaxed commune experienced the sharpest decline in population of any village I have sampled. In 1365 it was one of the largest villages in the *contado* of Santa Maria Novella. With 220 families (probably about a thousand individuals), it was twice the size of Sesto.[27] But, while Sesto's population remained stable over the last thirty-five years of the Trecento, Mangona's fell to eighty-six families and 278 persons in 1401 – a third of its 1365 post-Black Death population. After further onslaughts of war and peasant flight between 1402 and 1404, its population was cut in half again, falling by 1412 to its lowest point of only forty-seven families and 138 individuals, about a quarter of Sesto's size. Nor was Mangona alone in its population disaster. The demographic trajectories for villages in the mountains were decidedly downward from 1356 to 1427, and the decisive moment were the years 1394 to 1402 (see figure 3.1).

On the other hand, the post-Black Death population history of the plains stands in striking contrast to that of the mountains. As the figures show, after 1348 populations in the plains hardly changed over the long term, and in no case did a village's population in the lowlands turn suddenly downward from 1394 to 1402 as happened almost

---

[25] The schedules and amounts of these payments can be seen in the exemptions Florence granted villages in times of difficulty; for Mangona, see Provv. reg., 92, 215r–16r, 1403.xii.18.

[26] I have traced these coefficients by using the fiscal decrees found in the *provvisioni* and the income and expenses records of the Florentine treasury: Camera del Comune: Povveditori e Massai, Entrata e Uscita, 1–32 (1383–1428).

[27] No returns survive for the *plebis* church of San Martino a Sesto in 1356, but in the next survey of 1365 it posted 125 households. The difference in the population of Mangona and Sesto as well as of other large villages in the lowlands may have been even greater before the Black Death. Mangona was the only village singled out as badly struck by the pestilence ("mortiferam pestem") and which received special consideration; see Provv. reg., 36, 8v–10v, 1348.ix.12.

without exception in the mountains. The suburban parishes of Novoli and San Lorenzo "outside the walls" even gained numbers in this interval (see figure 3.3). Finally, the hills fit neatly in between the two: while their households declined, 1356 to 1402, it was a more gentle decline than that experienced in the highlands (see figure 3.2).

Taxes were the lever which turned the demographic and economic history of the countryside during the last years of the Trecento. With the increased tax rates and tax inequalities of 1393, the wealth and population of the mountain villages dipped sharply downward both absolutely and relative to the hills and plains (see figures 3.5, 3.6, and 3.7). The assessments of 1401 marked the watershed in community tax inequalities. In August of that year the *Signoria* and the councils sensed that their peasantry could take no more, and they reduced the coefficients on the *contado*'s "extraordinary" taxes – from 1.5 florins to 1 florin on the *lira* even though the war with Milan raged on and Florence's fiscal and military crisis intensified.

The year 1402 was a turning-point for tax inequalities as well. While 1401 marked the apogee of tax rates and tax inequalities, 1402 was the first time in the *estimo*'s history that the city's final *lira* revisions of the village distributions lowered instead of raising the village tax base. While the tax inequalities between mountains and plains remained at their highest levels, the rates imposed on the mountains fell almost to their 1394 levels. The year 1402 had initiated a trend. With the next tax estimates in 1412 to 1414, the tax rates imposed on the mountain dwellers continued their decline, reaching their lowest intervals since 1365 and approximating the low percentages found in the hills and plains.

Finally, the *catasto* of 1427 eradicated these community inequalities altogether; at least in the *contado* all individuals were taxed according to the same criteria regardless of residence (see figure 3.1). As the decline in tax rates for the *contado* illustrates, the principles of uniform taxation in the countryside did not spring solely from the crisis of the 1420s. Rather, this change in political mentality developed over a longer period, with 1402 as the turning-point. It was in that year, moreover, that the first evidence of the idea of a universal *catasto* emerges in the debates of the *Consulte e Pratiche*.[28]

The events at the turn of the century marked other long-term consequences for Florentine peasants that followed from changes in taxation. First, 1402 was the high point in emigration out of the Florentine *contado*

[28] See Brucker, *The Civic World*, p. 181. Matteo Strozzi made the "first documented proposal for a *catasto*, or property register" in the *Consulte e Pratiche* debates of 1402.

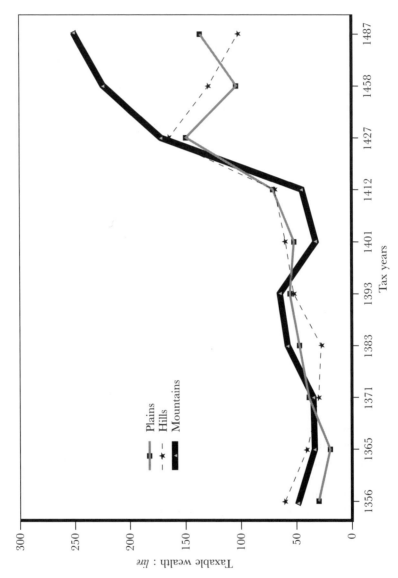

Figure 3.5 Wealth, including the propertyless: mountains, hills, and plains

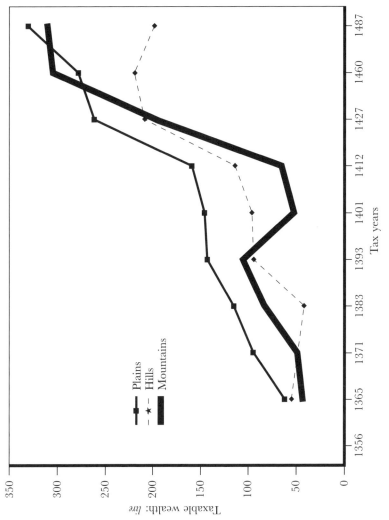

Figure 3.6 Propertied wealth: mountains, hills, and plains

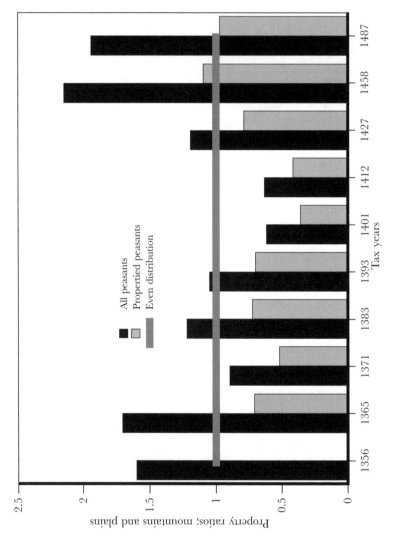

Figure 3.7 Wealth ratios: mountains vs. plains

and the low point in immigration from the countryside into the city. Second, although 1402 did not register a sudden upturn in the number of households across the three geographical zones, it did mark an increase in household size that would continue through my survey: from an average household size of 3.55 in 1402, the numbers gradually crept back to 3.77 in 1412 and reached their peak with 5.37 in 1487 (see figure 3.8).

More dramatic was the climb in household wealth. From 1365 to 1393, taxable wealth across the geographical zones of the Florentine *contado* edged upward without large discrepancies from mountains to hills to plains. But in the years 1394 to 1402 that phase ended. While household wealth in the plains remained the same and that in the hills even increased, the average wealth of mountain villagers plummeted from 58.46 to 31.80 *lire* – a 46 percent decline (see figure 3.5). In 1401/2 the average mountain family's assessed property was worth little more than half that of their neighbors in the hills. When only propertied peasants are compared, it dipped further still, to little more than one-third of those in the plains (52.34 vs. 146.28 *lire*), who had been spared the severe tax increases as well as the bloodshed and destruction of war. From 1402 to the next tax survey of 1412, as numerous pleas to the Florentine councils attest, large numbers of villages were unable or unwilling to pay their debts and taxes in the aftermath of plague, war, and rebellion. As we shall see, these petitions came overwhelmingly from Florence's mountainous periphery.

In part as a result of these successful petitions combined with the tapering off of taxes and the cessation of warfare in the Alpi, an astonishing reversal in fortunes appears in the opening years of the fifteenth century: both absolutely and relative to the hills and plains, the highlanders' economy improved steadily and rapidly. Although the wealth of those in the plains nearly doubled during the first half of the fifteenth century, by 1460, the ratio of wealth of highlanders to plainsmen had flipped from what it had been during the dark days at the turn of the century. From being the poorest in the countryside, mountain villagers sixty years on had become the wealthiest. Their wealth (210.60 *lire* per household) more than doubled that of the plains when all peasants are considered (98.07 *lire*), and for the first time the wealth of propertied mountain dwellers (286.92 *lire*) exceeded that of propertied plainsmen (261.94 *lire*).

Part of this reversal in relative fortunes no doubt stemmed from the spread of the *mezzadria* system in the hills and plains and with it the numbers of peasants with little or no taxable property. But the increase in the highlanders' taxable wealth as measured by successive *catasti* is

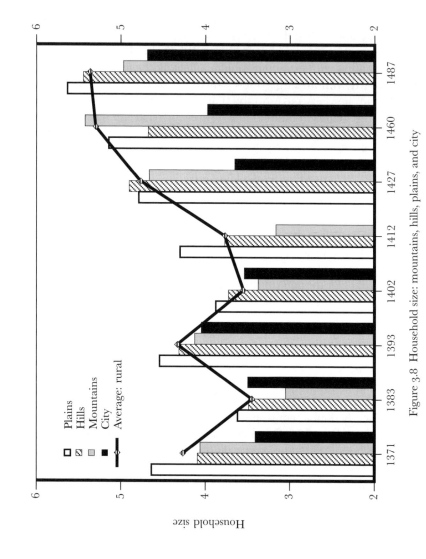

Figure 3.8 Household size: mountains, hills, plains, and city

impressive in absolute terms. In the years between 1402 and 1460, the highlanders' wealth had increased sevenfold (from 31.80 to 210.60 *lire*), and this in a period of stable wages and declining prices, at least as measured by the basic commodity of the peasant family – bread.[29]

By the Laurentian *catasto* in 1487, the *mezzadria* system may have been spreading more rapidly through the hills than even the plains. Since 1460 the hills' decline in wealth was absolute as well as relative to the others, whose wealth in nominative terms remained roughly the same as twenty years earlier. In real terms, however, the long ascent in peasant prosperity was over. While the value of peasant possessions and land started to edge downward, the costs of their basic commodities had begun to rise.[30]

How do we account for the these improvements in the wealth of the Florentine peasantry? Should they simply be attributed to the growth of a Florentine state that was more precise in its tax accountability and collection? First, as we have argued, the *catasto* evolved through the late Trecento and did not spring forth *ex nihilo* in the 1420s. The survey of 1401/2 was the first to analyze peasant holdings by itemizing them, specifying land measurements, and describing contiguous boundary holders as opposed to giving a single figure for the property's value. Yet this improvement in the tax collectors' scrutiny did not translate into higher assessments in peasants' values; instead the *estimo* of 1401/2 witnessed the nadir in peasant well-being since the Black Death.

But what about the *catasto* of 1427, when Florentine bureaucratic efficiency and fiscal administration reached their apex?[31] In addition to clear rules of assessment, the vicariate courts in the countryside came to the support of local officials in curbing the abuses of false reporting and a medley of devices for tax evasion in the countryside.[32] When all

---

[29] See Richard Goldthwaite, "I prezzi del grano a Firenze dal XIV al XVI secolo," *Quaderni Storici*, 10 (1975), p. 33, table B. Changes toward a more balanced diet evidenced by higher demands for meat, oil, and wine during the first three decades of the fifteenth century also attest to the general improvement in the condition of the Tuscan peasantry; see Herlihy, *Medieval and Renaissance Pistoia*, pp. 129–33. For a contrary view wholly lacking in statistical evidence, see Mazzi and Raveggi, "*Gli uomini*"; and Raveggi, "La condizione di vita," in *Prato: Storia di una città*, ed. by Giovanni Cherubini, I, part 2 (Prato, 1991), pp. 479–528.

[30] In addition to my samples, see Goldthwaite, "I prezzi del grano," pp. 33–4, tables B and C; and Brucker, "The Economic Foundations of Laurentian Florence," in *Lorenzo il Magnifico e il suo mondo*, p. 15. [31] See Herlihy and Klapisch-Zuber, *Les Toscans*, pp. 77–106.

[32] See the cases from the vicariate courts of the Florentine territory, Giudice, 76, 479v–87r, 1427.viii.30 and 562r–v, 1427.xii.20, where the authorities in Valdinievole and Marti in the former *contado* of Pisa cracked down on five rural communes, and over fifteen men were charged with taking bribes in exchange for lower *estimo* assessments. From these records, such corruption appears to have been normal in the outlying areas of the Florentine periphery. See also Herlihy and Klapisch-Zuber, *Les Toscans*, pp. 71–2.

peasants are figured, including the propertyless, who were usually charged a head tax,[33] the *catasto* shows a slightly sharper increase in property values from 1414 than the previous increase, 1402 to 1412. But, as historians have argued, the experiment of 1427 was brief and ended with the return of the Medici, if not before.[34] Yet wealth across geographical zones continued to climb between 1427 and 1458.

Although the 1412 to 1427 increase may reflect in part the administrative attention to detail and the more stringent endeavor of tax assessors to uncover hidden sources of wealth and income, it more likely charts the economic benefits of rising agricultural wages and of stagnant or even falling prices for landed property. After the devastations at the turn of the century, landless peasants and those with small plots finally were able to take advantage of the demographic consequences wrought by plague, war, and other forces of depopulation. With lower bread prices and higher wages, landless peasants in Florence as in Siena,[35] Languedoc,[36] and in many other places in Western Europe,[37] were able to buy back their land during the first half of the fifteenth century. This trend slowed by the second half of the century and ended by the 1470s.

Nor did these increases in the peasants' worth merely reflect an increase in the prices of property with no corresponding relationship to the income or produce from them. First, land prices remained relatively stable throughout the first half of the fifteenth century and may even have dropped in Tuscany as well as across Europe.[38] Second, with the *catasto* of 1427 (and probably earlier), the tax officials calculated property values not by the notarized prices they fetched, but from estimates of the properties' annual production in grain, wine, or other commodities.[39]

To estimate the relative differences in wealth and status of peasants across the Florentine territory, the historian can turn to another source

[33] On the head tax, see Herlihy and Klapisch-Zuber, Les Toscans, pp. 332–6.
[34] Petralia, "Imposizione diretta," p. 647.
[35] Cohn, "The Movement of Landed Property in Siena before and after the Black Death," unpublished ms.
[36] See Emmanuel Le Roy Ladurie, *Les paysans de Languedoc*, 2 vols. (Paris, 1966).
[37] See, for instance, Guy Bois, *Crise du féodalisme: Economie rurale et démographie en Normandie orientale du début du 14e siècle au milieu du 16e siècle* (Paris, 1976).
[38] I do not know of any price series for land in Tuscany for the later Middle Ages and Renaissance. On the low profits accrued from land from the late fourteenth through the early sixteenth century, see Goldthwaite, *Private Wealth in Renaissance Florence: A Study of Four Families* (Princeton, 1968), pp. 246–51; and for Europe more generally: B. H. Slicher Van Bath, *The Agricultural History of Western Europe, 500–1850*, transl. by O. Ordish (London, 1963), pp. 140–5, records the fall of land rents through 1450.
[39] Herlihy and Klapisch-Zuber, *Les Toscans*, pp. 59–67. The *catasto* of 1460 was the first to report notarized sales of rural properties, but the tax officials continued to estimate the produce from the property.

– notarized marriage records and dowries. Record linkage between the *estimi* and surviving marriage contracts show that even those without any taxable property somehow managed to assemble the resources necessary to dower their daughters or sisters for amounts as little as 40 *lire* plus the notarial fees to have them on record, even though the statutes did not require it.

From a sample of 506 marriage contracts collected from the plains around Sesto, the mountains of the Alpi Fiorentine, and mountains of the Aretine Casentino, dowry prices increased for the Florentine peasantry from a median of 40 *lire* at the time of the Black Death to 172 *lire* during the years 1451 to 1475. Then, following the trend traced by property values in the tax records, dowry prices fell in the last years of the fifteenth century and plummeted still further in the early years of the sixteenth century, reaching prices they had not seen since the late Trecento. At the same time, the cost of living was increasing, and dowries in the city continued to inflate. The dowries also show the same relative differences in wealth reflected by the tax returns during the fifteenth century: those exchanged by the alpine peasants consistently exceeded in value those from the plains around Campi, Sesto, and Santo Stefano in Pane.[40]

How then are we to understand these changes in the prosperity of the Florentine peasantry and in particular that of the mountain dwellers? Did climatic changes or plagues in the second half of the fourteenth century destroy men and crops more in the mountains than in the valleys? No evidence substantiates such speculations. Instead, man-made forces emerge from the documentation – first, war, and second, and more significantly, Florence's differential taxation. As taxes imposed on those in the mountains increased, their poverty deepened both absolutely and relative to the more favored peasants further down the slopes and nearer to the city (see figures 3.6 and 3.7). Demographically, these political facts were more devastating than the plague.[41] While in some other areas of Europe, population began to recover economically by the 1370s,[42] the heavy burden of Florentine tax policy retarded the economic recovery of

[40] See Cohn, "Marriage in the Mountains."
[41] On plague as an "exogenous variable," see Bruce Campbell, "Population-Pressure, Inheritance and the Land Market in a Fourteenth-Century Peasant Community," in *Land, Kinship and Life-Cycle*, ed. by Richard M. Smith (Cambridge, 1984), pp. 120 and 127; and Herlihy, *The Black Death*, pp. 4, 33–4.
[42] Campbell, "Population-Pressure," pp. 122–3; John Hatcher, *Plague, Population and the English Economy 1348–1530* (London, 1977), pp. 100–1; Hatcher, "England in the Aftermath of the Black Death," *Past and Present*, . 144 (1994): 3–35; A. R. Bridbury, "The Black Death *Economic History Review*, 2nd ser. 26, no. 4 (1973): 584–92;" and Cohn, "Insurrezioni contadine."

its *contado* and led to a further emptying of the countryside, especially in its mountain districts.

After the peasant uprisings of 1401 to 1405, these patterns changed. But less harsh taxation did not improve economic conditions evenly throughout the Florentine *contado*; as we have seen, household wealth increased faster in the mountains than elsewhere. Along with the changes in tax policy, other factors may have aided those from the mountains during the first sixty years of the fifteenth century. From the French Cévennes to the Val Demone in northeast Sicily,[43] highland peasants benefited from the rising prices of animals and crops other than cereals common to the lowlands. For Florence, moreover, the decline in warfare, after 1402 for the Alpi Fiorentine and after the Peace of Lodi, 1454, for the territory as a whole,[44] also favored the mountain zones first and foremost, which had previously borne the brunt of damages to crops, buildings, and manpower.

Even taxes, the bane of the highlanders' existence and reason for their emigration in the late Trecento, may have come to favor them over lowlanders. A decline in the rigor and efficiency of tax collecting after 1427, especially of liquid and mobile wealth, may well have profited remote mountain communities: first because of their inaccessibility, of which the tax collector would complain well into the early-modern period;[45] and second, because a greater proportion of their wealth was in livestock, which was more difficult to find and to assess. Thus the mountain villagers may well have been prospering through the fifteenth century even more than their returns tell!

If taxes were the lever for these long-term shifts, how do we explain Florentine fiscal policy in the last decades of the Trecento? Why did Florence hammer so brutally its mountain dwellers on its northern borders, forcing many to leave their lands?[46] I have not found any direct

---

[43] See Le Roy Ladurie, *Les paysans de Languedoc*, I, pp. 167–8; and Epstein, *An Island for Itself*, p. 220.

[44] On the chronology of warfare in late medieval Tuscany, see Molho, "Fisco ed economia a Firenze alla viglia del Concilio," *ASI*, 148 (1990): 807–44, esp. pp. 824–7, for warfare in the 1430s and 1440s in the Florentine territory; and "Lo stato," p. 263, for the years 1470–90. Also, see the remarks of Rucellai, *Zibaldone*, p. 122: "E per chagone che lla nostra città era stata in ghuerra e in grave spesa anni trenta, cioè dal 1423 al 1453 . . . che ssiamo stati tranquilla pace anni 20 di tenpo, cioè dal 1453 al 1473, eccetto un anno solo del 1467, ch'avremmo ghuerra in Romagna."

[45] See Braudel, *The Mediterranean*, I, pp. 39–41; and Wickham, *The Mountains*, pp. 349–80, on Florence's difficulties in disciplining the local elites in the Garfagnana highlands during the sixteenth century.

[46] On fiscality as a tool used by lords, communes, and states to spur migration, see Comba, "Il problema della mobilità," pp. 312–13.

testimony in either public documents – deliberations of the *estimi*, statutes, *provvisioni*, the *Consulte e Pratiche* – or private ones such as *ricordanze* that voiced explicitly Florence's rationale. But the logic or illogic of these patterns appears linked to economics and the long-term patterns of patronage.

The context of labor shortages and urban investment in agriculture suggests an explanation. Although David Herlihy originally argued that urban investment in land and the spread of the *mezzadria* system quickened from the Black Death through the early Quattrocento,[47] he later changed his mind: "The economic troubles of the late fourteenth century did not enlarge, but rather diminished the flow of urban capital into agriculture."[48] His evidence did not, however, follow the ebb and flow of *mezzadria* contracts or the flow of rural properties in or out of citizens' hands but instead relied on indirect evidence – changes in the tax receipts from the countryside. These showed an increase in tax revenue, which Herlihy took to mean a recrudescence in peasant ownership of the land. But, as we have seen, the tax the government levied on its rural hinterland hardly remained constant and reflected more about its politics than the demography or economy of the countryside. The rise in tax receipts from the *contado* in the closing years of the Trecento did not reflect their economic improvement or a flow of property back into their hands; rather it meant the opposite – increased taxes and increased economic deprivation.

On the other hand, other historians have continued to support Herlihy's earlier position with compelling new evidence from local studies of the Bisenzio valley surrounding the city of Prato, the Valdesa southwest of Florence, and elsewhere: the *mezzadria*, fueled by urban investment, spread "progressively and enormously" between the thirteenth and fifteenth centuries.[49]

None of these historians, however, have attempted to chart more precisely the ebb and flow of this movement of landholding over these three centuries. Further, Herlihy claimed that there is "no consistent run of documents which might illuminate the changing behaviour of Tuscan investors."[50] But notarial protocols redacted in the rural villages

47 Herlihy, "Santa Maria Impruneta: A Rural Commune in the late Middle Ages," in *Florentine Studies*, pp. 242–76.
48 Herlihy, "The Problem of the 'Return to the Land' in Tuscan Economic History of the Fourteenth and Fifteenth Centuries." in *Civiltà ed economia agricola*, p. 415.
49 Klapisch-Zuber, "Mezzadria e insediamenti rurali alla fine del medio evo," in *Civiltà ed economia*, p. 154; Pinto, *Città e spazi*, pp. 126 and 139; Raveggi, "La condizioni di vita," p. 549; and Muzzi, "Aspetti," p. 140.   50 Herlihy, "The Problem of the 'Return to the Land,'", p. 412.

surrounding the city of Florence are filled with land transactions, mostly sales and rents, and from these one can chart with greater precision the flow of landed rural properties in and out of urban hands at least for limited areas.

Once again we can rely on the notarial charters of the Mazzetti family, who worked the plains from Florence's city walls through the hills of Sesto. For this study I have recorded the sales and rents from only two of their books, both of near equal size for two different periods. The first covers the years 1364–71; the second, 1370 to 1401. In the first period the majority of sales (forty-one sales or 37 percent) took place between villagers. Of these, all were sales of scattered strips of land (*petie terre*). These years appear to have been a rare moment when the peasantry was recuperating some of its landed losses, at least as far as the numerical balance of transactions was concerned. Urban sales to rural clients slightly outnumbered rural sales to citizens (twenty-seven sales or 24 percent of all sales as opposed to twenty-three sales or 21 percent). In both cases the lands were mostly scattered strips and, more rarely, a plot with a house. In only one case was an entire farm (*podere*) transferred between a citizen and a *contadino*, and it was the citizen who acquired the property.

The next *filza*, that of Ser Piero di Talento Mazzetti, covers a longer, thirty-year period but contains slightly fewer land transactions than that redacted by his brother, Ser Giovanni, in the preceding six years. From this evidence, we cannot conclude that the land market's activity suddenly declined. Perhaps Ser Piero was less successful or less energetic than Ser Giovanni; perhaps other notaries now competed for the same business, or perhaps other protocols redacted by Piero covering the same period are now lost. These possibilities, however, would not affect the balance of buyers and sellers found in the land transactions that do survive in Piero's notary book.

This second volume shows a radical change from the years immediately after the plague of 1363. The presence of Florentines in the rural property markets of the nearby plains became dominant. First, rural properties exchanged exclusively between Florentine citizens within these villages climbed from 18 to 28 percent (twenty-three sales). In contrast to the smaller transactions of a few scattered strips common to the earlier period, more than half of these sales comprised either complete farms (*poderi*), houses with vineyards or arable lands attached, or large transactions of "many strips." These lands usually measured over a hundred *stiori* and were valued in the hundreds of florins. Furthermore, by the last thirty

years of the fourteenth century, artisans, small provisioners such as cob-
blers and butchers, and even disenfranchised workers – doublet-makers
and a wool-shearer – had begun trading in these more expensive lands.[51]
Second, exchanges exclusively between peasants declined from 37 to
less than 23 percent.[52] Third, and most significant, the pendulum had
shifted from the earlier transactions: while in the years immediately following the plague of 1363 sales of rural lands from Florentines to villagers prevailed, now the flow of rural lands had reversed direction; urban
buyers doubled the number of rural buyers in the acquisition of rural
lands.[53] In some cases, a second transaction followed on the same day
and place: a short-term lease or *mezzadria* contract converted the former
village proprietor into the urban landlord's tenant on the very property
which moments before he had owned.[54] Thus, from the 1370s to the end
of the century, at the very moment when tax rates were widening
between plainsmen and highlanders, urban interest in building up
estates in the surrounding plains was intensifying. As we will see, it was
also a time when labor shortages in the *contado* were on the increase.

The dominance of urban investment in the plains is shown even more
clearly in lease agreements. For both periods, the landlords in the surrounding villages were predominantly residents of Florence. But, in the
second period, no doubt reflecting the flow of rural property in urban
hands, this urban presence increased from less than three-quarters to
nearly 90 percent of all landlords.[55] All of these contracts, whether *ad
medium*, payments in kind, or (more rarely) in money, were of the short
term, never exceeding five years. Moreover, the character of the rural
landlord changed over these two periods. In the first, seven of the fifteen
rural landlords appear to have been mere peasants, identified simply by
a name, a patronymic or two, and their parish. The other eight were
local parish priests. By contrast, in the second period only one peasant
appears as a landlord in these transactions.[56]

---

[51] Not. antecos., 13521, 40r, 185r, 204v; *ibid.*, 125r, 163r, 188r; *ibid.*, 186r; *ibid.*, 54r, 146r, 154v, 169r, 227v, 231r; *ibid.*, 130v; *ibid.*, 106r; *ibid.*, 226r; *ibid.*, 155r, 193v; *ibid.*, 169r; *ibid.*, 61v, 69v, 70v; and *ibid.*, 130r.

[52] In both periods the exchanges rarely consisted of more than five strips of land and rarely exceeded ten *stiori* or three acres.

[53] In one-third of sales (twenty-six), Florentines purchased property from their rural holders as opposed to thirteen sales (16 percent) in which a villager bought property from urban specula-tors.

[54] See, for instance, the activity of the money changer (*campsor*) Giorgius f.q. Aldobrandini from the Florentine parish of San Lorenzo; Not. antecos., 13521, 187r, 1391.xi.20.

[55] From forty-three of fifty-eight rental contracts to forty-seven of fifty-three contracts.

[56] Not. antecos., 13521, np, 1397.x.28.

This increasing urban dominance in the rural land markets of the surrounding plains over the last three decades of the fourteenth century
contrasts markedly with their presence in the more distant and higher
lands of the upper Mugello and the Alpi. Here we rely on the mountain
notary Ser Antonio, who worked from Barberino and Scarperia north-
ward through the Alpi Fiorentine and across the Bolognese border
during the years 1428 to 1435.[57] In contrast to the Mazzetti's business,
Ser Antonio did not redact a single land conveyance of rural properties
where both parties were citizens of Florence. In addition, in only nine
transactions did properties move between rural and urban Florentine
hands, and here the balance of trade was almost equal.

Further, the residential status of some of these "urban" investors is
ambiguous. In one case I counted as a Florentine a Donna Gigia from
Santa Reparata in Florence, who sold a house with a sun porch to a
peasant in Galliano, but she was the widow of a man from the Ubaldini
clan who lived in the mountain village of Monti, and there is no reason
to believe that she had returned to Florence. To enter into the contract
she had chosen a *mundualdus* from the Alpine village of Valle, and all her
contracts were celebrated in the parish of Galliano – a former Ubaldini
stronghold.[58] A similar ambiguity is found with two members of the
Cattani family, both of whom were identified as residents of San Lorenzo
in Florence and as from Barberino del Mugello, where they possessed a
"palazzo" and where their presence on witness lists and as the initiators
of convocations and other notarial acts suggest they lived year round.[59]

In addition, not all of these urban investors bought property in
mountain villages. One sale was of rural property in the hills of the Val
di Marina closer to Florence,[60] and another was a house within the
walls of the new town of Scarperia.[61] But regardless of how these nine
contracts are counted, the preponderance of Ser Antonio's sales was
between the villagers themselves – forty-one of the fifty land sales
found in his book (82 percent). If the Cattani are considered as residents of Barberino and the Ubaldini widow as of Monti, the percentage rises to 90 percent. Moreover, unlike those for the villages in the
plains around Sesto, the land sales between peasants were not exclusively small strips of land, but often contained houses, huts, and
animals.

---

[57] *Ibid.*, 792. This is the earliest of the notaries I have found who worked extensively in the Alpi
Fiorentine.   [58] *Ibid.*, 166r–v, 1433.vi.4.
[59] To list only a few: *ibid.*, 70r, 1430.vii.2; 141v, 1432.viii.31; 150r, 1432.i.21; and 183v, 1434.iv.12.
[60] *Ibid.*, 128r, 1431.iii.2.   [61] *Ibid.*, 202v, 1434.viii.28.

The lack of urban interest in the mountain land markets to the north is further seen in the near absence of a rental market in the Mugello hills and Alpi. For the plains around Sesto, a third of the land transactions in the first period and over 40 percent in the second were rents, and in both the urban landlord was predominant. By contrast, Ser Antonio redacted only three rental contracts: two of these were not in the mountains but in the valley town of Barberino,[62] and in the third, a *mezzadria* contract of lands in Le Valli (Alpi Fiorentine), the landlady was the Ubaldini widow from Monte.[63]

The absence of urban investors in the upper Mugello and Alpi is further reflected in their rarity as contiguous property holders to the lands bought, sold, leased, or donated in Ser Antonio's protocol. Members of the Cattani family appear in the contiguous lists of only a handful of properties,[64] and a certain Cosimo di Giovanni de' Medici appears as the contiguous owner of "a piece of pasture land" measuring one *stioro* in the parish of Santa Maria a Casaglia "a pie d'alpe."[65] He was the only Florentine to appear with lands so far to the north,[66] and even this was still the Mugello and not yet the Alpi.

These differences form the context for understanding the tax rates across the Florentine *contado*. Since Nicola Ottokar (perhaps even Niccolò Machiavelli or Giovanni Cavalcanti), historians have stressed the importance of patronage for explaining Florentine politics.[67] For the most part, these studies have concentrated on clientage within the city and between members of the ruling class. Only recently have historians

---

[62] *Ibid.*, 163r–v, 1433.v.24.   [63] *Ibid.*, 166v, 1433.vi.4.   [64] *Ibid.*, 187r, 1434.iv.18.

[65] *Ibid.*, 151v, 1432.ii.3. In the *catasto* of 1427 Cosimo and Giovanni de' Medici owned land farmed by *mezzadri* in Mangona: see Mazzi and Ravaggi, *"Gli uomini"*, p. 158.

[66] He also appears as the contiguous owner of a plot of arable land in the Alpine parish of Santa Maria Caburaccio; Not. antecos., 792, 160v, 1433.iv.25; and in a property at San Martino within the parish of San Gavino; 209v, 1434.ii.4. One of Angelo Poliziano's *facezie* tells of Cosimo's father's "great friendship with some of the peasants from the Alps"; *Angelo Polizianos Tagebuch (1477–1479)*, ed. Albert Wesselski (Jena, 1929), p. 169. Before the Black Death, patrician landownership in the mountains may have been more diffused. For instance, the Bardi held important castles at Vernio and Mangona until 1340. In reaction to the Bardi's political influence and power, Florence passed a law in 1338 forbidding Florentine citizens to buy castles beyond the confines of the city of Florence (Armando Sapori, *La crisi delle campagnie mercantile dei Bardi e dei Peruzzi* [Florence, 1926], pp. 117–18, 124, and 130). On earlier citizen landownership in the area of Casaglia (Crespino), see Pirillo, "Uno caso di pianificazione," p. 194.

[67] Nicola Ottokar, *Il comune di Firenze alla fine del dugento* (Florence, 1926). More recently, see the work of D. V. Kent, "Dinamica del potere e patronato nella Firenze dei Medici," in *Ceti dirigenti nella Toscana del Quattrocento* (Florence, 1987); *The Rise of the Medici*; D. V. and F. W. Kent, *Neighbours and Neighbourhood*; F. W. Kent, *Household and Lineage in Renaissance Florence: The Family Life of the Capponi, Ginori, and Rucellai* (Princeton, 1977); *Bartolommeo Cederni and his Friends: Letters to an Obscure Florentine*, ed. by F. W. Kent and Gino Corti (Florence, 1991); and Molho, "Cosimo de' Medici: 'Pater Patriae' or 'Padrino'?" *Stanford Italian Review*, 1 (1979): 5–33.

begun to investigate such ties between the city and countryside,[68] but these remain within the ambit of the ruling classes and have concentrated on a later period. Yet, as readers of Florentine *ricordanze* know, the tentacles of patronage extended down the social ladder and beyond the city walls of late-medieval and Renaissance Florence into villages where Florentine citizens concentrated their rural holdings and exploited the resident labor force.

The diary of Bernardo Machiavelli mixed entries of his farm hands' economic dealings, marriages, and misfortunes with those of his own family.[69] Giovanni di Pagolo Morelli's advice to his future progeny demanded regular visits and rigorous surveillance over their rural holdings, enjoining them to compare the work habits and production of one farm with that of another and to reward and punish accordingly.[70] Similarly, Giovanni Rucellai's *Il governo della famiglia* dealt exclusively with the ways his sons should administer their rural estates and treat their "fattori."[71]

Numerous *ricordanze* and the records of the *Monte delle doti* show patrician landowners intimately involved in dowering and arranging the marriages of their rural tenants.[72] Such *noblesse oblige* went beyond prescriptive statements and entered the pious bequests of the Florentine elite. Giovanni Rucellai bequeathed a dowry fund to benefit only young girls from the parish of San Piero a Quaracchi, the closer to the city walls of his two rural estates,[73] and he chose his place of burial not within his own urban parish of San Pancrazio but in this rural parish church, where he left funds to light two lamps above his grave.

According to his *zibaldone*, these deeds gave him a particular "sweetness and happiness, because they showed honor to God and to my remembrance."[74] Indeed, by Rucellai's account, these ties of affection

---

[68] See chapter 1, note 14.   [69] Machiavelli, *Libro di ricordi*.

[70] Morelli, *Ricordi*, pp. 234–9: "E facendo questo dovrai essere poco da loro ingannato e sarai amato più che gli altri e sarannoti riverenti, secondo loro, e arai quello bene di loro ch'è possibile avere" (p. 236).   [71] Rucellai, *Il Zibaldone*, pp. 3–8.

[72] See Molho, *Marriage Alliance in Late Medieval Florence*, p. 122.

[73] *Il Zibaldone*, p. 26: "E' quali f.60 si debbono distribuire in perpetuo per la detta Arte [del Cambio] . . . E il resto per insino lla somma di f.60 si debbino chonvertire in maritare fanciulle, dando l.40 per ciascuna; le quali fanciulle sieno nate e allevate nel popolo di Sancto Piero a Quarachi, delle più miserabili, che parrà a' chonsoli . . . e allo abate della Settimo . . . e uno de' discendenti del detto Giovanni . . . gravando le loro choscienzie in piglare buone informazioni delle più miserabili."

[74] *Ibid.*, p. 122. Similarly, various members of the Sirigatti family who died during the plague of 1417 chose to be buried in the parish of their rural estates in the Badia di Passignano: Lapo di Giovanni Niccolini, *Il libro degli affari proprii di casa de Lapo di Giovanni Niccolini de' Sirigatti*, ed. by Bec (Paris, 1969), p. 135.

ran freely in both directions. He reported that the forty-three men of this rural village gathered "of their own free will" and voted to maintain the Rucellai gardens from their own expenses. They did so because of the "many benefits" received from him and because the "beauty and gentility of the Rucellai gardens bestowed fame on them" at the same time as they gave honor to the Rucellai.[75] Such sentiments between Florentine citizens and their peasants may have strengthened after the revolt of the Ciompi in 1378, when the practice of retreating to the calm of the country villa was reinforced.[76] Networks of dependency bound by debts may have further reinforced the ties of rent and respect between lowland peasants and citizen investors.[77]

It stands to reason that those villages where patricians such as the Machiavelli, the Morelli, the Corsini, and the Strozzi, along with druggists, bowl-makers, belt-makers, and other minor guildsmen of menial status, held their estates would be the ones offered tax advantages at the expense of others further removed, where Florentines possessed few, if any, landed properties and whose surplus hardly affected citizens' private interests. Indeed medieval economies were often structured by a competition between lords and the state for the limited surpluses of the peasantry.[78]

Further, as Becker and Molho have shown, Florentines faced a rapidly increasing public debt, resulting largely from the expansive military budgets of the late fourteenth century[79] but remained staunchly opposed to bringing direct taxes on themselves.[80] As a consequence, the Florentine oligarchy shifted the tax burden increasingly onto the shoulders of those in the *contado*. But this shift, as we have seen, was not felt equally throughout the *contado*. Heavy tax burdens on those from lowland and hill villages near the city, where citizens possessed their farms and profited from their sharecroppers' production and well-being, would have threatened the economic resources of these same urban

---

[75] Rucellai, *Zibaldone*, p. 23.   [76] See Brucker, *The Civic World*, p. 49.

[77] la Roncière, *Un changeur florentin*, esp. ch. 7.

[78] See, for instance, Frederic William Maitland, *Domesday Book and Beyond: Three Essays in the Early History of England* (Cambridge, 1987), pp. 323–4.

[79] Becker, "Economic Change"; *Florence in Transition*, II, pp. 234–6; and la Roncière, "Indirect Taxes," p. 142.

[80] One of the successes of the government of the Minor Guilds was a brief revival of direct taxes placed on Florentine citizens, but these were abolished immediately with the return of the oligarchic regime in 1382; see Provv. reg., 67, 72r–3r, 1378.x.29, "Pro extimo civitatis" and for the surveys compiled in 1379 Estimo 268, and Prestanze 367, 368, and 369.

rulers and proprietors; in effect they would have become a tax on themselves.[81]

Such concerns over the economic fortune and security of rural holdings may have proven even more problematic in the late Trecento than at any other time. How were these urban proprietors, whether wealthy patricians or small shopkeepers, to maintain, even increase, their rural investments in the plains and nearby hills (as the Mazzetti contracts reveal) during this period of acute labor shortages that followed in the wake of pestilence and depopulation?[82] The *estimi* reveal one solution practiced at least since the 1370s – Florence's increasingly unequal rural taxes.[83]

Indeed, radically inequitable tax rates forced highlanders more than others to forgo their independence and to abandon their homesteads. At the same time, the lowlands near the city were the very zones where taxes were lowest and where urban investment and the *mezzadria* system were highest, expanding most rapidly by the last decades of the Trecento.[84] As revealed by repeated inducements passed by the councils, the Florentines found themselves in dire need of agricultural labor. With increasing regularity, tax exemptions and moratoria on debts were promulgated from 1364 on, to induce foreign agricultural laborers to settle in the Florentine *contado*[85] and to entice back their own Florentine agricultural laborers who earlier fled from their debts and the Florentine tax official.[86] The earliest of these laws restricted exemptions to those who would work the land as *mezzadri* "ad medium vel affictu" and not as independent proprietors.[87]

---

[81] On the distribution of the *mezzadria* system, see Herlihy and Klapisch-Zuber, *Les Toscans*, pp. 268–72 and 285. Unfortunately, I know of no map showing the distribution of urban Florentine landownership in the *contado* for 1427 or for any other period during the late Middle Ages and early-modern periods. But surviving *ricordanze* of the late Trecento and early Quattrocento show that the rural properties bought and sold by Florentines were relatively near the city. See, for instance, the numerous properties recorded in the *ricordanze* of Niccolini, *Il libro degli affari*. Fifty years later Giovanni Rucellai considered his estate at Poggio a Caiano to be far from the city: *Il Zibaldone*, p. 120.

[82] Herlihy, "Santa Maria Impruneta"; "The Problem of the 'Return to the Land' "; and Klapisch-Zuber, "Mezzadria e insediamenti."

[83] For a similar conclusion for the maritime Alps of Piedmont, see Comba, "Il problema della mobilità," p. 312.

[84] See the comparison between 1427 and 1469 in Herlihy and Klapisch-Zuber, *Les Toscans*, pp. 268–72. The greatest change was in the Quarter of Santa Maria Novella, where the percentage of *poderi* with *mezzadria* contracts increased from 22.4 to 32.4 percent. Also, see Bec, "Introduction," to Niccolini, *Il libro degli affari*, p. 19.

[85] Provv. reg., 52, 34v, 1364.viii.8; 72, 171r, 1383.x.20; 74, 204r–5r; 1385.xii.8; 80, 197r–8r, 1391.xii.2.

[86] *Ibid.*, 88, 226r–7r, 1399.xi.7: "Laboratores absentes possint redire": "Laboratoribus terre jam absentibus propter debita succurrere cupientes cum etiam ex reditu ipsorum videatur utilitas varijs respectibus perveniret."   [87] *Ibid.*, 52, 34v.

But regardless of the Commune's logic, another logic prevailed on the land. As might be expected, peasants were hard pressed to pay, and many did not. As the *estimo*'s figures on migration and the disastrous declines in mountain population between 1393 and 1402 reveal, the mountain dwellers' first means of resistance was with their feet. But they did not move downward to greener valleys as the Florentine ruling class may have wished. Instead they fled Florentine taxes altogether, crossing the border into higher villages of Pistoia, Bologna, and Romagna.[88] This exodus meant that those who stayed behind were forced to pay even more. As a consequence, 1401 saw a new wave of resistance – this time one of direct confrontation. Were the Florentines so blind as not to see that their tax strategies were backfiring? Were they wedged irretrievably within the mindset of past policies? Before exploring Florentine reactions and government policy toward the hinterland in the early fifteenth century, part II will examine the events that propelled the Florentine oligarchy to abandon their "medieval tax" and to reexamine their stance toward the well-being of their *contadini*.

---

[88] The *provvisioni* to attract foreign agricultural labor into the *contado* of Florence specified that immigration to the former *contadi* of Arezzo, Pistoia, and Volterra would not result in forgiving past debts and taxes. In 1400, the Bolognese offered tax exemptions to attract foreign agricultural laborers; see Pini, "Un aspetto dei rapporti," p. 406.

PART II

Peasant protest in the mountains: three views

4

Peasant insurrection in the mountains: the chroniclers' view

As the previous chapters have shown, trends in household wealth, the differential in wealth between plains and mountains, rates and direction of migration, and changes in tax rates point to the end of 1401 or 1402 as a fundamental turning-point in the long-term history of Florence's domination over its hinterland. This is not the first time in recent Florentine historiography that the same date has been signaled as a turning-point in Florentine history. Following the propagandistic histories of Goro Dati and Leonardo Bruni, Hans Baron described Florence's war with Milan as the last stance of "liberty" against the rising sea of Milanese "tyranny." From this crisis in the summer of 1402, a new intellectual movement was born – civic humanism[1] – which ultimately gave the Italian Renaissance its distinctive character and through the writings of Machiavelli would cross the Alps as the intellectual basis of seventeenth-century republican consciousness.[2] But other than the key date of 1402, my theses and Baron's have little in common. Indeed, our notions of what were the underlying causes of change may even be contradictory. As Baron boldly announced in his introduction, the originality of his work was explaining ideas within the context of politics. Yet, while he reacted against a simple "history of ideas," he was even

---

[1] While Baron carefully built this thesis in a number of articles from the 1920s and continued to support it through his life, its cardinal statement was *The Crisis*.

[2] See also William Bouwsma, *Venice and the Defense of Republican Liberty* (Berkeley, Calif., 1968); and J. G. A. Pocock, *The Machiavellian Moment* (Princeton, 1975); Quentin Skinner, *The Foundations of Modern Political Thought*, I, ch. 6. In contrast, Bec, *Cultura e società a Firenze nell'età della rinascenza* (Rome, 1981), "Introduzione," has argued that Florence's period of civic humanism was over by 1440 and what it exported to other courtly societies in Italy and across the Alps was instead a "courtly humanism." The Baron thesis continues to attract proponents. See, for instance, Lanza, *Firenze contro Milano*, which sustains Baron's thesis through works of literature as well as historiography and Witt's more tempered defense, "The *Crisis* after Forty Years." The thesis has also had its critics; see most recently, Hankins, "The 'Baron Thesis' ".

more hostile to explaining ideas in the context of economic and social forces.[3]

As far as the day-to-day legislation of the Florentine ruling elites allow us to probe the consciousness behind the Florentine oligarchy's rule over its region, Baron was correct: the revolt of the Ciompi and the subsequent rule of the Minor Guilds did not alter Florence's attitudes and policy toward its hinterland. At least the government's decrees do not suggest any sudden change in its taxation of the *contado* or in its relief to communities hit by war, disease, or other disasters.[4] But another "internal struggle" did coincide with the abrupt changes in our graphs and go a long way toward explaining the long-term changes in peasant wealth, rural population, and fiscal burdens within Florence's *contado*. This struggle was between Florence and its peasant communes along the mountainous periphery bordering the territories of Modena, Bologna, Imola, Arezzo, and Siena.

At best, historians have seen only hazy outlines of these revolts and assume that central and northern Italy and especially Tuscany were spared from "true" peasant uprisings until the "Ave Maria" revolts of the 1790s, if then. They have developed models to explain the supposed absence of peasant uprisings in late-medieval and early-modern Italy between Piedmont and Sicily.[5] Even outside Tuscany,

---

[3] Baron, *The Crisis*, p. 8: "No revolt with either social or economic overtones occurred in Florence between the 1370s and the Savonarolian revolution at the end of the Quattrocento; and the unsuccessful rising in 1378 of the 'Ciompi,' the workers of the Florentine woolen industry, had not left any traces that might have shaped the outlook and culture of the citizenry about 1400."

[4] For these statistics, see chapter 9.

[5] Peter Burke, "Mediterranean Europe 1500–1800: Notes and Comparisons," in *Religion and Rural Revolt: Papers Presented to the Fourth Interdisciplinary Workshop on Peasant Studies, University of British Columbia, 1982*, ed. by Janos M. Bak and Gerhard Benecke (Manchester, 1984), pp. 75–85; and for early-modern Europe see Oscar Di Simplicio, *Le rivolte contadine in Europa: I grandi movimenti che scuotono le campagne nell'epoca moderna* (Rome, 1985), pp. 121–2. In the most recent work on peasant revolts in medieval Italy, instead of describing peasant conflict, the authors go to pains to explain its absence; see especially the excellent essay on the *mezzadria* system in central Italy, Roberta Mucciarelli and Gabriella Piccinni, "Un'Italia senza rivolte? Il conflitto sociale nelle aree mezzadrili," in *Protesta e rivolta contadina nell'Italia medievale*, ed. by Cherubini, in *Annali dell'Istituto "Alcide Cervi"*, no. 16 (1994), pp. 173–205. Even for southern Italy, where an older historiography described peasant uprisings such as in Angevin Sicily, the authors play down their significance, claiming that they were not "true" peasant revolts; see Giovanni Vitolo, "Rivolte contadine e brigantaggi nel Mezzogiorno angioino," in *ibid.*, pp. 207–25. On late-medieval peasant revolts in general, see Maire Vigueur, "Per una periodizzazione delle lotte contadine nell'Italia medievale," in *ibid.*, pp. 261–8; R. H. Hilton, *Bondsmen Made Free: Medieval Peasant Movements and the English Rising of 1381* (London, 1973), ch. 3; Comba, "Rivolte e ribellioni fra Tre e Quattrocento," in *La storia: I grandi problemi dal Medioevo all'Età Contemporanea. Il Medioevo*, II: *Popoli e strutture politiche*, ed. by Nicola Tranfaglia and Massimo Firpo (Turin, 1993), pp. 673–91; Guy Fourquin, *Les soulèvements populaires au Moyen Age* (Paris, 1972).

according to the latest historiography, "one will not be able to talk
about peasant 'revolt' but only of peasant 'unease' in the Veneto";[6]
"one cannot talk about 'peasant revolts' in the strict sense in
Umbria";[7] "there does not exit a single example of a peasant revolt
properly so-called in the Marche, Lazio, and Umbria."[8] Not even in
southern Italy, in either Sicily or Calabria, according to this latest literature, did "true" peasant revolts (*veri e propri movimenti insurrezionali*)
arise, with the possible exception of one outbreak in Calabria,
1459–60, which was quickly and brutally suppressed.[9] As Philip Jones
long ago concluded: "Peasant hatred, and even armed risings were
mostly short and bloodless."[10]

Before passing judgment on the social and political activities that
swept across the mountainous perimeter of the Florentine state from
1401 to 1404, it is necessary to describe these actions from the perspective of the different sources that reported them. Such descriptions
place us in a quandary of multiple and contradictory realities. If it
were not for the coincidences of dates and places, it would sometimes
be difficult to conceive that the three sources for these events – chronicles, judicial records, and legislative documents (the *provvisioni*) – were
describing the same events. Let us begin with those sources that tell us
the least but which historians to date have relied on most: chronicles
and the surviving diaries and recollections of Florentine citizens, the
ricordanze.[11]

These narrative sources reveal more about the revolts in the mountains
of Pistoia than elsewhere, perhaps because these stemmed from an urban
factional conflict between Pistoia's two principal families, the Panciatichi

[6] Sante Bortolami, "Lotta e protesta contadina nel Veneto dal Medioevo all prima età moderna:
un bilancio." In *Protesta e rivolta contadina*, pp. 45–64; for evidence to the contrary, see John E. Law,
" 'Super differentiis agitatis Venetiis inter districtuales et civitatem' – Venezia, Verona e il
contado nell' 400," *Archivio Veneto*, 116 (1981), p. 10.

[7] Maria Grazia Nico Ottaviani, "Sistemi cittadini e comunità rurali nell'Umbria del Due-
Trecento," in *Protesta e rivolta*, p. 92.

[8] Claudio Regni, "Fiscalità cittadina e comunità rurali: Perugia, secoli XIV e XV," in *Protesta e
rivolta*, p. 139.

[9] Vitolo, "Rivolte contadine," p. 225. Even the Marxist historian L. A. Kotel'nikova, *Mondo contadino e città in Italia dal XI al XIV secolo dalle fonti dell'Italia centrale e settentrionale* (Bologna, 1975
[Moscow, 1967]), pp. 330–5, has difficulty finding more than indirect evidence for peasant insurrections in northern Italy from the tenth through the fourteenth centuries.

[10] Jones, "Italy," in *The Cambridge Economic History of Europe*, I, ed. by M. M. Postan (Cambridge,
1966), p. 430.

[11] For the most thorough catalog of Florentine *ricordanze*, see Fulvio Pezzarossa, "La tradizione
fiorentina della memorialistica," in *La "Memoria" dei mercatores: Tendenze ideologiche, ricordanze, artigianato in versi nella Firenze del Quattrocento*, ed. by G. M. Anselmi, Pezzarossa, and L. Avellini
(Bologna, 1980), pp. 41–149.

and the Cancellieri.[12] This conflict, however, quickly spread into the countryside, leading to Ricciardo Cancellieri's siege of Sambuca in the Montagna di Pistoia, his three-year armed assault and robberies of villages sympathetic to the Panciatichi, his alliance with the Duke of Milan, and his resistance to Florentine military pressures (1401–3).[13]

But rightly or wrongly, this resistance has been seen exclusively from the perspective of vying urban elites, whose rivalry in Pistoia (seemingly unlike Florence) extended through the countryside even into the mountainous periphery. The question of peasant discontent and uprising has not been addressed. Once we move east from the Pistoiese into the northern fringes of the Mugello, the Alpi Fiorentine, the Podere Fiorentino, the Romagna, and Casentino, the picture becomes more opaque. Few historians have mentioned the northern realm of the Florentine state as the scene of internal resistance and conflict, and those who have, have seen these events as the recurrence of old feudal hostilities between Florence and its ancient enemies, the Ubaldini, aided by the Milanese war effort and Florentine exiles.[14]

The recollections of Scipione Ammirato senior[15] filled only a phrase within a sentence that also reported the urban insurrection of the Cancellieri and Florentine military pacts with the lord of Faenza:

---

[12] Much has been written on this rivalry in the primary and secondary sources; see Giovanni Sercambi, *Le Cronache di Giovanni Sercambi*. ed. by Salvatore Bongi (Lucca, 1892), III, pp. 42–3, 48, and 58–9; Iacopo Maria Fioravanti, *Memorie storiche della città di Pistoja* (Lucca, 1758), r. 24, pp. 341–6; D. M. Bueno de Mesquita, *Giangaleazzo Visconti, Duke of Milan (1351–1402): A Study in the Political Career of an Italian Despot* (Cambridge, 1941), p. 287; Herlihy, *Medieval and Renaissance Pistoia*, pp. 198–239; Conti, introduction to *Le "Consulte" e "Pratiche" della repubblica fiorentina nel Quattrocento*, I *(1401) (Cancellierato di Coluccio Salutati)*, ed. by Conti (Pisa, 1981), pp. lxix–lxxii; and most recently, William Connell, *City of Sorrows*, ch. 4.

[13] See Chittolini, "Ricerche sull'ordinamento," p. 313; Brucker, *The Civic World*, pp. 172–3; Herlihy, *Medieval and Renaissance Pistoia*, p. 204, only mentions "the great uprising against Florentine power" led by Ricciardo, which he notes will be discussed on pp. 229–30 but is not.

[14] The historian who has paid the most attention to internal struggle in the countryside in these years is Brucker, *The Civic World*, p. 166.

[15] On Scipione Ammirato and his son, Scipione Ammirato, the Younger, see *La Letteratura italiana*, XXXI, part r: *Storici e politici fiorentini del Cinquecento*, ed. by Angelo Baiocchi (Naples, 1994), p. 273; and Eric Cochrane, *Historians and Historiography in the Italian Renaissance* (Chicago, 1981), pp. 284–6. The *Istorie fiorentine*, ed. by Luciano Scarabelli (Turin, 1853), first published in 1600, was reissued with additions from his son Scipione the Younger in 1647, who added to his father's account for 1401 a few details about Florence's suppression of the Ubaldini in the Podere Fiorentino at Susinana and Lozzole, the corruption of its officials in the Podere, and the need to apply severe penalties (*Istorie fiorentine con l'aggiunte di Scipione il Giovane* (Florence, 1848), part r, IV, pp. 126–7).

Scipione the Younger is also the only chronicler or historian to allude to the massive number of benefits Florence doled out to the mountain villagers in 1403, but he misrepresents them as Florentine charity rather than as the result of peasant negotiations, claiming that, because of the damage of the war, many left their homes, and the Commune granted them tax exemptions similar to those enjoyed by the inhabitants of Firenzuola (p. 114).

Ricciardo Cancellieri ran through the mountains of Pistoia, the Ubaldini recovered the Alps and the Podere [Fiorentino], Astorre da Faenza made several pacts with the Florentines and then broke them.[16]

By contrast, Ammirato, both senior and junior, described with greater detail the failed revolt of San Miniato four years earlier, when members of the Mangiadore family, the indigenous rulers of San Miniato before Florentine accession in 1370, stormed the palace of the vicariate and killed Florentine officers by hurling them out of the windows, but (according to Ammirato) were repulsed by the people of San Miniato, who chanted "Viva il comune di Firenze" and railed against the Mangiadore leader, "traditore e assassino."[17] By contrast, from the perspective of the criminal records and the government's decrees, these events register little more than a ripple in comparison with the numerous inquests, sentences, and peasant petitions unleashed by the insurrections of the opening years of the fifteenth century in the Alpi Fiorentine.

But perhaps even more indicative of Ammirato's bias and zeal to rewrite Florentine history with triumphant soundings is the contrast between the words he placed in the mouths of the "people of San Miniato" and those reported in the original archival sources from which he drew his raw materials. According to the *Podestà*'s inquest, the people of San Miniato "exclaimed loudly," "Long live Vanni da Piano, liberty, and Benedetto Mangiadore, and death to the Estimo!"[18] This is the first insurrection I have found in the court cases that targeted Florence's direct taxes on the *contado* – the *estimo* – as the cause of rebellion. Since the beginning of the decade these taxes had increased fivefold and, in the year of this revolt, its coefficients increased again, to the highest levels seen from the Black Death to the return of Cosimo.[19]

The nineteenth-century historian Gino Capponi, whose *Storia della Repubblica di Firenze* is still the most detailed political narrative of Florence for the fourteenth and fifteenth centuries, provides another perspective on the activities in the Alpi and upper Mugello, but his account is also limited to a single sentence. After describing the threat of

[16] Ammirato, *Istorie fiorentine*, IV, pp. 337–8.   [17] *Istorie fiorentine con l'aggiunte*, p. 47.
[18] CP, 2199, 95r–6r, 1403.ix.12: "Viva Vanni da Piano libertà et Benedecto Mangiadore et Moya l'estimo!" Sercambi, *Le Cronache*, II, pp. 175–6, described the incident as the results of Florentine military maneuvers in the territory of Pisa: "si mossero alquanti ribelli di Sanminiato con alquante brigate di Pisa." On praise for the Ammirati's impeccable archival research, see Cochrane, *Historians*, pp. 284–6; and Rado, *Dalla Repubblica fiorentina*, p. 12.
[19] See appendix 2. For the anti-Florentine sentiments of the people of San Miniato and "vere e proprie cospirazioni antifiorentine" provoked by fiscal pressures in 1377 and 1381, see Pinto, "Controllo politico e ordine pubblico nei primi vicariati fiorentini: Gli atti criminali degli ufficiali forensi," *Quaderni Storici*, 49 (1982), pp. 234–6.

Giangaleazzo's conquests in the summer of 1402, Capponi adds: "the *contado* [was] fatigued by taxes and in the Mugello the peasants gave a hand to those in the Alps [Fiorentine], where the Ubaldini, even though exhausted, were able to take the mountain crest together with others fed up with the Republic."[20] Later in the same passage Capponi reports that the Florentine military command, the Ten of War (*Dieci di Balìa*)[21] assisted by 2,000 Ciompi were sent to secure the fortresses in the Alps.

Although Capponi generally relied extensively on archival sources and especially on the Florentine *provvisioni*,[22] his chronicle of events here rests exclusively on previous chronicles and *ricordanze* (Minerbetti, Buoninsegni, and Morelli). There is no notice of the siege of Firenzuola, the spread of the revolt through the Podere Fiorentino and into the Romagna and Casentino, and nothing about the peasants' negotiations or diplomatic victories in 1403. Although Capponi does mention peasant discontent, the conflict was clearly one between disgruntled lords – the Ubaldini and patrician malcontents – and the Florentine Republic; it was not a peasant uprising.

Even less ink has been spilled on these events in the twentieth century. Drawing on both Tuscan and Lombard sources, D. M. Bueno de Mesquita referred to Giangaleazzo's support of "his friends in Tuscany," meaning Ricciardo Cancellieri, during the summer of 1401, as a side-show to his major objective, the conquest of Bologna. He further maintained that the only internal attack "which the Florentines had to meet was that of the Ubaldini." Relying on the chroniclers – Minerbetti, Delayto, and Malavolti – he interpreted this attack as a fledgling feudal revolt against the city; peasant discontent was not at play: "from their fortresses in the Alpi di Podere and the Mugello, [the Ubaldini] had renewed their old feud with the Republic." By 23 August 1402 the Florentine army had defeated the Ubaldini and the Milanese army of 400.[23]

Similarly, Gene Brucker's magisterial study of the period gives scant notice to these events, interpreting the unrest in the Apennines and the

---

[20] Gino Capponi, *Storia della Repubblica* (Florence, 1876; repr., 1976), II, p. 91.

[21] The Ten came to life with Florence's acquisition of Arezzo in 1384; on this "extraordinary commission," see Fubini, "Dalla rappresentanza sociale alla rappresentanza politica. Sviluppi politico-costituzionali in Firenze dal Tre al Cinquecento," in *Italia Quattrocentesca: Politica e diplomazia nell'età di Lorenzo il Magnifico* (Milan, 1994), pp. 48–9 and 54–5; and "From Social to Political Representation," p. 229.   [22] See his appendices of transcriptions to volume II.

[23] Bueno de Mesquita, *Giangaleazzo Visconti*, pp. 287–9. Francesco Cognasso's "Il Ducato Visconteo da Gian Galeazzo a Filippo Maria," in *Storia di Milano*, VI: *Il Ducato Visconteo e la repubblica Ambrosiana (1392–1450)* (Milan, 1955), pp. 30–67, does not even discuss Milan's forays into the Florentine countryside.

Casentino as a "conspiracy" of nobles provoked by Giangaleazzo's agents, most prominently Paolo Giraldi, which testified to the "success of Visconti proselytization." To this picture Brucker adds the layer of exiles from the city of Florence as agents of unrest, but peasants fail to appear as actors.[24]

Of the contemporary accounts which have guided modern historians, the most famous and enduring has been Leonardo Bruni's *Historiarum Florentini Populi* written in the 1420s. The humanist Bruni refers only obliquely to these events in the Alpi, describing the insurgents as "Ubaldinorum clientes" who rebelled only after the Milanese had made incursions into the Alpi Fiorentine and Podere Fiorentino. Moreover, by Bruni's compressed account, like the previous insurrections of the Cancellieri (which also receive short shrift from Bruni), the Ubaldini raids were quickly suppressed and were of no consequence.

Bruni makes no reference to peasant discontent, cries of anguish over escalating and excessive taxation, peasant poverty, or mass migration from the highland communities. Nor does he tell us who these Ubaldini "clientes" were, what they were after, or what they may have gained. Crucial events such as the formation of rebel peasant troops in the mountains above Firenzuola, the building of fortifications, the capturing of old strongholds such as the Castel di Pagano near Susinana in the Podere Fiorentino, and the siege of Firenzuola do not make it into his record of the events.[25] Bruni's later *Rerum suo tempore gestarum commentarius*, completed in 1441 toward the end of his life, covered the Florentine wars with Milan again and extended his account into the fifteenth century. Yet it added nothing new about the events in the Alps of 1402; the second time around they were deleted altogether.[26]

Brief and oblique as Bruni may have been, he tells us more about these events than any other Florentine humanist historian of the fifteenth or sixteenth century. Poggio Bracciolini's *Historiarum Florentini Populi* (written at the end of his life in the 1450s) does not mention Ricciardo Cancellieri's revolt in Pistoia or the spread of factional

---

[24] Brucker, *The Civic World*, p. 172.
[25] Leonardo Bruni, *Historiarum Florentini Populi: Libri XII*, ed. by Emilio Santini, in *RIS*, XIX, part 3 (Città di Castello, 1914–26), p. 288: "Itaque, cum multi subinde dies intercessissent, nec hostes cum exercitu venirent, civitas, resumptis paulatim animis, insurgere ac reparare vires perrexit; et adversus Ubaldinorum clientes, qui post victoriam hostium rebellaverunt, et adversus Ricciardum pistoriensem, cuius sectatores post adversum praelii casum multa invaserant loca, missae auxiliares copiae illorum conatus repressere."
[26] Bruni, *Rerum suo tempore gestarum commentarius [aa. 1378–1440]*, ed. by Carmine di Pierro, in *RIS*, XIX, part 3 (Città di Castello, 1914–26), pp. 432–3.

warfare and resistance to Florence from the heights of Sambuca. His only reference to the Alpi Fiorentine for the years 1401 to 1403 was that the Ubaldini led the cavalry and foot soldiers from Bologna, attacked the citadel of Firenzuola with war machines, but were "easily" repulsed and forced to retreat across the border.[27] By the time of Machiavelli's and Guicciardini's histories of Florence in the 1520s, the Florentine intelligentsia had either completely forgotten or suppressed these events. Their fundamental histories of Florence leave no traces to them; nor did later historians from the court of Cosimo I – Iacopo Nardi, Benedetto Varchi, and Bernardo Segni – recall them.[28]

Even if an aversion to such lowly matters as peasants and their demands for lower and more equal taxes may have played a part, the reasons contemporary patricians left them out of their chronicles and diaries may have had more to do with the success of these uprisings than with any humanist principles about the proper materials for history writing.[29] This thesis is suggested by the selected memories of high-ranking patricians who served in the Florentine hinterland as *Podestà*, *vicarii*, and members of the Ten of War during the crucial years at the turn of the century.

Two such valuable reports from the hinterland come from Bonaccorso Pitti and Jacopo Salviati.[30] Pitti's first appointment in the Florentine government was as Captain of Pistoia in 1399. Thus he was at the eye of the storm when conflict erupted between the Cancellieri and the Panciatichi and certainly would have been privy to the events of the following two years when unrest spread to the countryside and Ricciardo occupied Sambuca and much of the Montagna di Pistoia.[31] Shortly thereafter Pitti's contemporary Jacopo Salviati served in the war-torn

[27] Poggio Bracciolini, *Historiarum Florentini Populi*, ed. by Fubini (Turin, 1966), bk. 3, pp. 151–2.

[28] Iacopo Nardi, *Istorie della città di Firenze*, ed. by Lelio Arbib (Florence, 1842); Bernardo Segni, *Storie fiorentine dall'anno MDXXVII al MDLV* (Florence, 1835); Benedetto Varchi, *Storia fiorentina*, ed. by Arbib (Florence, 1843).

[29] See Felix Gilbert, *Machiavelli and Guicciardini: Politics and History in Sixteenth-Century Florence* (Princeton, 1965), pp. 203–18; and Cochrane, *Historians*, pp. 3–9.

[30] The literature on Bonaccorso Pitti and his *Ricordi* is substantial; see Vittore Branca's introduction to *Mercanti Scrittori: Ricordi nella Firenze tra medioevo e rinascimento*, ed. by Branca (Milan, 1986), pp. lv–lxxi and lxxxi; and Bec, *Les marchands écrivains*, ch. 2. There are at least two modern editions of this chronicle–diary, and it has been translated into English, French, Spanish, and Russian. By contrast, the equally fascinating accounts of Salviati still await a modern edition and have received little attention despite recent interest in Florentine family diaries and chronicles. On Salviati, see Bec, *Les marchands écrivains*, pp. 16 and 280; and Zorzi, "Giusdicenti e operatori di giustizia nello stato territoriale fiorentino del XV secolo," *Ricerche Storiche*, 19, no. 3 (1989), p. 533; "I fiorentini e gli uffici pubblici nel primo Quattrocento: Concorrenza, abusi, illegalità," *Quaderni Storici*, 66, no. 3 (1987), p. 739; and Brucker, *The Civic World*, pp. 220 and 263.

[31] Buonaccorso Pitti, *Ricordi*, in *Mercanti Scrittori*, pp. 414–15.

Casentino as a member of the Ten of War and Captain to quell the uprisings spurred by the Ubertini lords. In 1404 he was knighted for his military success.[32]

Although both these high-ranking officials must have played major roles in combating unrest and negotiating with mountain rebels in their respective districts, neither mentions peasant discontent, negotiations with the peasant rebels in 1403 and 1404, or the favorable outcomes for the rebels and their communities as evinced in hundreds of acts of Florentine legislation. Instead, these patricians described their service in these war-troubled lands as marked by harmony between their benevolent and sagacious rule and the devotion of their subjects.

By his account, Pitti was showered with the "tears and sighs" of his subjects when at great peril to the advancement of his career he defended the liberties of the citizens of Pistoia against the demands of Florence's highest councils, which had ordered him to turn over a "famous" Pistoiese thief to be tried in Florence instead of Pistoia.[33] Later, as *vicarius* in the Valdarno Superiore, which stretched into the mountains of the then insurrectionary Casentino, Pitti claimed to have ruled with pleasure, executed his office well (*feci bello e buono uficio*), and returned to Florence with honor.[34] He made no mention of the Guidi recapturing their ancient castles or of the favorable negotiations their "fideles" made with Florence for tax concessions in 1401 and 1403.[35]

Similarly, Salviati reported the honors he gained for himself and Florence through his rule in various offices in the Florentine territory in these years, from the Alpi Fiorentine in the north to Montepulciano at the southernmost corner of the Florentine regional state. As *Podestà* of Montepulciano in 1399 he claimed "to have filled the office well and with honor, winning the satisfaction of his subjects,"[36] and as *vicarius* of the Alpi Fiorentine in 1407, he claimed to have won the devotion of his subjects because of his "gentle rule." He made no reference whatsoever to the insurrections five years earlier or to the sweeping tax exemptions and legal concessions which the Florentine state had been forced to concede to these subjects, which continued into his term as vicar.[37] Thus, these

---

[32] Iacopo Salviati, *Cronica, o memorie di Iacopo Salviati dall'anno 1398 al 1411*, in *Delizie degli eruditi toscani*, XVIII, ed. by Fr. Ildefonso di San Luigi (Florence, 1784), pp. 175–381; see Brucker, *The Civic World*, p. 263.   [33] Pitti, *Ricordi*, p. 415.   [34] *Ibid.*, pp. 537–8.
[35] Provv. reg., 90, 156r–7v, 1401.vi.7: "Plures comunium Vallis Florentine"; 92, 113r–15r, 1403.viii.27: "Comunis Romena."
[36] Salviati, *Cronica*, p. 182: "L'uffitio feci bene, et con honore, et con tale contentamento degli huomini di Montepulciano, che al sindicato non vi fu niuno, che porgesse contro di me nè petitione, nè altra cosa, che m'havesse a dispiacere." See also Zorzi, "Giusdicenti," pp. 537–8.

patricians not only would have known of the widespread insurrections
that swept across the Florentine Apennines in the early years of the
fifteenth century; they were in prominent positions to advise and negotiate for the government against the demands of these mountain peasants.[38]

The evidence from the *novellista*, poet, and career judge in the provinces Franco Sacchetti[39] is perhaps the most striking of all. What certainly ranked as one of the more trying decisions of his long career was
the condemnation to death of the ringleaders of a revolt in the
Romagnol market village of Rocca di San Casciano, in which the villagers in 1398 turned to their earlier feudal lords to assist them in freeing
themselves from Florentine "tyranny."[40] The men were condemned in
their absence, and two months later Florence's highest councils reversed
Sacchetti's judgment. Not only were the rebels absolved; they gained a
five-year exemption from all taxes for their commune. Yet in the year of
this revolt Sacchetti wrote a long poem on his experiences as Captain of
the province in which he decried the torments of war and praised peace
but did not mention this revolt or any internal strife then brewing within
the Romagna Fiorentina.[41]

Similarly, Sacchetti's *Il Trecentonovelle* reveled in the satire of peasants,
mocking them for their animal manners and poverty, but rebellion was
not a subject he cared to breach. Was it a conspiracy of silence among
the Florentine ruling elites to enhance their own honor? Or did their
claims of local harmony and obedience across Florence's mountainous
perimeter at the turn of the century arise more from the desire to
propagate a triumphalist view of the history of Florence, whose manifest destiny was to rule Tuscany? I believe that it was a combination of
both.

Curiously, the diary of a patrician outsider of lower social ranking
than the powerful Pitti and Salvati gives us a closer look at the events of
the upper Mugello at the turn of the century. Giovanni di Pagolo

---

[37] See Salviati, *Cronica*, p. 284; and Brucker, *The Civic World*, p. 220.

[38] In praising his 1404 victory over the Ubertini and the counts da Bagno in the Casentino, Salviati, *Cronica*, p. 220, admitted that about a thousand peasant soldiers were under their command ("e circa mille fanti paesani di quel d'Arezzo, di Casentino, e d'altronde").

[39] On Sacchetti's political career, see *La Letteratura italiana: Gli Autori, Dizionario bio-bibliografico e Indici*, ed. by Giorgio Inglese, 2 vols. (Turin, 1991), II, pp. 1558–9; Larner, *The Lords of Romagna*, pp. 162–4; and *Storia della letteratura italiana*, II: *Il Trecento*, ed. by Enrico Malato (Rome, 1995), pp. 894–901.   [40] On this revolt, see my *Women in the Streets*, pp. 122–3.

[41] "Canzone distesa di Franco Sacchetti, fatta a Portico di Romagna, dove era capitano per lo Comune di Firenze, anno MCCCLXXXVIII," in Lanza, *Firenze contro Milano*, pp. 175–7; and Sacchetti, *Rime*, pp. 456–60.

Morelli, a member of the wool guild who even practiced as a dyer, was marginalized from politics until 1403 because of his family connections with the Alberti.[42] But despite these connections, similar to those of political insiders such as Goro Dati and Bruni, Morelli saw Giangaleazzo's threat to Florence during the summer of 1402 as pivotal in the history of the Republic. As Morelli put it, "all seemed lost, beyond any help."

While Giangaleazzo had just spent the fabulous sum of 120,000 florins to construct his citadel in Milan, Morelli reports that Florence had been unable to receive grain supplies from the countryside for two months; the land was torn by divisions in both the city and *contado*, but matters were worse in the countryside, where the peasantry had been impoverished by frequent taxation. According to Morelli, "there was not a peasant who would not have been willing to come to Florence to burn it down."[43] Earlier, in his memoirs, when he had praised his ancestral Mugello for its abundance and beauty and the pleasantness, honesty, and piety of its peasants, he also commented on the Mugello's decline in population over the previous fifty years. He attributed the decline to plague, war, and taxation, "for which" he added, "many had fled to avoid being imprisoned."[44]

But, despite these revelations, when he arrived at the crucial years 1401–3, he devoted only two sentences to Ricciardo Cancellieri's take-over of Sambuca, followed by a single sentence on the affairs in the Alpi Fiorentine: "And then many of the Ubaldini, who we thought had been finished off, reemerged and took the Podere [Fiorentino] and stirred up the Mugello, and many in the region came out in their favor."[45] He adds that much the same happened in Arezzo, Prato, and Volterra, where the old Ghibelline exiled lords were able to take back their lands and castles. In Morelli's judgment, had Giangaleazzo ridden through the *contado* it would have fallen at once.[46]

Although Morelli gives us a closer description than any other chronicler thus far examined, pointing to high taxes and peasant discontent, he nonetheless presents the events of the Alpi and Podere as a feudal revolt led by the Ubaldini and fails to report the siege of Firenzuola, the

---

[42] The literature on Morelli is immense; see Branca, *Mercanti Scrittori*, pp. xxv–li; Bec, *Les marchands écrivains*, ch. 1; and Leonida Pandimiglio, "Giovanni di Pagolo Morelli e la ragion di famiglia," in *Studi sul Medioevo cristiano offerti a Raffaello Morghen* (Rome, 1974), II, pp. 553–608.
[43] Morelli, *Ricordi*, p. 392.   [44] *Ibid.*, p. 113; see Bec, *Les marchands écrivains*, pp. 74–5.
[45] Morelli, *Ricordi*, p. 396: "Appresso, riuscirono fuori molti degli Ubaldini, i quai pensavamo essere ispenti, e tolsono il podere e feceno sommuovere tutto il Mugello; e molti di quel paese si scoersono in loro favore."   [46] *Ibid.*

takeover of particular castles, or the successes of the peasantry and their independent negotiations with Florence in the following years. Moreover, in his opening preamble to his *ricordi*, where he praises the virtues of the Mugello, he contradicts any hint that the peasants of the Mugello might have been deterred in their devotion to Florence. Much like his contemporary Dati, he praises the peasants of the Mugello, reporting that they "always remained steadfast in their devotion and loyalty to the Commune of Florence," despite the Ubaldini's attempts to "contaminate them with their many promises and great gifts."[47]

This tendency to eradicate such peasant successes from what the Florentine chroniclers and patrician diarists wished to preserve even within the ambit of patrician family memoirs is best revealed in the one Florentine chronicle that reports most on the deeds of the *alpigiani* in 1402. Whatever the name of the chronicler of Florentine events, 1385 to 1409, whose work traditionally was attributed to Piero di Giovanni Minerbetti,[48] he was certainly a high-ranking patrician, privy to state papers, governmental deliberations, and secret ambassadorial reports. Most likely he was a member of the influential Minerbetti family, in whose private archives the text was discovered.[49] His chronicle shows knowledge of precise troop movements and military expenditures both at home and abroad. Yet, despite this insider knowledge, his short summary reveals no sense of the scale of these uprisings or their subsequent successes:

Certain of the Ubaldini in exile in Bologna were in the employ of the Duke of Milan and had their hearts set on retaking l'Alpe del Podere . . . They knew that the men of that region were all discontent with Florentine rule because of the heavy taxes imposed on them. And of these people certain corporals nearby incited them: "Come quickly and we'll all be with you." Thus, in August they stole a number of cattle . . . and invaded as far as Firenzuola, making threats and attacking the people there. And the Alpigiani, almost all of whom supported them, rebelled against the Florentines, laid out several bulwarks on the hilltops, and constructed ramparts with moats and wood. Here they posted many thieves for guard duty, and others went through the region of the Podere, which is in the Romagna, and many of these countrymen supported them, and rebelled against the Florentines, laying out more bastions on the highest hilltops and strengthening them with armed men. Thus the Alpi and the Podere were

---

[47] *Ibid.*, pp. 97–8.
[48] Minerbetti, *Cronica volgare di Anonimo Fiorentino dall'anno 1385 al 1409 già attribuita a Piero di Giovanni Minerbetti*, ed. by Elina Bellondi, in *RIS*, XXVII, part 2 (Città di Castello, 1915–18).
[49] Bellondi, "Prefazione" to Minerbetti, *Cronica volgare*, p. iii; and Rado, *Dalla Repubblica fiorentina*, p. 7, surmise that it was Andrea di Niccolò Minerbetti, who would have been between fifty-five and sixty at the time his chronicle begins in 1386.

almost entirely in rebellion, which greatly upset the Florentines, to whom such matters appeared as a very bad beginning.[50]

Although Minerbetti supplies us with more details, he recounted other peasant uprisings of much less political importance and geographic extent in more grueling detail. The difference between these other riots and the tax revolts of 1402 that ran through the Apennine ridges down to the Chianti is that the ones he related in greater detail failed and thus provided "lessons" for neighboring peasants as well as for patrician rulers.

One such lesson concerned the wealthy peasants from Puleggio in the territory of Ferrara, who in 1395 entered Ferrara yelling: "Long live the House of the Este and death to the gabelles and other taxes."[51] The armed soldiers in the city repulsed the peasant advance, killing a hundred of the assailants and sending the rest fleeing back to their villages in the *contado*. But this was not the end of the peasants' misadventure. The ruling despot of Ferrara assembled a force of 1,200 specially chosen cavalry, 200 crossbowmen, and a sufficient number of foot soldiers (*fanti*) together with troops from Florence. They invaded the villages of Puleggio and with little effort won the day (*e con poca fatica li vinse*), killing or capturing all the peasants who had participated, which the Minerbetti chronicler numbered at 600 or more killed and 2,000 captured. Yet this was still not sufficient retribution for the Marchese of Ferrara. He granted his troops and the Florentines "license" to rob the countryside for all they could take, and because these peasants were rich and the land fat (*grassissimo*), the booty was "inestimable" and the troops returned to Faenza "enriched."[52]

In an earlier example dated 1391 and taken from the village of Raggiolo in the Montagna Fiorentina on the eastern flank of the Casentino, Minerbetti makes his lessons more explicit. For unexplained reasons, the peasants of this village newly incorporated into the *contado* of Florence petitioned the troops of their former feudal lords of Pietramala to assist them in regaining control over their village.[53] With their aid they regained their castle, but the victory was short-lived. Florentine troops stormed the castle, won it over, and burnt it to the ground. The Florentines then took advantage of the opportunity to run through the village stealing all they could lay their hands on. Frightened by the soldiers' violence, the women and children carried away their

[50] Minerbetti, *Cronica volgare*, p. 279.
[51] *Ibid.*, p. 194: "Viva la casa da Esti, e muoiano le gabelle e' dazi."   [52] *Ibid.*
[53] On earlier treaties between the "men" of Raggiolo and the Guidi lords, see La Roncière, "Fidélités," p. 37.

most valuable possessions and hid in their parish church, but without
hesitation the Florentines burnt it to the ground filled with those women
and children, "killing and devouring them all." The troops then set fire
to the rest of the village, littering its streets with "many charred bodies."
Fifteen surviving "rebels" were led back to Florence, where they were
either hanged twice by the neck or sentenced to jail for life. In both cases,
the Commune of Florence confiscated all their goods. The Minerbetti
chronicler ended his report:

> And thus the village of Raggiuolo, which formerly had counted 150 households
> or more, was entirely destroyed along with its castle, and all the houses together
> with its church were burnt to the ground, and the place now remains uninhab-
> ited and broken. As a good example to the surrounding villages, the Florentines
> were more evil than they needed to be to show that they would do the same to
> others.[54]

In fact, to hammer home his lessons about effective rule, the
Minerbetti chronicler overstated the Florentines' brutality and its consequences for Raggiolo. The village did not disappear from the face of
the earth but has survived to the present, and throughout the fourteenth
and early fifteenth centuries it continued to receive tax relief and other
concessions from Florence.[55] The Florentines were less brutal with the
peasant rebels as well. A decree of 26 August, 1391 liberated thirty-five
rebels from the July revolt of Raggiolo, all of whom the *Capitano del Popolo*
had condemned to life sentences in Florence's prison, the Stinche. "For
the devotion of Jesus Christ" they were led to the Baptistery of San
Giovanni and allowed to go free.[56] The following year the Florentine
government renewed a five-year exemption on various payments for all
the people of the Montagna Fiorentina (including Raggiolo), because of
the widespread destruction these mountain villagers had suffered during
the rebellion.[57] Evidently, such acts of compassion and compromise
were not the sort of government action that merchant chroniclers
wished their future readers to remember.

Despite the silence of later humanist historians and of Machiavelli
and Guicciardini, the Minerbetti chronicle certainly circulated within
oligarchic circles during the fifteenth and early sixteenth centuries.
According to Vittorio Fiorini, it was Machiavelli's principal source for

---

[54] Minerbetti, *Cronica volgare*, pp. 127–8.
[55] Provv. reg., 81, 17v–19v, 1392.iv.25; 84, 257v–9r, 1395.xii.22; 86, 66r–8v, 1397.v.29; 87, 367v–8v, 1398.xii.27; 91, 55v, 1402.vi.5.
[56] *Ibid.*, 80, 88v–90r, 1391.viii.26; their goods, however, remained confiscated.
[57] *Ibid.*, 81, 17v–19v, 1392.iv.25.

the years 1385 to 1409.[58] Yet, in reporting the "thirteen-year" war between Milan and Florence, Machiavelli appears completely oblivious to Minerbetti's sections on the Alpi Fiorentine; the only dissent that Machiavelli reports came from rival Florentine patrician factions residing within the city of Florence and those then in exile in Bologna – the Ricci, Adimari, Medici, Mannegli, "and many other families who followed them."[59] He ends this chapter of Florentine history by extolling the "great wars and glory" of the years 1381 to 1434 and "the acquisition to its empire" (*allo imperio suo*) of Arezzo, Pisa, Cortona, Livorno, and Montepulciano.[60]

However, for lesser historians of the second half of the fifteenth century, Minerbetti's chronicle served as the *Urtext* for the events of 1402 in the Alpi Fiorentine. Domenico Buoninsegni largely paraphrased him from Italian into Latin, seeing the Ubaldini's incursions as a feudal revolt staffed by exiled noblemen, which he compared to Ricciardo Cancellieri's revolt in the Montagna di Pistoia.[61] According to Buoninsegni these events were not only known to many back in the city of Florence, but struck fear and caused consternation.[62]

The only chronicler to report more on the disturbances in the Alpi Fiorentine and the Podere Fiorentino than Minerbetti was an outsider, Ser Luca di Bartolomeo Dominici of Pistoia. His first concerns were not the political affairs of Florence but those of his own city-state, Pistoia, where he served as notary of public offices for fourteen years and was elected to the highest council, the *anziani*, during the crucial years of his chronicles.[63] Ser Luca's two chronicles are only roughly consecutive. The first, compiled after his death by his brother Ser Paolo (also a Pistoiese notary) in 1415 had a rich manuscript tradition and was published in part by Lami in 1657. It focuses with microscopic detail on the plague of 1399–1400, the flagellant movement called the "whites," and the spread

[58] Vittorio Fiorini, *Istorie Fiorentine di Niccolò Machiavelli.* (Florence, 1894); also see Bellondi's Prefazione, p. iv; and Roberto Ridolfi, *Vita di Niccolò Machiavelli*, 2nd edn. (Rome, 1954), pp. 296–7.
[59] Niccolò Machiavelli, *Istorie fiorentine*, ed. by Franco Gaeta (Milan, 1962), p. 266.
[60] *Ibid.*, p. 270.
[61] According to Molho, "Domenico di Leonardo Buoninsegni, *Istoria Fiorentina*," *Renaissance Quarterly*, 23 (1970), p. 263, "the sole authority of the sixth book which narrates the events of the years 1385–1409 is the *Cronica volgare . . . Minerbetti*." Also, see "Buoninsegni, Domenico," in *Dizionario biografico degli Italiani*, XV (Rome, 1972), pp. 251–2.
[62] Domenico Buoninsegni, *Historia Fiorentina* (Florence, 1580), p. 772.
[63] Giovan Carlo Gigliotti, "Introduzione," to *Cronache di Ser Luca Dominici*, ed. by Gigliotti, 2 vols. (Pistoia, 1933), I, p. 11–12.

of religious fervor through Pistoia, Tuscany, and Italy at the end of the century. It ends in 1402 with Florence surrounded by its enemies, the allies of Milan, Bologna, Lucca, Pisa, Siena, and Perugia, and concludes with a Florentine triumphalism that would have enriched Baron's text had he known of it:

> And the entire country was under the control of the tyrannical lords [of Milan] except for Florence and what the Florentines held. Amen.[64]

The second chronicle is wholly different in its manuscript tradition, content, and political sentiment. Ser Paolo chose not to transcribe the materials of this volume, evidently not finding them "notable deeds worthy of remembrance" to be "selected and abridged" for his one volume.[65] Instead, only an autograph copy survives, discovered in a private archive at the end of the nineteenth century.[66]

The editor of the chronicles, Gigliotti, tried to explain the difference in the manuscript traditions of the two and why Ser Luca's brother did not transcribe the second or even intersperse parts of it into his abridged single volume. He argued that the second was more provincial, more lodged within the events of Pistoia, and thus of less interest to contemporaries than the first.[67] But both chronicles center with minute detail on the affairs of Pistoia, and the second more than the first concentrates on interregional politics and would have drawn greater interest from observers beyond the borders of Pistoia. It placed the civil war between Pistoia's two ancient rival factions, the Panciatichi and Cancellieri, within the frame of the Italian wars, where, as we have seen from Ser Luca's own perspective, Florence was the last bastion in Italy defending republican liberties against the threat of Milan. Indeed, Gigliotti claimed these political events "among the most calamitous in the history of the Florentine Republic," observing that Italian republicanism would have been crushed had it not been for the sudden death of Giangaleazzo.[68]

A better explanation, though still speculative, would focus on the context of the political events, which the second chronicle recorded for the most part dispassionately. This second volume ends in 1403 after Florence's continuous efforts to squash Ricciardo Cancellieri and his peasant supporters in the Montagna di Pistoia had failed. The negotiations chronicled in the *Consulte e Pratiche*[69] and formalized in Florentine

---

[64] Dominici, *Cronache*, I, p. 292: "E tutto questo paese è sotto i Signori tiranni, salvo che Firenze e ciò che i Fiorentini tengono. Amen."   [65] *Ibid.*, p. 24.   [66] Gigliotti, "Introduzione,", p. 40.
[67] *Ibid.*, pp. 18–28.   [68] *Ibid.*, p. 21.

legislation show the rich concessions these rebel forces won at the hands of Florence. In return for control over the castles at Sambuca, Calamecca, and Piteglio, Florence absolved Ricciardo and certain followers of all crimes of war and rebellion, granting them handsome exemptions from all taxes and gabelles. Florence even agreed to rebuild brick by brick Ricciardo's city palace "il Pantiano," destroyed as a reprisal while Ricciardo was encamped at Sambuca.[70]

By Ser Luca's death in 1415, when Ser Paolo took up the task of editing his brother's papers, such an ending of compromise or even defeat for Florence would not have been popular with Pistoia's regional rulers – the Florentines – or with the philo-Florentine faction, the Panciatichi, now at Pistoia's helm.[71] The second chronicle differs from the first also in its political sympathies. After enumerating Florence's population, the number of soldiers it could raise, the amount of taxes it collected, and its territorial conquests, Ser Luca's praise of Florence quickly becomes muted. The section, "Here comes the bad news," describes with undisguised bitterness Florence's punitive reforms of 1401, which restricted the powers and liberties of Pistoia's ruling council of elders (where Ser Luca sat) and the city's rights of taxation.[72]

While this second chronicle concentrates on the civil war between the Cancellieri and the Panciatichi, it also gathered hearsay evidence from Florence and further afield, showing among other things that the events in the Alpi Fiorentine were known outside Florence's ruling elite. On eight separate occasions his second chronicle reports events in the Alpi and Podere Fiorentino in 1402, leaving us more detail of the conflicts and rebellion than that left by any chronicler from Florence. These events include the siege and burning of Florence's northernmost town, Firenzuola, the peasant and feudal recapturing of ancient Ubaldini castles, such as Cavrenno and Palazzuolo, and the building of new bastions on the hilltops above Firenzuola. Moreover, we learn that Florence's victory was neither swift nor wholly successful (as the

[69] See *Le Consulte e pratiche della repubblica fiorentina (1404)*, ed. by Renzo Nenci (Rome, 1991), p. xxxii. On this source, see Brucker, The *Civic World*, ch. 1; and Fubini, "Italia quattrocentesca," pp. 21–2.
[70] Provv. reg., 92, 153v–8v, 1403.x.10: "Pro negotiis Sambuce et aliter"; 159r–6or, sd, "Pro factis Sambuce et domini Ricciardi."
[71] Another foreigner writing in the new philo-Florentine ambience of the early fifteenth century describes the Cancellieri's negotiations with Florence as coming from defeat and desperation: Sercambi, *Cronache*, III, pp. 58–9.
[72] Herlihy, *Medieval and Renaissance Pistoia*, pp. 223, 229; Gigliotti, "Introduzione," p. 9; Dominici, *Cronache*, II, p. 32ff.

Florentine chronicles report), but that after the death of Giangaleazzo troops under the command of the Ubaldini remained encamped in strategic positions in the mountains above Firenzuola.[73]

Despite his additional details, Ser Luca's big picture differs little from the fragments pieced together from the writings of Bruni, Morelli, and Minerbetti. For all of them, conflict in the Florentine Alps was directed and fueled by the Milanese onslaught and supplied with forces from Bologna and Sambuca. The internal struggle, if it existed at all, was one between Florence and its ancient feudal enemies, the Ubaldini, assisted by Florentine exiles. Peasant discontent or ruinous taxes, if presented, remained in the background. Indeed, for Ser Luca leagues of peasant troops under the command of Florentine captains forced the enemy from its strongholds above Firenzuola and brought to an end the conflict in the Alpi.

Perhaps, had Florence's more famous chroniclers of earlier years such as Marchionne di Coppo Stefani, Giovanni Villani, or Giovanni's brother Matteo survived into the early fifteenth century, more would have been reported on these mountain dwellers, their discontent, their military actions, and their successful negotiations with the Florentine oligarchy. But I doubt it. Their triumphalist vision of Florentine history would also have deterred them from leaving any such bad memories and lessons. In fact, these earlier chroniclers described Ubaldini and other feudal revolts against Florence, but like the later chroniclers, they seized on those revolts that failed, that gave them the occasion to boast of Florence's military successes and its manifest destiny to conquer its feudal foes.

At most, these chroniclers reported feudal successes as only temporary setbacks in the history of Florentine power and conquest,[74] and the theme of Florentine "liberty" versus feudal "tyranny" was well in place with Giovanni Villani's chronicle. When Florence brought the lands

---

[73] *Ibid.*, II, pp. 95, 182, 194, 200, 203–4, 207, 215, and 224.

[74] See, for instance, Stefani, *Cronica*, for the period from 1348 through Florence's first war with Milan in the early 1350s: r. 639, p. 233; r. 641, p. 234; r. 645, p. 236. For the same period, Matteo Villani, *Cronica*, I, r. 25, p. 49, describes the defeat of the "fedeli degli Ubaldini," and gives one of the few examples of a peasant revolt against their lords. It is described with Florentine triumphalist tones as the defeat of Count Galeotto [Guidi], whose peasants turned over the "dominion" of San Niccolò to the city of Florence; r. 24, pp. 49–50: "Come i fedeli del conte Galeotto si rubellarono da lui e dieronsi a' Fiorentini."

Matteo's book 2 is replete with uprisings of rural lords against Florence and its efforts to control its mountainous periphery: r. 6, pp. 202–3. "Come gli Ubaldini arsono Firenzuola, e presono Montecolloreto"; r. 7, pp. 202–3: "Come gli Ubertini, e" Tarlati, e i Pazzi assalirono il contado di Firenze"; r. 13, pp. 215–16: "Come il conte di Montecarelli si rubellò a' Fiorentini e

above Firenzuola into its dominion in 1332, it not only extended its territory, it "liberated and freed the serfs and followers [*servi e fideli*] of the said Ubaldini."[75] For Giovanni's brother, Matteo, the march of Florentine liberty was the organizing principle that gave meaning to his narrative. For the abortive revolts in the Mugello of 1351, he reported that rebels went from one village piazza to the next, organizing resistance to the Florentines and conscripting labor from places as far apart as Sambuca and the lands of the Podere to rebuild Ubaldini fortifications. Their rallying cries "death to the foreigners [i.e., the Florentines] and long live the villagers" (*muoiano i forestieri, e vivano i terrazzani*) might further suggest that the leaders of this opposition were the peasants themselves. However, Matteo is fast to explain that this was not the case. Instead, the hand of the Ubaldini was behind the scenes, "corrupting their followers with every subtlety of deceit."[76]

On the other hand, when the peasants supported Florence against the Ubaldini, Matteo proudly celebrates their heroism. Thus, in 1352, although "few and poorly armed," the mountain villagers of Vagliano in the Podere Fiorentino defended the Florentine state against Ubaldini troops, ultimately winning the day, when thirty of its village women, "screaming without stopping," chased seventy well-armed Ubaldini soldiers "out of their hilltops and over the slopes."[77]

To my knowledge, none of these chroniclers mentions a single peasant uprising that had even a glimmer of success against Florentine might. The one potential exception may have come from the more obscure chronicler Naddo di Ser Nepo di Ser Fallo da Montecatini, whose account unfortunately ends in 1398, on the eve of the eruption of social unrest in the Montagna di Pistoia and the Alpi.[78] His last entry describes the fall of Civitella near Arezzo to the Sienese. But, while the criminal records and the *provvisioni* describe the actions of

venne al capitano"; r. 18, pp. 221–4: "Come i Tarlati, Ubertini e i Pazzi furono cacciati"; r. 55, pp. 287–90: "Come la Scarperia fu furata e racquistata"; r. 58, pp. 292–3; "Come que' da Ricasoli rubellaro Vertine a' Fiorentini."

[75] Giovanni Villani, *Nuova Cronica*, II, r. 200, pp. 763–4.

[76] Matteo Villani, *Cronica*, I, bk. 2, r. 55, pp. 287–90, esp. 289.

[77] *Ibid.*, r. 41, pp 374–5. Further, see the prologues to books 6 (pp. 713–14) and 11 of Matteo's chronicle: the first is a discourse on the nature of tyrants, who turn out to be the feudal enemies of the Florentine Commune; the second contrasts the riches and liberties enjoyed by the Florentines to "the most cruel yoke of tyranny." Also, see his description of Florence's "liberation" of the mountain village of Rezzuolo in the Mugello from the "seige" of their former feudal lords, Count Ruberto da Battifolle, when it came under Florentine dominion in 1356; *ibid.*, I, bk. 7, pp. 289–90.

[78] Naddo da Montecatini, *Memorie storiche cavate da un libro di ricordi scritto da Naddo di ser Nepo di Ser Fallo da Montecatini, dall'anno 1374 all'anno 1398*, in *Delizie*, XVIII.

locals (*terrazani*), in both the town and the surrounding countryside, the chronicle attributes its fall to Milanese tactics, a 1,500-florin bribe from the Sienese, and the treachery of the town's guard (*castellano*). Ser Naddo insists "that the men of the town knew nothing of the treachery".[79]

The Minerbetti chronicler and Sozomenus, a mid-fifteenth-century humanist historian of Pistoia, are the only others to refer to the events at Civitella. Minerbetti's account was much the same as Ser Naddo's,[80] only the castellan's bribe increased to 2,000 florins and the "terrazzani di Civitella" either died or were taken in defense of their *borgo* against Florence's enemies. Sozomenus' report was briefer and more confusing. He presents the Florentine reincorporation of Civitella in 1398 as though Florence had acquired it for the first time in that year and the revolt and overthrow of Florentine rule in the previous year had never happened. Moreover, in this humanist account the acquisition came about not from negotiation with its peasant captors, who gained lifetime tax exemptions, as Florence's own *provvisioni* spell out in detail,[81] but by Florence sending the supposed Sienese rulers fleeing.[82]

As short, oblique, and even misleading as these memoirs, chronicles, and histories may have been in regard to the uprisings of the Alpi, Podere Fiorentino, and Civitella, the majority of those covering the period make no mention of them at all.[83] In cases such as the *ricordanze* of Niccolò del Buono di Bese Busini[84] and Falcucci Paliano di Falco,[85] whose memoirs were contemporaneous with the events of Florence's "third war" with Milan, we might dismiss their silence on the grounds that their *ricordanze* deal with little beyond land transactions and the vital statistics of birth, marriage, and death. But both these Florentine patricians had their ancestral holdings in the Mugello and bought and sold farms and strips of land during the opening years of the fifteenth

[79] *Ibid.*, pp. 169–70.   [80] Minerbetti, *Cronica volgare*, p. 223.
[81] Provv. reg., 87, 74v–8r, 1398.v.17.
[82] *Sozomeni pistoriensis Specimen historiae*, ed. by Muratori, in *RIS*, XVI (Milan, 1730), col. 1166: "1398 à Nativitate de mense aprilis . . . Castrum Civitellae in Valle Ambrae à Fiorentinis recipitur, fugatis Senensibus, qui illud tenebant."
[83] See Giovanni Cambi, *Istorie di Giovanni Cambi*, in *Delizie* xx–xxiii; Gino Capponi, *Monumenta Historica de Rebus Florentinorum . . . ab anno 1378 usque ad annum 1419 cum continuatione Nerii illius filii usque ad annum 1456*, ed. by Muratori, in *RIS*, XVIII (Milan, 1731), pp. 1097–220; Benedetto Dei, *La Cronica dall'anno 1400 all'anno 1500*, ed. by Roberto Barducci (Florence, 1984); Gregorio Dati, *L'Istoria di Firenze di Gregorio Dati dal 1380 al 1405*, ed. by Luigi Pratesi (Norcia, 1902); Giovanni di Iacopo Morelli, *Ricordi fatti in Firenze (1385–1437)*, in *Delizie*, XX, pp. 1–164; *La Cronica di Bologna*, ed. by Muratori, in *RIS*, XVIII.
[84] Carte Strozziane ser. IV, 564: Ricordanze di Niccholo del Buono di Bese Busini.
[85] *Ibid.*, ser. II, 7: Falcucci Paliano di Falco, *Ricordanze*, 1382–1406.

century (at San Martino a Vaglia in the first instance and Borgo San Lorenzo in the second). Not only would these two patrician memorialists have been aware of the peasant disturbances of the Mugello, the peasant raids into the Mugello, made evident in the *provvisioni*, reached as far south as Borgo San Lorenzo and thus may have even threatened their property and security.[86] But both failed to remember them.[87]

Other sources written later in the century, but with the same eye for daily detail and statistics that earlier characterized the Villani brothers and Minerbetti,[88] also fail to report peasant discontent in the Alpi Fiorentine and Florence's failure to quell them by force. Benedetto Dei opens his chronicle triumphantly with the lone stand of encircled Florence against the "most powerful lord and tyrant," Giangaleazzo, followed by his death, and the victory of Florentine republican liberty.[89] He then skips to 1406 when "the most powerful and glorious people of Florence" embarked on its "enterprise against Pisa."[90]

Still other sources such as Goro Dati's famous history of the Milanese war go further, denying that the Milanese incursions into the northern parts of the Florentine *contado* had any impact whatsoever on Florentine resistance: Rambo-style, chapter 54 is entitled: "How the troops of the Duke came into the *contado* of Florence, but were not able to achieve anything by it." Thus rewriting the history of Florence's "third war" with Milan with a triumphalist Florentine gusto (which historians such as Hans Baron and Antonio Lanza have accepted at face value),[91] Dati goes on to describe "the marvelous fortifications" that the Florentines maintained along their mountainous borders and the fierceness of its numerous peasant defenders, "each peasant the equal of two foreign invaders." Unlike Morelli, Dati papers over any hint of high taxes, peasant discontent, or depopulation in the mountains, insisting that "Florence possessed a great number of men in its *contado*." Instead, he turns to the enemy to describe peasant and city-state rebellions in "the lands" of Lombardy immediately following the death of Giangaleazzo.[92]

---

[86] Provv. reg., 92, 29r–30r, 1403.iv.26.
[87] Similarly, Niccolini's *ricordanze*, *Il libro degli affari*, stretched across the years of this war without any comment on the war or peasant discontent.
[88] See Molho's preface to Dei, *La Cronica*, pp. 10–11.   [89] Dei, *La Chronica*, p. 39.
[90] *Ibid.*, p. 40. Curiously, another mid-Quattrocento chronicler, Filippo di Cino Rinuccini, *Ricordi storici di Filippo di Cino Rinuccini dal 1280 al 1460*, ed. by G. Aiazzi (Florence, 1840), p. xlv, reports for May and June 1402 the return of Bolognese exiles, who, with the aid of the Duke of Milan, "took many castles in the *contado* of Bologna," but fails to mention that the same took place in July closer to home in the Alpi and Podere.
[91] Dati, *L'Istoria di Firenze*, r. 54, pp. 49–50: "Come le genti del Duca vennono in sul contado di Firenze, e come per la loro venuta in sul detto contado niente n'acquistarono."

Similarly, the unedited, anonymous Panciatichi chronicle, in covering the events of Florence's "third war" with Milan (1399–1404),
remains silent about the internal dissension between Florence and the
Ubaldini, the bombarding of Firenzuola, the capture of old castles,
and the building of new bastions. Nor does he report anything about
excessive taxation in the Florentine *contado* or peasant discontent.
Instead he displaces this reality of fiscal strain onto the shoulders of
the Milanese, describing how the Duke's subjects "groaned under the
weight of his war taxes." He claims that they could not possibly pay
half of what he demanded. As a result they grew "bad tempered" (*male
pazienti*) and became his enemies.[93] Like Dati and Bruni, the
Panciatichi chronicler glories in the Lombard rebellions against the
Visconti and in the collapse of the Milanese empire following
Giangaleazzo's death but denies that the same was happening in
Florence.[94]

Perhaps had a chronicle tradition existed or survived in Milan at the
time of Giangaleazzo's "third war" with Florence,[95] the resistance and
success of the Florentine mountain dwellers might have been in turn triumphantly recorded. But the narrative left by chroniclers from Bologna
and Ferrara suggests that a Milanese account would have simply stressed
the leadership of the Facino Cane and the role of the exiled Ubaldini
lords, who accompanied Cane's Bolognese troops into the Florentine
Alps. At least this is as far as either the Bolognese chronicler or the
Ferrarese chronicler Jacobo de Delayto would go.[96]

Did a counterculture of peasant proverbs, songs, or poetry keep alive
the memories of these peasants' resistance to the Florentine state? Did

[92] *Ibid.*, chapter III, pp. 83–4.
[93] Biblioteca Nazionale di Firenze, Panciatichi, 158, 201v: "Eglie saputo a firenze a punto tuti cio
che il duca avea d'entrata da potere spendere e sapevasi tuta la spesa che egli portava tra in
soldati e indonare a signori e anbasciate e providigioni di terre che da pertenelle a sua divozione e sapevasi che questa spesa li manchavano tanto l'entrate massimamente che al tempo di
ghuerra no gli risponde ano la meta che a lui era forza gravare e suoi popoli di gravissime imposte
delle quali sapeano che essi popoli erano male pazienti e per questo venia ad avere per nimici
tutti i suoi sudditi."   [94] *Ibid.*, 202r.
[95] For the period of the Sforza, see Gary Ianzitti, "A Humanist Historian and his Documents:
Giovanni Simonetta, Secretary to the Sforzas," *Renaissance Quarterly*, 34 (1981): 491–516; and
Humanist Historiography under the Sforzas: Politics and Propaganda in Fifteenth-Century Milan (Oxford,
1988).
[96] *Cronica di Bologna*, pp. 241–791, esp. p. 575; and *Corpus Chronicorum Bononiensium*, "Cronaca A," ed.
by Albano Sorbelli, in *RIS*, XVIII, part 1 (Città di Castello, 1905), pp. 487–8: "On 22 July, Facino
Cane made camp in the Florentine territory to wage war against the Florentines, carrying with
him our big cannon [*la nostra bombarda grossa*] and many other war machines; they went to
Cavrenno, where they were joined by [those with] more Bolognese cannons . . . On 23 August
the Florentines defeated the armies of the Duke of Milan; they lost everything." Delayto tells

contemporary artisans and shopkeepers even know of these events in the distant hills? To answer the first question would require a trawl through the folklore of the Apennines from the earliest surviving indigenous poetry to the present. (I know of no scraps of such evidence for the fourteenth or fifteenth centuries; nor are they recounted for subsequent centuries by the local historians and antiquarians of the early twentieth century.)[97]

To answer the second: three chroniclers report that news of the affairs in the Alps caused "much fear" in Florence – Minerbetti, the mid-fifteenth-century Buoninsegni, who paraphrased him, and the Pistoiese contemporary of Buoninsegni, Sozomenus, who copied Buoninsegni. Most likely the Florentines they perceived as being afraid were the political elites. On the other hand, governmental decrees refer to these events as being well known in Florence.[98] But well known to whom? Did news of these events circulate beyond the Ten of War, the Priors, *Gonfalonieri*, and the broad level of four hundred or more office holders in the two councils who deliberated and decided favorably on the final negotiations with the rebels from the mountains?

The chronicle of the vintner Bartolomeo del Corazza, which begins at the end of the war with Milan (1405), may give us some insight into Florentine propaganda and the perceptions of such "foreign affairs" at street level beneath the chambers of the oligarchy. Illustrating the richness of Florentine ceremonial life – processions and grand entries of ecclesiastics, foreign ambassadors, and other notables – Bartolomeo's descriptions make clear that the ruling elites indulged in such displays for more than their own self-glorification and entertainment. Banquets, bonfires, and dancing spilled out of patrician *loggia* into public squares, where the vintner Bartolomeo provisioned the wine for heavy, all-night drinking. Florentine propaganda was an act of participant observation.

On the other hand, as the editor of this chronicle has pointed out, Bartolomeo was silent about all reports of Florentine defeats and military difficulties over the thirty-five years he covered.[99] It is impossible to know

much the same story, placing more emphasis on the Ubaldini exiles and their ancient friendship with the Bolognese, adding that the siege of Firenzuola lasted twenty days, after which Facino Cane was forced to retreat with only 100 horsemen (Jacobo Delayto, *Annales estenses Jacobi de Delayto . . . ab anno MCCCXCIII usque ad MCCCCIX*, ed. by Muratori, in *RIS*, XVIII, pp. 971–2).

[97] No such poetry came down to the early-twentieth-century historian of Firenzuola, the local mountain priest of one of the rebel villages, Cornacchiaia, who collected works of poetry from the nineteenth century (see Casini, *Dizionario*).   [98] See Provv. reg., 93, 99v–100r, 1403.x.3.

[99] Bartolomeo del Corazza, *Diario fiorentino (1405–1439)*, ed. by Roberta Gentile (Rome, 1991), p. 7.

whether he had heard of events such as the Florentine defeat of Zagonara (1424) or of Valdilamone (1425) or whether he had internalized the propaganda that the Florentine oligarchy wished to preserve for its present morale as well as for the creation of its "myth of Florence."[100] My suspicions are that as a member of a minor guild with representation on the councils that voted on fiscal and still to some extent on military matters,[101] he would have known of these events. But either way, the effect on the memory of Florentine deeds was the same.

Compared to criminal records and governmental decrees, which listed hundreds of peasants, first as rebels condemned to death, then as the successful negotiators of handsome tax exemptions, the chronicles and patrician memoirs either left in silence or reported only fragments of the internal resistance that Florence faced at the height of its war against Milan. In the case of Buonaccorso Pitti and Jacopo Salviati their selective memory resulted from a desire to leave behind for posterity an image of their fair and effective rule in the territorial outposts of Florence, where instead of provoking uprisings they were loved by their subjects. A ruling statesman such as Minerbetti was zealous to teach the proper historical lessons: that if a village such as Raggiolo should ever resist Florentine rule, the consequences would and should be horrific. Finally, for the triumphalist Dati and the anonymous Panciatichi, what mattered was to rewrite Florentine history in a fashion that has carried "the myth of Florence" into the twentieth century: it was a myth of the cultural and political superiority of "civic" Florence over feudal "tyranny" and would explain why Florence would become the spearhead of a reputedly new republican civilization.

By contrast, it was a foreigner and notary from a subject city, disgruntled with Florentine imperialist encroachments on home rule, who has left us the most details of these events. But even his account, which in effect was suppressed by his brother and did not come to light until the end of the nineteenth century, tells only a portion of the story. It

---

[100] On contemporaries' formation of "the myth of Florence" – late-fourteenth- and fifteenth-century Florence as a mighty military power, the beauty of its city, and the first-born of a new Renaissance culture, see Bec, *Cultura e società*, pp. 323–35. Also, see Donald Weinstein, "The Myth of Florence," in *Florentine Studies*, pp. 15–44. On popular poetry against Giangaleazzo and the ideal of Florentine "liberty" against Milanese "tyranny," see Nino Valeri, *L'Italia nell' età dei principati*. 2nd edn, *Storia d'Italia*, IV (Milan, 1969), pp. 233–4; and Conti, introduction to *Le "Consulte" e "Pratiche"*, I, p. lxviii.

[101] With the establishment of the Council of Eighty-One in 1393, the new elitist regime of the Albizzi took matters such as the hiring of mercenaries and the election of the Ten of War out of the hands of the councils of the People and the Commune; see Guidi, *Il Governo*, II, p. 146.

leaves out what Florentine patrician patriots as well as local leaders of smaller subject cities would have found disturbing – Florence's failure to quell their peasant subjects and its need to negotiate with them as equals.[102]

---

[102] Najemy, "The Dialogue of Power," has shown the reluctance of historians from the civic humanists to the present to admit that Florence's elites needed to negotiate with the wider guild communities much less lowly peasants.

5

Peasant insurrection in the mountains as seen in the criminal records

▼

The events in the Alpi Fiorentine and their spread across and down the northern and eastern perimeters of the Florentine state take a different shape in the judicial sources from their obscured shadows cast by the chronicles and *ricordanze*. First, the uprisings' temporal and geographical dimensions are much more extensive; second, the criminal records bring into question the chroniclers' assertions that the revolts were simply the rising of Florence's traditional feudal enemies assisted by a few Florentine patrician malcontents. Instead, these records show peasants as the bulk of the rank and file, part of leadership, and at times even planning military strategy.

Yet the criminal records are no less neutral than the chronicles and can no better claim to tell the whole truth. While imbrued with the ritualistic aura of notarial and juridical accuracy, they present only the state's view, tending to portray the defendants in the worse possible light even when they were absolved of their purported wrongs. The inquests report often in meticulous detail military maneuvers, the exchange of secret letters, the conversations of co-conspirators on plans to besiege castles and to overthrow lands under Florentine suzerainty. But they remain silent about the political, economic, and human motivations of the peasants who filled the long lists of the condemned for so-called conspiratorial and rebellious behavior.

By the notarial reckoning the motivation behind their "evil" was in fact not human at all but instigated by the devil (*spiritu diabolico instigati*). Even less than in the reported insurrections of urban Ciompi a generation earlier, the rallying cries of these rural rebels are rarely heard and, when reported, mostly tell us little more than their hatred for the Florentine state.

In addition to these predilections and prejudices, the judicial view of insurrections is complicated by overlapping and missing records. For certain semesters, the initial inquests (*inquisitiones*) as well as the final sentences survive. In addition, some cases were tried in more than one tribunal and some by as many as three, while others are missing altogether. The problems of these records' survival through the centuries were compounded by the flood of 1966, which damaged this section of the state archives at Florence as badly as any other. Slowly some records are being restored, but great gaps remain. Luckily for the present analysis, however, the flood left completely unscathed the critical period of peasant insurrections and conspiracies, 1398 to 1405, for the three main criminal tribunals that adjudicated such cases – the *Podestà*, the *Capitano del Popolo*, and the vicariate courts.[1]

Because of the number of books (*filze*) in the criminal tribunals (one of the largest sections of the state archives), I have concentrated on the period of revolts from 1397 to 1406. For these years, I read all the sentences and inquests from the surviving criminal tribunals – the *Esecutore*, the *Capitano del Popolo*, the *Podestà*, and the vicariate court records.[2] None of the records from the *Otto di Guardia* survive for this period.[3]

In addition, I have searched through the *Podestà* from its earliest surviving records in 1343 to the end of the mountain peasants' hostilities in 1406. This tribunal tried the majority of cases of peasant revolts and acts labeled as "conspiracy" or rebellion during the fourteenth century. From this trawl I endeavor to show the variety of cases that the law considered rebellion and how these crimes changed over time. From these records I will attempt in part to construct a counter-chronicle of events, which the original chroniclers chose largely to ignore in their histories.[4] In so doing,

---

[1] The flooded volumes for the Atti del Podestà until 1410 are 177–239, 377–579, 726–812, 2188–546, 3441–678 (years 1347, 1348/49 to 1349–50, 1350/1 to 1352, 1369 to 1372, 1394 to 1397/8); for the Capitano del Popolo, 77–534 and 1773–2091 (years 1348 to 1372 and 1388/9 to 1398/9); for the Esecutore, 94–497 and 1433–841 (years 1347/8 to 1366 and 1401 to 1415). These gaps affect most seriously the uprisings of San Miniato in 1369. But even here an inquest survives describing the events and listing some of the accused rebels. While the Esecutore was a principal tribunal for urban rebels across classes, it rarely adjudicated cases of insurrection in the countryside, and by the end of the Trecento, largely stripped of its earlier judicial responsibilities, it specialized in curbing the neglect, excesses, and corruption of the other criminal courts and their officers.

[2] Except for a few fragmentary inquests, these court records mistakenly filed in the archive of the Giudice degli appelli e nullità begin in 1398; see my *Women in the Streets*, pp. 98–9 and 198.

[3] One slim volume of deliberations and sentences survives from 1406–7 and then nothing until 1460; see Cohn, *Women in the Streets*, p. 21.

[4] The Statutes of the Podestà, 1325 and the Capitano del Popolo of 1321–5 use the terms "rebelles," "rebellio," "conventiculum," "tumultus," and "seditio" sparingly and never define them. Often "rebelles" or "rebellio" were used in conjunction with exiles ("exbanniti"). The penalties for such crimes of illicit congregation, sedition, or revolt were left to the discretion of the *Podestà*; see *Statuti della repubblica fiorentina*, II, ed. by Romolo Caggese (Florence, 1921), bk. 3, cii, pp. 257–8: "De congregatione non facienda nisi certo modo." For other statutes that use the terms for rebellion, see *ibid.*, I, bk. 1, liii, pp. 47–58, "De offitio notarii super bonis rebellium et eius sindicatu"; bk. 5, cxxii, p. 317: "De habendo capitaneo pro capiendis rebellibus et exbampnitis in districtu Florentie"; II, bk. 5, liiii, p. 397: Quod rebelles exbanniti aut cessante a factionibus non possint vendere."

I hope to bring into relief the remarkable change in the frequency, magnitude, and outcomes of peasant uprisings of the years 1401 to 1403 for its late-medieval past.

Acts called "rebellion" or "conspiracy" that involved peasants (those who tilled the soil) dot the criminal records before the fifteenth century; however, they are rare and almost all of them were led by feudal lords who sought to restore their ancient rights and territories against Florentine claims of suzerainty. Other "rebellions" found in these records concerned the sedition of small towns, such as San Miniato, which tried to revive their ancient liberties through an alliance with foreign armies invading the Florentine territory. In addition to galvanizing support from artisans and nobles within their own walls, these "revolts" also relied on peasant support from nearby parishes. Acts called rebellion usually meant an attempt to cast off Florentine rule and are present from the earliest surviving criminal records.

In December 1344 the *Podestà* sentenced eight peasants, identified only by a patronymic and their place of residence, for the rebellion of the walled village (*castrum*) of Cennina in the Valdambra, at that time the southeasternmost reaches of the Florentine territory. Armed with "spears, knives, swords, crossbows, and other arms," they were allied with an invading troop of thirty-four soldiers (*militibus armigeris*) from Pisa. Together these two forces assisted the old feudal family that once controlled the majority of castles in the Valdambra, the Ubertini. With tambourines, drums, trumpets, and raised banners, they besieged the castle of Cennina, then invaded the nearby village of Averiolla in the curia of Montevarchi, assaulted eight peasants, killing four of them, and captured five others, whom they led back to Cennina for ransom. While the motives of the Ubertini are clear – the recapture of their ancestral lands – those of the peasants are left blank by the tribunal's inquest. We have only the description of their actions and the phrase: "all those living in the said *castrum* [of Cennina] rebelled [*rebellati*] against the Commune and People of Florence." But it was the peasants and not the Ubertini who were rounded up, charged with rebellion, and sentenced to be hanged.[5]

The 1360s produced a wave of continued feudal uprisings in the mountainous zones of the Florentine state, whose rank and file, as with the siege of Cennina, was filled by peasants. First, fifty-two men from five mountain parishes along with "many other armed men," not named

---

[5] AP, 116, 18r–v.

by the court, besieged and occupied one of Florence's principal strongholds in the northern Mugello, the castle of Mangona. Here the list of
men began with Tano, the Count of Montecarelli, an Alberti lord.
He summoned "the congregation" of over one hundred men and
women armed with offensive and defensive weapons to his castle of
Montecarelli[6] and led the siege of Mangona, "subverting the peace and
tranquility of the Commune and people of Florence." But ultimately
Tano and his band of mountain followers failed to keep the castle.[7]
Perhaps as a result, the sentencing was light for an act of armed rebellion, which almost invariably drew death penalties. Only five peasants
were fined, four at 400 *lire* apiece and one at 600. The others including
Count Tano escaped sentencing.

Later that year, two of the unsentenced peasants were convicted
again, this time for delivering messages and holding secret meetings with
those in the Alpine village of Cornacchiaia to prepare the siege of the
castle of Monte Vivagni in the Alpi. According to the inquest, these
peasants appear in leadership roles, having "congregated many armed
men . . . against the people and army of Florence." The second time
around, the mountain rebels were not as lucky. Before the siege could
materialize, they were captured, and "because of the enormity and
intolerable evil of their crimes," before being hanged they were to be
dragged backward on a mule through the city of Florence to the place
of justice.[8]

This attempted seizure in the Alpi was not an isolated case; 1361
opened with another uprising organized by the feudal enemies of
Florence in the same area of Cornacchiaia. Ubaldino di Cardacio of the
Ubaldini clan allegedly bribed the castellan of the castle of Monte
Fremoli, located in a place called "Montanea alpinorum." According to
plan, Ubaldino and his army of "associates" (*sotiis*) found the castle gates
open to their charge. Unfortunately, the sentence does not name these
"associates," but it is probably safe to assume that they were not unlike
the mountain peasants who comprised Count Tano's band. Given the
proximity of the location, some probably were the same. At any rate, the

---

[6] AP, 1486, 8r–10r, 1360.vi.20: "fecit invitationem et congregationem gentium et mulierum [et]
hominum armatorum numero centum et ultra et in dicta invitatione congregatione."

[7] *Ibid.*, "non stetit quin dictum castrum Mangonis invaderent et occuparent." Also, see Matteo
Villani, *Cronica*, I, bk. 2, r. 13, pp. 215–16 and bk. 3, r. 62, p. 400 for feudal revolts by Tano in 1350
and 1354. According to Villani, Count Tano was captured and decapitated by the Florentines;
ibid., IV, bk. 9, r. 108, pp. 328–30.

[8] AP, 1486, 107r–8r, 1360.ix.9: "traatur ad caudam muli et per civitatem Florentie traginetur usque
ad locum justitie."

siege was abortive and the "corrupted" castellan beheaded, but the feudal leader, Ubaldino, escaped sentencing.[9]

While these descriptions leave the motives of the mountain peasants and their feudal leaders obscure, an examination of the list of condemned men in Count Tano's entourage and their linkage to contemporary tax records (*estimi*) might supply some definition to the hazy picture left by the criminal records. Of Count Tano's fifty-one listed followers, twenty came from the count's own parish of San Michele a Montecarelli, and sixteen were from neighboring Alpine villages – Santa Maria de Casaglia (seven) and San Gavino Adimari (nine). Three came from further south in the Mugello (Mucciano, near Borgo San Lorenzo, and San Lorenzo Mozzanello, near Barberino) and one from slightly further afield, Vernio, across the Calvana mountains. But twelve were residents of the besieged commune of Mangona itself.

In terms of social status only Count Tano carried a feudal title; none of his followers possessed a family name; two were *sers* (though it is not clear whether they were notaries or priests), one a son of a *ser* and two were smiths (*faber*). The rest were local mountain peasants.

From the tax registers of Montecarelli, Casagli, and Mangona, only three rebels are found in the *lira* of 1365, constituting a far worse success rate of linkage with the tax registers than is possible in connecting even those who exchanged the smallest of notarized dowries. For the latter record linkage, I found 90 percent of marriage partners or their fathers in the *lira*, even though some were propertyless.[10] Perhaps, the difference arises because, even more than impoverished peasants, rebels were forced to be mobile. To escape conviction, they most likely had long since fled their parishes and crossed the frontiers of the Florentine state. Perhaps the low success in record linkage resulted also because it was the young, yet to assume the mantle of household heads, who formed the rank and file of these insurrections. In fact, for the next redaction of the *estimo* in 1371/3, when these rebels would have aged by twelve years, I was able to double the number of linkages for those then residing in the communes of Montecarelli and Casaglia.[11]

However, the *estimo* of 1371 – the first to list family members by age – contradicts this second hypothesis: the rebels were certainly not confined to the young; rather, they headed households with wives and children and were mostly middle aged or even elderly by late-medieval stan-

---

[9] AP, 1525, np, 1360.ii.13.   [10] See my "Marriage in the Mountains."
[11] Estimo 284, 172v–5r.

dards.[12] Five of those who can be traced were aged between forty and forty-five in 1371 and had wives and children.[13] One of the smiths was sixty-five in 1371, was married, and had a daughter age fifteen; and a Lottino di Ghinello, age seventy, headed a three-generational joint family with his wife, a twelve-year-old daughter, a married son, age twenty-five, this son's wife and two grandchildren, ages nine and two.[14] Of the eight who can be linked to the tax records, only one might not have been a family head in 1360. In 1371, Francesco di Ducciolino, at thirty, still lived with his mother, but was then married with two sons, one seven, the other four. At the time of the revolt he would have been around nineteen.[15]

Further, none of the eight were marginal or impoverished by village standards. In 1365, when only the final *lira* assessments were recorded or survive, the rebels from Montecarelli were assessed amounts slightly above the village mean, which based on subsequent *estimi* would have corresponded to a small holding or a few animals.[16] In 1372, their *lira* assessments edged slightly upward.[17] All were property holders, even if of modest values, ranging from 15 to 50 *lire*.[18]

At Montecarelli the average tax base in 1372 was 1 *lira* 4s 1d and the average property value 17.52 *lire*; at Casaglia, 14s 9d and a mere 8.48 *lire*. In neighboring Mangona, they were slightly better off – 1 *lira* 7s 16d and 29.37 *lire*. Overall the mean tax base and property values for my sample villages in Florence's rural Quarter of Santa Maria Novella was 1 *lira* 6s 8d and 36 *lire*, respectively. Thus, these rebels were certainly not the wretched of the earth. None was propertyless as compared with 15 percent of the population of Mangona, 16 percent in Montecarelli, and 42 percent across the plains and mountains of Santa Maria Novella in 1372. On the other hand, these peasant rebels, sometimes described as "fideles" and "vassallos" were neither village aristocrats nor the village rich. Instead, they were a middling group with property values at 26.75 *lire*, slightly above the average of their neighbors but beneath that of the Quarter of Santa Maria Novella as a whole.

Tax rates provide a clue to their discontent. The epicenter of rebellion, Montecarelli, paid the highest rates in 1371–2 of any village or

---

[12] On notions of aging in the later Middle Ages, see Herlihy and Klapisch-Zuber, *Les Toscans*, pp. 606–13; and Herlihy, "Veillir à Florence au Quattrocento," *Annales, E.S.C.*, 24 (1969): 1338–52.

[13] Estimo 215, 812v, 813r, 815r, 812v.   [14] *Ibid.*, 812v.   [15] *Ibid.*, 816v.

[16] *Ibid.*, 283, 157v–9v. The three linked rebels were charged 1 *lira* 5s, 2 *lire* 5s, and 1 *lira*; the average tax assessment for Montecarelli in 1365 was 1 *lira* 6s and for Mangona 1 *lira* 7s 9d.

[17] 1 *lira* 15s, 2 *lire* 9s, and 1 *lira* 9s; Estimo 284, 172v and 173v.

[18] Estimo 215, 812v and 813v; 284, 173v, 172v; 215, 813r and 820v; 215, 347v and 348r; and 284, 28r.

commune within my sample. Its base rate of 5.7 percent of its inhabitants' wealth[19] was considerably higher than the 2.2 assessed on average across the rural Quarter. But was this high tax a reprisal against Montecarelli for its rebellion of 1360? Or did such burdensome and unequal rates stretch back to the *estimo* of 1356 and thus underlie the motives of Tano's large peasant following in 1360? Because these earlier *lira* assessments lack village registers that surveyed household assessments, we are unable to view the mosaic of community taxation before 1372 and thus will never know.

The early 1360s saw a further array of acts the Republic of Florence labeled as "rebellion." In April the *Podestà* sentenced eight peasants from the county (*comitatus*) of Belforte on the eastern mountainous fringes of the Florentine state.[20] Many unnamed armed men "congregated, conspired, and drew up their plans" near the Florentine frontier to take the castle of Belforte. It was held, however, not by Florence but by Count Guido Battifolle, who ruled the upper Casentino and was an ancient enemy of Florence. In this instance, for unexplained reasons, Florence supported its feudal foes against their peasant insurgents. Perhaps Florence was meeting its obligations of an earlier treaty (*accomandigia*) with the counts of Battifolle,[21] but whatever the justification for Florentine force and afterwards their legal action, these peasants not then subject to Florentine jurisdiction were condemned to death for their unsuccessful attempt to free themselves from their lords.[22]

This is one of the rare cases that sentenced peasants who revolted against their feudal lords instead of having allied with them against the state of Florence. No doubt other peasant uprisings against lords were occurring along the feudal fringes of the Florentine state but did not concern the Florentine authorities.[23] Instead, as we have seen, Florence

---

[19] The rebels' rates were comparable at 5.2 percent.
[20] Florence purchased the castle of Belforte in 1375; the peasants were from the parishes of San Lorenzo a Fabbiano, San Lucia Casanova, San Martino a Coreglia, and San Mano a Comano. Although a part of the Florentine state in 1427, none of these parishes appear in the *catasto* of 1427. According to Repetti, *Diz.*, I, pp. 292–3, the castle guarded one of the most treacherous passes dividing the Mugello from the Romagna.
[21] On a treaty made with the Battifolle in 1344, see Giovanni Villani, *Nuova Cronica*, III, bk. 13, r. 36, p. 382; an *accomandigia* was drawn up in 1357. On the *accomandigia* or *accomandiga*, see *Le Consulte e pratiche* (1404), p. 345; Fabrizio Barbolani di Montauto, "Sopravivenza di Signorie feudali: la accomandigie al Comune di Firenze," in *I Ceti dirigenti nella Toscana tardo comunale: atti del III convegno, Firenze 5–7 decembre 1980* (Florence, 1983), pp. 47–55; and la Roncière, "Fidélités," pp. 38 and 45.   [22] AP, 1486, 26r–v, 1360.vi.15.
[23] The chroniclers describe some of these; for the second half of the fourteenth century, see la Roncière, "Fidélités," p. 49.

often encouraged such insubordination in the name of liberty against feudal "tyranny and treachery."

Later in the year, the court of the *Podestà* charged eight men and a woman from San Niccolò della Pila further south in the hills of the Mugello (this time squarely behind Florence's borders) for "sedition and rebellion," for disturbing the peace and tranquility of the parish of San Niccolò, and for acting "against the liberty and people of Florence." None was identified by more than a patronymic and parish; all were charged with illegal gathering and conspiracy and for planning the rescue of one of their neighbors, a certain Megliore, from the hands of the *Podestà*'s police. While Megliore was being led off for unpaid debts to Florentine citizens, the eight attacked the police, yelling: "to arms, to arms, let them be killed." In addition, Megliore further "impeded Florentine justice" by stealing one of the policemen's swords, valued at a florin. The eight were tried as rebels and condemned to be beheaded.[24]

In my survey of the judicial records I have found fifty-two cases of villagers attacking the police to free their neighbors (almost invariably charged with indebtedness to Florentine citizens), but this is the only one defined as rebellion and hence sentenced so severely.[25] Even when a villager killed an officer of the state, the courts did not brand him as a rebel; almost invariably the perpetrators received fines and not death as was usually the sentence for rebels.[26] Perhaps the villagers' inflammatory words did spread sedition through the village, or perhaps these acts incurred such harsh treatment because of Florentine anxieties in the Mugello in the early years of the 1360s. For the most part, the courts restricted the word rebellion to attempts at wresting castles and territory from Florentine suzerainty.

In the middle years of the 1360s peasant uprisings are harder to spot, and cases called seditious were more matters of internecine village rivalries than armed combat against the centers of Florentine control. In 1365 two rival clans (*domo et stirpe seu proienie*) in Carmignano – the

---

[24] AP, 1540, np, 1361.ix.25.
[25] For references to similar cases, see my *Women in the Streets*. It was a form of protest in which women were particularly prevalent as the accused. Also see AP, 1569, 34r–v, 1362.vii.14.
[26] Numerous cases involved peasant attacks on Florentine officers, sometimes resulting in their death, but these were not normally labeled as acts of sedition, conspiracy, or rebellion. See, for instance, AP, 1657, 1r–v, 1365.viii.4; 1693, 221r–v, 1366.xi.28; 2039, np, 1368.i.3 and 3695, 58v–60r, 1399.vi.4. Such freeing of neighbours from Florentine officers might involve large numbers; for instance, in 1401, sixteen armed men of Santa Maria a Peretola attacked the officers of the *Capitano del Popolo*, while they were leading one of their neighbors to prison in Florence; the parishioners were not tried as rebels; CP, 2129, 135r–v.

Caniglari and Marenghi – tried to oust each other from the community.[27] Similar rivalries struck further down the social scale. In one from Civitella in the Valdambra three men without noble status or family names led a siege of more than a hundred men against the town of Montepulciano. The three ringleaders were condemned as rebels,[28] but Florence was more conciliatory with Civitella's community at large and later passed legislation to ratify verbal agreements "for the peace and harmony" of the communities.[29]

  This absence of direct attacks against Florentine strongholds and territory continued through the early 1370s and is especially surprising given Florence's offensive in the mountains of the Mugello and the Alpi, its war in 1373 "to exterminate the Ubaldini," and the wave of pestilence, war, and famine from 1374 to 1375. The few cases called rebellion that come to light hardly match the feudal insurrections of the 1340s and early 1360s. In 1373, over sixteen highway robbers from Montecuccoli wounded a citizen of Florence;[30] another case condemned three men from the mountain villages along the Mugello–Romagna border for harboring a "rebel" Ubaldini.[31] But the war seems not to have stirred peasant discontent or rebel followers in support of the Ubaldini. Perhaps Florence's strategy of divide and conquer in 1373 had worked: the offer of tax exemptions and guarantees to protect the peasants against paying their feudal dues had dampened their appetites for defending their ancient lords.[32]

  The only feudal revolt of 1374 to appear in the *Podestà* came northwest of the Ubaldini's territory and was guided by a branch of the Alberti who held Bruscoli, then beyond Florence's borders. Four Alberti lords with over sixty armed followers attacked present-day Castiglione dei Pepoli, possessed by another branch of the Alberti, then allied with Florence. Although these events took place beyond Florence's borders, the *Podestà*'s sentence denounced them as acts of rebellion and

[27] AP, 1657, np, 1365.ix.9. For similar cases of rival village clans in Colle Valdelsa, see AP, 1693, 37v–8v, 1366.x.7.

[28] AP, 2208, 24r–5r, 1369.v.23. Also, two men from San Leonino in the Valdambra were charged with conspiracy and rebellion for plotting with "many other men" to besiege Montepulciano; *ibid.*, 57r–v, 1370.v.24.

[29] Provv. reg., 57, 27v, 1369.vi.22: "Pro parte comunis de Civitella Vallis Ambre districtu Florentie . . . quod propter quasdam controversias et scandala mota in castro de civitella." Also see the rivalries in San Miniato whose participants were labeled "congregates tumultuosos et seditonses ac etiam turbatores et molestratores"; AP, 1657, 34r–5v, 1365.x.27.

[30] AP, 2562, np, 1373.vi.30.   [31] *Ibid.*, 45r–6r, 1373.vi.17.

[32] Provv. reg., 61, 39r–42r, 1373.iv.28.

subversion that threatened the peace and tranquility of the people of Florence.[33]

In 1376 similar cases of extra-territorial rebellion entered the sentences. One involved the Manfredi lords of Faenza who led a group of peasants from Marradi and Pratovecchio (both then outside Florence's jurisdiction) in an attack against the Battifolle's castle of Biforco, also beyond Florence's borders.[34] Another came from further afield: the counts of Modigliana (Mutiliana) with their vassals (*vasallos*) laid siege to their own castle of Porciano,[35] on the eastern fringes of the Casentino, which was beyond Florence's borders but, according to Florence, threatened its "liberty".[36]

The relative quiet in the countryside continued through the decade, despite the revolt of the Ciompi and the stormy years of Minor Guild rule (August 1378 to January 1382) when exiles threatened Florence's borders and stability almost daily.[37] Only the odd armed conflict between rival clans in the mountains[38] and minor assaults on officers of the Florentine state, but not defined as rebellion, appear in the sentences.[39] Nor did the restoration of oligarchic rule provoke as much insurgency in the countryside as it did in the city.[40] Feudal revolts staffed by peasant followers appear only at the end of the 1380s and were confined to the mountains of Arezzo, recently annexed into the Florentine dominion (1384–5).

For some the stimulus to revolt may have come from the old feudal families of Arezzo – the Tarlati, Battifolle, or Ubertini – who sought to restore old prerogatives. For others, however, no such behind-the-scenes pressure appears. In 1387, five men without family names or distinctions and one called "ser," from Pertine, were accused of attacking and occupying their castle, but were found not guilty.[41] In 1390 a group of thirteen

---

[33] AP, 2732, np, 1374.xii.29. Also, on the Casentino frontier to the east, the Battifolle occupied five villages; see la Roncière, "Fidélités," p. 46.   [34] AP, 2812, 25v–7r, 1376.xii.19.

[35] On this castle, see Francovich, *I Castelli del contado*, p. 126.   [36] AP, 2812, 141r–2r, 1376.i.19.

[37] See, for instance, AP, 3053, and Cohn, *The Laboring Classes in Renaissance Florence* (New York, 1980), pp. 142–54.

[38] See the conflict of rival groups in the Alpi Fiorentine, AP, 3006, np, 1381.vii.9; and in the Chianti, *ibid.*, np, 1381.vi.19.

[39] In 1381 a mix of noblemen and their servants (*famuli*) attacked the *Podestà* of the league of Monte Tignosi, who was a cobbler from the Florentine parish of San Lorenzo – evidence of a shift in the social hierarchy of these political appointments during the rule of the Minor Guilds (AP, 3006, np, 1381.v.28).

[40] On these "conspiracies" and attempts of artisans to regain power, see Cohn, *The Laboring Classes*, pp. 144–5; Brucker, *The Civic World*, pp. 67–7; Rado, *Dalla Repubblica fiorentina*, 193ff.

[41] AP, 3268, 17r–v, 1387.xi.2.

without titles attempted "to subvert and change the present liberty of the people and Guelf state of Florence" by retaking their *castrum* of Cacciano (Valdambra),[42] handing it over to undisclosed "enemies of the Florentine state" (probably their previous Aretine lords). Perhaps as a lesson to neighboring mountain villagers, their sentence was more grue-some than previous condemnations: before hanging and the confiscation of their property, they were to be tortured with red-hot pincers, their bodies lacerated.[43] This and other forms of torture before execution would become the norm with rebels in the 1390s and early fifteenth century.

But other revolts show more clearly the hand of Arezzo's previous feudal lords. In 1390 five Tarlati lords led an unspecified number of armed men both on foot and horseback to retake the castle town of Bibbiena.[44] In the same year one of the Tarlati rebels accused in the revolt together with another nobleman of Pietramala and his "cancel-larius" invaded Gaenna (Gahene)[45] with fifty named men from this *castrum* and "over one hundred" others whose names were concealed to make possible future arrests. All of the fifty-three named, this time including the noblemen, were to be subjected to the same condemna-tions and tortures as had been meted out earlier that year to the Aretine rebels – laceration by red-hot pincers before hanging.[46] They were not, however, brought to justice. Six year later the *Capitano del Popolo* reviewed the case, listing most of those condemned in 1390 and adding several new names and details of the case, such as the Tarlati's organization of secret meetings. Again, *in absentia* the men were condemned to the same forms of mutilation and hanging as six years earlier.[47]

By 1397 the resumption of Milanese and Sienese incursions into the Florentine countryside and the consequential stiff increases in taxes placed on Florence's traditional *contado* provoked new waves of farm vio-lence and insurrection, mostly along Florence's southern mountainous periphery. "Out of bitterness, deprivation, opportunism, and the designs of the devil" Florentine villagers joined enemy troops in their assaults against the Florentine state. Among these turncoats was Luca di Brizzio of Montepulciano, guilty of "crimes perpetuated against his own country." He had gone to Siena to join a 400-horse cavalry under the command of Martino de Papia, the corporal of Lord Brolio of Milan. With this regiment, he rode from Sinalunga to raid the villages of

[42] Repetti, *Diz.*, I, p. 378.   [43] AP, 3351, np, 1390.vi.4.   [44] *Ibid.*, 3371, np, 1390.ix.19.
[45] See Repetti, *Diz.*, II, p. 368: Gaenna or Gajenna was in the Valdichiana, in the jurisdiction of Civitella.   [46] AP, 3351, np, 1390.vii.4.   [47] CP, 2040, 55r–9r, 1390.vii.4.

Colunnata[48] and "many others" along the Sienese–Florentine border, capturing animals and men for ransom. In Colunnata the raid was successful, not only because of the troops' ability to strike "the fear of war" into the residents, but also because they were aided by thirty peasants (*rustici vel circa*) from the village itself.[49]

Other "rebels" appear not to have enjoyed substantial support from local villagers such as a Florentine foot soldier named Baptista accused of rebellion and treason (*lese maiestate*, rarely found as a charge for these rural uprisings). While in charge of the fortified village of Cacciano, the alleged traitor held meetings with "an old woman" from neighboring Selvole, who served as a "mediator" between him and the Lord Angelo of Selvole. First for 1,000 then for 500 florins, Baptista settled "to give over" Cacciano to Lord Angelo. The takeover was to be prepared by Baptista's breaking a hole in the *castrum*'s walls and the siege to occur when only three villagers (*rustici*) would be within the village walls, suggesting that the locals may not have favored this transfer of suzerainty.[50]

Similarly, Nanni di Mignano from the village of Larniano near San Gimignano may have been no more than a traitor employed by enemy forces. But the inquest suggests that he was able to tap peasant discontent within San Gimignano for reasons the criminal records do not disclose. In May 1397, "accompanied by many associates," he laid siege to a farm in San Gimignano. Later that month he seems to have graduated from a primitive rebel of farmland violence to a military captain. Leading a large contingent of armed cavalry from Siena to San Gimignano, he captured animals and men for ransom,[51] striking "many times and in many places" and especially in the mountainous region around the Villa Colle Muscioli, 5 kilometers northwest of San Gimignano.

Far more serious to Florentine hegemony than these border rebels and traitors was the revolt of the Valdambra's principal town, Civitella, in 1397 – one of the few revolts to be recorded at all by contemporary

---

[48] The name corresponds to a number of places in Tuscany – Colognola, Colognole, Colognoli, Colonnia, Colonica, Coloniola; see *Diz.*, I, p. 778.

[49] CP, 2065, 45r–9r, 1397.xii.29: "et quia triginta rustici vel circa de dicta Villa Colunnate armati invaserunt."

[50] CP, 2065, 34v–5v, 1397.xii.10: "Dictus dominus Angnelus veniret ad accipiendum dictum castrum cito et de nichilo dubitaret quia in ipso castro erant solomodo tres rustici de quibus non dubitabat."

[51] CP, 2065, 14r–15r, 1397.x.23: "hostiliter equitando conduxit et guidavit magnam communitatem gentium armorum [i]nimicarum de Senis supra territorio Sancti Gemingnani."

chroniclers.[52] These narrative accounts, however, placed the blame on foreign troops and bribery and did not portray it at all as a rebellion of an indigenous population. The first inquest regarding Civitella's loss accused the Florentine castellan not of treachery or bribery as reported by the chroniclers but instead of simple negligence in performing his "honor-bound" duties to supply the castle with food, wine, and water and for his failure to resist the Milanese surprise attack.[53] Subsequent inquests, however, went further, pinpointing Civitella's loss to an internal uprising. A certain Minuccius of Civitella, whose patronymic the officials expunged from the record because of the gravity of his crime – *lese maiestate* – had allegedly signed a pact with Milan's corporal Lord Brolio to hand over Civitella to the Duke of Milan.[54] Who this Minuccius or Minutius was, how he had the power to turn "the possession of the *castrum*" over to Lord Brolio, or why he chose to do so, are left without explanation.

The case against Civitella's rebels was to last longer than most. In 1401, the *Podestà* arrested Dominicus del Ciocto from Torre a Castello, accused of having congregated over one hundred men in 1397. Although they had been armed with lances and crossbows, the court did not identify them as enemy soldiers (*gens armigera*), who might have been employed by the Duke of Milan or his officers. Instead they were simply called "men" and were accused of conspiracy and rebellion. From this late inquest, we are told that they killed Florence's *Podestà* at Civitella, invaded the *castrum*, seized it from Florentine rule, and occupied it "for many months." But for undisclosed reasons the *Podestà* found the accused Dominicus not guilty.[55] As we will see, the criminal courts do not fully reveal the success of these indigenous rebels; further clues about these "men" and their activities come to light in the Florentine decrees to be discussed in the next chapter. Half a year after its seizure, Florence was still unable to regain Civitella and was forced into negotiations with the local rebels.[56]

With direct taxes mounting on those from Florence's traditional *contado*, the final years of the fourteenth century sparked further plots

---

[52] Civitella had a history of insurrection against Florence; see the insurrection of 1369 above.
[53] CP, 2065, 21r–2r, 1397.xi.21.
[54] *Ibid.*, 54r–v, 1397.xii.31: "Et exequendo dictam perditionem et tractatum idem minutius inquisitus predictus preditorio modo dedit et assignavit dicto domino Brolie possessionem et dominium dicti castri Civitelle . . . exspoliavit et privavit possessionem et dominio dicti castri Civitelle contra voluntatem et in gravissimum danpnum, preiudicium, et periculum dicti magnifici comunis Florentie eiusque pacifici status et catholice partis Guelfe."
[55] AP, 3823, 13r–14r, 1401.i.16.   [56] Provv. reg., 87, 74v–8r, 1398.v.17.

and unrest. In 1398 local insurgents tried to regain independence in another Florentine town, this one from within the Florentine *contado* – San Miniato al Tedesco. This is the first rebellion to state explicitly the underlying reasons for rebels' discontent with Florence – the direct taxes or *estimo*, whose charges for the "taxa straordinaria" had risen by a multiple of six during the decade (see appendix 2). Curiously, the earliest surviving criminal records for the February 1398 rebellion do not appear until 1403. A resident of Pisa, Simone d'Andreuccio, probably under the pressure of torture, "confessed to the truth of the *Capitano*'s inquest" that charged him with organizing secret meetings and congregating a force "to bring rebellion to San Miniato, against the good and peaceful state of the city of Florence." Among his band of armed associates were Benedetto Mangiadori and his sons – the family that had led San Miniato's resistance to Florence's forced incorporation in 1369–70.[57]

Approaching the palace of the *vicarius*, they chanted loudly (*semper vocificando alta voce exclamando*): "Long live Vanni da Piano, liberty, and Benedetto Mangiadori, and death to the Estimo!"[58] The band stormed through the gate called "la porta dello succurso," and enjoined their townsmen to rebel. According to the inquest, had the Florentine army not arrived "swiftly" and fought "valiantly," the town would have fallen, causing "grave damage and indecorous shame to the status of the people and the liberty of the Commune of Florence."[59] Against the triumphalist claims of the Florentine historian Ammirato, these archival sources give no hint of counterrevolt or antagonism against the Mangiadori rebels; instead their chants railed against Florentine rule and in particular the rise in the dreaded *estimo*.[60]

Yet between this insurrection of townsmen and the peasants' military movements in the Alpi Fiorentine during the fall of 1402, the traditional *contado* of Florence appears remarkably quiet, especially given the war with Milan and the unprecedented escalation of taxes placed on the countryside. The most threatening insurrection at the end of the century came from the territory not yet subject to the *estimo*, in the

---

[57] On the 1369 revolt, see Brucker, *Florentine Politics and Society, 1343–1378* (Princeton, 1962), pp. 238–40. Also, Pinto, "Controllo politico," reports a revolt in San Miniato against Florence's salt tax.

[58] CP, 2199, 95r–6r, 1403.ix.12: "Viva Vanni da Piano liberta et Benedecto Mangiadore et moya l'estimo!"

[59] CP, 2199, 95r–6r, 1403.ix.12. A subsequent case vindicated the Pisan Simone, admitting that he had been unjustly tortured and hanged based on false testimony; *ibid.*, 98r–100r, 1403.xi.25.

[60] *Ibid.*, 95r–6r: "Et nisi fuisset gens armigera dicti comunis Florentie que subito velociter venit et dictis se viriliter opponuit et eos expulit."

recently acquired lands of the Florentine Romagna. It differed from other insurrections led by feudal lords and backed by their peasant *vassalli* in that it came from a small market town and was the only revolt clearly organized by what might be pointed to as a middling, local bourgeoisie.

A Ser Matteo di Calandrino and Maestro Giovanni di fu Niccole, both of Rocca di San Casciano and described by the Florentine notary as plotting to subvert the peace and "wishing that the people of Romagna should live in tyranny," sold their bread gabelle without authorization from the district's *Podestà*. According to the court's scribe, they "had acted as tyrants by speaking injurious and ugly words to the Florentine authority in the district," charging that the Lord Captain (who happened to be Florence's most famous *novellista* since Boccaccio, Franco Sacchetti) ought not to interfere in their business. Several days later Ser Matteo appeared before the court to defend himself along with Maestro Giovanni, an elected councilman of this rural commune. Ser Matteo protested against the band of exiles placed on them and claimed indemnity for all penalties and expenses.

Sacchetti, seeing that he did not have the force to arrest them, demanded that they report back to his court on the following day. Ser Matteo replied, "yes we shall appear, and we shall bring with us men and women from throughout the province of Romagna." "Among the many other vituperous and offensive words against the Magnificent Commune of Florence," Ser Matteo's counterclaims and attacks evince the Florentine ruling class's sensitivity toward the use of the heavily-laden words, "tyranny" and "liberty." He left the courtroom with the challenge: "One day, we will escape from this tyranny once and for all" (*Noi usciremo pure una volta di questa tirapnia*).

Later that month, Ser Matteo and Maestro Giovanni held secret meetings, constructed ladders for scaling the *borgo*'s walls, and appealed to their former feudal lords of Romagna to block Florence from further encroachments into the economic liberties granted to them in their original treaty of submission to Florence in 1382.[61] In their absence, the two ringleaders were sentenced to death but within two months had petitioned the Florentine councils and were absolved of their crimes.[62] By

[61] *I Capitoli*, I, pp. 109 and 354: "Che quegli uomini possano esigere i pedagii, salvo dai cittadini, contadini e distrettuali di Firenze, o per le loro mercanzie o per robe che fossero del C. di Firenze."

[62] Giudice, 97, 28r–9v, 1399.iii.6. Also see Cohn, *Women in the Streets*, pp. 122–3. The cancellation is written in the margins of this document. See Provv. reg., 88, 50v–1v, 1399.iv.29.

then, increasing warfare and the threat of peasant insurrection elsewhere may have conditioned Florence's mercy as it did later for cancellations of death penalties charged against peasant insurgents across the
northern borders from Sambuca to Palazzuolo in the Podere Fiorentino.

In 1399 and 1400 further acts branded by the Florentine courts as
rebellion followed in the wake of foreign military incursions along the
mountainous perimeter of the Florentine state. Again, they flared not
in the heavily taxed *contado* but in the district – the Montagna
Fiorentina,[63] the Casentino lands of the Ubertini lords,[64] the
Valdambra,[65] and the town of Montepulciano.[66] Several of these
"rebellions" hardly fit our present-day notions of insurrection and
appear instead simply as military operations conducted by foreign
troops without any connection to internal strife. Such was the invasion
of the Chianti mountain stronghold at Monteluco.[67] Its plot was
hatched in Siena at the behest of the Duke of Milan and assembled
men as prominent as the Bishop of Novara, four Ubertini lords, Count
Guido of Modigliana, a Piccolomini of Siena, and soldiers from as far
away as Imola, Padua, Venice, and lower Germany. None were indigenous to the Chianti. Their rallying cry was that of a military company:
"Long live the company and death to the Commune of Florence'[68] and
"Saint George! Long live the company and death to the Commune of
Florence."[69] Instead of liberating the indigenous population, the
invaders either expelled Monteluco's inhabitants or "tied them up for
ransom."[70]

Although not labeled as conspiracy or rebellion, the most explicit case
of peasant resentment against Florentine authority during these years
came from the *contado*, in fact from the *prope Alpes* of the upper Mugello
where Florence's tax rates were the highest. Again, fiscal pressures and
the inability of mountain peasants to meet Florentine demands appear

---

[63] AP, 3712, np, 1399.xii.1; CP, 2107, np, 1399.xii.1; Esecutore degli ordinamenti di Giustizia (here-
after Esecutore), 1383, 17r–20r, 1399.xii.17; 23v, sd; 24r–v, 1399.i.10.

[64] AP, 3695, 75r–7r, 1399.iv.7.

[65] See the cases relating to the raids on Capannole: CP, 2103, II, 23r–4v, 1399.xii.2; CP, 2107, np,
1399.xii.20.   [66] AP, 3712, 9r–10v, 1399.xii.31.

[67] Repetti, *Diz.*, III, p. 411; *AG*, p. 687, Monteluco is 780 meters in altitude. See AP, 3712, booklet
II, 5r–6r, 1399.x.31; 11r–12v, 1399.xii.10; CP, 2103, II, 15r–16v, 1399.xi.22; CP, 2111, 25r–7r,
1400.iv.27; CP, 2113, np, 1400.v.11.

[68] AP, 3712, booklet II, 5r–6r, 1399.x.31: "Viva la compagnia et mora el comune de fiorenza."

[69] CP, 2111, 25r–7r, 1400.iv.27 and also, CP, 2123, np, 1400.v.11: "Sancto Giorgio, viva la compagnia
et mora el comune de fiorenza." On the history of this company, see William Caferro, *Mercenary
Companies and the Decline of Siena* (Baltimore, 1998), pp. 10–11.

[70] Also see the case of the Aretine "robber, conspirator, and rebel," whose company's battle cry was
"Sancto giorgio viva la compagna"; CP, 2123, np, 1400.v.10.

as the cause of conflict. A father, his wife, and their two sons from San Niccolò at Montecarelli attacked officers and a notary of the *Podestà*, stabbing one while they were capturing a neighbor who had not paid his taxes (*estimo*) to Florence. During the attack, the wife hurled abuse at Florence, exclaiming: "Run, run men! that we should have lost our feudal lords only to end up with so cruel a tyranny."[71]

In short, the years immediately following the sharp rise of Florentine taxes in 1395 did register the first outright assaults by townsmen and peasants against the *estimo* and the tax collector that I have found in the criminal records. But despite this unprecedented escalation of taxes, most of the crimes called rebellion appear not as internal conflicts but as military invasions organized by Florence's enemies, the Duke of Milan, the commune of Siena, the Ubertini and Battifolle lords, and marauding soldiers of fortune. As the tax records testify for the mountains of the upper Mugello and Alpi, the first means of opposition to Florence's spiraling *estimo* was not open revolt but a more atomized form of protest – flight from the *contado*.

The opening years of the fifteenth century marked a change in protest emanating from the countryside. In 1401, the Florentine tribunals chart geographically and temporally one of the most extensive rebellions in Florentine history. Planned by secret meetings held in the city of Pistoia in January 1401, this revolt began as a typical factional conflict between rival patrician clans in a subject city. Like other such conflicts in Italian history, a disputed marriage and its resultant new alliances of consanguinity[72] rekindled conflict between two ruling factions, in this case, the Panciatichi and the Cancellieri.[73]

What distinguished this internecine conflict from others was its interregional dimensions made possible by the "third war" between Florence and Milan and its rapid transition from an urban to a rural conflict fought mostly in the mountains of Pistoia. Within weeks, the patrician rebel Lord Ricciardo Cancellieri fled Pistoia to establish an impregnable

---

71 CP, 2107, np, 1399.v.17: "Acuromo, acuromo, che noy perdiamo el nostro Signore et noi aviamo si crudel tiranno."

72 See, for instance, the 1215 marriage conflict between the Buondelmonti and degli Uberti, which according to Villani initiated the Guelf–Ghibelline conflict in Florence: *Nuova Cronica*, I, bk. 6, r. 38, pp. 267–9. On how peace was "fortified and made firm with many marriages" between the Panciatichi and the Cancellieri in 1351, see Matteo Villani, *Cronica*, I, bk. 1, r. 99, p. 190. For other examples, see Trevor Dean, "Marriage and Mutilation: Vendetta in Late Medieval Italy," *Past and Present*, 157 (1997), pp. 17–18.

73 For the origins of this conflict, see Michelangelo Salvi, *Historie di Pistoia e Fazioni d'Italia*, 3 vols. (Pistoia, 1656–62), II, pp. 198–219.

mountain base at Sambuca, from where he raided villages in the former *contado* of Pistoia and occasionally crossed into the Florentine Mugello. Along with other conquered villages within the Montagna di Pistoia, Sambuca did not return to Florentine suzerainty until a treaty of October 10, 1403, which granted the Cancellieri and some of their followers extensive protection from Florentine criminal retribution, along with privileges and tax concessions.[74] Moreover, perhaps because of its urban origins, this was the only rural revolt of which extensive discussions within Florence's highest chambers have survived in the records of the *Consulte e Pratiche*.[75]

At least four separate criminal cases and inquests for 1401 alone describe Lord Ricciardo's siege of Pistoia and the capture of Sambuca, condemning sixty-three men to death for rebellion.[76] Cases of cattle raids, kidnapping, murder, and the burning of villages continued to be adjudicated in the *Podestà*, *Capitano*, and vicariate courts until October 1403. Of the men listed, most were from the mountain commune of Sambuca, followed by several from Pistoiese villages in the plains – Montale, Agliana, and Montemurlo. All of these villagers appear as simple peasants without titles, family names, or any marks of the old nobility (which still persisted in some mountain regions of Tuscany). Furthermore, with the exception of Ricciardo, his notary, and three close friends from the Cantasanti family, those named from the city of Pistoia do not appear to have been socially distinguished. Besides the notary, only two were identified by profession; both were tailors, including Ricciardo's personal tailor. But the sixty-three listed rebels represent only a small tip of the over 1,500 men and women the inquests claim filled Ricciardo's ranks when he captured Sambuca.[77]

---

[74] Provv. reg., 92, 153v–8v: "Pro negotiis Sambuca et aliter."

[75] Consulte e Pratiche, 35, 164v–5r; 36, 18r, 71r, 84v–7r, 117v–23r; *Le "Consulte" e "Pratiche" (1401)*, pp. 195–6 and 200. After the abortive revolt of the Pratese, a brief discussion of the punishments to be meted out to the Guazzalotri entered these debates (Consulte e Pratiche, 35, 119r, 1402.vi.8–9). On nonurban insurrection, the only clear case within these records that has come to my attention was the 1426 revolt of Pontenano; see Consulte e Pratiche, 46, 180v, 1426.vii.31; and Cohn, *Women in the Streets*, pp. 123–35. The *Consulte* debates mention military tactics and difficulties with the Ubaldini and the prospect of losing the Mugello in 1402, but little discussion centered on the mountain communes of the Alpi, the Podere, and the Casentino (see Consulte e Pratiche, 35, 171v–3v, 1402.xi.20–21; 36, 2r, 1402.xi.22). Only the hint of a popular insurrection emerges from the laconic texts; see *ibid.*, 109r, 1403.ix.18; 115r–v, 1403.x.13; 117r, 1403.x.14; 135v–6r, 1403.xi.11; 37, 2r, 1403.xi.26.

[76] AP, 3821, I, 66v–70r, 1401.xi.4; 81v–2r, 1401.xi.8; 3823 (3rd booklet), 33r–4v, 1401.i.28; 56v–7r, 1401.ii.23.

[77] AP, 3821, I, 66v–70r: "tum multis comitatinis et amicis de dicta civitate . . . et intromictere bene mille quingentos homines armatos et ultra" (p. 68).

The earliest sentence against Cancellieri and his followers, dated November 4, 1401, condemned to death Ricciardo, seven others from the city, and thirty-three from the Pistoiese countryside. The style of execution is the first of its kind that I have spotted in the numerous executions of rebels. The rebels were to be first tortured with red-hot pincers and led to the place of justice (*attanaglando ducantur . . . ad locum justitie*), where they were to be hanged upside down with their heads buried alive (*cum capitibus deorsum plantentur ita et taliter*) and their property confiscated. Prompted by widespread rebellion through the Florentine territory, this ritual of execution would become more popular with Florence's judges for political rebels in the countryside in the early fifteenth century with added flourishes: buried alive, the rebels were to be hanged once dead but never buried thereafter; their bodies were to rot on the gibbet.[78]

A second sentence condemned to death by the same means the two Florentine castellans of the fortifications of Sambuca for "infidelity, disobedience, and treachery."[79] A third condemned eighteen others from Sambuca, Montemurlo, Montale, San Quirico, and Agliana, who left Sambuca "to make war" on the valley village of Montale, where they killed two men.[80] In a fourth, nine men from Montale were tried for harboring rebels from Sambuca.[81]

By 1402, smaller-scale guerrilla activities in the plains and mountains of Pistoia replaced cases of rebellion comprising long lists of insurgents. These included cross-border cattle raids, kidnapping for ransom, murder, burning houses, secret meetings, and several attempts to capture entire villages. These assembled peasants from villages across the Montagna di Pistoia with soldiers of fortune from villages from Bologna, Genoa, Parma, and Milan.[82]

The criminal records here paint a picture similar to that seen in Ser Luca's chronicle: robbery and ransom were the means of rebellion, and villages with long-time loyalties to the Cancellieri attacked those loyal to the Panciatichi or of mixed allegiances. From the revolt's beginnings in the city, Ricciardo's success depended on ancient networks of patronage spread throughout the city and countryside. According to Ser Luca,

---

[78] AP, 3821, I, 70r. Also, see Cohn, *Women in the Streets*, p. 131. [79] AP, 3821, I, 81v–2r, 1401.xi.8.
[80] AP, 3823, III, 33r–4v, 1401.i.28.
[81] *Ibid.*, 56v–7r, 1401.ii.23; however, these men were found not guilty.
[82] AP, 3856, 10r–11r, 1402.viii.4; CP, 2183, 20r–1v, 1402.xi.3; 67r–8r, 1402.xii.18; 133r, 1402.iii.10; 2188, 9r–16v, 1402.x.19, 70r–3v, 1402.iii.5; 2192, 36r–7r, 1402.iii.22; 2207, 25r–v, 1403.i.21; Giudice, 97, 215r–17r, 1402.ii.26; and 218v–19r, 1403.viii.9.

these passions consumed the cares of all *contadini* down to women and little boys.[83]

In the numerous reports, no chants or allusions to peasant discontent with taxation or Florentine rule seep through the seemingly dispassionate enumerations of robbery and murder. Was the revolt of Sambuca and its almost three years of resistance simply a matter of urban factional rivalry that had spread to the countryside? Were the insurgents mere opportunists who took advantage of the anarchy in the countryside to further their individual economic ends? Although it is difficult to resolve these questions from the Dominici's chronicle or the criminal records, it is certain that these revolts differed markedly from those that would break out a year later further east in the Florentine Alps. Unlike the negotiations that settled scores between Florence and its peasant rebels in the Alpi and Podere, those between Florence and Ricciardo extended guarantees and privileges almost exclusively to himself and his clan. Indeed, Florence singled out the three most loyal villages to Ricciardo – "Sambuca, Calamecca, Pitegli" – not for special privileges or exemptions but to meet new obligations – to relinquish their castles and to maintain or destroy them as Florence saw fit.[84]

Although chroniclers and later historians have reported more often and with greater detail the Cancellieri revolt and seizure of Sambuca than any other rural uprising of the early fifteenth century, the 1402 firing on Firenzuola, the recovery of old castles once belonging to the Ubaldini, the building of new bastions in the Alps, and the spread of peasant uprisings through the Alpi and Podere Fiorentino were more extensively recorded in the surviving judicial records of Florence. Many more men were condemned as rebels, and more criminal cases of conspiracy were brought to trial than in the three years of Cancellieri guerrilla warfare. In one case alone almost four times the number of insurgents were listed (215) than were named in all the cases brought against Ricciardo and his band (63).

Moreover, the consequences of the revolts in the Alpi had longer and more significant results than those in the Montagna di Pistoia. The treaty of October 10, 1403 with Ricciardo doled out benefits mostly to him and

---

[83] Dominici, *Croniche*, II, pp. 12–13. Also see Connell, *City of Sorrows*, chapter 4 and map 1.
[84] Provv. reg., 92, 153v–8v; 1403.x.22 and 159r–60r: "Pro factis Sambuce et domini Ricciardi"; Salvi, *Historie di Pistoia*, II, pp. 208 and 214–15, summarizes the treaty between Florence and Ricciardo, but discrepancies arise between his account and the *provvisioni*. He may have been relying on other sources; he gives no references.

his family, and factional bickering between the Cancellieri and Panciatichi continued to dominate Pistoiese politics much as before. By contrast, the negotiations between the highlanders of the Alpi Fiorentine unleashed a tidal wave of tax concessions benefiting a hundred villages across the mountain perimeter of the Florentine state. Some of these privileges would endure until the rise of the Medici and even beyond.

At the end of 1402 and in 1403 at least seven separate sentences and inquests describe the plans and attacks of Ubaldini and peasant insurgents on Firenzuola and the conquest of territory in the Alpi Fiorentine, followed by numerous other sentences for rebellions in the Podere Fiorentino, the Romagna Fiorentina, Casentino, and Valdambra. As for the revolts in the Alpi, fifty-seven individuals were sentenced to death for insurrections in the summer and autumn of 1402, and the courts maintained that many more were involved whose names they withheld. The first of these sentences lists forty-one men beginning with eleven Ubaldini whose places of residence show that their years of conflict with the Florentine state had dispersed them across the Romagna and Tuscany; they now hailed from Pignole (Pignuole)[85] Caprile,[86] Cardaccia, Carda,[87] Visano,[88] and even as far south as Città di Castello. Despite this geographic diaspora, they joined together in Bologna to plan the siege of their former homeland, the "Alpe degli Ubaldini", renamed the Alpi Fiorentine by a Florentine law of 1373.[89]

A twelfth Ubaldini was listed further down; otherwise the list contains names of countrymen from the mountain parishes of the Alpi and the Podere – eight from Caburaccio, four from Cornacchiaia, one from Rapezzo, one from San Piero a Santerno, two from Tirli, three from Pignole, six from Castro, and three without place names. Of these, only three were identified by a profession or title – a cobbler from Rapezzo, the parish priest of Caburaccio, and a Ser Vannino from Caburaccio. Unlike those condemned in the skirmishes that germinated in Sambuca and spread through the Pistoiese, this list contains no obvious examples of soldiers of fortune from distant parts of Tuscany or Italy or of "vagabonds" without fixed abodes. Beneath the ranks of the Ubaldini, those who planned and fought to regain the Alpi Fiorentine were countrymen

---

[85] It is in the Alpi Fiorentine, the parish (*pieve*) of San Giovanni de Camaggiore; see Provv. reg., 61, 39r–44v, 40v, 1373.iv.28. This place name does not appear in Repetti, *Diz.*

[86] Five kilometers north of San Godenzo, in what would have been the Romagna Fiorentina; Repetti, *Diz.*, I, p. 471.   [87] An Ubaldini castle in the Romagna; *ibid.*, p. 473.

[88] On the border of the Podere and Romagna, 1.5 kilometers northeast of Palazzuolo, *ibid.*, V, p. 792.   [89] Provv. reg., 61, 39r–42r, 1373.iv.28.

from the region; none came from its town, Firenzuola, or from Scarperia further south.

From the court descriptions five men emerge as the leaders who conceived strategy and commanded military operations that tore through the Alpi during the summer and autumn of 1402. The criminal records cast the revolts in a wholly different light from that seen in the few chronicles which mentioned them at all. Instead of an Ubaldini-led feudal reaction against Florentine dominion, the judicial acts highlight only one nobleman in a leadership role, Galeotto called Troncha; the other listed Ubaldini are not even mentioned as interlocutors in the secret meetings.

Galeotto had already played a key historical role in 1373, when Florence waged its successful war against the Ubaldini.[90] He was one of four grandsons of the patriarch Attavianus (the Pignole branch of the Ubaldini) who made peace with Florence by relinquishing the Ubaldini castle at Lozzole in the Podere Fiorentino[91] for the extraordinary sum of 7,000 gold florins plus a monthly allowance of 5 gold florins for ten years. In addition, Florence had abolished all condemnations and renounced all "vendettas and reprisals" against them and had granted them citizenship as commoners ("popolani") that would pass to their descendants down each of their male lines.[92] Twenty-eight years on, this Galeotto changed sides again, rejoining his hunted clansmen.

But Galeotto's leadership does not emerge as more senior or important than that of four villagers, none of whom bore a family name or a title of nobility; all were taxed as commoners in the *estimo* as opposed to noblemen in the *gabella seu page nobilium*. The first of these, Cinuccino (sometimes Cinaccio) the son of Bertino from the mountain hamlet of Castro under the Futa pass was present at the initial secret meetings with Jacopo dal Verme, the famous *condottiere* then serving as the Duke of Milan's lieutenant and captain of the army at Bologna.[93]

Because the *lira* of Castro in 1402 does not list tax assessments and its *estimo* of 1401 does not survive,[94] the earliest property assessment for

---

[90] AP, 3886, 9r–10v, 1402.xii.9; and *ibid.*, 84r–5r, 1402.xii.22. The second sentence repeats much of the description of the first sentence, with thirty-seven instead of the forty-one charged earlier and condemned in their absence (*in contumacie*) to be beheaded.

[91] In the commune of Palazzuola at 610 meters; its earliest documentary notice comes in 1223; see Francovich, *I Castelli del contado*, p. 96.

[92] Provv. reg., 61, 101r–5v, 1373.viii.26 (three distinct *provvisioni*).

[93] On this *condottiere*'s career, see Caferro, *Mercenary Companies*, p. 13.

[94] Castro is the village nearest to the Futa pass (902 m) and is at an altitude of 572 meters (*AG*, p. 284).

Cinuccino is in the *lira* and *estimo* of his father Bertino di Cini in 1393. At eighty-five years old, his father then headed a complex household comprising three married couples and their children, those of Berinus and two of his sons, Cinuccino and Giusto. They were the wealthiest peasants in the village with property assessed at 400 *lire*[95] and paid the highest tax, 2 *lire* 14s.[96] Like others at Castro, they owed a perpetual rent in kind (*census perpetuus*) to their Ubaldini lords, though at 10 *staii* of wheat a year, it was lower than that owed by most in the village. As these records show, Florence had not been able to keep its promise of 1373 to the peasants of the Alpi – the abolition of feudal and other perpetual rents owed to the Ubaldini.[97] In 1393, Cinuccino was thirty-nine with a wife of thirty-two and four children ranging in age from fourteen to two. In 1402 he would have been forty-eight with a family and, even with Florence's punitive taxation, probably with something to lose had the rebellion failed.

The second rebel villager was Ser Vannino di Cenni from the mountain commune of Caburaccio, seven kilometers northeast of Firenzuola.[98] Neither the significance of Ser Vannino's "ser" nor his profession is specified in any of the criminal lists, *estimi*, or *lire*, but as evinced by his payments of annual fees to the guild of notaries and judges of the Commune of Florence, he was a mountain notary in good standing.[99] Further, in the criminal record, he is called a *stipendarius* employed by Florence. One of his functions as seen in the *estimo* of 1393 was drafting the local assessments to be sent to Florence. In addition to his own village, he drafted the returns for other villages in the Alpi[100] and continued to do so after the revolts, appearing again as a Florentine "commissioner" in the last *estimo* of 1414.[101]

In 1401, like Cinuccino, he was the richest man in his village, assessed at 285 *lire*. At thirty-five he was younger than his comrade and headed a

---

[95] Estimo 218, 280v.   [96] *Ibid.*, 286, 65v.   [97] See Provv. reg., 61, 39r–42r, 1373.iv.28.

[98] *AG*, p. 186. Caburaccio is 558 m high and today has a population of only nine. Also, see Repetti, *Diz.*, I, p. 377.

[99] He appears as Ser Vanninus Cenni, Arte dei Giudici e notai, 95 (1393) and 97 (1398) – the only two years of the last decade of the fourteenth century for which these registers survive. None of his notarial protocols survive. I thank Franek Sznura for searching his databases of Florentine notaries for Ser Vanninus' name.

[100] Ser Vanninus signed the returns of the parishes of San Lorenzo al Peglio (Estimo 218, 235r), San Cristofano a Visignano (253r), San Michele a Monti (277r), and his own village of Caburaccio (289r).

[101] See Estimo 224 for 1414; the return for San Benedetto delle Valle ends with "facta per Ser Vanninum Cennis de Caburaccio commissarium dicti populi que iuris et etc." In 1427 these tasks were handed over to a specially trained corps of tax officials from the city of Florence; see Herlihy and Klapisch-Zuber, *Les Toscans*, pp. 77–94.

family consisting of his wife, age 30, and three sons between two and thirteen.[102] Because he had fled across the border to the mountains of Bologna, he does not appear in the *lire* records for Caburaccio in the following year, but was estimated in the village *estimo* to be assessed at 43s[103] – the same as in 1393–4, when, even as a young man of twenty-three, he was listed as a household head and assessed the highest in his village of 103 households.[104]

Similar to Cinuccino and Ser Vannino, the third village ringleader, Viviano alias Nasso, the son of Stefano di Viviano alias Tanaya (in one document, Travagia and Tanaia in a third) from Castro,[105] came from a propertied family, was married, and was among the wealthiest of his village. But he was younger than his co-conspirators and had no children. At the time of the revolt of the Alpi Fiorentine and the siege of Firenzuola, he was twenty-two with a wife of only fifteen.[106] In the *estimo* of 1401/2, his father, fifty-five, headed a household with his son, and at 200 *lire* was tied with three others as third wealthiest and taxed accordingly.[107]

Finally, the fourth village rebel leader was Bonone di Bertolo from the Alpine village of Cornacchiaia between the Futa pass and Firenzuola. Because of the fragmentary remains of its fiscal returns at the turn of the century, less can be said about him or his family than for the others; he does not appear in the *lira* of 1402 or 1414, but does appear in the *estimo* of 1401. However, perhaps as a sign of collective protest against taxes, the returns from Cornacchiaia in 1401 did not abide by *estimo* regulations: they lacked the usual lists of household members, ages, and property assessments; only household heads appear with their proposed tax base.

Bonone shared the head of his household with three brothers and was assessed at 43s, which along with another household was the highest in the village.[108] Unfortunately, Bonone is not listed in any other *estimo* or

---

[102] Estimo 224, np, village 43. His property consisted of "una casa cum capanna et aia et orto posto nel detto popolo . . . vale libre 50; uno pezzo di terra lavoratoia e soda cum quercie di staiora tre a seme posto nel detto popolo luogo detto di capo di sala vale libre 20; uno pezzo di terra lavoratoia di staiora sei a seme posto nel detto popolo luogho detto burano . . . val libre 30; uno pezzo di terra vignata posto nel detto popolo luogo detto le costarelle . . . vale libre 20; uno pezzo di prato posto nelle corte di peramora luogo detto le lame vale libre 5; uno pezzo do terra lavoratoia d'uno staioro a seme luogo detto sala vale libre 10. Libre cclxxxv a debito sopra la persona e asii più che non vale il suo."   [103] Estimo 287, 217v–19v.   [104] *Ibid.*, 286, 68v.

[105] AP, 3886, 9r; and *ibid.*, 3v; CP, 2207, 3v–6v, 1402.xii.9. The *Capitano* prosecuted only Nasso and Galeoctus.   [106] In the *estimo* he is called Johannes but in the *lira*, Vivianus.

[107] He was assessed 1 *lira* 5s, Estimo 287, 200r; for his property value see 218, 280r. Castro had a population of sixty-five households.   [108] Estimo 224, np, village 51.

lira records from 1383 to 1414, but in the *lira* of 1372 a certain Buono di
Bartolo is named among the heads of what most likely was a large and
complex family with four heads, taxed at 3 *lire* 7s, again suggesting that,
like his comrades, he came from among the wealthiest households in the
Alpine communes.[109]

Thus these rebel leaders were neither young free-wheeling vagabonds
nor "miserabili," and they were wealthier than the "fideles" who earlier
filled the rank and file of the insurrectionary bands headed by feudal
lords such as Count Tano in the 1360s. The social composition of these
later rural rebels fits the character of their revolts: it was the village elites
and not the propertyless who were hardest hit by Florence's escalating
taxes at the close of the fourteenth century and had the most to lose.

The *Podestà*'s sentences of 1402 and 1403 reported that these "traitors
and rebels" had gone to Bologna with many others whose names the
courts withheld. At "many, many, many times, on diverse days, day and
night, during the months of July and August 1402" Lord Galeotto and
Cinuccino with many of the above-listed rebels held meetings with
Jacopo dal Verme to plan the siege of Firenzuola. At this point in the
court description, Lord Galeotto fades into the background and the
principal interlocutors communicating with Jacopo dal Verme were the
three commoners Cinuccino, Ser Vannino, and Viviano alias Nasso.

Indeed, these highlanders and not the Milanese captain or the
Ubaldini lords were the strategists of the first siege of Firenzuola; it was
they who gave the commands to Jacopo dal Verme. According to the
Podestà's description:

With the said Cinuccino, Ser Vannino ordered Lord Jacopo the above-mentioned lieutenant and captain, saying: "We have organized a plot for the takeover of this *vicariatus* of Firenzuola and its Alpine region, which should proceed
as follows: when the bell-tower chimes, you are to have your army of foot soldiers and cavalry ready at the [entrance of] the *castrum* of Firenzuola." Ser
Vannino, Cinuccino, Nasso, and many of their friends, whom they requisi-
tioned, would be armed with both offensive and defensive weapons. And when
they felt that they were strong enough, they would call on the Milanese troops
to enter the town and together they would murder the *vicarius* of Firenzuola, kill
the Florentine soldiers, and provoke the town into rebelling for the Ubaldini
and against Florentine rule.[110]

---

[109] *Ibid.*, 284, 189r. In the *lire* a Teus, the diminutive for Domenicus, is listed as Buonus's brother,
most likely the same Domenicus listed as his brother in 1412.

[110] AP, 3886, 9r–10v, and CP, 2207, 3v–4r: "videlicet Dictus Ser Vanninus qui omnia infrascripta
ordinaverat cum dicto Cinaccio et pluribus aliis de suprascriptis dicendo eidem domino Jacobo
locumtenente et capitaneo supradicto: 'Nos habemus in dicto vicariato Florenzole et Alpibus

According to the court, "by divine grace and providence" and through the Florentine *vicarius*'s "industry and security" the revolt was nipped in the bud.

Nonetheless, the highlanders were not caught and continued to travel back and forth between Bologna and their mountain fortifications to deliberate with Lord Galeotto Ubaldini and the Milanese captain of war during the summer of 1402 when, "at the will of Jacopo dal Verme," Cinuccino, Ser Vannino, and Galeotto led "a great quantity of armed men and horsemen of the Duke with many cannon, iron assault weapons, and other machines to take Firenzuola." They first camped in the Alpi Fiorentine at a place called "el Pogio de Montecoloretio," between the villages of Pignole, Brenta, and Brenta Orsania, which was the site of an old Ubaldini castle that had been acquired by Florence in 1361.[111] Numerous others joined the Milanese forces whose names the court refused to disclose – presumably local highlanders from the surrounding district not unlike those listed in the inquests. Following the instructions of the Duke of Milan's lieutenant and the Ubaldini, they built a bastion of stone and wood, where "they remained for many days, inflicting maximum damage, disgrace, and shame on the people of Florence."[112]

The description of their rebellion continues: "Not being content with this but adding evil to evil" and together with the fourth village rebel leader, Bonone di Bertolo, and an unspecified number of foot soldiers and cavalry under the command of Jacopo dal Verme, Cinuccino descended from Montecoloreto and made camp at a place called "la bastia da Castro," which lay in the Alps between Cornacchiaia, Casanuova, and le Valli. From this position the rebels built another bastion of wood between Cornacchiaia and Casanuova called "el pogio de Castello Guirino" and then descended into the *vicariatus* of

ipsius vicariatus tractatum ordinatum hoc modo, videlicet: Vos mictetis exercitum vestrum armatorum tam pedestrum quam equestrum a[d] dictum castrum Florenzole procere quam campane pulzabutur ad martellum.' Et predictus Ser Vanninus, Cinaccius, Nassus, et plures alii de suprascriptis de quibus vicarius Florenzole multum se confidit ibunt ad dictum castrum cum pluribus aliis eorum amicis requisitis ab eis et in dicto castro cum eorum armis offendentibus et defendentibus paulatim intrabunt ut moris est quam talia contigunt. Et cum dicto Ser Vannino, Cinaccio, et aliis prenominatis videbitur in dicto castro Florenzole esse fortiores dicto domino vicario atque stipendiariis comunis Florentie ibidem permanentibus ipsum dictum vicarium et stipendiarios gladio interficient et morti tradibunt. Et castrum Florenzole predictum et rebellabunt a dicto comuni Florentie pro Ubaldinis. Et in casu quo predicto ordine et modo predicti Ser Vanninus et Cinaccius una cum supradictis non possent eorum pessimum pravum."

[111] Repetti, *Diz.*, III, pp. 373–4. It is at 970 meters.

[112] In the text from the *Podestà*'s sentence, the phrase is "in maximum dampnum preiudicum et verecundiam populi comunis Florentie"; in the *Capitano*'s it is "in maximum dampnum prividicium et verecundiam populi comunis Florentie."

Firenzuola, "making war, robbing and capturing" Florentine subjects as well as messengers, who were carrying letters from Florence's Priors and the Ten of War (the *Dieci*). Further, they used these bastions and hilltops to besiege Firenzuola (this time with success as is suggested by Minerbetti and made explicit in later trials). Again, the insurgents were not captured but were sentenced to death *in absentia*.[113] Later that year, the *Podestà* condemned thirty-seven of these rebels for meetings, plotting with Jacopo dal Verme, and "for rebelling and occupying Firenzuola." But they too were condemned *in absentia*.[114]

While all of these insurgents were indigenous villagers or Ubaldini, later charges were brought against two men described as "vagabundos" with no fixed residence, most likely soldiers of fortune, who, according to the court's descriptions, rode on many occasions from Bologna to Firenzuola "with raised banners to make war against Firenzuola." Unlike the local rebels, they had also assisted Ricciardo in his takeover of Sambuca.[115] Finally, a third case partially confirms Ser Luca's and other chroniclers' claims that disgruntled Florentines in exile might have been involved. However, the courts condemned only four Florentines, and none came from prominent families, as Ser Luca and Machiavelli claimed. Instead, they were without family names and had lived in the mostly artisan neighborhoods of San Pier Maggiore and Sant'Ambrogio.[116]

From the Alpi Fiorentine peasant uprisings spread southward to the Mugello's *prope Alpes* where two from Mangona with other unnamed villagers sought enemy aid to throw out their Florentine commissioner and return the keys of the village gates to their own men.[117] But more troublesome for Florentine defenses and territorial stability was the spread of mass armed insurrection through the ancestral lands of the Ubaldini

---

[113] AP, 3886, 9r–10v, 1402.xii.9; on the same day, the *Capitano del Popolo* also adjudicated this rebellion and condemned to death Lord Galeoctus and Vivianus alius Nasso, but did not list the other thirty-nine rebels listed in the *Podestà*'s record. Otherwise, the descriptions are almost identical; see CP, 2207, 3v–6v, 1402.xii.9.

[114] *Ibid.*, 84r–5r. 1402.xii.22. Perhaps the *Podestà* had caught the other four, who were not listed the second time.   [115] CP, 2199, 1403.vi.21; CP, 2207, 37v–9v, 1403.vi.21; 58r–6or, 1403.ix.22.

[116] CP, 2199, 45r–7r, 1403.vii.12. On the social composition of these parishes see Cohn, *The Laboring Classes*, ch. 4; and Alessandro Stella, *La révolte des Ciompi: Les hommes, les lieux, le travail* (Paris, 1993), ch. 5.

[117] CP, 2183, 31r–v, 1402.xii.18: "dixerunt et protulerunt verba iniuriosa, obbrobriosa, et victuperosa contra et adversus prefatum comixarium et officialem predictum et in eius victuperium et verecundiam et etiam dicti comunis Florentie, videlicet: dictus Lemmus dixit et protulit hec verba 'Esset bonum et bene faceremus accipere claves porti dicti castri ab isto comixerio et ipsum comixarium proiecere extra muros.' Et dictus nero dixit et protulit 'Bonum esset quas dictas claves non retineret dictus comissarius sed alique terigena de dicto castro.'"

across the Apennine crests and into the Podere Fiorentino. In November 1402 the Ubaldini assisted by the Lombard army and the forces of the Count of Imola invaded the commune of Tirli[118] and began building fortifications of wood and stone for which they imported provisions, building materials, and twenty-five master masons from Imola. On May 23, 1403, the *Capitano* drew up an inquest listing 221 rebels, the longest list of insurgents I have found in the criminal archives for any insurrection, urban or rural, for the entire fourteenth and fifteenth centuries – three times the number found for any sentence of Ciompi insurgents, 1378 to 1382, and almost four times as many as indicted in all Ricciardo's Pistoiese insurrections combined.

The constituency and leadership of this rebellion differed from the siege of Firenzuola and the building of bastions in the Alpi Fiorentine during the previous summer. Here, control and leadership were more clearly in the hands of the Ubaldini, and, as against the Alpi revolts, whose rank and file were almost wholly indigenous to the region, the majority in the Tirli uprising came from immediately across the border, principally from the mountains of Bologna and Imola. Forty resided at the Bolognese castle of Co' di Ronco (Codronco),[119] at Massa Alidosia,[120] but none were from the village of Tirli itself.

On the other hand, the mass of those indicted were peasants from the mountains, undistinguished by family names or titles, and many were also identified as previous inhabitants of places within the mountains of the Florentine *contado*, such as Putei (Pozzo) in the Montagna Fiorentina. Others came from the Florentine mountains of the Podere and Alpi – seven from Susinana, two from Piedimonte, three from Bibbiana, fourteen from Rapezzo, nineteen from Valmaggiore, and twenty from Piancaldoli.[121] Most likely, these *émigré* rebels had been among the swarms of peasants to have abandoned their fields, fleeing Florence's ruinous taxation during the preceding five to ten years.

In addition to building the bastion at Tirli and attempting to wrest this strategically important territory from Florence, the inquest charged the rebels with pillaging the countryside of "grain, wine, chestnuts, and many other goods," which they brought back to their bastion at Tirli. In

---

[118] Tirli was one of the border communities to be incorporated into the new vicariate of the Alpi Fiorentine in 1373. Its first castellan was a Medici, Zanobus Grisi de Medicis, elected by the Florentine councils; Provv. reg., 61, 145v.
[119] The commune of Codronco became allied to the Alidosi in 1382; see Larner, *The Lords of Romagna*, p. 176.
[120] It was the seat of the Alidosi counts of Imola, now above Castel del Rio; see *ibid.*, p. 22.
[121] Repetti, *Diz.*, IV, pp. 162–4, 15 kilometers northeast of Firenzuola, on the border with Bologna.

January and February 1403 they attacked the village of Casaglia in the
Alpi Fiorentine, torched it, stole many oxen, asses, and horses, and captured four villagers whom they led back to the castle at Susinana for
ransom. On January 21, 1404, eight months after the inquest, none of
them had been arrested or had appeared in court.[122]

In the same month as the siege of Tirli (November, 1402), mountain
peasants further east in the Podere Fiorentino "rebelled," using the
castrum of Valle Maggiore in the *contado* of Imola as a base, and invaded
and occupied Susinana. In contrast to the rebellion at Tirli, the *Capitano
del Popolo* sentenced 115 men – the second longest list of indictments
found in these sources and the longest list of those actually sentenced.
"At the bidding of the Ubaldini" (*pro Ubaldinis et ad ipsorum petitionem et
instantiam*), the rebels built a bastion of stone and wood and held the
castle "at great damage, opprobrium, and shame for the Commune of
Florence." The men "added evil to evil" by raiding houses in Susinana
and "robbing and pillaging for the remainder of the year."

Unlike the siege of Tirli, and in contrast to the rhetoric of the inquest,
which pictured these men as the enemies and invaders of the Podere
Fiorentino, these rebels, condemned to be beheaded, were mostly from
the region: the largest group in fact came from Susinana itself (twenty-
five men). A separate inquest of the siege listed slightly fewer insurgents (109) than the *Capitano*'s sentence, but twenty-nine were from
Susinana.[123] In both records, men of the Podere Fiorentino predominated: Palazzuolo[124] (twelve), Campana[125] (eleven) and Castel Pagano[126]
(eight), Bibbiana, Piedimonte, Frassino, Crespino, Salecchio, della
Rocca, and Val di Senio. Few, if any, were foreigners. In addition, of the
115 men, only five were Ubaldini.[127] Among other matters, these cases
show that threats to Florentine territorial security certainly did not end
in the summer of 1402 with the death of the Duke of Milan, as contemporary chroniclers and many modern historians sometimes assert.[128]
Instead, along Florence's frontiers invasions from outside and rebellions
from within increased in severity.

Further, the criminal acts provide numerous examples of how the
old feudal powers of the Valdambra, Arezzo, and Modigliana, either

---

[122] CP, 2199, 34r–8r, 1403.v.23 and 1403.i.21. Also see further raids through the Podere in the winter
of 1402; CP, 2203, 12r–14r, 1403.iv.18.   [123] CP, 2203, 126r–30r, 1403.vii.7 to 1403.ix.1.
[124] The central village of the Podere Fiorentino.
[125] Five kilometers northeast of Palazzuolo, Repetti, *Diz.*, I, p. 411.
[126] This was the castle of Maghinando Pagani, whose lord by the time of his death in 1302 was
effective ruler of Faenza, Forlì, and Faenza; see Larner, *The Lords of Romagna*, pp. 24, 47–51.
[127] CP, 2206, 17v–19v, 1403.viii.16.   [128] Brucker, *The Civic World*, p. 184, is an exception.

actively or by proxy, used this period of disruption to claw back possessions lost to Florence after its acquisition of Arezzo in 1384. In these,
military pressure from the south – the commune of Siena – increasingly played a role. After Civitella's successful rebellion in 1397 little is
heard from the Ubertini lords of the Valdambra other than an occasional cattle raid.[129] Then, in April 1402, Giangaleazzo's lieutenants in
Siena bribed locals from the Valdambra to stage an insurrection of the
castle of Galatrona.[130] In November a man from Montichiello in the
former *contado* of Arezzo and a soldier (*famulus*) placed by Florence's
Priors at the castle of Montebonico (Montebenichi) in the Valdambra
"to preserve the peace" held secret meetings with exiles and rebels and
negotiated with members of the Ubertini to "prepare" the overthrow
of the castle.[131] In January 1403, the *Capitano* indicted the son of the
Count of Modigliana, the wife of an Ubertini, and a man simply called
Castio for instigating a rebellion among their armed followers (*compli-
cis et fidelissimi servitoris*), which led to the plunder of men and goods for
booty and the takeover of the castle of Corezo (Coretio)[132] in the
former *contado* of Arezzo.[133] Meo from Castro in the Valdarno
Superiore was convicted of treason, sedition, and rebellion for engag-
ing in secret meetings with the enemy and the lords of Palazzuolo in
the Valdichiana at the castle of San Gosimey in the *contado* of Siena,
where he and his feudal supporters planned to wrest the castle of
Montay (Montalla)[134] from Florentine dominion and return it to the
lords of Palazzuolo.[135]

In January and February, 1403 Count Piero the son of Count Biagio
of Palazzuolo led a group of nineteen named rebels, all from
Palazzuolo and identified only by patronymics or nicknames, to rebel
and turn over the castle of Palazzuolo to the enemy, the commune of
Siena, and thus place it within the "dominion of Milan."[136] In the same
year, the *Capitano* indicted three from Castelfranco, Valdarno Superiore,

---

[129] For cattle raids in the Casentino and the Valdambra organized by the Ubertini clans, see
Giudice, 97, np, 1399.iii.29; np, 1399.iv.8; 38v–9r, 1399.vi.26; 103r–4r, 1400.iii.17; 97, booklet II,
39r–v, 1401.vi.25; 98, booklet II, 23r, 1405.x.21.   [130] CP, 2199, 23r–4r, 1402.ii.2.
[131] CP, 2178, 16r–v, 1402.v.13.
[132] Repetti, *Diz.*, I, p. 799: in the Casentino, 11 kilometers north of Chiusi Casentinese, in the district of Poppi.   [133] CP, 2192, 28v–30r, 1402.ii.26.
[134] Repetti, *Diz.*, III, p. 313: Montalla in Valdichiana, three kilometers southeast of Cortona.
[135] AP, 3922, np, 1403.ix.12.
[136] Giudice, 97, 205r–206r, 1403.iv.17; and 98, 6r–v, 1403.vii.30; and AP, 3886, 28v–9r, 1403.iv.1: "et
dictum bastium Palaccuoli abdicare, subtrahere, et rebellare a dicto comune ordinaverunt, trac-
taverunt, et deliberaverunt et tradere, dare, et applicare dictum castrum comuni civitatis
Senarum, in locumteneti in dicte civitate pro dominio Mediolano, inimicis comunis Florentie."

for raiding their village, kidnapping men for ransom and bringing them back to the castle of Pietraviva in the Valdambra held by Count Andreino Ubertini.[137]

But not all of the disruption in the Casentino and Valdambra was organized or sponsored by Arezzo's old feudal lords. Some of the rebels were indigenous to the communes whose Florentine rule they wished to overturn, and on occasion they used this period of hostilities to turn against their former feudal lords as well as the Florentine state. In October 1402 two men and a woman from Montebonico in the Valdambra[138] along with unnamed associates invaded the Florentine territory and stole twenty-five pigs from the lords of the Ricasoli family, now citizens of Florence.[139] In February 1403 four others without titles from this castle "rebelled," trying to seize the castle again, and again failed.[140] Later in the year, the *Capitano* condemned four men without titles from the same *castrum* for invading and attempting to incite rebellion in their village. The four were to be beheaded and their children and descendants labeled forever as rebels.[141]

Further west, three men styled as vagabonds, but identified from Monte Rinaldi in the Chianti, Largenina, and Castel San Giovanni, along with thirty unnamed followers, brought the castle of Monteluco in the Chianti to rebellion, but according to the court's description were unsuccessful because of resistance from Florentine soldiers and the "terigeni" of the castle.[142] In 1403 the *Podestà* condemned to death as rebels two men from villages in the Chianti (San Leonino and Ricciano) who had moved across the border into the territory of Siena. Along with associates from Siena and supported by a German military company of Domino Rappi and the Sienese army, they raided villages near the southern borders of Florence from San Gimignano through various places in the Chianti – Staggia, San Leonino, and Selvole – stealing farm animals and kidnapping men. They successfully occupied the *castrum* of San Leonino, "against the will of its men," but failed to take Selvole.[143]

By 1404, except for the so-called insurrections centered on Gambacorta's attempts to preserve Pisan independence within Pisan territory,[144] the countryside of Florence had returned to normal. Among

---

[137] CP, 2214, 100r–2r. For further reprisals against the Ubertini in the Romagna during 1403, see Dieci di Balìa: Missive Legazioni e commissarie, 3, 17r–v, 1403.v.7.
[138] It does not appear in Repetti, *Diz.* but is identified in the document as in the Valdambra.
[139] AP, 3886, 59r–v, 1402.i.8.   [140] CP, 2203, 147r–8r, 1403.viii.17 to viii.29.
[141] CP, 2206, 26r–v, 1403.xi.4.   [142] AP, 3856, 91r–2v, 1402.ix.27.
[143] AP, 3922, np, 1403.ix.12.
[144] CP, 2264, 74r–5v, 1405.ii.17; 136r, 1406.iv; 2269, 100r–1v, 1406.iv.7.

the usual cases of theft and assault, the occasional magnate rape or murder punctuates the otherwise monotonous inquests of rural crimes.[145] The closest approximations to rebellion (but not labeled as such) were a cattle raid and kidnapping for ransom in the mountains of Pistoia (Colle Lupo)[146] staged from the Bolognese castle of Casio and an armed protest against the *Podestà* at San Donato in Poggi.[147] In place of rebellions of mountain villages, collective protest had returned to handfuls of family members resisting the arrest of fathers and husbands for overdue debts to Florentine citizens, jailbreaks, illegal cutting of trees, and neglect of work.[148]

Except for two abortive "rebellions" in 1402, the internal disruptions of the war years 1397 through 1404 took place on or near Florence's frontiers and mostly in the mountains. In one, a soldier of the Duke of Milan held secret meetings in Florence and Lucca to equip men in Fucecchio and Santa Croce in the Valdarno Inferiore to revolt against Florence but was caught before his plot was hatched.[149]

The second was more significant. Similar to San Miniato's revolt of 1397, the leaders of Prato's revolt against Florentine domination in 1402 came from a former ruling family of Prato – the de Guazalutis (or Guazzalotri). Staffed by a priest, notaries, and other "friends and confidants" of the Guazzalotri, their clientele differed from the followers found in the rural insurrections studied above. A later inquest of the case in 1404 shows the centrality of the priest Guccio di Ser Angelo in the organization of the revolt. Secret meetings were held with these "conspirators" in his private room in Prato's church of San Marco. In addition the rebels negotiated with the duke's agents in Lombardy and Ravenna and promised "to place their *castrum* in the hands of the duke."[150]

Further, the revolt's strategy clearly came from the top: Lord Ugo Guazaluti tried to mislead the Florentine Ten of War into thinking he was about to attack Florence with a force of fifty to seventy lances, while he was leading his army of at least 1,200 foot soldiers from

---

[145] See the cases involving the Cavalcanti, Altoviti, and the Adimari; AP, 4003, 3r–7r, 1404.xii.3; 39r–40r, 1404.xii.24; 64r–5r, 1404.i.24; 66r–v, 1404.ix.20.

[146] This place name is not found in Repetti or the *catasto* of 1427.

[147] CP, 2232, 42r–4r; and 2264, 80r–2r, 1405.iii.11.

[148] For resisting arrest see CP, 2264, 116r–21r, 1405.iv.16; 2282, 27r–9v, 1406.i.25; 2309, 17r–19v, 1407.vi.7; for jailbreaks, 2269, 61r–4r, 1405.ii.2; 2309, 17r–19v, 1407.vi.7; for cutting trees, 2269, 69r–77r, 1405.ii.13; 2309, 100r–2r, 1407.x.22.   [149] AP, 3856, 30r–1r, 1402.ix.13.

[150] CP, 2232, 42r–4r, 1404.vii.1: "ipsumque rebellandum et abdicandum a dominio, jurisdictione, et potestate magnifici comunis Florentine pro duce Mediolani et ipsum castrum ponendum in manibus domini ducis" (42r).

the mountains of the Garfagnana into Prato's Porta Travaglia at night.[151]

The notaries' closer attention to the motivations that lay behind this city revolt lends insight into those taking place at the same time in the Alpi Fiorentine and soon afterwards in the Podere. In these, however, the court scribes wasted no ink in explaining the peasants' reasons for risking their lives. More than the recovery of ancient liberties or the general opportunities wrought by war and disruption, the cause made explicit in Prato's revolt was taxation.

As the principal leader of the insurrection, Lord Ugo Guazzalotri charged: "the massive forced loans and direct taxes imposed on us by the Commune of Florence, you know, are so great that we cannot possibly pay them."[152] He then promised to free Prato from Florentine domination to "liberate us from their forced loans." For Prato and other communities within the Florentine *contado* these "forced loans" were not the privileged *prestanze* charged on citizens of Florence with favorable rates of return but instead the "extraordinary" taxes based on the *estimo* that so ate into the wealth of the *contado* with the Albizzi tax of 1393 and its steep rise up to the turn of the century. As our figures showed earlier, these taxes were far heavier in the mountains than elsewhere; yet even the wealthy and privileged merchant class of Prato found them "impossible" to pay and risked rebellion.

The picture of internal dissent in the countryside takes on a different complexion in the criminal records from that obliquely exposed by the few chroniclers who conceded that such action might have been conceivable given Florentine republican liberty. First, the siege of Firenzuola, the recapturing of old Ubaldini strongholds, and the building of new bastions in the Alpi and the Podere Fiorentino were not simply military operations conducted and staffed by the Ubaldini lords and the armies of the Duke of Milan alone. Not only was the rank and file comprised largely of indigenous villagers from Florence's mountains, they were among those who devised strategy and led armed groups of "associates" in the siege of villages and towns. On at least one

[151] CP, 2159, np, 1402.vi.17; and 2169, 78r–80v, 1402.vi.13.
[152] CP, 2169, 78r: "scitis quod magne prestantie et imposite et ponuntur vobis et nobis pro comune Florentie et tam magne quod non possimus aliquo modo eas solvere." On the increasing laments in Prato over high taxation at the end of the fourteenth century, which led to emigration and the decline in the size of the city, see Franek Sznura, "Edilizia privata e urbanistica in tempo di crisi," in *Prato: Storia di una città*, I, part 2, pp. 305–6. The city shrunk from its second to its oldest city walls.

occasion they gave orders to men as exalted as the Duke of Milan's lieutenant at Bologna.

Nor did the invasions and building of mountain bastions end after a twenty-one-day campaign during the summer of 1402 as the chroniclers claimed. Instead of marking the end of hostilities, Giangaleazzo's death saw the intensification of resistance against Florence in the Alpi and its spread to the Podere, the Romagna Fiorentina, the Casentino, and southward through the Ubertini lands of the Valdambra.

Yet the criminal records only rarely report the peasants' own words beyond the details of military operations or afford any window into their motivations beyond the "spirit of the devil." They give only one face of Florence's rule – that of state violence – and only indirectly afford a glimpse of the rebels' successes by the numerous condemnations made *in contumacia* or *in absentia*.

We now turn to a source that gives another face to Florence's rule – that of negotiation and compromise after Florence had failed to shape its territorial state to its liking by military might.

6

Rebellion as seen from the provvisioni

Florence's day-to-day approval of petitions and promulgation of laws and decrees called the *provvisioni* show another side to the highlanders' revolts in 1402 not disclosed by the chronicles or the judicial records. In addition to portraying peasants as the leaders of insurrections in the Florentine Alps, even more so than the criminal records the decrees show a remarkable fact in the social history of Europe – villagers as victors of insurrection, who successfully negotiated special privileges and fiscal exemptions for themselves and their communities against their overlords, in this case the republican Commune of Florence.

The legislative machinery that approved these petitions and decrees relied on Florence's highest elected councils. The *Tre Maggiori*[1] (comprised of the Priors of the guilds and the *Gonfaloniere* of Justice, the *Gonfalonieri* of the sixteen companies or neighborhoods of the city, and the Twelve Good Men) determined which bills or petitions could proceed to be voted on by the larger legislative assemblies of the People (*Popolo*) and the Commune. Often other special committees, such as the Ten of War, assisted the *Tre Maggiori* in the selection of bills. The debates over some of these issues were preserved in volumes called the *Consulte e Pratiche*, but deliberations over matters such as peasant petitions, even when they involved issues as important as rebellion, find few traces in these records.[2] For these matters we must rely on two records – the *Libri fabarum* (or bean books), which did little more than sum up the votes on particular issues before the two councils,[3] and the *provvisioni*, which recorded these decrees and petitions fully but only those that passed the councils and became law.

---

[1] On these institutions, see Fubini, "Italia quattrocentesca," pp. 21 and 30.

[2] Most of the discussions in the *Consulte e Pratiche* concerning the rural districts of the territory dealt either with defense and fortifications or taxation. Only occasionally did humdrum matters such as the allocation of a *Podestà*'s duties within a rural district come up for debate in these chambers; see Consulte e Pratiche, 35, 70v, 1401.i.25.

[3] For this source, see Fubini, "Le edizioni dei 'Libri fabarum,'" in *I Consigli della repubblica fiorentina. Libri fabarum XVII (1338–1340)*, ed. by Francesca Klein (Rome, 1995), pp. xi–xxi.

These bodies passed laws ranging from what the Priors and *Gonfalonieri* ate to how much to feed the town lions, from the adjudication of citizen bankruptcies to the amount of jewelry patriciate ladies were allowed to wear. They were also intimately involved in the affairs of the territory, particularly with questions of defense. In conjunction with the Ten of War and the Officials of the Towers, they determined which localities were in need of new defenses, the dimensions and costs of repairs, and who was responsible for supplying the labor, the materials, the fees, and the munitioning of castles old and new. The *Tre Maggiori* and councils voted on the formation of special committees such as the board of the *estimo*, which authorized new tax surveys and determined the tax base for the countryside. Finally, these bodies heard petitions from individuals and communities from the city and the countryside, which pleaded for deliverance from condemnations, fines, public debts, and, most often, taxes.

This chapter will investigate the explosion between 1403 and 1406 of one type of petition that made it through the *Tre Maggiori*'s vetting and the two larger councils' voting. These were peasant petitions, lodged by peasant "ambassadors" on behalf of their communities.[4] To understand the distinctiveness of these years, we need to set them against a backdrop of earlier peasant pleas, and the ways these councils treated "rebels" from the countryside, whether feudal lords or peasants.

First, in the years 1347 to 1402 the councils approved on average 8.5 petitions annually from communities in the countryside or less than 4 percent of the business approved by them.[5] In 1403 that number increased by over five times, soaring to a record high of forty-four, then

---

[4] Local statutes established the procedures for electing the community's ambassadors; see *Statuti della comunità*, 420 (Mangona), c. 89, 47r: "Che i consiglieri possino elegiere imbasciadori." At Mangona, the ambassadors were elected when the need arose to send representatives to Florence. They were to note when they left and returned from Florence and were to be paid a salary of 15s each. Also, *ibid.*, 624 (Palazzuolo, Podere Fiorentino, 1406), c. 38, 22r: "Di dare ambasciadori a chi gli domanda"; *ibid.*, 13 (Anghiari, 1387), 116r: "De ambasciatoribus"; *ibid.*, 317 (Firenzuola, 1418), c. 18, 12v: "Del salario delli ambasciadori"; and c. 19, 12v: "Di quelli che andassino a firenze senza licentia in nome della comunita"; 171 (Castel Focognano, 1385), c. 7, 7v–8r: "De electione ambaxiatori et eorum salario et de pena non facientium ambaxiatam"; 447 (Montagna Fiorentina, 1396), c. 27, 26r: "De salario ambasciatorum comunis."

[5] With 294 folios, *Provv. reg.*, 91 was an average-sized volume. In the year covered by this volume, 1402, the councils met twenty-four times, approving 224 laws, decrees, and petitions. For that year (and I believe for many others) the *Libri fabarum* fail to report all the legislation finally formalized in the more authoritative registers of the *provvisioni*. According to the *Libri fabarum*'s abbreviated tallies of votes on individual bills and petitions, the councils met twenty-four times in 1402 (but on five of these occasions passed no legislation) and approved only 190 bills, thirty-four fewer than in the *provvisione*'s register.

tapering off to thirty-seven, then twenty-eight, over the next three years.[6] As for the villages awarded special concessions, from the absolution of condemnations to long-term tax immunities, the figures are even more impressive. In 1403, the government's awards of tax relief and canceled or reduced public debts and back taxes went to 117 rural parishes and villages; in 1404, 94; and in 1405, 71. These clustered along the mountainous periphery of the Florentine state, following closely the battle lines outlined by the insurrections adjudicated in the criminal tribunals (see map 4, p. 262).

In these years entire sessions of the councils on several occasions were devoted almost exclusively to quelling discontent in the countryside, reducing public debts owed by peasant communes, and awarding them tax concessions.[7] Such rural matters temporarily displaced the normal grist of the government's decrees – urban matters, most often the affairs of the patriciate such as bankruptcies, pleas for lowering their taxes (*prestanze*), elections to special committees, and appointments to posts in the territory.

In addition to this quantitative change, a qualitative one permeated the government's treatment of peasant rebels. Previously, the rhetoric of pleas from peasant communes for the remission of penalties, extensions of deadlines, or grants of tax concessions were pitched in terms of "humble supplication," invoking the state's "misericordia" or its "paternal piety" that would be "decorous in dealing with its children."[8] Before 1403, Florence rarely treated rebels or rebellion against Florence in these forums any less lightly than did its criminal tribunals. Instead, it often added military might to shore up the criminal courts' judgments.

For instance, in 1349 following the Ubaldini's robbery and massacre of merchants on the Alpine passes of the Mugello (one of whom happened to be a close friend of Petrarch), the councils voted to allocate 450 florins to purchase various war machines to retaliate and destroy this feudal family.[9] In 1373, the councils went further, allocating 30,000

---

[6] In 1403 (Provv. reg., 92) the councils met twenty-one times and passed or approved 240 laws, decrees, and petitions.   [7] See, for instance, the sessions in the *Libri fabarum*.

[8] See, for instance, Provv. reg., 38, 142r: "quod decet paternam pietatem consilium capere pro filiis."

[9] Provv. reg., 36, 89r–v: "Pro expensis exercitus contra Ubaldinos": "pro crochis panellis, funibus, scalis ligonibus, palis ferreis, bechastris, virgis ferreis, agutis, clovis, et aliis feramentis et rebus et hominibus et personis missis seu mitendis et emptis seu emendis pro fulcimento felicis cavalcate seu exercitus noviter missi seu facti contra Ubaldinos rebelles seu inimicos comunis Florentie seu terras per ipsos occupatas." On these raids, see Stefani, *Cronica*, r. 639, p. 233. On Petrarch's outrage, see his *Rerum Familiarum*, transl. by Aldo S. Bernardo (Albany, N.Y., 1975), I, bk. 8, letter 9, pp. 422–8; Cherubini, *Una comunità*, p. 10; and Casini, *Dizionario*, I, p. 151.

florins and declaring war on the Ubaldini to end once and for all their "treachery and tyranny" toward pilgrims, merchants, and, according to the Florentine councils, their own peasants.[10]

Beyond war, the councils used fiscal policy to break peasant ties with feudal lords and to draw them into Florentine allegiance. Immediately after the Black Death, Florence intensified its attempt to consolidate its power and authority within its own boundaries against its internal enemies – the Battifolle, Ubaldini, Pazzi, and Ubertini. In 1349 the councils allocated monies to "augment" the dimensions of the then frontier town of Scarperia to protect those *comitatini* who already lived there and to attract new peasants from the surrounding countryside by promising them protection and extinction of all feudal obligations owed to their lords, the Ubaldini.[11] In the same year, Florence offered protection to the commune of Burro in the Valdarno Superiore[12] after it had "rebelled against the enemies and rebels of Florence" (the feudal family, the Pazzi) who had held them "under the yoke of tyranny for many years." By their deeds, these peasants had proved themselves "faithful and devoted friends of Florence" and thus would be protected against the Pazzi and all other Ghibelline rebels of Florence.[13]

In the following year, the Florentines captured their feudal enemies Andrea di Francesco and Francesco di Biordo of the Ubertini clan, who possessed vast estates and castles in the Valdambra. Florence held them for ransom, demanding 2,000 florins for their release, 400 florins of which went to aid Bucine, which had lost many men and had suffered damages to its fortifications in Florence's war against the Ubertini.[14] The struggle to keep Bucine even produced a secular "martyr," Ser Arrigo, a Florentine

---

[10] Provv. reg., 61, 64r–6r, 1373.v.30.

[11] *Ibid.*, 37, 12r–13r, 1349.x.2: "Et pro liberatione ipsorum hominium et personarum . . . quod omnes et singuli facientes domum et habitationem saltem per decenium in dicto castro . . . et eorum filii et descendentes imperpetuum essent liberi et franchi ab omni vinculo, nexu, et jugo servitutis, fidelitatis, et homagii et accommadisgie et angarie et pangarie." In 1357, the government granted Scarperia tax immunities "in renumeration of its first defense against the armies of the Archbishop of Milan and rebels within the territory of Florence."

[12] Eighteen kilometers from Loro Ciuffenna in the Pratomagno.

[13] Provv. reg., 37, 27v–8r, 1349.x.23: "Quod prout notum est ipsi homines et universitas favore comunitatuum Florentie . . . dictum castrum rebellaverunt ab inimicis et rebellibus comunis Florentie supradictis Pazzis Vallis Arni Superioris qui eos jugo tirannico multo tempore tenuerant et ipsi facti se fecerunt amicos, fideles, et devotos comunis Florentie et tenuerunt et tenent partem quelfam et Sancta Romana Ecclesia contra de Pazzis et alios rebelles Ghibellines comunis Florentie."

[14] Provv. reg., 38, 12v–13r, 1350.iv.7. Also see the case of San Martino Leona (Arezzo), awarded exemptions from all taxes for one year and renewed the next year to reward its men and women for breaking their allegiance with their Ubertini lords; Provv. reg., 39, 54r–v, 1351.xi.22; and 40, 30v–1r, 1352.xii.3.

official and spy in the Valdambra, who was captured by the Ubertini. Wounded by their beatings, he took eight months to recover and because of his physical condition was easily captured again and tortured by extracting five teeth. To compensate Arrigo and his family, the councils fined his Ubertini captors and levied special taxes on six communes in the Valdambra, presumably for their Ubertini support and sympathies.[15]

With several exceptions, legislative measures to combat feudal enemies in the Mugello, Valdarno Superiore, and Valdambra quietened for the next two decades. After Florence had smashed the rebellion of the counts and commune of Montecarelli in 1360,[16] the government passed laws to encourage loyalty to Florence, granting this mountain commune certain privileges in its act of submission to Florence, including a six-year exemption from most taxes and annulment of condemnations to fifty-five of its men convicted as rebels.[17] But such a reconciliation to peasant and feudal rebels before 1403 was the exception. In 1361 Florence, instead, centralized its authority and judicial court structure by forming the new vicariate of the Mugello to help combat the problem of Ubaldini "rebellion and sedition."[18] Further, after San Miniato's abortive revolt of 1367, instead of abolishing condemnations and granting tax relief, the Florentine government forced this war-torn commune to accept a loan of 2,000 gold florins to hire "Guelf" soldiers to prevent the people of San Miniato from further attempts to free themselves from Florentine rule.[19]

The most serious expenditure by Florence to extirpate its feudal opposition, however, came in 1373 when the councils allocated 30,000 florins "to exterminate the Ubaldini."[20] For this exceptional sum, Florence charged the entire *contado* and district for the month of May an "extraordinary" tax of 10s on the *lira* in addition to the "ordinary" *estimo* at 12s.[21] The war did more than blunt the Ubaldini's threats to Florentine control or to merchants crossing mountain passes. State violence and taxation took its toll on the peasantry as well. Between the two redactions of the *estimi*, 1371 and 1383, the population of one of the epicenters of Ubaldini power, Montecarelli, was halved, from 116 families with 535 individuals to 62 families with 225.[22]

---

[15] *Ibid.*, 39, 179r–80r, 1352.vii.27.
[16] In the 1350s, Montecarelli had been an Ubaldini stronghold in its attacks on Scarperia; see *ibid.*, 40, 64v–5r, 1352.ii.19.
[17] *Ibid.*, 48, 1r–6v, 1360.viii.27. These were mostly the same as listed in the *Podestà*'s sentence earlier that year, including Count Tano and his extended clan.   [18] *Ibid.*, 48, 165r–6r, 1360.iii.23.
[19] *Ibid.*, 55, 88v–9r, 1367.xi.8.   [20] *Ibid.*, 61, 64r–6r, 1373.v.30.   [21] *Ibid.*, 73r–v.
[22] See figures 3.1, 3.2, and 3.8.

But violence was only one of several means to control the Alpi and upper Mugello. Even before electing a war committee for the 1373 massacre of the Ubaldini and their peasant followers, the councils had created the new "commune of Firenzuola." It comprised the three ancient *pievi* that formerly had formed the "Alpe degli Ubaldini" – Cornacchiaia, Camaiore, and Bordignano with their nineteen parishes (*populi*). The decree was richly infused with Florentine republican ideology on the virtues and vices of liberty and tyranny. According to its preamble, these communities had suffered "the cruel lacerations of thirty-two years of Ubaldini occupation, during which time they had been violently divested of their possessions."[23] The councils blamed the "tyranny of the Ubaldini" for these peasants' "cessation of obedience" to Florence. They now granted them the opportunity "to return to [Florence's] paternal dominion" and thus "to return to the path of truth, equality, and justice." To attract their loyalty, the councils (1) absolved all those from these *pievi*, except members of the Ubaldini, of all condemnations of crimes committed before February 15, 1373; (2) freed them from any taxes or long-terms rents, or feudal bonds (*ad afficttus seu census pensiones vel accomandigias*) due to the Florentine government before February 15; (3) granted them a five-year exemption from all taxes and gabelles, except the toll tax, the gabelle on contracts, and "payments to maintain an army and cavalry to defend their lands and other places in the Alpi and Podere Fiorentino." In return, these peasants were obliged to "construct and demolish castles" as benefited the Commune of Florence. Further, they were given the right (and obligation) to formulate their own statutes and to fight under the "arms and insignia" of the commune of Firenzuola.

Later in the year, Florence pursued another strategy of divide and conquer by buying off the members of one branch of the Ubaldini clan, granting them rights as citizens (*popolani*), and exempting them from the reprisals and condemnations due to rebels.[24] But, unlike the Pignole branch of the Ubaldini, no peasant rebels (that I know of) successfully engaged in negotiations with the Florentine government until after the rebellion of Civitella in 1397. In 1391 the Florentine councils granted the captured rebels of Raggiolo in the Montagna Fiorentina a reprieve from

---

[23] Provv. reg., 61, 39r–42r, 1373.iv.28: "iam sunt triginta duo anni vel circa et ab ipso tempore citra fuerunt occupati per nobiles de Ubaldinis et per ipsorum tirannidem crudeliter lacerati et bonis et rebus ipsorum per violentiam expoliati."

[24] *Ibid.*, 101r–2r, 1373.viii.26; also see previous chapter.

their life sentences in the Stinche. But here clemency came from God, not from negotiations with a victorious peasantry.[25]

By contrast, the negotiations following the fall of Civitella to enemy hands marked a new departure in Florence's treatment of peasant rebels. Unlike the law creating the commune of Firenzuola in 1373, the Florentine councils in 1398 did not cloak their grants to "disobedient" rebels in the usual rhetoric of "tyranny and liberty." Instead, at Civitella Florence presented its agreements more straightforwardly: "For the recuperation of the said *castrum* and its fortification certain agreements and promises have been made."[26] It admitted that Civitella and especially its keep was unassailable and could be regained only through negotiation.[27] The councils then canceled all death sentences to the four ringleaders of the revolt in the previous year, rubbed their names from Florence's register of rebels, the *libro maleabbiatorum*, and granted them privileges to carry offensive and defensive weapons anywhere in the city, *contado*, and district of Florence – a coveted privilege usually reserved to the urban nobility of Florence.[28] In addition, they were to have safe passage to move, live, and exchange money, salt, and goods anywhere in the territory of Florence. These rebels were not military captains, noblemen, or Florentine patricians in exile; they were commoners of this agrarian center seen earlier in the condemnations of the *Capitano del Popolo*, identified only by patronymics or their nicknames – the Plum, the Club, and the Cow.[29]

These guarantees and privileges evidently were not enough to sway the rebels into relinquishing control of their fortifications. Two weeks later the councils approved a second set of negotiations,[30] which again

[25] Florence liberated the defeated peasants in a ritual offering in reverence to Jesus Christ, Mary, and John the Baptist at the Baptistery of San Giovanni; *ibid.*, 80, 88v–90r, 1391.viii.26.

[26] *Ibid.*, 87, 74v–8r, 1398.v.17: "pro recuperatione dicti castri et eius casseri facta fuisse certa pacta et promissiones tenentes."

[27] *Ibid.*, "Legum subspensio pro factis Civitelle": "Ut qualiter assertum est quod dictum castrum et maxime casserum quod videtur qui in expugnalie aliter habere non posse. Et attendentes ut dicitur quod rehabere dictum castrum est summe utilitatis et honoris comunis predicti et ideo volentes."

[28] Such grants made to the Guicciardini, Strozzi, and other of Florence's most esteemed and powerful families can be found in the *pergamene* preserved in the Diplomatico of the Archivio Generale (ASF).

[29] Their names as drafted in the *provvisione* were Minuccius Angeli de Civitella sive dela casa de Civitella; Pierus Miglioris alius dictus del Mazzo de Ambra; Jacobus Francisci alius del Sucina de Ciggiano alius etiam dictus el Naccha sive Vacha; Pierus del Foresto vocatus Cortona de Sintigliano comunitate Aretii.

[30] Provv. reg., 87, 89r–93r, 1398.v.30: "Circa negotia civitelle."

conceded that the town could be reobtained only through negotiation. First, Florence sweetened the pill for the original four, plus another named Puccio di Meo, by granting lifetime exemptions from ordinary and extraordinary taxes and the rights to transfer these immunities to all their descendants down the male line forever. Second, it extended absolutions for crimes of rebellion and other concessions to another twenty-six men. Like the first four, they were commoners, identified by no more than patronymics and nicknames.

Contrary to the chroniclers' reports, this list of leaders does not link Civitella's fall to outside agitation. Of the twenty-six, twenty-two came from Civitella and the others from nearby villages in the former *contado* of Arezzo – Ciggiano, Battifolle, Castiglione Fibocchi, and Foiano. Yet further "chapters" in the agreements suggest that Civitella may not have been united in support of the rebels' cause. To ensure that the rebels "would have peace" with the rest of the community of Civitella, the Florentine Ten of War granted the original four plus Puccio a bevy of guards (*una bandena*) comprised of twenty-five "famuli" or soldiers, five for each rebel, to be employed during their lifetimes and paid from Florence's military coffers. In addition to a regional conflict against Florence, had this rebellion arisen from factional clashes between rival clans, like the Cancellieri's takeover of the Montagna di Pistoia only at a lower social standing?

Unlike in later negotiations between Florence and its *alpigiani* to the north, the leaders of Civitella negotiated only for themselves and a small coterie of followers; they won nothing (and, as far as the documents reveal, asked for nothing) for the people of Civitella. Instead, in a subsequent act the commune of Civitella came forward, not as victors but "as unhappy and desolate men and women" to beg for clemency before the Florentine councils because of the damages suffered in the rebellion. They claimed to have seen "all of their property destroyed" and many of their men captured by the enemy (who unfortunately was not specified). Saddled with heavy ransoms to free their neighbors, they asserted that if Florence did not grant them tax relief, they would be forced to go off begging (*per mundum pergere mendicando*). Although Florence answered their cries, they were not as well rewarded as Florence's adversaries in Civitella. The commune as a whole won only a two-year exemption from most of the taxes, including the salt tax and the honorific gift of wax to Florence on the feast of John the Baptist.[31]

---

[31] *Ibid.*, 93v–4v, 1398.vi.30.

While the threat of warfare with Milan, Siena, and the Ubertini may have conditioned Florence's negotiations with Civitella, no other group of peasant rebels or commoners bargained so well until 1403, despite the escalation of war in the interim. As in the criminal records, peasant protest appears to have been remarkably quiet between 1398 and 1403 as far as the *provvisioni* reveal. The only favorable treatment to rebels during the war was negotiated by noblemen, not commoners, when in 1399 and 1400 Count Robert of Battifolle made incursions into Florentine territory, occupied castles previously loyal to Florence, and "plundered men and animals" in a zone called the "Alpibus Cascie" on the western flanks of the Pratomagno.[32] By "returning to Florentine devotion" (which amounted to no more than a cease-fire), Count Robert convinced Florence to cancel death sentences against himself and his rebel followers.

By April 1403, this silence ended suddenly as peasant petitions began to fill the *Tre Maggiori* and councils' business in unprecedented numbers. These petitions were among the first to mention rebellion as a cause for deserving tax relief as well as to point directly at state extortion and high taxation as the root causes of peasants' inability to pay. The first came from the center, not the periphery – from Borgo San Lorenzo, which had not in fact attempted to overturn Florentine rule.

The decree shows more than the judicial records just how far the activities of the rebels had spread down the mountains into the hills and plains. In addition, a new spirit of negotiation and criticism of the Florentine state permeates Borgo's petition in marked contrast to the standard rhetoric of filial piety and supplication. The decree began by saying that the councils had heard from many of Borgo's ambassadors concerning "their taxes, public debts, poverty, and loss of men." It then specified the cause of this misery: "the expense of the extraordinary tax (*estimo*) forced on them in the past year because of the rebellions in the Alpi and the Podere."[33] In response, Florence shifted 1,300 florins of debts from Borgo's books to Florence's funded debt, the *Monte*.

On the next day, the councils approved another petition citing rebellion as the cause of the peasants' needs. This one came from "the many

[32] *Ibid.*, 89, 190r–2r, 1400.xii.11.
[33] *Ibid.*, 92, 29r–30r, 1403.iv.26: "Pro expensis extraordinarie pro quibus coactum fuit ipsum comune Burgi ab anno citra occasione rebellionum factarum in partibus Alpium et Poderis et multa alia eorum incommoda."

parishes near the Alps," near the Futa pass, claiming that "the rebellion" had broken out in the Alpi Fiorentine and the Podere and "had spread through large parts of the Mugello." It pleaded that their houses had been burnt, their men captured, and their property stolen as much by the rebels as by the enemy army.[34] On the same day, another petition was approved from the other side of Florence's territory in its southern-most corner, the parishes of the *pieve* of Presciano in the Valdambra, citing the rebellion of the Ubertini as the cause of these parishioners' inability to pay their debts.[35]

By June 1403 a new set of petitions came from the north, from the heartland of the rebellion. These were the petitions of the perpetrators as opposed to the victims of 1402 and were more in the form of demands than of traditional pleas. The first set out an agreement between Florence and the mountain dwellers who had found a safe haven across the border in the mountains of Bologna, where they continued to launch cattle raids and invasions against Florence and its stronghold, Firenzuola.[36]

Anxious to secure the castle of Cavrenno and its surrounding popu-lation of the commune of Pietramala,[37] the Ten of War and the Florentine councils had to go much further in their negotiations with these rebels than even earlier with the rebels of Civitella. In addition to favors passed on to the leadership, Florence's 1403 negotiations granted privileges to mountain communities in the Alpi Fiorentine on a scale not yet seen in previous acts of submission or peasant pleas.

The name of this act reflects its character. Unlike earlier "acts of sub-mission" where new territory came into Florentine hands by purchase, force, or desire on the part of the subjects, this one was called "nego-tium" and not "submissio." It differed from other Florentine acts of acquisition in another sense as well by pertaining as much to villagers

---

[34] *Ibid.*, 36v–7r, 1403.v.27.   [35] *Ibid.*, 38r–9r.
[36] *Ibid.*, 92, 87v–90v, 1403.vi.22: "Del Cavrenno, Petramala."
[37] On the strategic border separating Florence and Bologna, Pietramala (851 m) was higher than any village in the Alpi Fiorentine. On the Ten's reports from their agents, Pierozzo di Biagio degli Strozzi and Sino de Beffadi, on their negotiations with the men of Cornacchiaia, Pietramala, and Castro and their plans to seize other castles from the Ubaldini, see Dieci di Balìa: Missive Legazioni e commissarie, 3, 21r–v, 1403.v.29 and 1403.vi.1. On July 23, 1403, Matteo Castellani wrote from Volterra to the *Signoria* advising them of the "grande utile" of acquiring Cavrenno; Signori: Responsive originali, 4. For a short description of Cavrenno and its importance as a castle bastion, see Traversari, *Hodoeporicon*, p. 114. Repetti, *Diz.*, I, p. 466 (Caprenno) gives no information on the conditions of its 1403 submission to Florence but does note Pietramala's sub-mission (IV, pp. 212–13) and dates it 1404. In addition to Bruscoli, Cavrenno, Pietramala, and Piancaldoli and by similar negotiations with Florentine alpine peasants the Ten tried to seize Baragazza but did not succeed; it still remains in the *contado* of Bologna.

from other places in the *contado* of Florence (the Alpi Fiorentine), forced from their homes by high taxes and state violence, as it did to the new acquisitions of Cavrenno and Pietramala.[38]

First, Florence granted Pietramala one of the longest and most sweeping exemptions from taxes seen in these documents; "every man and woman" was exempted from all taxes and gabelles for fifteen years. Second, without explanation, eight men of Pietramala were granted perpetual exemptions from all taxes and the right to hand these privileges to their children down the male line. Third, Florence protected these men from any debts they might have incurred to the commune of Bologna or to any group or individual from Bologna. Fourth, Florence extended the fifteen-year exemptions to anyone from the *contado* of Bologna who would come to live in Pietramala. In return Florence asked of the peasants only one symbolic gesture of allegiance: the ceremonial offer of a silk banner (*palium*) worth 5 gold florins on the feast of John the Baptist.[39]

The second and longer portion of this exceptionally complex decree went beyond the rights of acquisition to the new commune of Pietramala and concerned negotiations between Florence and its 1402 rebels within the *contado*. They bargained to have their names rubbed from the book of rebels and their condemnations and banishments canceled, including "all crimes, condemnations, and delinquencies made, committed, or perpetuated" by anyone from Pietramala or from "any commune, parish, or village" within the Alpi Fiorentine from July 1402 (when the rebels began their siege of the Alpi and Firenzuola) until the day of the agreement's signing by the Florentine councils. Further, no official or rector of the city, *contado*, or district of Florence could pursue these men for any crime, including murder and rebellion.[40]

None of the listed rebels possessed a title or were identified by more than a patronymic and their place of origin. The first three were from Pietramala, in Bolognese territory at the time of the rebellion. But they

---

[38] Consider, for instance, the "pro submissionis" of the neighboring border village of Piancaldoli, which Florence acquired through negotiations with the papacy in 1405. The document promised the men of the village some exemptions from several taxes but did not even specify what these would be or how long they would last; instead, it left that for the *Signoria* to determine, "at their convenience"; Provv. reg., 94, 5v–6v, 1405.iv.4.

[39] On this "gift" and increasing resentment over it among subject communities both in Tuscany and Lombardy at the end of the fifteenth century, see Chittolini, "Civic Religion and the Countryside in Late Medieval Italy," in *City and Countryside*, p. 78. These negotiations became the core of Pietramala's and Cavrenno's statutes approved in 1403; Statuti, 577, 1r.

[40] Provv. reg., 92, 89r. Among the absolutions granted, the document adds: "especially the murder of Jacopino Nutelli sive Michaelis from Friene" but fails to disclose his special importance.

were the exceptions set apart from the main list of absolved rebels as a separate "item." Next came privileges to twenty men, seventeen of whom originated from villages in the Alpi Fiorentine.[41] They had migrated to Pietramala either during the revolt of 1402 or, as the document makes clear, in the last years of the fourteenth century, when Florentine taxation began to escalate and to charge especially severely mountain peasants in the Alpi.

Unlike the criminal sentences, these decrees show not a single Ubaldini or any other nobleman among the rebels, who now were to benefit from these negotiations. The tax registers yield further clues about these rebels. Of those from Castro singled out for special treatment, four can be traced to the *lira* registers of 1394 and 1402 and to the *estimo* of 1393. Two of them appear in the criminal records of 1402 – Cinuccino di Bertino and Stefano called Tanaio di Viviano – as strategists in the siege of Firenzuola and the building of bastions in the mountains over Firenzuola during the summer of 1402. The third was Cinuccino's brother, Giusto. The decree further reveals a point not disclosed in the criminal record of 1402: these brothers and Stefano, who had been among the wealthiest inhabitants of Castro, had abandoned their lands and probably the greater part of their furnishings and animals to escape Florentine taxation; from their mountain hamlet under the Futa they had moved upward across the border to the Bolognese commune of Pietramala.

The fifth rebel to receive privileges is an exception to this group of peasant ringleaders as well as to the other indicted peasant rebels whom we previously linked to the tax records. Agnolino del Merlo's assessed wealth and tax base were at the bottom of Castro's tax assessments in 1394 (a mere 2s),[42] and in 1402 for his joint household with his two brothers, Nanne and Cininus, it totaled only 5s.[43] In the *estimo* of 1393, Nanne and Agnolino were listed in a single household comprising eight members. They owed a long-term or feudal rent (*affictus perpetuus*) of 12.5 *staii* of grain a year to the Ubaldini but possessed no taxable property; the scribe described their household as "povero e miserabile." Nonetheless, Agnolino was neither young nor without family obligations. In 1393 he was thirty-eight with a wife aged twenty and two young

---

[41] The three exceptions were subjects of Florence; one from the city; another a mountain villager from further west in the district of Florence, Colognole in the Garfagnana; and the third from Corella in the Mugello. The list shows the importance of kinship ties in linking peasant rebels. Of the four from Cornacchiaia, all were brothers, as were the three from le Valle and two from Castro.   [42] Estimo 286, 65v.   [43] *Ibid.*, 287, 199v and 286, 65v.

children (four and two). In the revolt of 1402 he would have been middle aged at forty-seven.[44]

Next, Florence absolved six from the alpine villages of Cornacchiaia and Castro (including the brothers Cinuccino and Giusto) of all debts owed to Florence or to their communes. As with the first eight of Pietramala, the councils granted these migrant rebels, their children, and descendants down the male line other privileges not extended to Pietramala as a whole – perpetual exemptions from all taxes, forced loans, and gabelles due to Florence or to any other parish or village. They were never to be registered by the treasury or recorded in the *estimo*, and any officer who attempted to do so would be punished.

Three brothers from Cornacchiaia who had left their Florentine homesteads thirteen years earlier acquired further privileges – the right to return anywhere within the *contado* of Florence and fifteen-year immunities from all taxes and gabelles. In addition, they were given the unprecedented authority to select any man or woman from Cornacchiaia or Castro who had left his or her mountain hamlet for foreign places in July 1402 (the beginning of the siege on Firenzuola). If selected, these former neighbors would enjoy the rights "to return, stay, and live securely anywhere in the city, *contado*, or district of Florence notwithstanding any acts of arson, robbery, extortion, excess, or wrongdoing committed from July, 1402 to the present."[45] They would also gain exemptions from all taxes and gabelles for ten years. Further, six of the above-mentioned rebels plus all those nominated by the three brothers could not be forced to pay any previous debts to any individual for the next five years.

If the lists of "usciti" from the *estimo* of 1412 can be trusted, most of those selected may have opted to return to their previous abodes rather than leave for this newly incorporated mountain *borgo*, despite its appealing tax exemptions. Castro's 1412 survey does not list a family which had left for Cavrenno or Pietramala since 1402, and Caburaccio's *estimo* lists only one. But the earliest date of out-migration

---

[44] *Ibid.*, 218, 280r. Unfortunately, the *estimo* for this commune in 1401/2 does not survive.

[45] Provv. reg., 92, 89r: "Item quod omnia et singulares homines et persone de comuni Chornachiarii et de communi Castri qui se abstentaverunt a kalendari mensis Julii anno domini Mccccii citra et iverunt ad habitationem extra comitatem Florentie solummodo illi ex predictis qui erunt nominati per predictes Bonomem, Gianoctium, et Stefanum aut per maiorem partem supra inventium ex eis possint reverti a stare et habitare secure in civitate, comitatu, et districtu Florentie non obstante quacumque arsura, incendio, robaria, vel alia extorsione aut excessu vel malefitio per eos factis, commissis, vel perpetratis a dictis kalendari mensis Julii citra usque in presentem diem et sic ipsius effectualiter observetur."

recorded in Castro's 1412 register is 1404, after hostilities with Florence had ceased and after Florence's offer of tax exemptions had ended. Before that date, many may have migrated to these two border strongholds but in the confusion were not recorded by the village commissioner. Indeed, the opening lines of Castro's *estimo* suggests just this: "many had been lost" (*perduti*) and had left for the *contado* of Bologna.[46]

A further item granted licenses to carry offensive and defensive arms anywhere in the city, *contado*, and district of Florence to twelve of the previously listed twenty, plus to any four nominated by the three brothers from Cornacchiaia. The next item threatened with severe punishments anyone who violated the special rights extended to these rebels or any of the items within this decree. Finally, any village, parish, or commune within the *contado* of Bologna that wished to swear obedience to Florence in a public document within four months would receive exemptions from all taxes and gabelles for ten years, that is, if the above three brothers voted in favor of that village's annexation. Thus, in effect, the three rebel peasants were given prerogatives formerly reserved to Florence's highest councils – the rights to incorporate new territory into the dominion of Florence.[47] This long and unprecedented grant of privileges passed the council of the Commune by a wide margin of 174 black beans (pro) to 34 against.[48]

Later in the year, Florence agreed to a similar set of negotiations and privileges to rebels in the *castrum* of Bruscoli, again on the Bolognese border and again to acquire a strategic castle on the Apennine crest.[49] Again, the Ten of War were instrumental in the negotiations "for the honor and expansion of public matters." And again the acquisition had a positive impact on rebel villagers from within the Alpi Fiorentine. Fourteen rebels from the Alpi were absolved from all crimes including rebellion and their names rubbed from the book of misdeeds. They received the licenses to carry weapons through the territory of Florence, which could pass these privileges on to their sons down the male line; they gained perpetual exemptions from all direct taxes and some

---

[46] Estimo 225, 363r–v.
[47] Two other acts granted special favors to individuals. In one the Cornacchiaia rebels were absolved from a loan owed to a man in Scarperia and could not be charged for any other personal debt for twenty years. In another, two from Castro were freed of all debts for ten years.
[48] Provv. reg., 92, 90v. The next day the councils approved another act again absolving the twenty above-listed rebels, *ibid.*, 94v–96r, 1403.vi.27. Evidently, later scribes or lawyers who consulted these registers took notice of these *provvisioni*. Inside the wooden cover of this register "Cavrenna" is scribbled with the votes approving this act in two separate hands, one from the late fifteenth or sixteenth century, the other from the seventeenth century.
[49] *Ibid.*, 248v–51r, 1403.xii.22: "Bannitorum de Bruscoli."

gabelles but unlike the expatriate rebels of Cavrenno and Pietramala did not receive exemptions from the gate gabelles, those on contracts, retail wine, and meat.

What the commune as a whole won from these negotiations is hard to know. The act's next chapter began with a clause that signaled the commune's as opposed to the leaders' agreements – "Item. Quod Comune Bruscoli cum suis hominibus et personis" – but the notary left the next half page blank, probably awaiting the final negotiations. As in the negotiations with Pietramala, names and facts were later inserted by different scribes into spaces previously left blank by the notary of the *Riformagioni*. Evidence from the *estimo* of 1412, however, suggests that the Florentines must have agreed to community-wide exemptions not unlike those made to Pietramala and with attractive terms for new migrants. Bruscoli was not surveyed for taxes until the *catasto* of 1427. Moreover, in the *estimi* of other communities in the Alpi it appears to have been a haven for those seeking tax immunities. From the village of Casaglia alone, eleven of twenty-three families that had left their village since 1402 moved to the newly incorporated *borgo* of Bruscoli.[50]

After this blank half page, Florence made another unprecedented concession. Six of the rebels were nominated for life-time positions as military officers to be paid by Florence and given the authority to hire forty-four shieldsmen and crossbowmen (*pavesarios et balistarios*), paid and equipped by Florence to defend its borders.[51] Thus in these acts Florence's highlanders became transformed: from rebels against the state, they now received the pay and status as defenders of the Florentine realm, and more, even became the spearhead of Florentine expansion north into the Bolognese Apennines.

A year later Florence finalized negotiations with the thirteen parishes of the Podere Fiorentino and Casaglia which lay "juxta alpes" just below Crespino.[52] The grants and privileges were divided into two parts, those for the thirteen parishes of the Podere and that for the

---

[50] Estimo 225, 576r–v. By contrast, Bruscoli had not previously appeared as a destination for Florentine migrants from my sample villages in any *estimo* except 1393, when two households from neighboring Castro crossed the Futa pass into this Bolognese mountain commune (Estimo 218, 286r–v).

[51] This act was followed by another, which reiterated the cancellation of all crimes of rebellion for the previously listed fourteen men, *ibid.*, 257r–8r, 1403.xii.28.

[52] This parish does not appear in the *catasto* of 1427; see Repetti, *Diz.*, I, p. 494: Casaglia del Mugello, sixteen kilometers northeast of Borgo San Lorenzo on the Apennine pass between Florence and Faenza may have been the first of Florence's planned "terre nuove" in the Mugello; see Pirillo, "Uno caso di pianificazione."

single parish of Casaglia. The decree began by declaring that "the major part" of those from the Podere had rebelled against the Commune of Florence, whereas those from Casaglia had been faithful. Nonetheless the settlements for both were almost identical; as the decree's preamble explained, the Commune of Florence "desired the devotion and faithfulness" of all these mountain communes, and as a result Podere's rebels were absolved of "all acts of war, cavalry, rebellion, deprivations, and other crimes and excesses." However, unlike in earlier annulments, the men of the Podere were required to present all the goods they had stolen during the siege of Palazzuolo to the *vicarius* of the Podere, who would "administer justice" by reimbursing or restoring the goods to their former owners. Second, the Podere's peasant rebels were absolved from paying all taxes in arrears from the beginning of their rebellion in August 1402 until the day of the agreements and were given a one-year period of grace on all tax debts accumulated before August 1402. Further, Florence protected the rebel communities against all other debts incurred through August 1404 with payments extended to August 1405 for the first half and August 1406 for the second. Next, they were granted immunities from all taxes except the gate gabelle, that on retail wine, and half their salt quota. Finally, all those who had left their homesteads during the periods of high taxes, war, and rebellion were given the right to return to their villages with the same rights and privileges as their neighbors, provided they presented themselves to the *vicarius* of the Podere or his officers before October 1404.

Again, the precarious demographic levels of Florence's mountainous frontier were a prime factor in spurring on the favors Florence gave its rebel peasants. For these guarantees and privileges, Florence required only that one year after the treaty the villagers maintain an army and cavalry in the Podere. The decree then repeated almost verbatim, item by item, the same privileges and obligations for those in the parish of Casaglia, even including the absolutions from acts of arson, war, robbery, and any other crime or delinquency committed in August 1402, suggesting that "the good and faithful" of Casaglia may not all have been what the decree's preamble had proclaimed.[53]

As well as rewarding communities which remained loyal to Florence during the wars and rebellions of 1402, Florence sought to compensate and reward individuals in the Podere who had made sacrifices in

---

[53] Provv. reg., 93, 25r–7r, 1404.iv.24.

defense of the Republic. One such Florentine hero was a certain Paulo called Rosso of Palazzuolo. His appeal began: "as is known to all Florentine citizens, the recent rebellion had spread throughout most of the Podere Fiorentino, but this Paulo alone remained completely faithful and devout to the Commune of Florence."[54] As a result of attacks by "agents of the Ubaldini, bandits, and even soldiers of the Florentine Commune, his house was burnt to the ground and all his animals, both large and small, and all his movable property was either stolen or destroyed. Thus, his lands remain still today uncultivated, and Paulo must beg to feed himself and his family. And in the last *estimo* Paulo was assessed 19s but now finds this *estimo* not only difficult but impossible [to pay]." For his sacrifices, he won a ten-year exemption from all taxes, which was an extraordinary grant as far as individual petitions for tax concessions went but not as favorable as those granted to the rebels in the Alpi and Podere.

The same applied to the "most devoted servant" of Florence, Guaspar d'Odaldo of Palazzuolo, who had defended the Commune against the "inequity and tyranny of the Duke of Milan."[55] Attaviano Ubaldini and "his accomplices and followers" had burnt to the ground Guaspar's house in Palazzuolo and two others in Susinana after robbing him of all his possessions – all of which "Guaspar always bore patiently because of his love for the Commune of Florence." By his own strength and that of his band of supporters (*suorum setiorum*) he took custody of a bastion in the Valle degli Agnelli and restored to Florence the castle of Susinana. But for all Guaspar's heroism, he received less than his neighbors who had rebelled – a ten-year exemption from taxes and gabelles.[56]

Unlike earlier agreements between Florence and its rebels, where nobles cut deals and peasants were left unmentioned, none of these collective agreements in 1403 and 1404 within the ancestral lands of the Ubaldini – the Alpi or the Podere – mentioned a single member of that clan or any other nobleman or exiled Florentine. Instead, the Ubaldini remained "rebels" and presumably continued to be hunted by the Florentine army, the *Podestà*, and *Capitano del Popolo*. They may have

[54] *Ibid.*, 93, 99v–100r, 1403.x.3: "Et omnibus civibus Florentinis notum est occasione proxime preterite querre fere omnis de dictis partibus se rebellaverunt a domino et devotione comunis Florentie cum aliis inimicis comunis Florentie guerram contra comitatem Florentie facientes. Et quod ipse Paulus semper stetit et ibi solus remansit in perfecta fide et devotione dicti comunis Florentie."

[55] On 1403, the Ten relied on Guaspar's reports; see Dieci di Balìa: Missive Legazioni e commissarie, 3, 38v–9r.   [56] Provv. reg., 94, 277r–v, 1405.ii.25.

tried to negotiate separate deals with Florence, but only one member of this clan seems to have succeeded: Bartolomeo called Tronta was absolved from acts of war and rebellion and his name expunged from the book of misdeeds. But, unlike the peasant rebels of the Alpi and Podere, he received no tax exemptions or payoff such as had marked earlier Florentine negotiations with the Ubaldini and other rebel lords.[57]

Nor did the Ubertini or Guidi fare any better. In June 1405 Florence answered a plea from their "devout and loyal" friend Count Antonio, son of the former Count Bandino of Montegranello, whose possessions had been badly damaged in the war recently fought against the counts of Balneo (Modigliana) and Andreino the son of Lord Biordo and others of the Ubertini. But these Ubertini rebels were given nothing. Instead, because of Count Antonio's merit and in compensation for his losses, Florence granted him all dominion and possessions that had belonged to Count Guido of Modigliana, his nephew Ricciardo, Andreino, and to any other Ubertini who had been a subject of Florence before the rebellion of 1402.[58] With the exception of Ricciardo Cancellieri and his clan and unlike in fourteenth-century agreements, Florence favored the peasantry over the nobility in the negotiations that followed the revolts of 1402. Either Florence's rebel lords were not mentioned, as in the case of the Ubaldini, or they received added reprisals as in the case of the Ubertini and Guidi in the Casentino and Valdambra.

By 1404 Florence's negotiations with peasant rebels turned southeastward to the old trouble spots within the mountainous zones of the Arezzo. In negotiations with Marciano, Florence tried to put a positive face on this commune's rebellion against Florence, saying that "for many years, that is, almost fourteen, the commune had been obedient to Florence."[59] But Florence needed more than rhetoric or force "to induce this castle and its men and women to return to Florentine rule." The councils absolved these rebels of all crimes and acts of rebellion and listed thirteen of its leaders for special privileges. Like the rebels from the Alpi Fiorentine, none came from an old feudal family or bore a family name, and all were from rural Marciano. The government offered them

---

[57] *Ibid.*, 93, 5v–6v, 1404.iv.18 and 18r–v, 1404.iv.24.
[58] *Ibid.*, 94, 56v–7r, 1405.vi.5. On the Florentine recapture of these lands and castles, see Minerbetti, *Cronica volgare*, pp. 309–11; and Dieci di Balìa: Missive Legazioni e commissarie, 3, 41r.
[59] Provv. reg., 93, 4r–5v, 1404.iv.18: "Supra negotiis comunis Marciani de plano Aretii."

five-year exemptions from all taxes and gabelles except those on the gate tolls, contracts, and salt and guaranteed that no one from Florence or Arezzo could demand from them "any rent or profits from their harvests owed from the day Florence lost Marciano until the present."[60]

Further, Florence prohibited any creditor demanding debts from them for two years, and all debts owed to Florence were annulled. In return for these concessions, these Aretine peasants had to maintain and provision their fortifications for the Commune of Florence at their own expense. While such grants may pale by comparison with those granted to Florence's peasants to the north, they are unique against the backdrop of Florentine acts of submission and treatment of rebels prior to 1403.

Further, by 1404, and perhaps as significant as the tax exemptions and other privileges won by peasant ringleaders, successful petitions for community-wide tax exemptions continued to dominate the business of the Florentine councils. These had shifted southward mostly to the mountains and hills of the Valdambra and the Chianti.[61] Along with war, the rebellion of places such as Monteluco Berardinga had led to peasant suffering, destruction, and their inability to pay taxes.[62] Unlike the pleas for the Alpi Fiorentine, the Podere, and the Casentino, none from the Chianti or Valdambra *pievi* such as Presciano or Rendola portray the peasant petitioners as rebels. And yet Florence heeded their cries for debt reduction, rescheduled their tax rates, and granted tax exemptions as it had never done before.

Why then were the peasants of the Valdambra and Chianti so successful in having so many pleas heard so favorably? Could it have been that the Ten of War and the Florentine councils had learned lessons from the north and were eager to forestall similar outbreaks of rebellion in the south as war heated up on their southern frontiers with Siena? Although the decrees do not give direct answers, they show that these

---

[60] *Ibid.*: "Item quod aliqua persona de civitate, comitatu, aut districtu Florentie vel Aretii non possit petere aliquo de Marciano seu quo usque nunc habitasset in comuni Marciani aliquid occasione redditum vel pro fructibus, tractis, vel recollectis, acceptis, vel habitis a die quo comune Florentie perdidit Marcianum usque in presentem diem. Et propterea aliquis molestrari non possit nec debeat ullo modo."

[61] While in 1403 only eight of forty-four petitions came from the Valdelsa, Chianti, and Valdambra, representing seventeen villages, in 1404 the numbers increased to sixteen of thirty-seven petitions from these zones, representing twenty-nine villages and in 1405 nine of twenty-eight petitions, representing thirty-two villages.

[62] Provv. reg., 93, 146r–7r, 1404.xii.9: "Et iam sunt quattuor anni vel circa fuit in castru Montis Luchi predicti ut notum est proditio per vim et violentiam ab esbannitis tam comunis Florentie quam comunis Senarum et aliorum rebellatorum et tunc et cetera si quid eis superat de novo exiterunt combusti de residio ipsorum domum et de mobilibus nichil eis remansit."

pleas were unlike those that preceded the revolts to the north. They were not simply filial supplications made at the feet of the Florentine *Signoria* as they had been before 1403. Instead, even if not as emboldened as the peasant demands from the north, a new spirit of negotiation ran through them. They made clear to Florence's rulers that if their requests were not met, the villagers would leave the territory, thereby further weakening the *contado*'s already fragile tax base.

In addition, the Minerbetti chronicler gives us clues unrevealed by either the judicial or legislative records. By his report, the peasants of the Valdambra had engaged in secret negotiations with Florence. In exchange for billeting Florentine troops in their homes and for breaking their loyalties to the Ubertini, they gained "buoni e larghi patti" from the Florentines. While Minerbetti did not clarify what these "good and generous deals" were, the *provvisioni* from 1404 to 1406 spell them out in detail as numerous parishes in the Valdambra and Chianti won tax exemptions and had their debts wiped from their books. As in the north, Florence had turned its potentially rebellious peasantry into the defenders of its realm and the spearheads of territorial expansion and consolidation. But, unlike the north, where the chroniclers eradicated from memory any part played by the indigenous peasantry, in the south, the Minerbetti chronicler conceded them an active role in shaping Florentine history, claiming that their disloyalty to their lords led to Andreino Ubertini's defeat in the Valdambra.[63] This time, through massive grants of tax exemptions and cancellation of debts, Florence made sure that the peasants were allied to the Republic against their former feudal lords.

Even in the north, the petitions dated after 1404 show mountain communes more as victims than as tough-minded negotiators who a year earlier had held their own with humanist ambassadors. Moreover, these later petitions suggest that the mountain peasants had not mounted a united front across the Alps and Mugello highlands. In 1407 villages near the Alps in the upper Mugello petitioned successfully for state intervention into their desperate financial affairs, portraying themselves as the victims of rebel incursions. A petition from the peasants of Santa Maria

---

[63] Minerbetti, *Cronica volgare*, p. 309: "Di che gli uomeni di tutte le castella di Valdambra, ch'erano fedeli al detto Andreino, vedendosi disfare del tutto e non veggendo d'avere soccorso niuno, non ne aveano da persona e difendersi non poteano, presono partito per loro migliore darsi a' Fiorentini, e segretamente intesisi co' Dieci della Balìa e con loro suti di concordia prima, a dì otto di aprile tutti si rubellaro e diersi a' Fiorentini, e ricevettono in casa le loro genti, e da' Fiorentini ebbono buoni e larghi patti per loro."

a Casaglia confirmed that the rebels invaded this parish and captured men for ransom "so that nothing remained."[64]

But, as in the south, these pleas did not simply replicate the earlier rhetoric of supplication. Seven years after the revolts, the men of Montecarelli still pleaded and won concessions from Florence as the victims of these wars and rebellions. In a sense these peasants had, however, pursued an unarmed resistance to Florence ever since: from Florence's military escalation in 1399 until the day of the approval of their petition on 20 April 1409 they had not paid their taxes. As a result, they had accumulated a colossal debt of more than 500 florins in one account and more than 2,300 *lire* in another. But instead of begging for mercy and recalling the horrors of war suffered at the hands of Florence's enemies as would have been customary earlier, they placed the blame squarely on Florence and its fiscal policy – its "massive and immense taxes."

Further, this plea elaborated more on the crimes of Florence than on the enemy: "Most of the men of Montecarelli were captured or forced to emigrate, leaving their animals and goods behind. And beyond these punishments once peace came, these peasants took loans at high rates of interest that now spell their final destruction." In concluding their plea the highlanders could not have made their criticisms more poignant: "And thus these people do not live according to the rule of men but like animals."[65] Despite these barbs against Florentine republican rule, the councils listened sympathetically and transferred 1,000 *lire* of Montecarelli's debts to the *Monte del Commune*. These debt reductions came from forty-three separately listed items of unpaid taxes and gabelles from 1399 to 1409, leaving few taxes that the peasants of Montecarelli may have actually paid.

In conclusion, the Florentine decrees give a third face to the rebel actions at the turn of the fifteenth century. Before Florence's attempt to regain Civitella in 1398, the councils treated rebels and rebellion with no less severity than did the criminal tribunals. In return for their castle and allegiance the rebels of Civitella won extraordinary privileges. But Civitella was an isolated case. It was one, moreover, in which the ringleaders negotiated for themselves alone and won nothing for the com-

---

[64] Provv. reg., 96, 87r–8v, 1407.viii.9.

[65] *Ibid.*, 98, 25r–6r, 1409.iv.20: Et quod ultra hec poena tempore pacis credentes ipsi homines adversus tales causas posse resurgere, acquiserunt sub gravi fenore certos denarios a certis qui fuerunt causa finalis eorum destructionis. Et quod ipsi non ut homines sub regula viventes steterant sed fuerunt in totum et steterunt ut bestie" (25r–v).

munity as a whole. A more significant change came five years later, after waves of peasant revolts in the Alpi and the Podere Fiorentino. Like the criminal records, the decrees show that the revolts of 1402 were not a matter that ended with the death of Giangaleazzo or the retreat of Bolognese and Milanese troops from the Alpi in August. Instead, the chronology of troubles for Florence was almost the opposite: revolt spread in the late fall and winter of 1402, when the rebels besieged Firenzuola, conquered the castles of Palazzuolo and Pagano, and built new ones through the Alpi and Podere. Moreover, like the criminal records, the decrees show that the revolts were certainly more than a feudal reaction to Florentine rule in the mountains.

The government decrees give a third view concealed by chroniclers and only obliquely suggested by the criminal courts' failure to bring hundreds of condemned rebels to justice where they were to suffer new horrific forms of torture and death. Even more than in the judicial records, villagers instead of magnates appear as the leaders and negotiators of their fate. In the collective negotiations following the revolts, members of the Ubaldini clan do not even appear. But more remarkable for peasant uprisings for any place or time that have thus far come to light in European history was the very fact that after the revolts negotiations followed at all and not the usual mopping up operations resulting in the brutal suppression of the state's enemies.[66] Instead of reprisals, the village negotiators won unprecedented rewards as Florence attempted to restore control along the northern, eastern, and southern frontiers and expand its territory across the Bolognese border.

Besides the privileges granted to village leaders – lifetime exemptions and sinecures and rights to carry weapons and even to choose who could immigrate into Florence's new border communities – rebel communes as a whole won the longest and most sweeping tax exemptions seen in these documents. Even more spectacular was the outpouring of tax exemptions and cancellations of public debts awarded to hundreds of other villages mostly within the mountains and within the traditional *contado* of Florence. In addition to slowing peasant emigration, these fiscal concessions became weapons in Florence's resistance to feudal control in the south and the expansion of its dominion in the north.

For three years (1403–5), consideration of peasant pleas – previously a minor chore for the urban elites – took center stage in the Florentine

---

[66] Even for a reading of the European past sympathetic to the impact of "ordinary people," such as Te Brake's *Shaping History*, little evidence of such successful peasant negotiations is related.

councils. Yet no one from the political elite left any trace of them in family diaries, chronicles, or histories even though individual decrees declared that the events in the Alpi and Podere Fiorentino were "known to all citizens of Florence." In addition, a large segment of the Florentine adult male population – those who sat for short stints as members of the ruling councils – heard descriptions of these revolts and voted in favor of the peasants' demands.[67]

The writers who did leave records of their public service and of Florentine history – Minerbetti, Buonaccorso Pitti, Jacopo Salviati, and Franco Sacchetti – all served in prestigious and politically active positions during these years. In addition to knowing about the rebels' successes and the spread of favors to hundreds of villages, they would have been active in determining the course of these events, but they chose to remain silent about them. Their "realism" (for which all four writers have been praised[68]) was a selective one that carefully skirted those issues that would have tarnished their reputations as fair and able governors. But more was at stake for these republican ideologues of the early Renaissance: by choosing feudal and Milanese "tyranny" over republican rule, the peasant rebels had struck at the heart of Florence's myth of liberty that remains even today ingrained in Florentine literature and historiography.

---

[67] The short terms of office and the numbers elected to the two popular councils plus to the *Tre Maggiori*, the Ten of War and other committees such as the Officials of the Towers meant more than five hundred men would be privy to such discussions at any given moment and many more over the course of the rebels' three to four years of revolt and negotiations. On the numbers approving laws, see Najemy, *Corporatism and Consensus in Florentine Electoral Politics, 1280–1400* (Chapel Hill, N.C., 1982), p. 236.
[68] On the realism of Pitti, see Bec, *Les marchands écrivains*, pp. 90–4.

PART III

Governmental clemency and the hinterland

7

Florentine peasant petitions: an institutional perspective

Recent studies on peasant revolts in Italy have challenged an earlier historiography, claiming that even those in Angevin Sicily were not "true" peasant revolts[1] and for others "a concept of 'class struggle' can be applied only with great strain."[2] While the participants carefully systematized the range of peasant acts of violence over the central and later Middle Ages,[3] they failed to clarify exactly what would constitute "true and proper 'insurrections'" as opposed to what one has called "small-change criminality."[4] One criterion used by historians to deny that certain peasant uprisings constituted "true" rebellion is the supposed absence of any long-term consequences. Such a yardstick has been brought to bear on insurrectionary activity even as widespread as the fourteenth-century Jacquerie or the English Uprising of 1381 – the usual benchmark of a "true" peasant revolt of the later Middle Ages. For the English Uprising the debate goes on about just how profound or long-lasting were its effects on English government and serfdom.[5]

Following the definitions of rebellion used by contemporaries in chronicles, criminal records, and the government decrees, this study has defined a peasant revolt simply as an attempt staffed primarily by villagers, most of whom tilled the soil, to wrest castles or other territory from their feudal lords or the Republic of Florence, regardless of the leadership or the outcome. As far as such acts are concerned, the Florentine countryside was hardly absent from peasant revolts from the earliest surviving judicial records. As I have argued, in 1402 these uprisings changed

---

[1] Vitolo, "Rivolte contadine," p. 224. For an earlier historiography, see Caggese, *Roberto d'Angio e i suoi tempi* (Florence, 1921).   [2] Bortolami, "Lotta e protesta contadina," p. 51.
[3] See Maire Vigueur, "Per una periodizzazione."
[4] Bortolami, "Lotta e protesta contadina," p. 58.
[5] See Sir Charles W. C. Oman, *The Great Revolt of 1381* (Oxford, 1906), pp. 152–7; Michel Mollat and Philippe Wolff, *Popular Revolutions of the Late Middle Ages*, transl. by A. L. Lytton-Sells (London, 1973), p. 315; J. A. F. Thomson, *The Transformation of Medieval England, 1370–1529* (London, 1983), p. 31; and *The English Rising of 1381*, ed. by R. H. Hilton and T. H. Aston. (Cambridge, 1984).

fundamentally in their leadership and intensity as they emerged from isolated castle assaults to insurrections that swept across the northern and eastern perimeter of the Florentine territory, challenging the security of the state in a way they had never done before.

But did they have long-term consequences or, as the chronicle tradition and historiography of Florence might suggest, were they quickly forgotten blips on the surface of history? The most graphic evidence to support the opposite view comes from the tax records themselves. As part I of this study has shown, 1401–2 was the turning-point in the well-being of those in the countryside and in particular of those in the mountainous zones where the insurrections took place and where the rebels won extraordinary benefits.

Even more important, the insurrectionary years at the beginning of the fifteenth century marked a change in Florence's governance of its *contado* in at least one critical area – fiscality. The differential in taxation between the mountains and plains reached its peak in 1401 and narrowed with the following *estimi* of the fifteenth century until the tax reforms of 1427 eradicated the old medieval mosaic of community inequalities altogether. Second, 1401–2 marked a shift in the balance between Florence's traditional *contado*, subject to the escalating rates of the *estimo*, and its more privileged *districtus*, mostly under the aegis of older formerly independent city-states – Pistoia, Volterra, and Arezzo.[6] These areas were subject to the fixed rates of a military tax called the *lance*, but, like the city of Florence, were freed from the *estimo* and direct taxation.

One index of this difference in privilege and tax burdens before 1402 was the mass migration of peasants from the *prope Alpes* and the Alpi Fiorentine, not only across the border into foreign lands such as Bologna, but across territorial boundaries into the lands of Pistoia. As a consequence, in its early tax incentives to draw foreign agricultural laborers into the depopulated lands of its *contado*, Florence specifically ruled out any tax exemptions to foreign laborers who migrated into the *contadi* of Pistoia, Arezzo, and Volterra. They even went so far as to attempt to poach agricultural workers then residing in these *contadi* by offering them the same tax breaks to migrate into the Florentine *contado* as they offered foreigners.[7]

---

[6] The acquisitions of Pisa, Cortona, and Livorno came later – in 1406, 1411, and 1421.
[7] Provv. reg., 72, 171r–2r, 1383.x.20: "Et ad maiorem declarationem quod quilibet de Pistorio aut de Vulterris seu de Aretio vel de comitatu aut territorio vel districtu aliquorum dictorum locorum veniens et stans ut prefertur possit gaudere benefitio supradicto." Those from Arezzo were given

The Florentine oligarchy began to see the need to increase taxes on the district as early as 1396,[8] but it was only in 1404 that it realized its need to restructure taxes on the *districtus*, equalizing them with the *contado*. It extended the onerous "extraordinary" tax onto the backs of communities within the district (at that time set at 4 *lire* to be multiplied by the assessed *lira*).[9] The Florentine councils repeated such calls to equalize the burdens across the Florentine territory through the early decades of the century. Even the language of the legislative sources in the early fifteenth century began to blur the old distinction between *contado* and district, fusing them together with the single Roman term "territorium" to give a sense of "a unified jurisdiction."

Further, Florence incorporated newly acquired provinces as though they were a part of the Florentine *contado* ("verum et originale territorium et comitatus de territorio et comitatu Florentiae").[10] In 1419 a five-man commission of Florentine councilors was appointed to survey the procedures by which taxes were imposed on subject lands and to ascertain the precise amount of tax imposed on each administrative unit.[11] The ultimate aim of these decisions was to destroy the fiscal autonomy of former city-states, which after their submission to Florence had enjoyed self-determination in fiscality.[12] From 1415 through the 1420s governmental decrees gave further evidence of the Florentine efforts to extend and clamp down on payments owed by communities in the district. Numerous acts were passed to scrutinize those communities in mountain and valley outposts as well as in the cities of the Romagna, Aretino, Valdinievole, Pisano, and Pistoiese that had managed to slip through the net in the assignment of salt taxes. To insure that the state salt monopoly was upheld, Florence sent its agents throughout its dominion to survey the "number of mouths" in communities not yet

---

further securities for coming to live and work within the Florentine *contado*. Also, see *ibid.*, 74, 204r–5r, 1385.xii.8, and 80, 197r–8v, 1391.xii.2, in which Florence singled out the agricultural workers from Volterra and Pistoia and their *contadi* as especially welcome to move to the *contado* of Florence and enjoy tax immunities.

[8] *Ibid.*, 85, 214r–v, 1396.x.27: "Pro augendo taxas districtualibus."
[9] *Ibid.*, 93, 92v–3r, 1404.ix.18: "Quod districtuales debeant solvere impositam terminus aliis ordinaris et extraordinaris hic": "Consideratis neccesitatibus rei publice et gravibus expensis factis et continue occurrentibus pro defensu et subdictorum et obedientium comuni Florentie et aliorum qui sub umbra dicti comunis conservantur."
[10] Fubini, "La rivendicazione," esp. p. 51; and Chittolini, "The Italian City-State," p. 602.
[11] See Molho, *Florentine Public Finances*, pp. 42–3; and Mazzi and Raveggi, *"Gli uomini"*, p. 56.
[12] Molho, *Florentine Public Finances*, pp. 43–4; also see Chittolini, "Ricerche sull'ordinamento," p. 325; and Provv. reg., 109, 226v–9r: "Electio V. civium comitatus."

taxed, to calculate how much salt they were to consume and what price per *staia* they should pay.[13] If communities bought their salt from sources other than Florence, they would be fined a hefty sum of 1,000 florins.[14] Finally, in preparation for the *catasto* of 1427, Florentine patricians pointed to the example of Venice in arguing for universal and equal taxation across the Florentine dominion.[15]

Significantly, when war erupted with Milan in 1424, bringing about perhaps the most disastrous fiscal crisis in Florentine history by 1427,[16] the mountain communes of the Florentine *contado* in the Alpi Fiorentine and the Podere were noticeably quiet. This time, areas hardly touched by the previous wave of insurrections rose up against Florentine taxation. Again, they were in the mountains, but not in the *contado*. The new hot spots of revolt were further east in the district of Arezzo – Pontenano, Castel di Ranco, and Castel Focognano.[17] Again, government petitions make clear that the spark of insurrection was excessive taxation.[18]

As in 1403, in 1427 the *provvisioni* exploded with concessions dealt out to rebellious peasants. This time around, the councils did not always wait

---

[13] See Provv. reg., 104, 123v–4v, 1414.ii.15: "Comunia Romandiole accipiant salem a comuni florentie"; 105, 168r–v, 1415.x.22: "Balia gubernatorum gabelle salis pro factis comunis piancaldoli"; 105, 297r–8r, 1415.ii.17: "Quod certu comunia de districtu accipiant salem a comuni Florentie et non aliunde"; 113, 6r, 1423.iv.20: Comunia Romandiole pro sale habendo"; 113, 148r–v, 1423.ix.28: "Magistri gabelle salis debeant taxare certa comunia Aretii ad accipiendum de salia et alia"; 263v–3v, 1423.ii.7: "Fratrum sancti Augustini de Niccosia [de Valle Calci districtu Pisis] pro sale"; 114, 118v–19v, 1424.i.24: "Comunia comitatus Aretii taxari debeant quantum salum quolibet eorum accipere quolibet anno."

[14] *Ibid.*, 105, 297r–8r; and 110, 99r, 1420.ix.28: "Contra salis gabellam fraudantes." An exception to this trend was a decree of 1409, which began: "it is just" that those from the *contado* and district should bear more of the tax burden, "considering the great and heavy expenses of defending the free state of the subject lands of Florence and being attentive to the many forced loans imposed on Florentine citizens." The tax measure then raised the coefficient on the *estimo* imposed on those from the *contado* by 10 gold *soldi* on the *lira* but said nothing about increases to be paid by those in the district (as implied in the document's preamble, "de imponendo comitatinis et districtualibus certam quantitatem pecunie"); *ibid.*, 98, 91r–2r, 1409.xi.14.

[15] Herlihy and Klapisch-Zuber, *Les Toscans*, pp. 21 and 32–3. Despite these efforts to blur the distinctions between *distrettuali* and *contadini*, the legislation of the *Monte delle doti* (founded in 1425) continued to distinguish between them, granting those from the district higher rates of interest on their investments than those from the *contado*; see Molho, "Investimenti nel Monte delle Doti di Firenze: Un analisi sociale e geografica," *Quaderni Storici*, 61 (1986) pp. 163–4. The difference did not, however, attract greater numbers of deposits from the district; see Molho, *Marriage Alliance*, p. 113. [16] See Molho, *Florentine Public Finances*, pp. 153–82.

[17] The only area where the insurrectionary waves of 1402–4 and 1426–30 overlapped was in the Florentine Romagna, outside Florence's traditional *contado*. See Giudice, 102, 219v–20r, 1430.iv.21: eleven men from Oriolo were condemned to death for rebellion in an attempt to hand over their *castrum* to the enemy forces of Lucca in March, 1429.

[18] On these insurrections, see Cohn, *Women in the Streets*, pp. 123–5.

for the peasant communes to petition them formally before intervening with tax concessions and reductions of fees such as the salaries paid to local *Podestà*. In 1427 alone the Commune dealt out twenty-five tax exemptions and other concessions to villages in the countryside. While in 1403 thirty-six of the forty-four approved petitions from the territory came from the *contado*, the ratios reversed in 1427; eighteen of twenty-five went to the district. Between 1346 and 1427 only two years showed more successful petitions from the district than the *contado*, and in both the differences were negligible.[19] Before 1427 successful petitions from the *contado* almost trebled those from the district,[20] while afterwards (1428 to 1434) district petitions predominated in every year and as a whole nearly doubled the *contado*'s numbers[21] (See figure 8.3).

With the war against Lucca following in the wake of the Milanese war, the subject towns and their districts were now the ones forced to bear increased taxes, and they responded in kind with revolts in Volterra (1429), Arezzo (1431), and Pisa (1432) along with numerous villages through the Pisan plains, and the mountains of the Valdinievole and Arezzo.[22] These revolts were the consequences of Florence's attempt to redistribute tax burdens across its territory; by unburdening its *contado*, it stripped away the former privileges of its *districtus*.

Apart from these long-term structural developments in fiscality and the narrowing of the distinction between the *contado* and *districtus*, did these revolts change Florence's governance of its dominion after 1403? As we have seen, the councils exempted the rebellious communes of the mountains from taxes for as long as fifteen years and the insurgent ringleaders in perpetuity. But by 1406, the flood of peasant petitions had ended and at least in quantitative terms Florentine grants of clemency to its territorial subjects appear to have returned to normal. Did the

---

[19] In 1385 two petitions were approved from the district and one from the *contado*; in 1387, seven from the district and four from the *contado*.

[20] The councils approved 571 petitions from the *contado* and 215 from the district.

[21] The councils approved seventy-one from the district and thirty-six from the *contado* in these years.

[22] For Volterra, see Herlihy and Klapisch-Zuber, *Les Toscans*, pp. 21, 89–92; for the prosecutions of the rebels, see Giudice, 102, 290r–1r, 1430.vii.30; and Provv. reg., 120, 284r–5r, 1429.viii.17; 406r–9v, 1429.xii.23; 121, 56v–7v, 1430.vi.26. (To my knowledge, no one has made use of these documents.) For Arezzo, see Ubaldo Pasqui, "Una congiura per liberare Arezzo dalla dipendenza dei Fiorentini (1431)," *ASI*, ser. 5 55 (1890): 3–19. For Pisa, see Petralia, "'Crisi' ed emigrazione dei ceti eminenti a Pisa durante il primo dominio fiorentino: L'orizzonte cittadino e la ricerca di spazi esterni," in *I ceti dirigenti nella Toscana del Quattrocento* (Florence, 1987), pp. 314–15 and "Imposizione diretta," p. 648; and Pietro Silva, *Pisa sotto Firenze dal 1406 al 1433* (Pisa, 1910), pp. 134, and 529–60; for the Pisan countryside, see Petralia, "Imposizione diretta," p. 648; Brucker, *The Civic World*, p. 505; and Cohn, *Women in the Streets*, ch. 6.

period of revolts mark a qualitative change in what rural communities could expect from their Florentine rulers?

Before addressing this question of policy and what it may reflect about the mentality of the Florentine ruling class, we need to look at the institutional arrangements by which community petitions came before the Florentine councils and how they may have changed over the near-century of our analysis. As far as I can see, the original reports, presented by peasant ambassadors or "oratores" from the towns before the *Tre Maggiori*, have not survived. Indeed, most may never have been written but were presented orally. What we know of them comes from summaries of the successful ones by the notary for the government (the *Riformagioni*), now preserved in the notary's Latin. No doubt these summaries altered what the peasant ambassadors originally said or asked for. Unlike in slander cases brought before the criminal tribunals, no attempt was made to recapture the sound, orthography, or syntax of the peasant in these petitions.[23]

On the other hand, these summaries were far from formulaic, listing specific damages and costs to villages due to war, pestilence, or brigandage; the numbers of peasants who died or fled from their villages; whether the peasants threatened to leave if their requests were not granted; the exact figures of their public debts and why their communities were deserving of government clemency. Nor were these peasant complaints believed without investigation; regularly two citizens were sent to inspect damages and the villagers' ability to bear their tax burdens or other fees. By the 1420s, the final *provvisioni* often named these citizens and briefly summarized their reports. The *Tre Maggiori* and councils would then vote on whether to approve the petition and, if it was passed, would specify their concessions – which public debts were to be reduced or canceled and what should be the conditions, such as paying the nonexempted taxes or other back taxes by certain deadlines.

Beyond these records, precious few scraps of evidence inform us about how these cases were argued, how the ambassadors were chosen, or who they may have been. On rare occasions, walled villages and towns might first employ a notary to present their demands as seems to have been the case with the demands negotiated by the rebels of

---

[23] John Najemy is now working on individual petitions for remissions of penalties incurred in sex crimes. He finds that around 1400 the notaries began to present the evidence of these cases by attempting to recast the plaintiff's words in the Tuscan dialect.

Civitella in 1398[24] or, for more run-of-the-mill demands, with those from Castiglion Aretino, who used their notaries in 1396 and 1399 to plead for the cancellation of fines.[25] But such use of notaries or written documents for pleading before the *Tre Maggiori* seems to have been the exception, even for towns within the district. Instead the documents refer to "oratores." Tales of such rural representatives even seep into contemporary literature, such as Franco Sacchetti's story 31 of his *Trecentonovelle*, which poked fun at two ambassadors from the mountains of the Casentino sent to negotiate with Bishop Guido of Arezzo: on arrival they forgot why they had been sent and what they were supposed to say.[26]

In addition, the decrees themselves tell us that even the wealthier towns in the *contado* close to Florence, such as Prato, could be hard strapped by the "fatigue paid in labor and expenses" from sending, lodging, and maintaining those from their communities entrusted with arguing their pleas before Florence's highest elected officials. An appeal from Prato of 1389 was one of the few to speak of this pain, but it must have been common. According to the petition, since 1385 its "oratores" had made numerous appeals to the *Tre Maggiori*, insisting that earlier exemptions granted to them pertained to all their gabelles including that on contracts. Nonetheless, Florence had continued to demand this tax along with stiff penalties for failure to pay it. In response, Prato had sent ambassadors to Florence to present their appeals on numerous occasions without success until 1389 but had incurred great expense from these trips and stays in Florence.[27] At the same time, junkets to the big city must have been attractive to local villagers and townsmen and could cause excessive expenses and scandal even as they continue to do today.[28] In 1415, Florence passed a law prohibiting any elected ambassador from any place within the *contado* or district from staying in Florence on business for more than fifteen days under a penalty of 100 *lire* for each offense.[29]

The executive committees which deliberated and voted on decrees comprised five of the highest rungs within Florence's political and administrative hierarchy. At the apex was the *Tre Maggiori*, comprised of the *Signoria* and its two advisory colleges. It was these bodies that first sifted through,

[24] Provv. reg., 87, 89r–93r, 1398.v.30.
[25] *Ibid.*, 84, 285r–6v, 1395.ii.21; and 88, 121r–2r, 1399.viii.9: "Pro parte notarii oratoris comunis."
[26] *Il Trecentonovelle*, novella XXXI, pp. 59–63.   [27] Provv. reg., 77, 306v–8r, 1388.ii.18.
[28] Note the present spending scandals around Glasgow city councilors' junkets, 1996–7.
[29] Provv. reg., 105, 108r–9r, 1415.viii.9.

deliberated on, and vetted all decrees, laws, and petitions. If approved by a two-thirds vote, the bills passed on for further scrutiny and voting by two larger bodies, the council of the *Popolo* and that of the *Comune*. Even when a bill passed on to the wider councils, few recorded the votes they received within the *Tre Maggiori*. As the formula that introduced each act within the *provvisioni* put it, these matters had been deliberated by the Priors, the *Gonfaloniere* of Justice, and *Gonfalonieri* of the Companies in "solemn secrecy" with "sufficient numbers of black and white beans."

While the votes from these two wider councils have been preserved in at least two places – the *Libri fabarum* and, if passed, the *provvisioni* – only a small portion of the discussions held and decisions made previously in the chambers of the *Tre Maggiori* surface in the deliberations of the *Signoria*[30] or the *Consulte e Pratiche*. Of the thousand peasant petitions and negotiations between 1347 and 1434 that I have coded and analyzed for this study, few left any trace in the *Consulte e Pratiche*. Historians have yet to discuss the procedures by which the *Signoria* and colleges selected issues for debate.[31] Moreover, the discussions scribbled down by the chancellor in his Latin shorthand are often so elliptical that it is sometimes difficult to sense what the bill or petition may have concerned. Such was the case of debates around the negotiations with the communes of the Alpi and in the Podere in 1403. During the rebellion in the Alpi, it is clear from these debates that Florentines desired to banish the Ubaldini from the Alpi and Podere, and some even proposed the forced migration or extermination of the highlanders.[32] On the other hand,

---

[30] Not all of the surviving records for the Signori e Collegi, Deliberazioni fatte in forza di ordinaria autorità or speciale autorità concerned weighty matters of state; some regarded issues no more important than the routine hiring of the *Signoria*'s musicians and their salaries (see for instance, Collegi Deliberazioni fatte in forza di ordinaria autorità 28, 2r) or the election of the salt gabelle's functionaries (*ibid.*, 8r). The series of speciale autorità on occasion did concern the countryside and absolved rebels of fines and death sentences (see 11, 34r–6v), but none of the records for 1402 and 1403 dealt with the crimes of the rebels from the Alpi, Podere, or Casentino. Further, other records of the *Signoria*, such as the Signori carteggio: Rapporti e relazioni di oratori, reported nothing on peasant petitions and uprisings, at least during the critical years 1401–3; see 1 in this series which covers the period September 12, 1395 to May 12, 1403. The earliest records of the Cinque dei conservatori del contado begin in 1428 (1 bis) and record successful petitions for tax relief from the *contado* and district, but provide only shortened versions of what can be found in the *provvisioni*. On occasion, however, these deliberations name the "oratores," who presented their communities' arguments for fiscal need.

[31] See Demetrio Marzi, *La Cancelleria della Repubblica Fiorentina* (Rocca San Casciano, 1910); Rubinstein, *The Government of Florence*; Brucker, *The Civic World*, p. 13; Conti, Introduction to *Le "Consulte" e "Pratiche" (1401)*; Nenci, Introduction to *Le Consulte e pratiche (1404)*.

[32] Consulte e Pratiche, 36, 109r, 1403.ix.18: "Quod contra Ubaldinos fiat quicquid fieri poterit ut expellantur ab alpibus et podere; *ibid.*, 2r, 1402.xi.22: "Et quod gentes quas sunt in alpibus revocentur et mittantur alii."

they leave no trace of the outcome of these negotiations or even that widescale cancellation of criminal condemnations and fiscal exemptions might have been at issue.[33]

Despite the absence of these debates, this first screening of petitions by Florence's *Tre Maggiori* was crucial. When the government became disgruntled over the number of exemptions from the *estimo* they had granted to peasants in the *contado* and district for fortifications during the 1370s, they turned their attention not to the councils for limiting the number of successful petitions but instead to the *Tre Maggiori*, ruling that petitions from any village, *popolo*, *pieve*, or commune within the *contado* or district would have to receive at least thirty-four votes in their first screening before proceeding to the councils.[34] In addition, both larger councils were dependent on the *Tre Maggiori* in other ways. They were elected by it and could speak only in favor of what these three higher bodies had already decided. If they were against a motion, they had only their votes. For most legislation the bill or petition had to pass both colleges by a two-thirds vote to became law.

Another body of documents, the *Libri fabarum*, theoretically[35] gave the bean votes for each of the two larger councils on all decrees and petitions that passed the *Tre Maggiori*'s scrutiny. In these books the bill was jotted down along with its votes, whether or not it passed into law. However, unlike the *provvisioni*, which described the details of the petition and the reasons the peasants purportedly put forward to win governmental clemency, the bean books' versions are highly abbreviated. Rarely was the petition described in more than a four- or five-word phrase; often only "petitio" appeared before the name of the commune followed by the number of votes against, and whether it passed: *placuit* or *displacuit*.

An unremarkable petition from the commune of Gangalandi, which became law on April 13, 1400, may serve to illustrate the differences in information conveyed by these two sets of documents. The *provvisione* version of the petition fills six large quarto folios, well over 3,000 words. It relates that in the past, the men and women of Gangalandi had suffered many losses in population and in property from Florence's enemies and other armed companies passing through Florentine territory. As the commune possessed no fortifications to protect its rural population in wartime, the report argued that it would be useful to fortify the village

---

[33] *Ibid.*, 37, 2r, 1403.xi.26: "Quod placeat eis facta per diecem in alpibus nostris pro recuperateione locorum," and "Et quod expediant facta Tirli."   [34] Provv. reg., no, 65, 23r–4r, 1377.iv.22.
[35] See chapter 6, note 5.

called "dela lastra" on one side of Gangalandi's district and "Malmantile" at the other.

Given the scale of the project, the report further argued that Gangalandi could not afford the expenses without Florence's help. As a consequence, Florence authorized building both forts and specified which parishes could seek security in each of the two castles. It further made specifications about the walls, towers, and gates, indicating the length, height, and the materials to be used in the construction. In compensation, Florence allowed the commune of Gangalandi "to convert" its gabelle on retail wine worth 1,300 *lire* per annum, its meat gabelle at 70 florins, and its gabelle on sales of wine in bulk (200 florins) for a three-year period to cover the costs of the new construction, guaranteeing that these rates would remain the same for three years. The *provvisione* continued with other details, such as indicating that Gangalandi's gabelle rates were tied to its *estimo* and were not an actual account of sales.[36]

In contrast to this long document detailing the peasants' reasons for requesting governmental assistance, their need for new fortifications, the details of Florence's tax concessions, and specifications and conditions for the building of new fortifications, the *Libri fabarum* simply indicated that the petition passed the council of the *Popolo* by all but thirty-six votes (*40 petitio comunis gangalandi displ. 36*) and that of the *Comune* by all but eighteen (*petitio comunis gangalandi displ. 18*).[37] But from it we have no idea what the petition was for, why it was granted, or what the grant entailed.

Despite the paucity of information given in the *Libri fabarum*, it is possible to count how many petitions came from the countryside and whether the percentage of failed petitions changed over time. From a counting of all the petitions in the books from 1394 to 1407, I have found that the success rate of peasant petitions was relatively stable and high – around 70 percent – in years of peace, war, and rebellion alike, even though over these years the actual number of petitions that were granted fluctuated dramatically from three in 1396 to forty-four in 1403.[38] Surprisingly, the percentage of successful petitions from the towns and villages of the hinterland was higher than that of petitions presented by citizens of Florence, which included many from Florence's most prominent families.

---

[36] Provv. reg., 89, 13v–16r, 1400.iv.13. On the detailed specifications for the building and repairs of lowland fortifications, see Alessandro Monti and Sznura, *"Riparo della città", Il Castello di Campi nel Trecento: Un caso di ristrutturazione urbanistica* (Signa, 1997).   [37] LF, 47, 4r 1400.iv.14, and 5r.
[38] Fubini, "Dalla rappresentanza," p. 55, has computed the success rate of petitions in the years 1412 to 1419, but instead of tallying individual petitions, he has calculated the percentage of sessions when all the petitions were approved. Such sessions could approve from one to more than twenty petitions. He finds that of forty-seven sessions only sixteen approved all the petitions.

Like the villagers, these citizens petitioned for matters such as the annulments of condemnations, tax relief (*prestanze*), and the reduction of debts, as well as for a range of nonelected positions within the Florentine administration, most commonly as castle guards in the provinces (*castellani*). In certain periods, the doling out of such jobs had become a form of state charity for citizens who had fallen on hard times (*poveri vergognosi*).[39]

But we know nothing of the absolute or relative success rate of these petitions at their first screening. From the frequent repetition of bills from citizens, it is reasonable to speculate, however, that petitions from the city had a far greater likelihood of being presented, heard, and eventually passed than did those from the countryside. As illustrated by Ambrogio Traversari's attempts to argue for clemency for his friend Cosimo de' Medici in 1433, securing a hearing before the College of the Priors even for someone as respected as Traversari demanded prior behind-the-scenes negotiation with those high up in the office-holding elite.[40] Despite the massive documentation on the wider councils' decisions, it was the *Tre Maggiori*'s decisions, shrouded in secrecy, that played the dominant role in the promulgation of Florence's laws.[41]

Would changes in the composition of Florence's elected councils and the weight played by them have influenced the success of peasants' petitions? The voting procedure for filling all elective offices was by lot or scrutiny. The names of eligible citizens were drawn from electoral bags by officials called the *accoppiatori*.[42] The mechanisms by which these names were drawn, who was eligible, and who was made "divieto" because of fiscal or political improprieties was a political concern of central importance to contemporary chroniclers[43] and has been a major area of research over the past half century.[44]

---

[39] In the registers around 1405, such appointments made for charitable reasons increase in the *provisioni*; see, for instance, the appointments of Niccolai Nerli de Quarantensis of Florence as a castellan, "because at present he had no work that would bring in money" (*ad presentem aliquod exercitium lucrativum non habet*), and Marci Mei Luce Mei, citizen of Florence, "because his work at present brought in so little income he could not support his sizable family" (*Quod ipse de dicta sua arte ad presens modicum lucratur et eius substantia parva est cum no parva familia*); Provv. reg., 94, 100v and 101r, both 1405.vi.22.   [40] Traversari, *Hodoeporicon*, p. 168.   [41] Guidi, *Il Governo*, II, p. 140.
[42] On the crucial importance of these officials, see Rubinstein, *The Government of Florence*; and Clarke, *The Soderini*, pp. 44ff.
[43] It was a major preoccupation of the chroniclers Matteo Villani and Marchionne di Coppo Stefani.
[44] See Rubinstein, *The Government of Florence*; D. V. Kent, *The Rise of the Medici*; D. V. and F. V. Kent, *Neighbours and Neighbourhood*; Clarke, *The Soderini*; Najemy, *Corporatism and Consensus*; and Brucker, *Florentine Politics*; Herlihy, "The Rulers of Florence, 1282–1530," in *City States*, pp. 197–221.

The social and political composition of the larger councils of the *Popolo* and the *Comune* changed several times over the period under discussion.[45] After the Black Death, chroniclers such as Filippo Villani bemoaned the entry of new citizens ("novi cives") and "mezzani" to Florence's highest offices.[46] With the victory of the Ciompi followed by the Government of the Minor Guilds, the actual numbers who sat in the larger councils did not increase, but the proportion of offices held by those from the lesser guilds expanded, and magnates were excluded from office-holding. By contrast, with the fall of this government in 1382, followed by the reforms of the Albizzi regime in 1393, office-holding centered increasingly on members of the upper guilds, and entry to magnates opened.[47]

In addition, the Albizzi government created new councils which limited the power of the councils of the People and the Commune. First, the Council of Eighty-One[48] took matters such as the election of the Ten of War, the hiring of mercenaries, and even some decisions on taxation away from the wider councils and monitored their voting on other matters of legislation.[49] In 1411, the Council of Two Hundred was created, which constituted a virtual Florentine Senate of old elites close to the Albizzi and ushered in the major reforms that would structure a new elitism to endure until Lorenzo's further controls and narrowing of

---

[45] Throughout, they comprised citizens twenty-five years or older, who held four-month terms of office.

[46] Matteo Villani, *Cronica*, V, bk. 11, r. 65, pp. 224–6: "Dello stato della città di Firenze in que'-giorni."

[47] With the Reforms of 1328, the *Popolo* consisted of 300 members; by the period of the Arti Minori, 1378–82, it shrank to 160, but half had to be chosen from the minor guilds (forty per quarter). With the return of the oligarchy in 1382, the *Popolo* expanded to 285 citizens, but its constituency became more elitist; two-thirds were to come from the upper guilds. The Council of the Commune was the more elitist of the two councils. In 1328 it comprised only 150 members, expanding to 200 in 1356 – 160 citizens of *popolano* or commoner status and forty magnates. In 1378, the council retained its numbers, but half the *popolani* had to come from the minor guilds. In 1382 it increased to 252 – 192 *popolani*, forty magnates – but without requiring half the *popolani* to be minor guildsmen. Its membership stayed the same through the Statutes of 1415 but by the *catasto* of 1427 had shrunk to 208 – twelve from each of the sixteen districts or *gonfalones* of the city, plus sixteen elected magnates. These legislated numbers rarely corresponded to the actual numbers who showed up for any session or cast votes. In times of plague, for instance in 1375, it was difficult to assemble a quorum of 150 members. However, the *provvisioni*'s voting records show that attendance was generally high. At the beginning of the fifteenth century, 400 or more men deliberated and voted on the bills and petitions handed on from the *Tre Maggiori*. See Becker, *Florence in Transition*, II; Brucker, *Florentine Politics; The Civic World*; and Guidi, *Il Governo*, II, pp. 133–4 and 145–73; Najemy, *Corporatism and Consensus*; and Herlihy and Klapisch-Zuber, *Les Toscans*, pp. 38–9.

[48] On the composition and significance of this body, see Molho, "The Florentine Oligarchy," and "Politics and the Ruling Class."   [49] Guidi, *Il Governo*, II, p. 146.

political offices in the 1480s.[50] This innovation fundamentally changed the constitution of Florence and, according to Guidubaldo Guidi, was more instrumental in shaping the Florentine constitution than even the changes wrought by the Medici after their return in 1434.[51] Similarly for Brucker, 1411 was the key date when Florentine politics changed "from corporate to elitist: from a polity controlled and guided by corporate interests to one governed by a cadre of statesmen – experienced, skilled, professional."[52] Did these constitutional changes and shifts in the socio-economic composition of Florence's ruling class influence Florence's policy toward its hinterland?

---

[50] On these later developments, see Alison Brown, "Lorenzo, the *Monte*, and the Seventeen Reformers," *in The Medici in Florence: The Exercise and Language of Power* (Florence, 1992), pp. 151–83; and Fubini, *Quattrocento fiorentino*.

[51] Guidi, *Il Governo*, II, p. 147; also see Fubini, "Dalla rappresentanza," pp. 51–4, 56, and 59; "Diplomazia e governo," p. 72; and "Italia quattrocentesca," who dates its inception to 1411.

[52] Brucker, *The Civic World*, p. 11.

8

The reasons for assistance

To chart changes in public policy and in the mentality of the Florentine ruling elites, I have looked at what the oligarchy accepted as legitimate grounds for awarding governmental clemency to the hinterland and what these subjects actually won. This chapter will look at the reasons peasants and subject townsmen presented in their petitions in arguing for tax relief or, perhaps closer to the truth, what the ruling oligarchy saw, interpreted, and transcribed as these peasants' legitimate reasons. Before turning to these reasons, we will glance over the broad trends in peasant petitioning from the Black Death to the return of the Medici.

First, the numbers of approved petitions from the countryside show no correspondence between shifts of political regimes or changes in the Florentine constitution and swings in the number of successful petitions. For instance, the opening of the councils to greater proportions of minor guildsmen, 1378 to 1382, made no difference in the number of peasant petitions that passed through the councils: in the three years prior to the Ciompi revolt, the government approved twenty-three petitions from the hinterland; in the three years of Ciompi and minor guildsmen rule, it approved nineteen. Nor did the number change significantly with the restoration of the oligarchy in 1382 (see figure 8.1). Perhaps one might have expected the numbers to have risen to pay off *contadini* for their support in the suppression of the Ciompi, but instead they declined to sixteen, probably because of increased stability and reduced warfare.

Nor did the rise of the Albizzi and their elitist reforms alter in any apparent fashion the trends of approved petitions. In 1392 fourteen petitions passed the councils; with the reforms in 1393, fifteen. Nor did the monumental constitutional reforms of 1410–11, which severely limited the scope and power of the councils, affect the ebb and flow of the hinterland's successful pleas for fiscal mercy. In 1410, the number of successful petitions increased from six to nine, then fell to two but rose the next year to ten. None of these cardinal dates of Florentine political history

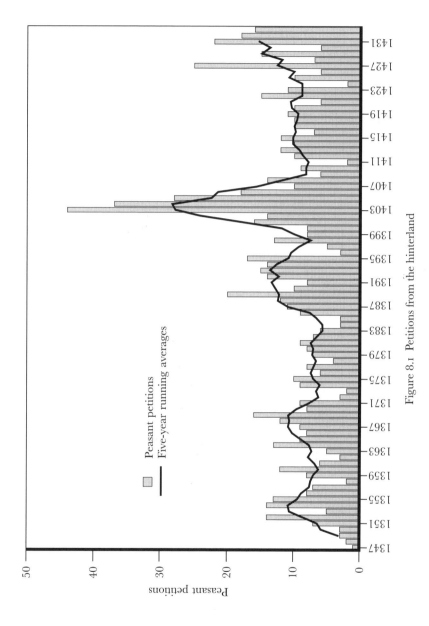

Figure 8.1 Petitions from the hinterland

shifted the balance between approved petitions and other decrees to regulate the countryside (see figure 8.2) or between petitions from the *contado*
and district (see figure 8.3). We shall also see that these changes in constitutional politics had no impact on changing the arguments marshaled
by those from the territory to gain the ear and sympathy of the government.

These petitions show two long-term patterns over these eighty-seven
years, 1347 to 1434. First, they rose or fell according to the ebb and flow
of warfare and invasion by foreign troops into Florentine territory at
least until 1402. In times of war the approval of petitions generally
increased – as with the war against Milan (Bernabò Visconti) followed
by the adventures and brigandage of the *condottiere* Fra Moriale
(1351–6),[1] the war with Pisa (1362–4), the revolt of San Miniato
(1369–70),[2] the war of Eight Saints (1375–8), war with Siena and
Giangaleazzo, Duke of Milan, at the end of the 1380s, followed by three
more wars with Milan with brief interludes from 1391 to 1404, the war
with Francesco Maria Visconti, Duke of Milan, 1424–9, and the war
with Lucca in the early 1430s.[3] With peace, peasants and townsmen continued to plead for assistance because of the lingering damages of war,
but the numbers usually eased off.

More striking than this correlation was a division of this eighty-seven-
year period into two parts around 1402, corresponding to the changes in
demography, fiscality, and the condition of the peasantry. This turning-
point even broke the correlation between war and the government's
approval of petitions. With the death of Giangaleazzo and the decline
in external warfare by 1403, the numbers of approved petitions, instead
of falling, shot up by over 400 percent and remained at levels not seen
before for the next three years. With Florence's "glorious war" and
acquisition of Pisa in 1406, the numbers of petitions sank and did not
rise substantially. Nor did King Ladislaus of Naples' invasion of
Florentine territory in 1411 send them upward. More remarkably, with
the ensuing decade of peace and prosperity after 1413, successful peasant
petitions, instead of falling, rose. Finally, 1427 saw another sharp rise in
the number of approved petitions. Even though 1427 was a war year, as
in the period 1403 to 1405, these petitions were not provoked by suffering
from war but by a new wave of peasant insurrections, this time from the
districtus (see figure 8.1).

[1] On Fra Moriale's career, see Caferro, *Mercenary Companies*, p. 5.
[2] Brucker, *Florentine Politics*, pp. 151 and 238–9.
[3] For these wars see Brucker, *Florentine Politics* and *The Civic World*.

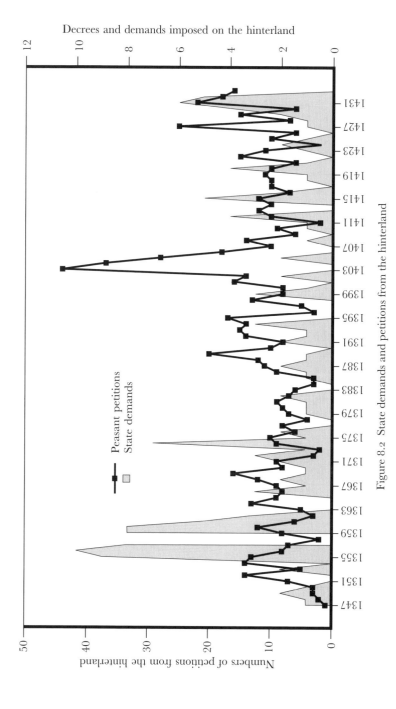

Figure 8.2 State demands and petitions from the hinterland

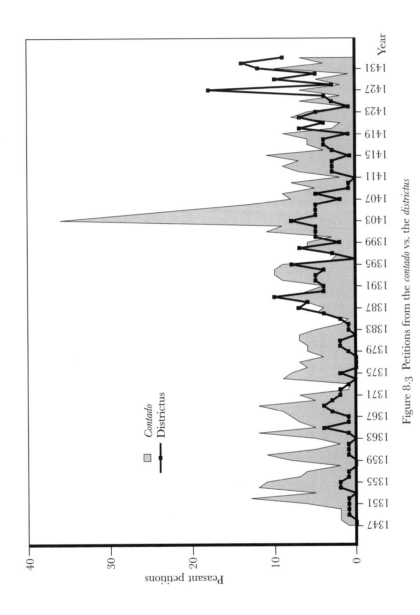

Figure 8.3 Petitions from the *contado* vs. the *districtus*

Second, the sheer numbers of successful peasant petitions increased after 1402. From 1347 to 1402 the government approved 8.3 community petitions a year from the hinterland; after 1405, the numbers increased by a third to over eleven per annum, and if the years 1403 to 1405 are added, the post-insurrectionary period then increases to 13.4. These increases did not arise from a decline in the government's bureaucratic rigor in examining peasant petitions. Rather the opposite seems to have been the case. In 1377 the councils increased the *Tre Maggiori*'s vote required to pass on a peasant petition for the councils' scrutiny.[4] By 1405, petitions were regularly examined by two citizens from the *Signoria*'s colleges, who often traveled to out-of-the-way places and reported back on peasants' claims.[5] Finally, in 1432 the government imposed yet further layers of bureaucratic procedure: rural villages as well as towns were now required to list the amounts of their *estimi* and any grants or terminations of grants that had been awarded to them within the previous five years.[6] As a result, the petitions of the 1430s become longer, with histories of past tax concessions that often extended back even before the mandatory five years. But the added red tape did not lower the numbers of approved rural petitions.

The increase in petitions from the hinterland after 1402 is still more remarkable when considered in the context of the pressures that had initially spurred the government into approving peasant petitions – rising taxes and war. First, the tax burden on the *contado* eased by 1406 and the huge inequalities between communities began to narrow. Second, the period 1402 to 1434 appears to have been more peaceful than the years from the Black Death to 1402 despite Ladislaus's incursions and the wars with Milan and then Lucca from 1423 to the return of the Medici. From the peace with Siena in 1404 until 1411, Florence experienced a rare interval without major incursions into its countryside. In the 1470s, Benedetto Dei compared the thirty-two years of war that culminated in 1402 (according to Dei) with the sixty-four months of peace before the Florentines embarked on their conquest of Pisa.[7] And in 1411, the guild community, tired of war, passed an exceptional law forbidding future wars. Florence was not to join any leagues or confederations or to make cavalry charges beyond its own borders and could hire armies of

---

[4] See chapter 7.
[5] Provv. reg., 97, 21r–2r, 1408.iv.26: "Et inde secutum est quod per vos fuerunt dati duos auditores qui examinatis omnibus concluserunt prout infra dicetur." Before 1405 "auditores" from the colleges or tax officials (*regulatores introitus*) might inspect a community's claims before a plea was approved by the councils, but evidence of such inspections appears only sporadically in the final *provvisioni*.   [6] *Ibid.*, 122, 371v–2v, 1431.ii.23.   [7] Dei, *La Cronica*, pp. 39–40.

sufficient size only to defend its borders, that is, no more than 500 lances or 1,500 archers or shield bearers (*panesarios*).[8]

Even though the law was short-lived, peace became the order of the day through the second decade of the fifteenth century. The collapse of the King of Naples' attempt to conquer Tuscany in 1413 opened a decade of peace and prosperity long remembered in Florentine history from the wine-dealer chronicler del Corazza to Machiavelli.[9] Further, it proved a rare moment in Florentine fiscal history, when the steady mounting of the communal debt – the *Monte* – was temporarily reversed. As Giovanni Rucellai recollected in the 1450s, this remarkable decade of peace also meant prosperity for the countryside. References in peasant pleas to war, invasion, and the devastation of villages corroborate the historians' impressions: only fifteen years between 1347 and 1402 (less than one-fourth) appear with no complaints of war as against ten years (nearly a third) from 1402 to 1433.

Behind these quantitative changes were qualitative ones reflecting the reasons peasants and small townsmen put forward to plead successfully for governmental clemency and what the Florentine oligarchy would accept as legitimate grounds for listening to and approving peasant petitions. Throughout this eighty-seven-year period the predominant cause for petitions from the hinterland winning government approval was war.[10] The peasant ambassadors' appeals often told stories of near total village destruction as in October 1352, early in Florence's first war with Milan. According to a peasant plea, the enemy cavalry had run through its village (Santa Maria Tartigliese in the Valdarno), burnt it to the ground, killed many men, captured others and taken booty. To raise ransoms for the return of their families, the survivors were forced to borrow 500 florins – a strikingly large loan for a small peasant village – from private banks at high interest rates.[11]

---

[8] Provv. reg., 99, 168r–9r, 1410.ii.4: "Quod non possit fieri guerra et alia."
[9] The contemporary chronicler and wine dealer Bartolomeo del Corazza, *Diario fiorentino*, pp. 32 and 48, celebrated the "perpetual peace" pacts during this decade made between the pope and Braccio of Perugia and those between Florence, Milan, Siena, and Naples. In the mid-fifteenth century Bracciolini, *Historiarum Florentini Populi*, bk. 5, p. 198, singled out these years as ones of peace. Rucellai, *Il Zibaldone*, p. 46, went further, seeing them as a golden age; agriculture became "profitable and rich," because the suspension of heavy expenditures to mercenaries meant low taxes. Niccolò Machiavelli, *Istorie fiorentine*, bk. 3, ch 29, p. 270 and bk. 4, ch 2, p. 272 continued to commemorate it into the next century, recalling it as a rare moment of peace and tranquillity.
[10] On war and the threat of mercenary violence as the cause of devastation and peasant petitions in Siena, see Caferro, *Mercenary Companies*, ch. 4.   [11] Provv. reg., 40, 37v–8r, 1352.xii.17.

At the same time, the commune of Barberino claimed that the war sweeping through the Mugello had "annihilated" their village, destroying all their homes, so that this large mountain commune now lay totally abandoned. Because of their misery, they argued, they would not have the wherewithal (*materia*) to return to their commune, rebuild their homes, or cultivate their crops unless Florence granted them tax relief.[12] In neighboring Galliano, Villanouva, and Pulicciano, the villagers said that they did not even "dare" return to their "annihilated homes and fields."[13]

Nor had the horrors of war abated by the end of my survey. The market town of Foiano, formerly in the *contado* of Arezzo, was at the strategic head of the Val di Chiana and vortex of invading troops from the north and south. From the moment it had become part of Florence in 1384 it had pleaded for "mercy" because of war damages. Besieged by Ladislaus of Naples' troops in 1411–13 and by the Duke of Milan in the 1420s, it continued to plead for fiscal concessions well into the 1430s, claiming that war had forced its population to flee and had made the sowing and reaping of crops impossible.[14]

Over this eighty-seven-year period, war-related causes constituted 57 percent of the reasons behind the petitions from the territory passed before the *Tre Maggiori* and councils.[15] The percentage was probably higher because occasionally the petitions were vague, referring simply to villagers' misery and "hard times" (*temporis asperitatem*). Such was the appeal of Poggibonsi in 1376 during the War of Eight Saints[16] and of the twelve communes of the Florentine Romagna in 1412, after they had been invaded by the King of Naples.[17]

Yet the predominance of war as a legitimate cause for tax relief shifted over time. Before the 1402 uprisings, almost two-thirds of the approved petitions from the countryside were war-related; afterwards the proportion sank to less than half.[18] Further, the preponderance of war-related petitions in the second half of the Trecento did not rest solely on the fact that it may have been more war-torn than the three decades that followed. War underlay the hinterland petitions even in peacetime far more frequently before 1402 than afterwards. In the

---

[12] *Ibid.*, 184r, 1353.xii.12. [13] *Ibid.*, 113v, 1353.vi.12. [14] *Ibid.*, 124, 108v–9r.

[15] Four hundred and nineteen of 733 petitions. For the eighty-seven-year period I found 904 petitions, but I excluded 171 that failed to explain or argue why a community was making its appeal. For a further thirty-nine petitions the reasons listed were only the formulaic ones of poverty and too many expenses. If these are also subtracted, war-related causes rise to 60 percent.

[16] Provv. reg., 64, 231r–v, 1376.xii.19. [17] *Ibid.*, 101, 15v–16v, 1412.iii.18.

[18] From 1347 to 1402, 233 of 359 petitions (65 percent) were war-related; 1402 to 1434 counted 185 of 369.

second half of the Trecento, Florence used periods of peace to demand the repair and construction of fortifications from its rural inhabitants. Such demands came with increased taxes and levies of labor from villages often already wrecked by war and high taxes, and provoked new complaints about the impossibility of shouldering new charges.

Thus, it was the first wars with Milan (1352–6) which prompted Florence to make plans for major fortifications and the building of village walls at strategic places along Florence's frontiers and trade routes. In 1354 the Commune drafted plans to fortify San Casciano ad Decem. Initially, Florence estimated the costs at 10,000 *lire*, but after two years the work had not been completed and proved to be more costly than calculated; a decree passed in 1356 raised the allotment to 17,000 *lire*.[19] Even more elaborate plans were imposed on Figline Valdarno from the late 1350s through the early 1360s.[20] At Staggia the call came at the end of the war with Siena in 1371;[21] at Pontassieve, at the end of the War of Eight Saints in 1381,[22] and at San Martino a Maiano in Valdelsa, again in peacetime, in 1389.[23] The only exception to this correlation between demands for large-scale expenditure on fortifications and periods of peace was the castle at Castellina in Chianti.[24] This project originated during the war with Milan in 1400, but when war was raging in the north and had yet to reach Castellina near the Sienese border.

Such fortifications involved large outlays of money, and their construction could last for years despite Florence's unrealistic deadlines imposed on dependent communities. As seen earlier for Gangalandi, they were regional strongholds where peasants from 8 kilometers or further could seek refuge in wartime, bringing their possessions and storing their harvests. Florence charged not only the places where the fortifications were built, but also the surrounding villages with special taxes and new labor obligations. In the case of Castellina, the expenditures were so great that Florence imposed a new tax based on the *estimo* across the entire *contado*.[25] Of the war-related causes put forward for government assistance, matters of fortification, whether it was the build-

[19] Provv. reg., 41, 94v–5r, 1354.x.25; 43, 82v–3r, 1356.v.28; 116r–v, 1356.vii.7; 152v, 1356.ix.27; and 46, 124v–5r, 1359.iv.12.

[20] *Ibid.*, 44, 85r, 22.ii.1356; 47, 148v, 22.ii.1359; and 52, 100v–1r, 22.i.1364. Also, see Matteo Villani, *Cronica*, II. bk. 3, r. 38, pp. 370–1.   [21] Provv. reg., 59, 81r–v, 1371.viii.21.

[22] *Ibid.*, 70, 141r–2r, 1381.xi.21.   [23] *Ibid.*, 77, 132r–3r, 1388.viii.27.

[24] *Ibid.*, 89, 3r–4v, 1400.iv.1.

[25] *Ibid.*, 89, 3r–4v; 91, 1r–2r, 18.iv.1402; further, in the petitions of 1403, villages as far away from Castellina as Borgo San Lorenzo, Cerbaia, and Mangona in the Mugello recorded their unpaid subsidies to build Castellina's castle; *ibid.*, 92, 29r–30r, 1403.iv.26; 138r–v, 1403.viii.28; 93, 135v–6v, 1404.xi.27; 149v–50v, 1404.xii.9.

ing of new forts or the munitioning of old ones, appeared most frequently.[26] But 1402 marked a change. From 1347 to 1402 such appeals appeared in 30 percent of the peasants' war demands; afterwards they fell to half that proportion and to only 5 percent of all petitions from the territory.[27]

What then were the nonmilitary causes that moved citizens' sympathies to assist their territorial subjects and filled the gap left by the diminished war claims after 1402?[28] On occasion, peasant petitions made clear that no matter how meticulous the Florentine merchant mentality, Florence's books were not always in order and even peasants could point to errors in Florentine accounting. As early as 1352 a village in the *pieve* of Cascia petitioned the councils, claiming that the village owed 27 *lire* 18s and not the 112 *lire* 10s as Florence had calculated; they added that payment of the extra 84 *lire* 12s would spell its "total destruction."[29]

Not all of these mistakes were innocent clerical errors. Peasants succeeded in winning tax concessions against previous acts of fraud and scandals involving dishonest officials both from Florence and within their own villages. In 1356, the Priors extended the deadline for compiling the new tax assessments in Prato and its district because of the discord, scandals, and divisions unleashed among the *comitatini*. According to the officials of the *estimo*, secret deals had been struck between certain privileged taxpayers and local officials.[30] In 1401, a syndic of Gangalandi absconded with 1,200 florins of his villagers' taxes through fraud and usury.[31] In 1403, the men of Santa Felicità a Larciano were credited 200 *lire* because the Florentine tax official had run off with their *estimo* payments back in 1390.[32] But these cases go no further in explaining the shift to non-war-related petitions after 1402; all but two of the fraud cases and over two-thirds of petitions that spotted the government's errors came before.[33]

The success of other territorial petitions turned on arguments about

---

[26] One hundred and eighty-three of 741 petitions.
[27] Before 1402, 70 of 233 war-related petitions and of 471 in all were for assistance with fortifications; afterwards, they fell to 22 of 186 and of 433 petitions in all.
[28] Poverty was the most common reason peasants and townsmen put forward; present in most petitions, it rarely stood alone as a reason for government assistance.
[29] Provv. reg., 40, 184r–v, 1352.v.4.   [30] *Ibid.*, 43, 115v–16r, 1356.vii.7.
[31] *Ibid.*, 90, 34r–36v, 1401.iv.27. A similar case of fraud happened in 1419 with the small parish of Santa Chiara alle Sodera; *ibid.*, 109, 116r–v, 1419.viii.14.
[32] *Ibid.*, 93, 221v–2v, 1403.xii.18.
[33] Sixty-eight of ninety-nine for accounting errors and eleven of thirteen for fraud were petitioned prior to 1402.

the damages suffered because of civil strife within individual villages or conflict between villages. Peasants appealed to Florence to settle scores between their rival families, as with an ongoing feud between two magnate families in Montevettolini in 1379.[34] In Barga the internal conflicts were so great that the villagers claimed that without Florentine intervention "in a short while the village will wind up exterminating itself."[35]

Internal feuds were also given as the reasons for prorogating deadlines for tax payments without penalties.[36] The majority of these cases arose over claims of unfair internal distributions of the *estimo*. To achieve "peace and tranquility" within Castelfranco in the Valdarno Superiore, their men petitioned in 1374 to elect new local officials to redraft their village's *estimo*, "making new measurements and assessments of the villagers' possessions."[37] In its preambles for new *estimi*, Florence often pointed to such internal squabbling as the cause for new distributions.[38] Given the wide discrepancies and inequalities between *estimo* burdens imposed on communes and parishes, especially before 1402, it is surprising that such complaints about unequal taxation did not surface more often. Perhaps they were implicit in numerous complaints, especially after 1402, when villages protested that their tax burdens were so ruinous, as one petition put it, that its villagers could not "breathe," because of the excessive vexations of over-zealous tax collectors.[39]

Disputes between villages also hinged on natural disasters as with the Arno's periodic flooding and changes of course that led villagers to seek Florence's intervention in newly created boundary disputes. Others centered on disputes over the local administration of justice. Several of these concerned the *Podesterie* of San Niccolò a Calenzano and its surrounding villages.[40] The smaller and weaker villages within its administrative ambit complained that the men of San Niccolò had bullied them into castle duty and had unjustly extracted munitions payments from them. As a consequence, they petitioned Florence to leave Calenzano's jurisdiction. Subject communes such as Montemurlo even accused Calenzano of "tyranny" to argue for secession as did Santa Maria a

---

[34] Provv. reg., 68, 72r–v, 1379.vi.22.   [35] *Ibid.*, 79, 203v–9v, 1390.x.19.
[36] *Ibid.*, 44, 116r, 1357.iv.27.   [37] *Ibid.*, 62, 64v, 1374.vi.16.
[38] *Ibid.*, 44, 78v–9r, 1356.v.28: "Auditis infinitis fere querelis factis per comitatinos et alios supportantes extimum ordinarium comitatus"; also see 112, 137v–40r, 1422.x.18; 117, 38r–43v, 1427.v.21.
[39] *Ibid.*, 63, 89r–90r, 1375.viii.11.
[40] On the history of Calenzano, see Daniela Lamberini, *Calenzano e la Val di Marina: storia di un territorio fiorentino*, 2 vols. (Bologna, 1987).

Querceto, Santa Lucia a Settimello, Santa Maria in Padule, Santa Maria a Carraia, and Santa Margherita a Torri from 1378 through to the end of my survey.[41]

Such intercommunity conflict could even lead to armed struggle, as when squabbles between Foiano and Monte San Savino in 1390 involved strategic meetings (*conventiculum seu congregationem*) and the death of a man from Monte San Savino.[42] Later, in the same curia, the men of Marciano went further to resolve their boundary disputes. With hoes, spades, hammers, and other farm tools, twenty-four villagers destroyed the boundary markers, throwing them into the river Elsa along with wood, branches, and other garbage to dam the river, causing it to break its banks and flood their neighbors' crops. They were sentenced for these acts but appealed to the councils and were absolved because "they were weak, poor, and agricultural workers."[43] Although these dispute settlements may give flesh to the largely unrecorded village life of late-medieval Tuscany, like petitions against fraud and bad accounting, they fail to fill the gap caused by the shift in petitions from war-related pleas after 1402; just the opposite, 80 percent of them were lodged before.[44]

On occasion, Florence granted remission of fines because villagers pleaded to being confused or ignorant of their obligations. Even stupidity or "simplicity" might stand as an excuse for avoiding taxes or breaking the law. In several instances, rural communes claimed to have forgotten their obligations. One of the most remarkable of these cases came immediately after the Black Death, when Mangona claimed that no one remained who remembered what the commune owed Florence.[45] Other rural villages pleaded that they had misunderstood the exemptions Florence had granted them either in their acts of submission to Florentine dominion or in later grants of immunity. Often the misunderstanding revolved around the gabelle on contracts, which communes believed was included in their packages of immunities.[46] Pleas of ignorance could even stem from the government's script. In 1356, the hill

[41] Provv. reg., 65, 298r–v, 1377.ii.26; 67, 130r–1r, 1378.i.27; 68, 166v–7r, 1379.xi.24; 75, 14v–15r, 1386.iv.2; 123, 113v–14r, 1432.v.27; 125, 46r–7r, 1434.iv.27.   [42] *Ibid.*, 79, 100r–1v, 1390.ix.25.

[43] *Ibid.*, 96, 183r–4r, 1407.xii.17: "In dicta curia Montis et dictum terminum devasterunt et inciderunt et lapides et lignaminia quibus muratus et affixus erat dictus terminus proierunt in flumine Else . . . et cum pluribus aliis de dicto Marciano renplenerunt fluminem Else . . . proierunt multa lignamina, spinos, et immoditas."   [44] Twenty-five cases before and six after 1402.

[45] Provv. reg., 36, 8v–10v, 1348.ix.12.

[46] *Ibid.*, 79, 120v–2r, 1390.vi.21; 80, 32v–4v, 1391.v.29; 83, 37v–9r, 1394.iv.27; 177v–8r, 1394.x.14; 93, 152v–3r, 1404.xii.9.

village of San Bartolomeo a Molezzano argued that they had not paid
Florence their correct *estimo* and gabelles because the treasury's notary
did not "write clearly and distinctly." Florence conceded and canceled
its fines.[47]

Still other petitions tell stories of the Commune's condescension
toward rural subjects it believed too backward and crude to understand
their accounts properly. These communities lay mostly on the mountainous frontiers of the Florentine state and reflect citizen prejudices against
mountain villagers that can be seen in other contemporary writing.[48] In
1381, citizen inspectors for the *Signoria* reported to the councils that the
notary and men of Pietrabuona in the Florentine district were ignorant
of Florentine municipal customs (*jura municipalia*) and for that reason
incurred certain penalties due to their mistakes in accounting. But,
because the commune was so distant from Florence, located in the wilderness (*in loco silvestro*), and its inhabitants were simple rustics who had
grown rigid from the cold (*rustici sunt morantes olbricitur*), Florence waived
the fines.[49]

In 1383, the parish priest of Santa Maria a Cintoia in the Chianti,
described as a "simple and ignorant man," misunderstood his obligations in paying the tax on priests and sold the village mill to pay the
officials. The Commune refunded the mill.[50] In 1411 the commune of
the Montagna Fiorentina had run up a debt of 7,300 *lire* by failing to pay
its castle duties over a seventeen-year period, arguing that it had not realized that the 432-*lire* a year payment to furnish munitions to the castle at
San Niccolò was a part of its obligations. After months of deliberations,
Florence demanded the payments but waived the fines, believing the
mountain peasants' ignorance was genuine; those sent to examine the
case reported that the men of the Montagna were indeed "homines
rudes et grossi."[51]

Finally, in 1428 the mountain men of the Podere Fiorentino incor-
rectly completed their self-assessments or "portate" for the new *catasto* of
1427, in this case to their detriment, listing sterile lands as productive.
The Commune refunded their overpayments, because they were unciv-

---

[47] *Ibid.*, 43, 95r, 1356.vi.9.
[48] See my *Women in the Streets*; and Sermini, *Le Novelle*, novella XII: "L'autore e ser Cecco da
Perugia," in which the author goes to live with mountain people outside Siena to escape the
plague of 1424 and criticizes their way of life from their religious beliefs to their gestures and
underwear. Also see Poggio Bracciolini, *Facezie*, esp. story xii, p. 21: "Di alcuni contadini ai quai
venne chiesto dall'artefice se volessero il Cristo, che dovean per incarico comprare, o vivo o
morto."   [49] Provv. reg., 70, 60r, 1381.vi.6.   [50] *Ibid.*, 72, 25v–6v, 1383.iv.17.
[51] *Ibid.*, 100, 110v–11v, 1411.xii.23.

ilized and stupid (*rudes et ignari*).[52] But, again, such tolerance toward the confused, ignorant, and uncivilized of the territory fails to account for the 1402 shift in clemency. Instead, the balance again tilted in the opposite direction. Of these grants of *noblesse oblige* three-quarters came before the peasant uprisings of 1402.[53]

How then did the non-war-related petitions change? After the revolts of 1402, Tuscan peasants appear to have grown leery of their republican lords meddling in their daily affairs, and this may explain the decline of petitions that pleaded for state intervention to settle internal scores and other business. Despite the formulaic language which continued occasionally to express the peasants' filial piety and supplication at the feet of their urban masters, their petitions for financial relief and tax breaks after 1402 display a new emboldened zeal to pin the blame directly on their rulers for their present predicaments and inability to pay their taxes. It was a new rhetoric that seeped through even after the notaries' Latin had no doubt sanitized the original pleas, whether spoken or written. Before 1402 only 2 percent of the successful community petitions alluded to mistreatment by over-zealous tax officials or to the enormity of tax burdens that had brought a community to insolvency; afterwards the proportion of such complaints more than trebled.[54]

In 1412 a community as small as the mountain parish of San Jacobo a Frascole in the commune of Pozzo with an assessment of only 31 *lire* placed the blame for their poverty and indebtedness directly on the government of Florence and its fiscal oppression.[55] In 1415 another small parish complained that its salt tax was too high given the numbers left in the village. Instead of referring to the usual reasons for a sharp decline in population – warfare, brigandage, the destruction of crops, death, and capture for ransom – the village syndics criticized Florence directly, blaming its onerous obligations both public and private for the village's troubles: "it is for these reasons that so many men had been forced to leave their village."[56] They further threatened that if their injuries were not redressed, those who remained would leave. Others held the Commune directly responsible for their depopulation, pointing their

[52] *Ibid.*, 120, 385v–7r, 1428.x.20. According to the government report, these men sustained themselves for most of the year on chestnuts and water alone (*pro eorum victu expedit ut fere in toto anno castaneis et aqua se substentent*).   [53] Fifteen cases in the first period, five in the second.
[54] The increase climbed from 10 of 471 to 29 of 438 petitions.
[55] Provv. reg., 101, 11v–12v, 1412.xii.23: "propter nimis magnam taxationem extimi vigentis."
[56] *Ibid.*, 105, 29r–31r, 1415.iv.26: "Et quod multi ex hominibus dicti populi tum publicis oneribus tum privatis obligationibus molestati relicta patria ab ierunt."

fingers at the tax collector (*propter vexationes exactorum*[57]). Still others cited their *estimo* assessments and "the daily vexation to pay their communal debts" to explain why their parishioners had left and why without clemency the rest were soon to follow.[58]

This new criticism and change in political sentiments on the part of Florence's rulers can also be seen in laws passed after 1402, in which Florence admitted that its officials were often guilty of "molesting those from the *contado*, extorting from their labor or possessions payments for taxes and communal debts."[59] Such was the 1403 law "Contra offitiales comitatium" directed against officials who unjustly "extorted" taxes from dwellers in the *contado*.[60] At the beginning of 1406 another law prohibited Florentine tax collectors and police (*exactores et nuntios*) from capturing and imprisoning those from the territory because of public debts or forcing property from them without a special "license" issued by the Priors themselves.[61]

In 1404 Florence passed laws to end the exploitation of the countryside through usury, first by outlawing it altogether,[62] then by regulating it. In 1405 a law prohibited Jewish money lending in the countryside. Although the subject communities protested against this law, repealing it in one commune after another,[63] the Florentine councils continued to see usury as the cause of peasant exploitation and of peasants' inability to pay their taxes. In 1420 and again in 1422 laws elected new bodies to regulate usury with the express intent of protecting *comitatini* from the "the useless expenditures" of usury, admitting that such exploitation had "greatly damaged" them.[64]

It was not only in the petitions and negotiations of the insurrectionary years, 1403–5 and 1427–30, that peasants stood up to their republican lords, blaming them for their misery. In addition to outright revolt, peasants had another card to play in their bid to lessen their fiscal burdens. The emptying of the countryside had begun to weigh on the minds of Florence's rulers more after 1402 than even after the catastrophic mortalities of 1348 or successive plagues of the second half of the fourteenth century. Aware of Florence's need for agricultural labor to feed the city, sustain its tax base, and to protect its borders from foreign invasion, peasants threatened increasingly after 1402 to leave their vil-

---

[57] See, for instance, Raggiolo's appeals for reductions in their debts; *ibid.*, 102, 117r–18r, 1413.x.28.
[58] *Ibid.*, 102, 67r–8v, 1413.vi.27.   [59] *Ibid.*, 94, 257v–8r, 1405.ii.19.
[60] *Ibid.*, 92, 150v–1v, 1403.x.10.   [61] *Ibid.*, 94, 257v–8r, 1405.ii.19.
[62] *Ibid.*, 93, 149r–v, 1404.xii.10: "Per alcuno modo non si possa prestare ad alcuno comune popolo o villa alcuna contracta di danari sotto pena di libri V[c] per ogni volta."
[63] *Ibid.*, 94, 232v–3v, 1404.i.24; see note 148 below.
[64] *Ibid.*, 109, 236v–8r, 1419.ii.13; and 111, 247r–8r, 1421.i.19.

lages and the territorial state of Florence altogether if their pleas were not answered favorably. In their petitions they argued that such abandonment would not only lead to the further misery and the ultimate destruction of their villages, it would also be of no "utility" to Florence.

To be sure, such threats can be spotted before. As early as 1351 during Florence's first war with Milan, the peasants of the mountain communes of San Godenzo and Babila argued that they were being burdened to "an unaccustomed degree" by Florence's war against Milan and the Ubaldini and for their forced conscription as soldiers and guards of the Alpine passes that led into the Florentine Mugello. If they did not receive compensation for their patriotic duties, the highlanders threatened to leave their fatherland (*patria*).[65] Yet before the uprisings of 1402, such threats were exceptional and, as in the example above, occurred on the strategic frontiers of the Florentine state and during periods of warfare. Nearly three-quarters of these threats (sixty-eight of ninety-four cases) came after the 1402 waves of insurrections, and by contrast with the earlier period over 80 percent of them were now passed in peacetime.[66]

Peasants and townsmen of the subject towns placed their pleas for relief more often in a demographic context than within any other except war – in nearly a quarter of the petitions which stated a cause.[67] These included claims of village desertion and the loss of men, women, or entire families either through death, disease, or emigration. But, despite the fact that the ravages of plague and war etched deeper scars into the population of Tuscany during the second half of the fourteenth century than afterwards (as in other regions of Italy), the councils favored peasants' pleas that turned on demographic arguments far more often after 1402 than before. Earlier, only 11 percent of the petitions referred to village population decline as a reason for needing fiscal concessions; afterwards such reasons more than quadrupled, rising to a quarter of all approved petitions.[68] Moreover, before 1402 the majority of petitions that cited demographic decline to elicit governmental sympathies were framed in the context of war; afterwards, 84 percent of them came in peacetime and did not hinge on the ravages of war.

Within this demographic context the most important cause cited after 1402 was disease and, most often, plague, whereas before it had been war. Again, this is counter-intuitive: nearly two-thirds of the plague petitions came after 1402, that is, after the plague of 1400 – the last plague to inflict

---

[65] *Ibid.*, 39, 64v, 1351.xi.22.   [66] Fifty-five of 68 petitions.
[67] One hundred and sixty petitions of 733.
[68] Fifty-one of 471 petitions in the first period; 109 of 433 in the second.

devastating mortality levels in Tuscany until at least the end of the fifteenth century.[69] Per annum, the results are even more surprising: after 1402, successful peasant petitions citing plague almost trebled their earlier appearance in approved petitions across the plague-ridden second half of the Trecento, when plague was more frequent and more virulent.[70]

To judge by contemporary chronicles and estimates made from tax records and other sources for demographic growth and decline, no plague between 1402 and 1434 was comparable to the devastation wrought by plague in 1348, 1363, 1374, 1383, or 1400. Indeed, only one or two plagues stand out for special mention at all in contemporary accounts between 1402 and 1434: that of 1417 and perhaps 1424. Yet between 1409 and 1432 at least one petition in all but five years claimed that plague was the source of a village's misery and passed the councils' scrutiny for tax relief or the diminution of public debts.

Many of these so-called plagues were certainly not of epidemic proportions (whatever the disease might have been).[71] Most must have been localized diseases of the sort that had brought populations in check throughout the preindustrial past – food poisoning, cholera, yellow fever, smallpox, typhoid, and other illnesses.[72] Yet the significance of such minor plagues in peasant petitions should not lead us to conclude that diseases other than "true plague" were becoming more rampant in the countryside after 1402. If anything, the Black Death may have created new immunities to other bacteria or viruses; diseases such as leprosy appear to have been on the decline – perhaps, as some historians have speculated, as a result of the Black Death. The decline in the frequency and mortality due to the Black Death coupled with rising standards of living at least by the *estimo* of 1412 was probably making Tuscany a healthier place to live than it had been in the late Trecento.[73] What had changed was the Florentine oligarchy's sensitivity to the demographic realities of its territorial state and their consequences for fiscality, military defense, and the economy.

---

[69] See Ufficiali della Grascia, I Libri di Morti, 187: 1398–1412; and Ann Carmichael, *Plague and the Poor in Renaissance Florence* (Cambridge, 1986), p. 62. This plague killed over 12,000, at least 20 percent of the city's population but probably more.

[70] Sixteen mentioned plague in the first period, thirty-three in the second, or less than one petition every 2.25 years to one a year.

[71] On the Black Death, see Graham Twigg, *The Black Death: A Biological Reappraisal* (London, 1984); and Herlihy, *The Black Death*, pp. 6–7 and 25–31.

[72] On the "penumbra" of preindustrial diseases, see Christopher Wills, *Plagues: Their Origin, History and Future* (London, 1996); and Carmichael, *Plague and the Poor*, pp. 18–35.

[73] This seems to have been the case in other regions of Europe as based on changing figures of life expectancy; see Christopher Daniell, *Death and Burial in Medieval England 1066–1550* (London, 1997), pp. 133–4.

The republican rulers' change of heart and finance is seen as much from the silences within their day-to-day legislative decisions as from their actions. Such silences were most deafening in the year of the most devastating of plagues, that of 1348, which may have been as severe in the countryside as in the cities, if not more so, and may have wiped out as much as half the population in parts of rural Tuscany.[74] In neither that year nor the next did Florence pass ordinances to assist plague victims or to readjust the fiscal burdens on peasant communities despite the mammoth changes in population and what they spelt for communities meeting their fiscal obligations to *estimo* and salt tax, which had been calculated on communities' pre-Black Death numbers.[75]

The only general legislation the plague prompted was labor regulation. Like the Ordinance and Statute of Laborers passed at the same time in England,[76] these laws were repressive and in no way sought to alleviate peasants' pain and dislocation. In 1349, the Commune passed severe penalties against rural laborers who did not meet the conditions of their work contracts or who neglected to work in search of better contracts. The legislation was repeated with added conditions and penalties in 1352, 1356, 1359, and during the plague year of 1363.[77] The only carrot to attract new laborers to Florence immediately after the Black Death was a decree motivated by politics, not demography. In 1349 the skirmishes between Florence and the Ubaldini heated up as the Ubaldini stepped up raids on merchants and pilgrims crossing the transapennine highways between Bologna and Florence. In response, on July 2, 1349 Florence sought to weaken the Ubaldini's infrastructure by offering ten-year exemptions from direct taxes and absolution from all crimes to all those living on Ubaldini lands who would abandon their allegiances to the Ubaldini and move into the Florentine *contado*. Yet, despite the fact that this decree was passed only a year after the Black Death, plague was not even mentioned.[78]

[74] Herlihy, *Medieval and Renaissance Pistoia*, pp. 55–77; and Herlihy and Klapisch-Zuber, *Les Toscans*.
[75] On October 9, 1348 the councils elected a committee to redistribute the *estimo* "because many who had been rich might now be poor and the poor, now rich", but the global tax base was not altered (Provv. reg., 36, 15v–6r). On September 16 1349, it was lowered from 125,000 (see Provv. reg., 35, 141r–v) to between 75,000 and 100,000 *lire*, but the plague was not mentioned as the cause and the new distribution would not have any effect until the 1350s (Provv. reg., 37, 3v–4r).
[76] The standard work remains B. H. Putnam, *The Enforcement of the Statutes of Labourers during the First Decade After the Black Death* (New York, 1908).
[77] Provv. reg., 40, 27r–v, 1352.xii.3; 43, 146v, 1356.xi.12; 46, 101r, 1358.ii.22; 51, 71v–2r, 1363.xii.2.
[78] *Ibid.*, 35, 141r–2r, 1349.vii.2. Florence declared as rebels and threatened to confiscate the lands of those who did not accept its offer. Other clauses outlawed marriage between the Ubaldini and Florentines and even "any communication with any member of the Ubaldini house by letter, messenger, or ambassador." Finally, the decree posted bounty of 1,000 gold florins for each member of the family captured alive, and 500 florins if brought in dead.

Like the laws, petitions from individual villages and towns failed to evoke significant governmental clemency by citing the demographic and economic havoc of the early plagues. Only two petitions which won government approval focused their arguments on the Black Death and the consequential colossal losses in population, but neither won special exemptions, tax adjustments, or even remissions from their communal debts. The first to pass the council's scrutiny was Mangona's plea on September 12, 1348, which sought clemency from the heavy fines charged for missing its last payments on a 1,800-florin land deal made with Florence in December 1345. Mangona's syndics pleaded that the plague (*mortiferam pestem*) had spread throughout all parts of Tuscany, that it had yet to subside, and that it had hit Mangona particularly severely. They reported that three-quarters or more of its population had been wiped out and that those who remained believed that everyone was about to die. In addition to arguing that they had missed their May and July payments because no one was left with any memory of these obligations, they further pleaded that they found it "most difficult if not impossible" to pay the May through October installments for 1348, much less the penalties added to them. But, despite the catastrophic consequences of 1348, the government answered Mangona's pleas only in part: absolving the fines, they insisted that Mangona meet its Black-Death installments on its debts within a limited time-frame.[79]

The second plea came from the lower Arno market town of Montevarchi in February 1349 and likewise won no tax exemptions or remissions on debts. Instead the community asked the councilors for a special ruling that would allow all testaments redacted during the plague year by "nonmatriculated notaries" (*alios notarios non matriculates*) to remain valid against the protests of the Florentine guild of lawyers and notaries. The men of Montevarchi argued that the plague (*pestiferam mortalitatem*) had killed or incapacitated all their matriculated notaries, thus forcing those writing last wills to turn to others.[80]

The government's deafness to pleas concerning plague persisted through the third quarter of the Trecento. No petitions arose out of the minor plagues reported by either Matteo Villani or Marchionne di Coppo Stefani in the late 1350s or, more astoundingly, for the plague of 1363. It was not until 1374–5 that a rural petition won governmental approval by citing the plague. These plague years coupled with famine may have been the worst since 1348, at least according to the chronicler Stefani, who

<hr/>

[79] *Ibid.*, 36, 8v–10v, 1348.ix.12.   [80] *Ibid.*, 36, 54v, 1348.ii.9.

recounted harvest failures in the countryside and a death toll of 6,000 out of 60,000 in the city of Florence.[81] Stefani's reports are matched in 1374 by the lowest numbers of councilors attending the meetings of the People and the Commune found in these documents. The massive fleeing of prominent citizens from the city of Florence almost brought the wheels of government to a halt. On July 14, 1374 the government passed special laws because of the difficulty of assembling the councilors "propter incumbentiam pestiferi temporis," and lowered the quorum necessary to pass legislation to 149 men until the end of November.[82]

Although these years were the first to see peasants make successful arguments for relief because of plague, all of the villages concerned were along the northern mountainous frontier that separated the Florentine state from Bologna or Romagna – the Alpi Fiorentine and Podere Fiorentino – and thus of prime military importance, especially given the new foreign invasions into these lands with the War of Eight Saints. Moreover, these petitions were fortified with descriptions of famine and the destruction due to warfare.[83] Unlike earlier plague years, 1374 brought together three of the four horsemen of the apocalypse: "the many wars, famines, and epidemics" as a petition from the Podere put it in 1376.[84]

Although 1374–5 was the first time plague opened Florentine minds to address the demographic plight of its territory with concrete fiscal measures, such concerns can be seen earlier in a shift in labor legislation from the stick to the carrot. As mentioned earlier, the Commune's immediate response to labor scarcity following the plague was to pass laws entitled "contra laboratores terrarum" in 1349, 1352, 1356, 1359, and 1363, which put stiff penalties on those who neglected their work on farms owned by citizens of Florence as well as on servants and wet nurses in the countryside who asked for more than their established salaries.[85] In 1355, the law even condemned as rebels (*per exbannitos et rebelles comunis Florentie*) those who "damaged" *poderi* by their failure to work. Although these laws remained on the books[86] and were used against

---

[81] Stefani, *Cronica*, r. 745, pp. 289–90.   [82] Provv. reg., 62, 104r–v, 1374.vii.14.

[83] *Ibid.*, 62, 191v–2v, 1374.xi.22; 63, 49r–50r, 1375.v.19; 89r–90r, 1375.viii.11; 92r–v, 1375.viii.11; 133r–4r, 1375.x.11; 149r–50v, 1375.x.25; and 64, 49r–v, 1376.vi.10.

[84] *Ibid.*, 64, 49r–v, 1376.vi.10: "propter multas guerras et propter magnas carestias et lipidimias."

[85] *Ibid.*, 36, 154v, 1349.viii.6; 42, 114v–15r, 1355.viii.21; 161r–v, 1355.xii.9; 43, 146v, 1356.ix.12; 46, 101r, 1358.ii.22; 51, 71v–2r, 1363.xii.2.

[86] See *Statuta Populi Communis Florentiae (1415)*, 3 vols. (Freiburg, 1778–83), III, "De Laboratorum Tractatu et Materia", rr. 11–26, pp. 393–404; esp. "Quod laboratores, et agricultores non possint dimittere bona inculta", r. 11, pp. 393–5.

peasants through the fifteenth century and probably beyond,[87] those passed in the aftermath of the 1363 plague show an about-face in the Commune's attitude toward its agricultural laborers and its strategy toward its demographically deteriorating rural economy.

The 1363 act was the last of the "contra laboratores" laws.[88] In the following year, the councils passed the first of a new type of act "in favorem comitatorum" to be repeated with varying exemptions and conditions through the first half of the Quattrocento. As with acts of piety seen in last wills and testaments across Tuscan and Umbrian cities, 1363 appears to have also registered the beginnings of change in Florence's rural politics and its consciousness toward suffering in the countryside.[89] Instead of struggling against the tide of market forces, tightening restrictions, and raising penalties on peasants who "neglected work" in search of better working conditions, Florence sought to compete for foreign laborers and to attract back their own peasants who, because of war, famine, debts, and especially excessive taxes, had skipped over the border.

The 1364 law exempted all those who "would come back to work the land" either as renters or as *mezzadri* for six years from all *estimo* payments, gabelles, and duties in the army and cavalry.[90] With different lengths of immunity and often slightly different conditions, Florence passed at least twenty-seven similar laws and decrees before the return of the Medici in 1434.[91] In some years, the city issued more than one such law; in 1429, for instance, five acts were promulgated attempting to attract labor into the Florentine countryside. But it was not until 1431 that such laws began to include urban artisans and other workers and not necessarily "laborers of the soil to come, live, and work with their

---

[87] See Cohn, *Women in the Streets*, pp. 25–7; and *The Laboring Classes*, pp. 186–90. In addition, AP, 2208 for 1369 and 1370 is filled with numerous urban prosecutions against peasants for trespass, cutting trees, and failure to work the lands belonging to Florentine citizens.

[88] One exception was a law promulgated during the famine of 1374 which gave special powers to the Podestà to punish those who worked the lands of Florentine citizens and were not "diligent" in cultivating or in caring for these citizens' animals; Provv. reg., 62, 73v–74r, 1374.vi.16. This was not, however, a revival of the old "contra laboratores" laws passed in the aftermath of 1348.

[89] See Cohn, *The Cult of Remembrance*.   [90] Provv. reg., 52, 34r–v, 1364.x.3.

[91] *Ibid.*, 65, 44v–6v, 1377.vi.4; 68, 113r–15v, 1379.viii.17; 72, 171r–2r, 1383.x.20; 74, 204r–5r, 1385.xii.8; 80, 197r–8v, 1391.xii.2; 88, 182r–3v, 1399.ix.14; 226r–7r, 1399.xi.7; 328v–9v, 1399.ii.23; 91, 146v–7r, 1402.ix.20; 93, 193r–v, 1404.ii.3; 101, 333r–4r, 1412.i.24; 334r–v, 1412.i.24; 105, 215v–16v, 1415.xi.22; 107, 215r–v, 1417.x.5; 112, 143r–4r, 1422.x.18; 113, 271r, 1423.ii.7; 114, 63v–4v, 1424.xii.5; 117, 122v–3r, 1427.vi.26; 123r, 1427.vi.26; 118, 116v–17v, 1427.xi.20; 120, 461v–2r, 1429.ii.8; 491r–v, 1429.ii.13; 121, 72r–v, 1430.x.26; 122, 2r–v; 2v–3r; 4r–5r, 1431.iv.16; 124, 167v–9r, 1433.vii.8. I wish to thank Gene Brucker for drawing my attention to some of these laws in the *Libri fabarum*.

families in the city, *contado*, district, or any other place where Florence possessed hegemony or custody."[92]

Despite these initial changes in the consciousness of the Florentine ruling class toward its hinterland, they fail to constitute a watershed in policy or opinion; after 1375 the next wave of pestilence in 1383 did not register a single successful petition whose justification for governmental clemency rested on the plague or turned on sudden demographic decline. Instead, the next mention of plague did not come until 1392 and that from a war-threatened zone near the borders of the Romagna. The men of Lozzole, a fortified mountain village in the Podere that once belonged to the Ubaldini, claimed it was unable to pay a fine for neglecting to apprehend a murderer within its borders due to a "magna epidemia" that struck in the winter of that year.[93] It must have been an isolated epidemic, perhaps influenza, as described by the Minerbetti chronicler in the Casentino in 1386.[94] Before 1402, other plagues and localized diseases also prompted the councils into granting villages some relief, but in every case cries about the damages of war formed the overarching context for these villagers' successful petitions.[95]

Further, not until after the plague of 1400 did Florence finally pass its first general act legislating welfare across the *contado* because of the economic and demographic damages of plague. After the councils had passed a special charity of 600 florins to assist impoverished citizens afflicted by plague,[96] they turned their attention to the plight of their *comitatini* on October 11, 1400. They argued that "because of the peasants' weaknesses and the invasion of pestilence," the government would grant a month's extension on the September salt taxes and the ordinary

---

[92] Provv. reg., 122, 4r–5r, 1431.iv.5. Perhaps reflecting a shift in Florentine demography and the need for new housing the councils passed a decree "Magistrorum forensium privilegium" in 1420, meant to attract stonemasons and carpenters (*magistri lapidum et lignaminis*) from Lombardy or elsewhere to immigrate into the city or territory of Florence. The law granted them protection against any coersion to join the Florentine guild of masons and carpenters, but they were required to pay the guild 1 *lira* 4s annually. Unlike the legislation to attract agricultural labor, these masters were not offered tax exemptions; *ibid.*, 110, 103v–4r, 28.ix.1420. In 1429 to attract silk workers (*quilibet tintor serici sive sete aut textor drapporum seu pictor operarum drapporum vel alius quicumque laborans suis manibus de dicta arte*) to the city, the government offered security for three years from paying any debts, whether to private individuals, businesses, or any other collectivity, but did not offer any tax incentives; *ibid.*, 120, 303r–5v, 1429.viii.23.

[93] *Ibid.*, 80, 272r–v, 1391.ii.26. Bartolomeo del Corazza, *Diario*, p. 29, describes another case of what may have been influenza, which spread across Tuscany in 1414, causing widespread suffering and death.   [94] Minerbetti, *Cronica volgare*, pp. iv and 23.

[95] See Provv. reg., 84, 13v–15r, 1395.iv.6; 90, 256r–7v, 1401.x.26 and 302r–3r, 1401.xi.23.

[96] *Ibid.*, 89, 93r–4v, 1400.vi.25: "Elemosina propter pestem."

estimo to every village, parish, commune, and *pieve* in the *contado* of Florence.[97] In addition, the pestilence of 1400 was the first to move the Florentine rulers to draw up a new *estimo*. Its preamble made the ruling councils' reasons clear: "There are two reasons for making the new survey – first war, then plague."[98] But only later did plague stand alone as the government's reason for enacting a new *estimo*, and it came after a much less devastating plague, in 1424 – Florence's last *estimo* before the *catasto* reforms.[99]

As reflected in the government's concessions to the mountain peasants during the plagues and famines in 1374–5, war continued to figure as the first and major reason for granting immunities to peasants even in plague years; afterward, twenty-nine of thirty-three that approved plague petitions (over 85 percent) did so without any mention of war or the advantages a frontier community might contribute to Florence's defenses if granted clemency. Further, of those pre-1402 peacetime petitions that did manage to win governmental clemency because of plague, all were of the stamp of the 1348 petition from Mangona; none won more than the postponement of payments or the lifting of fines. Afterwards, Florence took its rural communities' peacetime appeals more seriously. In addition to remission of communal debts, peasant communities hit by plague often won tax immunities and revisions of their *estimi* based as they were on population as much as on material resources.

Further, the post-1402 plague petitions that won clemency show a change in geography: before, these communities were almost all on Florence's strategic borders; afterwards, they came predominantly from within the heartland of the Florentine *contado*, nearer to Florence and lower down the hills and plains, in places such as Macioli, Colognole, Rignano, Borgo San Lorenzo, San Martino a Valcava, Cerreto, and Empoli (which after the conquest of Pisa was no longer on the frontier but in the center of the Florentine territory).[100]

Had the epidemiology of the plague (or of other diseases variously called "pestiferio morbo," "morte pestifera," "mortalitas," or "furor sevienter mortalitatis" and the like) changed? Given contemporary views that mountain air gave safe haven against the plague and present-

[97] *Ibid.*, 89, 150v–51r, 1400.x.12.
[98] *Ibid.*, 90, 133r–7r, 1400.vii.23. For the text, see chapter 3, note 23.
[99] *Ibid.*, 115, 1r–4r, 1425.iii.9.
[100] *Ibid.*, 94, 129r–31r, 1405.viii.17; 95, 169v–70r, 1406.viii.26; 102, 15r–16r, 1413.iv.22; 105, 66v–8r, 1415.vi.7; 105, 66v–8r, 1415.vi.7; 108, 108r–10r, 1418.vi.28; 109, 70v–1r, 1419.vi.20; 110, 126r–v, 1420.x.3; 113, 179v–80v, 1423.x.26.

day convictions that the plague was bubonic, it is surprising that any,
much less almost all, the pre-1402 approved petitions citing plague came
from the mountains. While I do not deny that plague did hit these mountain outposts, the shift in geography after 1402 owed much more to politics than to epidemiology. After 1402 the welfare of its rural inhabitants,
the threat of mass out-migration and depopulation played on the hearts
and purse strings of the government in a way that it had failed to do
earlier.

Petitions pointing to natural disasters as the reason for needing
government clemency follow no more accurately the chronology of disasters in the Florentine territory from the Black Death to the return of
the Medici than do plague petitions. First, the majority of petitions that
described crop failures as the reason for needing governmental clemency
before and after 1402 were more connected with acts of man – war –
than of God. Torching peasant crops and devastating the countryside
was a common weapon of enemy troops as well as of brigands to
terrorize peasants and to block food supplies to towns and cities.[101]
Nonetheless, nearly 60 percent of the petitions which pointed to crop
failure as a reason for deserving governmental relief followed the
peasant uprisings of 1402.[102] Had strategies of slash and burn become
more prevalent as tools of warfare after 1402, or do these descriptions
show instead a change in peasant rhetoric reflecting what would move
the councils toward sympathetic action – the disastrous demographic
crisis of the Florentine regional state?

Regardless of possible changes in warfare, not all the crop failures in
these petitions were connected with war. When only those petitions that
cited crop failures without any mention of war are considered, the post-
1402 proportion increases to two-thirds.[103] Certainly, the trends in grain
prices from the Black Death through the first three decades of the
fifteenth century do not suggest that these changes in rhetoric reflected
a sudden deterioration of climate at the turn of the century. If anything,
the opposite was closer to the truth. In the second half of the Trecento,
grain prices fluctuated wildly and generally increased from their pre-
Black Death levels, while in the early fifteenth century they stabilized
and began to decline.[104]

Furthermore, we know from the chroniclers that the second half of
the Trecento was rife with climatic disasters that led to crop failures and

[101] On such uses of warfare, see Caferro, *Mercenary Companies*, ch. 4.
[102] Seventeen before 1402, twenty-five afterwards.   [103] Six in the first period, ten later.
[104] See Goldthwaite, "I prezzi," p. 33, table B.

famines. The chronicler Stefani lists at least seven years when inclement conditions brought famine to the Florentine countryside and city. In June 1349, hailstorms destroyed vineyards and other crops throughout the *contado*, leading to a wine famine in Florence.[105] In 1367 through the fall of 1368, famines resulted from heavy rains;[106] conditions deteriorated further because of a heavy snow and a deep freeze in January 1369.[107] Heavy rains again led to crop failures in 1370, 1371, 1374, 1379, and 1383; in this last year, according to Stefani, they provoked the worst wine harvest ever remembered.[108] To these inclement years Matteo Villani adds others, such as in 1354 when hailstones "as big as mandarin oranges" fell, "killing animals and men and wrecking rooftops."[109]

Heavy snows and unusually cold temperatures also struck in the second half of the fourteenth century, punctuating the chroniclers' normal reports of military maneuvers and the elections of Priors. By these reports Tuscany was certainly much colder in the late fourteenth century than today.[110] In April, 1356, Florentine troops were halted in their campaigns against the Battifolle counts around Raggiolo because of the snow, winds, and "immeasurable cold."[111] In 1369 unusual cold and snows reached even the city of Florence and persisted for two months.[112] And in 1386 a cold wave led to widespread attacks of coughing, fever, and death, perhaps one of the first recorded flu epidemics in Italy.[113]

The decrees also hint that winters may have even been deteriorating in the latter half of the fourteenth century. On April 5, 1391, the councils voted to change the dates when one *vicarius* from Florence would replace another when traveling to the distant mountains of the Podere Fiorentino. Because of heavy snows and inclement temperatures, recent *vicarii* to the Podere had complained of the "great dangers and inconveniences" of crossing the mountains to reach these villages, often losing their horses and other animals along the way. As a result, the councils voted to move this changing of the guards from 14 February to 13 April.[114]

---

[105] Stefani, *Cronica fiorentina*, r. 638, p. 233.   [106] *Ibid.*, p. 268.   [107] *Ibid.*, p. 269.
[108] *Ibid.*, pp. 275, 290, 360, and 434.   [109] Matteo Villani, *Cronica*, I, bk. 4, r. 24, p. 507.
[110] For evidence of colder and wetter weather throughout Europe beginning in the fourteenth century, see N. J. G. Pounds, *An Historical Geography of Europe* (Cambridge, 1990), p. 11.
[111] Matteo Villini, *Cronica*, I, bk. 4, r. 21, pp. 737–78.   [112] Stefani, *Cronica*, p. 269.
[113] Minerbetti, *Cronica volgare*, p. 23; on years of bad weather after the Black Death, also see Leverotti, "La crisi demografica," pp. 120–1.
[114] Provv. reg., 80, 14r–v. For descriptions of blizzards and severe cold in the Aretine mountains near Soci in December 1431, see Traversari, *Hodoeporicon*, pp. 41, 48–9.

While the government was almost completely deaf to the cries of those in the countryside whose buildings and crops had been ruined by inclement weather before 1400, afterwards such pleas became more frequent and better served. The natural disaster most often mentioned – in fact, the only climatic disaster mentioned before 1402 in the petitions – was flooding and its destruction to town walls, fortifications, and crops. From the earliest registers I have examined, peasants and subject townsmen petitioned the government for help in confronting the damages caused by rivers and streams in the Arno basin changing their course.

Such natural disasters often had human causes. At the beginning of 1348, those who lived and possessed property along the Umbrone, Chielle, and Vigone rivers petitioned Florence, claiming that flooding caused by the Pisans damming the Arno had brought "maximum damages" and the ruin of their crops. In response, the government voted to elect several "good men and citizens of Florence" to take measurements and to study the problem of too many mills damming the streams but refused any relief through fiscal concessions.[115] In 1354, in roughly the same area, flooding had impeded traffic along the Florence–Pisa road, damaging the "goods, lands, and houses" of those in the parishes of Settimo, Gangalandi, and Giogoli as well as properties owned there by Florentine citizens. Again, instead of outright grants or conversion of tax payments, the councils elected "good citizens" to study the problem of too many ditches running off into the rivers.[116]

The next petition complaining of floods did not arise until sixteen years later. Again the petition came from the parishes around Settimo, but, despite the interval of silence, the plea made clear that the problem of inclement weather had not abated; nor had Florence's "good men" done much to solve the hydraulic problems of the lower Arno. The peasants of Santa Columba in Settimo began: "the Arno river now for a long time" had continued to overrun its banks, damaging greatly their possessions. But their pleas were answered once again, not by tax relief, but by election, this time of "six good men and citizens of Florence" to measure and redraw property and parish boundaries, where the Arno had changed its course.[117] In the same year Pontorme (downstream from Settimo) complained that the Arno had flooded its lands, damaging fortifications, crops, and trade. According to its report, the Florence–Pisa road was passable only by boat. They pinned the blame,

---

[115] Provv. reg., 35, 95r, 1347.i.22.   [116] *Ibid.*, 40, 207r–v, 1353.i.30.
[117] *Ibid.*, 58, 69v–70r, 1370.viii.20.

not on God, but on the many mills owned by the monastery of Settimo further upstream and the fishing ponds it had created. Florence again refused tax relief but did act against the monastery, ordering it to lower its dams and to demolish its pond (*peschariam*).[118]

Two years later flooding damaged this alluvial plain again, this time closer to the city in the parishes of Campi with the swelling of the Marina, Gavina, Degaia, and other streams that flow into the Bisenzio and the Arno, causing these rivers "to overflow their banks, change their courses, and destroy many possessions." Despite the villagers' claims that "many of their properties had been reduced to nothing" and that yearly they lost great quantities of grain to the floods, the government refused immunities, a reassessment of their *estimo*, or to provide any other financial assistance. Instead, "good Guelf citizens" again were elected to study the problem and decide on how best and how much to spend on repairing the banks of the Arno. Once decided, however, the monies were not to come from state coffers but were to be paid *pro rata* by those whose possessions would be improved by the government's intervention.[119] In 1374, again villages from around Settimo reported that "for a long time" the Arno's flooding and changes of course had damaged fields and caused confusion over boundaries and property rights. Florence came to the same resolution: its "mercy" did not include the allocation of funds or tax credits and was limited to the election of "good Guelfs" who would adjudicate disputes between property holders.[120]

In January 1380, the first petition in my survey from the upper Arno complained of damages due to flooding, but the report makes clear that floods were hardly new to those further upstream from Florence and further from the capital. The men of San Giovanni Valdarno reported that "for many years" during November and December the Arno was accustomed to flooding, "lacerating their possessions and turning the plains into places of sterility." The flooding had further caused serious damage to their walled town, reducing many places along the Arno to ruins. They pleaded that, given their poverty and the extent of the damages, they would find it impossible to provide the necessary expenses without governmental clemency. But, despite these pleas and their relevance to fortifications, the councils went no further than to elect Florentine citizens to study the situation with advice from the Officials of the Towers.[121]

---

[118] *Ibid.*, 91r–v, 1370.ix.25.   [119] *Ibid.*, 60, 59v–60r, 1372.viii.14.   [120] *Ibid.*, 62, 4v–5r, 1374.iii.27.
[121] *Ibid.*, 68, 225r–6r, 1379.i.30.

It was not until the end of 1388 that a commune received financial assistance for repairs caused by flooding, even in the indirect fashion of tax conversions for repairs. In December, the Officials of the Towers reported that the Arno had done great damage to San Giovanni Valdarno, destroying its fortifications and taking away almost all its wheat fields (*buono terreno da pane*). The Officials of the Towers estimated the damages at 2,000 *lire* or more, and the councils resolved to allow 1,000 *lire* from San Giovanni's *estimo* payments to be credited for the repairs so long as the Valdarno commune financed the other half and provided the labor.[122]

The government did not approve another petition to assist a rural village because of flooding until 1400, when the Arno caused 400 florins worth of damage to San Giovanni's walls and fortifications. Florence had become perhaps more concerned and certainly more generous; it converted the community's meat gabelle of 150 florins a year toward the costs.[123] By the next time those from San Giovanni complained of flooding, the councils were even more generous. To help defray the repair bills estimated in 1433 at 2,000 *lire*, the councils granted the commune exemptions from paying their meat and wine gabelles for two years and allowed it to recoup the *Podestà*'s salary by substituting a notary for four terms.[124]

The fate of the Valdarno Inferiore also changed around 1400. In 1410, Pontorme reported that the Arno had completely inundated over a thousand *braccia* of the main road to Pisa within the village, destroying buildings along the way. Florence's surveyors estimated the damages at 7,000 *lire* and agreed to help by exempting the commune from six payments of its *estimo*, amounting to 840 gold florins (about 3,360 *lire*).[125] In August, Pontorme received an extension, reporting that flooding had done more damage than previously estimated. In the meantime, plague had spread through the village, interrupting work on the repairs.[126]

In 1418, appeals to the government were finally heard for the first time from communities outside the Arno basin and considerably further from the capital. The commune of Corniolo in the Romagna pleaded for a "subsidy" because local flooding had damaged the mills they rented from Florence. The councils granted them an exemption from two payments on their mill rents owed to Florence and absolved them of any penalties, provided their men repair the mills within ten months.[127] Finally, in

---

[122] *Ibid.*, 77, 250v–1r, 1380.xii.12. [123] *Ibid.*, 89, 48v–50r, 1400.iv.27.
[124] *Ibid.*, 124, 48r–50v, 1433.iv.28. [125] *Ibid.*, 99, 50v–1r, 1410.iv.26.
[126] *Ibid.*, 148v–9r, 1410.xii.24.   [127] *Ibid.*, 108, 88v, 1418.vi.8.

January 1434 Florence heard the cries from its most distant outpost in the northeast; the newly incorporated commune of Modigliana complained that its fortifications, on which it had recently spent "vast sums," had collapsed because of floods. To rebuild the turrets, Florence granted Modigliana a six-year exemption on its lance payments provided the repairs were completed by 1436.[128] The old pre-1400 policy of merely establishing boards of citizens to study the problem or at best adjudicating how to divide the costs of repairs among property holders vanished from the government's repertoire of its so-called "clementia et misericordia." Afterwards, Florence dug into its own coffers, often offering substantial tax breaks to assist peasant and small-town victims.

Of climatic disasters flooding was the major one to win the oligarchy's sympathy and action, perhaps because often village fortifications and town walls and not just peasant fields and crops had been destroyed. But, as the chroniclers and other sources make clear, flooding was not the only climatic disorder to impoverish peasant villages.[129] Another scourge, hailstorms, did not register a single reference in the *provvisioni* before 1402, presumably because hailstorms, unlike flooding, do not wreck fortifications. Afterwards, however, they begin to appear without any references to war or destruction of a commune's defenses. In 1413 seventeen villages in the area of Monte Morello complained of a hailstorm in June that destroyed their vines and other crops. It had been so severe that the parishioners claimed they would not be able to feed their families without government subsidies, and if Florentine clemency was not forthcoming, they would leave "for alien lands."[130] Florence gave in, absolving them from three payments of the *estimo*.

In 1418, four parishes within the Mugello *pieve* of San Cresci a Macioli pleaded for tax exemptions because of their debts and plague. To these, they added that inclement weather had worsened their plight: not only had it destroyed their grain, it had uprooted vineyards and trees. These disasters, they argued, further impeded their ability to pay off their debts, thus leading to the arrest and imprisonment of many of their household heads, thereby compounding their fiscal plight. The government granted the communities an exemption from three payments of the extraordinary tax.[131]

---

[128] *Ibid.*, 124, 236r–7r, 1433.i.16.
[129] See, for instance, Stefani, *Cronica*, p. 233; in June 1349, "a great hailstorm [*grande tempesta di gragnuola*] destroyed crops throughout the entire *contado* of Florence."
[130] Provv. reg., 102, 101r–2r, 1413.x.20: "Cogerentur deserere comitatus et pro aliena territoria pro eorum victu mendicando discurrere."   [131] *Ibid.*, 108, 107v–8r, 1418.vi.28.

In 1421 storms again threatened the livelihood of peasants in the Florentine territory.[132] This time a storm (*quamdam tempestatem*) caused the Florentine Romagna to lose an entire harvest, which, the residents claimed, was responsible for the spread of famine through eleven of their communes. Florence responded by granting the Romagnoli a five-year immunity on their lance tax of 400 florins.[133] In the following year the councils reduced the public debts of the commune of San Pietro a Petrognano to 100 *lire* because storms had wrecked their harvest.[134] Finally, in the same year many parishes in the Chianti around the parish of San Martino a Monte Rinaldi[135] were exempted from two years of the *estimo* for roads and bridges, charged at 40s on the *lira*, because hailstorms in June had destroyed their wheat, olive trees, and vines. They explained that the damage not only struck the present year's crop but would cancel the following year's as well. In addition to these grants the councils provided the peasants with the "security" against Florentine tax collectors and other creditors hounding them for payments on all private debts for a year except those owed to landlords of farms rented out on *mezzadria* contracts.[136]

After 1402 Florence showed clemency toward its rural subjects for reasons that earlier either had not been mentioned or had registered only a scant appearance. One such body of petitions concerned local trade. Before 1402 only four petitions mentioned the loss of trade as a legitimate cause for a community's needs; afterwards it increased sixfold; twenty-five petitions persuaded Florence to help restore or stimulate local trade within the hinterland. Nor was this post-1402 increase in Florence's concern for the economic well-being of its territorial subjects simply a matter of Florence's expansion and incorporation of Pisa, Cortona, and Livorno after 1406.

To be sure, against an earlier historiography that saw Florence fleecing Pisa for all it could get and wrecking its economy,[137] Florence's decrees suggest a more complex history of Florence–Pisan relations. Almost from the outset of its domination, Florence began to reverse the harsh penalties of its conquest and became concerned about Pisa's rapid demographic and economic collapse, seeing the Pisan economy as vital

---

[132] See Leverotti, "La crisi demografica," p. 122. [133] Provv. reg,, 111, 152v–3v, 1421.ix.26.
[134] *Ibid.*, 112, 116r–17r, 1422.viii.28. [135] See Francovich, *I Castelli del contado*, p. 113.
[136] Provv. reg., 112, 176v–7v, 24.x.1422: "Eo salvo non . . . pro debitis . . . vulgo dicitur 'l'oste' aut ad quem tenetur occasione feneratorum cum quibus terrena laborantur."
[137] See Silva, *Pisa sotto Firenze*; and Michael Mallet's criticisms of this position in *The Florentine Galleys in the Fifteenth Century* (Oxford, 1967) and "Pisa and Florence in the Fifteenth Century: Aspects of the Period of the First Florentine Domination," in *Florentine Studies*, pp. 403–41.

to the larger economic fortunes of the Florentine territorial state. As early as 1409 Florence began to chip steadily away at the enormous tax burdens it had initially levied on the Pisans.[138] The Pisans successfully petitioned Florence almost yearly to lower their citadel costs, the new gabelles, and the special tax on Pisa and its suburbs. From 1409, through the records surveyed here and beyond,[139] Florence granted Pisa remissions of fines for late tax payments, revisions of gabelle rates, and grants of immunities.

In addition, the earliest decrees I have spotted that attempted to attract foreign artisans and merchants, as opposed to rural laborers, into the territory of Florence, concerned the urban economy of Pisa and not the city of Florence. "Desiring not only to conserve but to increase [the numbers] of the city of Pisa": thus began a Florentine decree of 1413 that granted exemptions first for ten years and then in 1419 for twenty years on all taxes and gabelles except the gate tax and the ordinary gabelle to any foreigner (except those then living in the *contado* or district of Florence) who chose to live with their families in the city of Pisa.[140] Further, in 1416 the Florentine councils granted Catalan merchants freedom to trade and settle in Pisa with immunities from taxes for five years, and although the stated reasons were political ("to conserve the mutual friendship between Florence and the King of Aragon"), the stimulus to trade within the region is also evident.[141] In 1419 the privileges were extended for another ten years, and in 1430 for another ten.[142] To assist further in the revitalization of the Pisan economy, the councils granted Catalan merchants in 1428 a license to transport grain from the Pisan Maremma.[143] The first attempts to attract foreigners to live and work in the city of Florence came later and were for only specialized trades – house builders in 1420 and silk workers in 1429.[144]

Yet only 12 percent of these petitions to improve local trade pertained to the newly acquired cities of Pisa, Cortona, and Livorno combined. The majority were launched not by the first tier of Florentine territorial cities – Arezzo, Pisa, Pistoia, Prato, Cortona, Livorno, and Volterra – but

---

[138] Provv. reg., 98, 106r–v, 1409.xii.12.   [139] See Mallet, "Pisa and Florence."

[140] Provv. reg., 101, 372r; and 109, 1419.xii.21; Petralia, "'Crisi'," pp. 317–18; Mallet, "Pisa and Florence," pp. 413–14; and Herlihy and Klapisch-Zuber, *Les Toscans*, p. 143.

[141] Provv. reg., 298v–301r, 1415.ii.4: "Catalanorum mercatorum capitula." The original statutes gave Catalans and all other subjects of the King of Aragon rights to trade freely and to settle in the city of Florence as well as Pisa. But the agreement's renewals do not include Florence.

[142] Provv. reg., 109, 32r–v, 1419.v.24; and 120, 444r–v, 1429.i.19. Neither Mallet nor Petralia mentions these laws.   [143] *Ibid.*, 119, 233v–4v, 1428.x.21.

[144] *Ibid.*, 110, 103v–4r, 1420.ix.28; and 120, 303v–5r, 1429.viii.23.

by market towns within the second or third tiers – Borgo San Lorenzo, Castiglion Fiorentino (Aretino), Montelupo, Empoli, Pontorme, and Barga – or even smaller markets such as Barberino in the foothills of the Mugello and Signa nearer to Florence's city walls.[145] To revitalize its local trade, Empoli received more concessions than any other place in the territory.

After 1402, Florence also intervened in the commercial affairs of its rural subjects with the intention of improving their economic plight. In addition to regulating the zeal and exploitation of its own officers in collecting taxes and imprisoning *contadini*, the Commune passed a law in January 1405 that regulated the lending practices of Christians in the territory and expelled Jewish money lenders.[146] Certainly this law was motivated by antisemitism;[147] it begins "considering that Jews and Hebrews are the enemies of our Lord Jesus Christ on the cross and of all Christians and exercise usury against the decrees of the Holy Church . . ." Nonetheless, its stated purpose was also to protect territorial subjects from unfair rates of interest.

Those in the hinterland, however, did not see it Florence's way and almost immediately began to petition to repeal the bans on Jews. Already by 1406 the city of Arezzo pleaded for licenses to be granted to Jews to return and to lend money. At least eight other towns followed their example, arguing as did the people of San Gimignano in 1410 that the law of January 1405 had done them "maximum damage"[148] and that they wished their Jews to be allowed to return and to lend money. Evidently the right must have been taken from Volterra after its abortive revolt of 1429, and it petitioned successfully again for the return of its Jews in 1432.[149] The only evidence I have spotted before 1402 that restricted creditors' freedom to exploit the hinterland as they pleased or listened to appeals from territorial subjects on questions of credit came from Arezzo in 1389. It successfully lobbied Florence to modify a law of

---

[145] On the demographic and economic hierarchy of cities and towns within Florentine Tuscany, see Herlihy and Klapisch-Zuber, *Les Toscans*, pp. 237–40.

[146] See Provv. reg., 94, 232v–3v, 24.i.1404; Umberto Cassuto, *Gli ebrei a Firenze nell'età del rinascimento* (Florence, 1918), pp. 362–3; and Molho, "A Note on Jewish Moneylenders in Tuscany in the late Trecento and early Quattrocento," in *Renaissance Studies in Honor of Hans Baron*, ed. by Molho and John Tedeschi (Florence, 1971), pp. 97–117; and *Florentine Public Finances*, pp. 38–9.

[147] See Molho, "A Note."

[148] Provv. reg., 99, 72r–v, 1410.vi.26: "Quod hoc cedit in magnum dannum et incommodum dicti comunis Sancti Geminiani." Also see *ibid.*, 102, 163r–v, 1413.ii.19; 110, 104r–5r, 1420.ix.28; 117, 86r–7v, 1427.vi.6; 122, 287r–8r, 1431.xii.6; 123, 5r–v, 1432.iii.29. On this rationale, see Fubini, "Prestito ebraico e Monte di Pietà a Firenze (1471–1473)," in *Quattrocento fiorentino*, pp. 172–3.

[149] Provv. reg., 123, 5r–v, 1432.iii.29.

the previous year prohibiting loans on the sale of beans, grain, and other crops.[150]

Over 85 percent of the state interventions to restore or encourage trade, either by granting market days without gabelles or tax relief because of damages to trade, came after the peasant uprisings of 1402.[151] The majority of these were requests for tax exemptions, usually the reduction of a commune's gabelles because of the decline or a temporary blockage of trade. In 1402 the men of Montelupo complained to the councils that they could no longer support the fixed tax of 2,000 *lire* on their gabelles on retail wine and 185 florins on meat because war had blocked their "free access" to Pisa, from which they claimed to have lost two-thirds of their trade. Florence responded by cutting these fixed gabelle payments accordingly.[152]

The neighboring communes of Pontorme and Empoli petitioned Florence on several occasions because trade in merchandise, usually meat and wine, had also been impeded by blockage of the Florence–Pisa road. In 1401, the reason had been plague.[153] In the next year, these communes pleaded that since 1392 trade had been interrupted or altogether blocked along this road as well as along the Arno because of war, but their case did not win a favorable hearing from the Florentine councils until 1402.[154] With the siege of Pisa in 1406, Empoli argued that the war had again impeded trade; as a result, it won further reductions on its meat and wine gabelles. Its arguments, however, were based on commerce and not on war: they pleaded that their goods could no longer "flow down the Pisa road" as they had when trade had been "free and frequent."[155]

Mugello communities near the Apennine passes, such as Barberino and Firenzuola, also won reductions in their gabelles during the first decade of the fifteenth century because of arguments about the hazards to trade and dangers along the road to Bologna.[156] In 1417, the commune of Barga, surrounded by Florence's enemies, petitioned Florence for tax relief. Instead of stressing the damages of war as certainly would have been their rhetorical slant before 1402, they pleaded for Florentine mercy on the basis of trade, arguing that in their present conditions "nobody could profit from trade" and therefore their gabelles should be cut.[157]

---

[150] *Ibid.*, 78, 258r–9r, 1389.x.27.   [151] Five before 1402, thirty-one afterwards.
[152] Provv. reg., 91, 1402.iv.26.   [153] *Ibid.*, 90, 76r–7v, 1401.x.26.
[154] *Ibid.*, 91, 9v–10v, 1402.iv.18.   [155] *Ibid.*, 95, 6r–7r, 1406.iv.22.
[156] *Ibid.*, 96, 228r–v, 1407.ii.12.
[157] *Ibid.*, 107, 24r–v, 1417.iv.16: "Quod nichil eorum personis lucrari possunt."

Except for the 1405 law outlawing Jewish money lenders, the difficulties for local trade, usually of grain, meat, and wine, had not changed dramatically from the mid-fourteenth through the first decades of the fifteenth century. Certainly, the wars against Milan in the 1350s and against San Miniato and Pisa in the 1360s and early 1370s, had blocked highways and waterways, and made mountain passages dangerous for merchants, as chroniclers and the decrees that sponsored retaliation against the Ubaldini proclaimed. Yet before 1401 not a single petition for tax relief made it through the councils that complained solely and explicitly about the damages or impediments to local trade. Instead of a sudden worsening in trade during the early fifteenth century, the approval of these petitions, as of those regarding plague, floods, and hailstorms, points in another direction – a change in the mentality of Florence's ruling class regarding what constituted legitimate grounds for state clemency.

9

What the peasants won

Certainly it would be opportune to examine those petitions that failed to go beyond the *Tre Maggiori* and how they may have changed over time or to judge the gap between what peasants may have initially asked for and what they finally got, but the original pleas simply do not survive. In addition, the notaries of the *Riformagioni* rarely intimated what peasants or townsmen may have first proposed before their petitions had run the gauntlet of bureaucratic hurdles and had been finalized in the *provvisioni*'s Latin parchments.

Nonetheless, from time to time discrepancies between requests and gains do emerge between the lines, as with the pre-1402 cases of flood examined earlier, where the petitions' preambles suggest that the peasants or townsmen sought financial relief but received only governmental studies or arbitration on local squabbles over boundaries. Compromises between the councils and villagers could, in fact, last months, as is clear from the petition argued by the "oratores" from Pisa who were running up their city's bills by so many trips to the big city. Although it is impossible to measure the differences in what villagers may have originally proposed and what they eventually won, it is possible to chart changes in what the government offered its territorial subjects to ease their suffering.

Before 1402 the most common governmental act of clemency granted to communities was directly connected with governmental military strategy and the defense of the realm. Peasants who found themselves in desperate straits, unable to pay their taxes usually because of war, won concessions only grudgingly. Rather than outright remissions of debts, reduction of taxes, or immunities, the government allowed the communities to convert their taxes into maintaining or building fortifications. Before 1402, 16 percent of the government's concessions merely took tax debits from one account in the Florentine treasury and transferred them to another. Afterwards such conversions declined by three-quarters, forming only 5 percent of what peasants and subject townsmen won.[1]

Next in importance among the pre-1402 grants of clemency were governmental absolutions of community-wide condemnations (14 percent of the petitions).[2] Various courts for various crimes and misdemeanors had imposed collective penalties on rural communities or towns. For instance, entire communities could be held responsible for the bad deeds of a small group of parishioners, and occasionally communes would appeal for relief or absolution from these fines. Peasants even petitioned to cancel fines and other punishments incurred because of armed insurrection against the Florentine state. Such was the case with a 1354 petition by the commune of Santa Maria in the Valdarno Superiore (Terranuova), whose men had been found guilty of armed conspiracy. It was one of the few pre-1402 petitions to challenge directly the authority of one of Florence's offices. The peasant ambassadors rebutted the charges, arguing that on many occasions the Executor of the Ordinances of Justice had vexed and tormented their community and that the court's inquest had been "mendacious".[3]

Rural communes might petition Florence to benefit only one of their members, as in 1365, when the commune of Bibbiena petitioned to reverse charges against a Giovanni di Berto of Bibbiena. Thirteen years earlier (on June 2, 1352) he had been condemned to death by fire for leading a siege with raised banners, armed cavalry, and foot soldiers that succeeded in "expunging" the castle of Giogatore in the Montagna Fiorentina. Giovanni's rebel troops then allegedly cut the trees around the castle and burnt the homes inside its walls.[4] But such reversals of fortune or even the use of the councils as an appellate court for collective village crimes were rare, at least before the uprisings of 1402, when numerous peasant villages won absolution from armed insurgency and rebellion, not because the government's charges had been false, but because of the peasants' positions of strength.

On the other hand, such petitions for absolution could rest on much less weighty matters, as with the appeals won by the communities of the Montagna Fiorentina on February 8, 1363, when each of its parishes was fined between 10 and 100 *lire* depending on their *estimo* assessments for their failure to appear in court.[5] The absolutions on occasion overturned condemnations against late or false returns in drafting new *estimi*, as with

---

[1] Before 1402 Florence granted seventy-three such conversions of taxes; afterwards twenty-three.
[2] Sixty-six petitions before 1402, thirty-three afterwards.   [3] Provv. reg., 40, 62r–v, 1353.ii.19.
[4] *Ibid.*, 53, 66r–v, 1365.x.21.   [5] *Ibid.*, 50, 106v.

the communities of Bibbiena and Pescia in 1365.[6] And often in their pacts of submission to Florentine dominion, villages won absolution for all their men who earlier had been under bans of exile.[7]

Before 1402, these absolutions from collective condemnations were most often directly tied to the government's principal preoccupation with its hinterland – its defense of the realm. Such was the case at the end of 1366, when the councils absolved numerous villages of the southern Chianti close to the Sienese border. Because of the war with Siena, the "perfidious acts" of military companies, and the inability of the villagers to harvest their grain, the men of nine Chianti parishes fled with their families instead of obeying Florentine orders to stay and defend their villages. With the end of the war, the peasants returned and begged Florence to absolve their fines.[8] The most frequent condemnations against which peasant communities pleaded before 1402 were fines for neglecting guard duty or failure to maintain and munition fortifications. Such condemnations might amount to fines of no more than 50 *lire*, as with the parish of Galatrona's neglect of castle duty in 1376,[9] but could run into thousands of *lire*, as with the condemnations that followed Prato's failure to meet its deadlines on rebuilding its city walls.[10]

Finally, the third most frequent concession granted to the communities of the hinterland before 1402 also did nothing to reduce debts or revise or diminish taxes. In 9 percent of these successful petitions, the councils met the peasants' cries for "mercy" by simply absolving them of the fines for failure to pay their taxes or other fees on time.[11] They granted new deadlines, usually no more than a month or two later, but the payments were not reduced. In no way did the government's clemency redefine the village's tax structure or debts that had brought it into insolvency and caused it to miss its payments in the first place.

With the peasant uprisings of 1402, the treatment of its hinterland changed radically. The two most important acts of governmental clemency in the pre-1402 period shrunk to near negligible proportions. Absolutions for fines of late tax payments dropped to 3 percent of successful petitions and conversions of taxes into castle-building to 5 percent. Only absolutions for collective condemnations against villages

[6] *Ibid.*, 53, 50v–1r, 1365.x.21.
[7] In addition to the *provvisioni*, see the numerous summaries of these acts in *I Capitoli*, I.
[8] Provv. reg., 54, 86v–7r, 1366.xii.10.   [9] *Ibid.*, 64, 110r–11r.
[10] *Ibid.*, 74, 109v–10v, 1385.viii.22; and 75, 98v–9v, 1387.viii.9.
[11] Forty-four of 471 before 1402; 13 of 433 afterwards.

and towns remained close to their previous proportion, though they too fell to less than 9 percent of governmental acts of clemency (thirty-eight petitions). But, as suggested above, the character of these condemnations had shifted. From a predominance of small fines for the neglect of castle duty, from 1403 to 1405 and again in 1426 to 1430, petitions prompted by peasant uprisings gained absolution from acts of rebellion that had called for the death penalty and the destruction and confiscation of villagers' property; different from the past, these concessions were coupled with massive tax and debt reductions.

After 1402, four categories of governmental clemency rose to the forefront which previously had put in only rare appearances. Unlike earlier makeshift responses that in no way altered what rural subjects owed the treasury, all four of these new governmental actions fundamentally changed what villagers owed Florence. First, in the early years of the fifteenth century the government answered the pleas of peasants and subject townsmen by cutting administrative costs to their local governments.[12] Foremost of these costs were the expenses of maintaining public order – the large salaries and expenses paid to Florentine officers of the peace, from the Captains in the larger subject cities of Arezzo, Pisa, and Pistoia to the *vicarii* and *Podestà* of rural regions, along with their bevies of notaries, soldiers, and horses.

In answering peasants' pleas to lower their expenses, the government began a program of rationalizing its policing of the *contado* and district. While it created larger secular zones of the *vicariatus* in the new acquisitions within the former *contadi* of Arezzo and Pisa,[13] it downsized podestral districts within its own *contado*. These administrative cuts usually came in response to community complaints of overbearing expenses and debts. Some were short-term measures during war that gave communities breathing space to recover. Such was the resolution to the woes of several communities in Valdinievole hard hit by the war with neighboring Lucca in 1431. Florence allowed Buggiano, Uzzano, Massa, Montecatini, Montevettolini, and Monsommano to unite into a single *Podestà* with a resident notary in each commune for as long as the war lasted. The savings in administrative costs went entirely into the locals' coffers and were not traded off to some other Florentine account for repairs to walls or other fortifications that would benefit Florentine defenses as had so often been the logic of Florence's pre-1402 clemency.[14]

---

[12] These comprised 10 percent of the post-1402 acts of Florentine clemency as opposed to only 3 percent earlier, forty-three and fifteen petitions respectively.
[13] Zorzi, *L'Amministrazione*; and Pinto, "Controllo politico."   [14] Provv. reg., 122, 5r–6r, 1431.v.15.

Other cuts served as longer-term measures. For instance, in 1400, because of losses suffered in "persons and substance" during the war with Milan, Florence answered the pleas for fiscal relief of the men of Foiano by allowing them to reduce the salary of their *Podestà* to 120 gold florins a semester and by cutting his staff and expenses to one notary, three soldiers, and one horse for a five-year period. Since the community succeeded in renewing this immunity continually through the early fifteenth century, it amounted in effect to a permanent change in Foiano's policing.[15] Similarly, in 1407, the councils answered the pleas of Barga by agreeing to assume half the expenses of the *Podestà* and his staff of six soldiers (*famulos*), a notary, and a horse, which saved the villagers 625 *lire*. Florence justified its clemency by arguing that Barga was a remote outpost on the Florentine frontier; moreover, the agreement was to be permanent.[16]

In numerous other cases the *Podesterie* of the traditional *contado* were reduced in number. In 1414, the administrative costs for Signa and Campi were cut in half by combining these two *Podesterie* into one.[17] In 1415, three *Podesterie* of the Valdarno Inferiore – Santa Maria a Monte, Castelfranco, and Santa Croce – were reduced to one.[18] Neighboring Gangalandi and Settimo were combined in 1417.[19] Such cost-cutting was also extended to the district. In the same year, several communes claimed they could no longer afford their contributions to the *Podestà* of Foiano and were hived off to Civitella with lower fees, while Marciano was fused in *perpetuum* with Foiano.[20] In 1420, Verghereto and Chiusi on the northeastern frontier of Arezzo's former *contado* were reduced to a single *Podestà*,[21] and in 1423, three former *Podestà* in the *contado* of Pisa – Lari, Respina, and Lorenzana – were reduced to one, their former staffs and expenses slashed by two-thirds.[22]

With war with Lucca and the subsequent economic strains placed on the countryside in the early 1430s, Florence answered more pleas than ever before by rationalizing podestral structures in the countryside, thereby cutting what peasants and subject townsmen paid to police their communities. In four years (1430 to 1433) Florence lowered the economic burdens of twenty communities by cutting their administrative costs, and with six other decrees it so acted without even being petitioned. These petitions constituted a third of Florence's acts of clemency toward its hinterland (twenty of sixty-two petitions) in these last years of my survey.

[15] *Ibid.*, 93, 140v–1r, 1404.xi.27.   [16] *Ibid.*, 96, 93r–v, 1407.viii.16.
[17] *Ibid.*, 103, 19r–20r, 1414.iv.18.   [18] *Ibid.*, 105, 168v, 1415.x.16.
[19] *Ibid.*, 107, 46v–7r, 1417.iv.22.   [20] *Ibid.*, 313v–15r, 1417.ii.18.
[21] *Ibid.*, 110, 118v–19v, 1420.x.15.   [22] *Ibid.*, 113, 14v–15v, 1423.iv.16.

Although slashing the number of staff or combining *Podestà* were the principal forms of Florence's administrative downsizing, on occasion it intervened by reducing other costs. Thus in 1416 it agreed to ease some of Arezzo's financial problems by assuming for a year and a half the local Priors' and their servants' food and drink bills, along with the expenses for clothing, feeding, and paying Arezzo's musicians (*tubatorum et naccherium ipsorum*). The subsidy ran to 300 *lire* a month and was renewed at least three times for three-year periods through 1425.[23]

Not every commune was happy with such cuts to its social services and security. On occasion peasant communes and towns petitioned Florence to reinstate their old *Podestà* with the forces he once enjoyed even though it meant facing higher bills. As early as 1368, Pontorme pleaded to end its sharing of a *Podestà* with neighboring Empoli and have its right restored of appointing its own *Podestà*, maintaining that "scandals" had arisen from the arrangement.[24] However, having a *Podestà* to itself was not a luxury Pontorme could afford for long, and with the crises of the early fifteenth century, it found itself sharing this Florentine law officer with three other communities. Nonetheless, in 1425 it petitioned the government again, claiming that the presence of this shared *Podestà* was inadequate and that "his absence was a detriment to the regulation of its trade and industry."[25] Similar desires can be seen in the numerous pleas Montemurlo brought before the councils in its attempts to break away from Calenzano; as we have seen, these petitions began in 1378 and continue to the end of my survey.[26]

In addition to these measures, Florence made other grants after 1402 that distinguished its clemency from the short-term, stop-gap measures it had awarded its hinterland before the peasant uprisings. After 1402, 11 percent of the petitions[27] won government action to recalculate and reduce gabelle or *estimo* assessments. Previously, despite the destruction of wars and the massive decline in population following the Black Death, communities had managed to convince Florence to recalculate their *estimi* and gabelles in only 3 percent of their petitions – twenty-three petitions, or less than one every two years.

The earliest one, in 1356, describes the near total destruction of the planned new town of Scarperia, one of Florence's most important military outposts protecting it from northern invasions. The reasons for the grant were directly tied to Florence's defenses, to remunerate those who

---

[23] *Ibid.*, 106, 20v–1r, 1415.v.19; 112, 174r–5r, 1422.x.22.   [24] *Ibid.*, 56, 76v, 1368.x.25.
[25] *Ibid.*, 115, 71v–2v, 1425.v.31.   [26] *Ibid.*, 65, 298r–v, 1377.ii.26; 123, 113v–4r, 1432.v.27.
[27] Forty-eight of 433 petitions; earlier, 23 of 471 or just under 5 percent.

had defended their town at their own expense in the war with Milan and "now had been reduced to penury." The people of Scarperia further argued that enemy troops and rebels had either burnt or robbed them of all their movables and household goods. Great numbers had died in the war, and those left were impoverished. Further, because of the "discordie et scandala" that had arisen among Scarperia's families (presumably because of the inequalities in previous governmental concessions), the villagers argued that Scarperia was in grave danger of "easily disappearing." As a result, the government granted all those households that previously had not been granted immunities a reduction in their assessments for all taxes by a third or 6s 8d off each household assessment.[28] Five years later, in 1361, the councils made their next adjustment in the taxes of a rural commune; again, this clemency was granted to a frontier commune, this time along the sensitive northeastern mountains that guarded the passes leading into the territories of the rebellious Ubertini lords. Florence lowered the *estimo* base for the commune of the Montagna Fiorentina to an unspecified sum (*ad minorem summam*).[29]

For the next petition that succeeded in rescheduling an *estimo*, the territory had to wait thirteen years. Again, the plea came from the northeastern mountain borders. The councils heard from the "fideles seu vassalli" of Count Robert of Battifolle, who had been assessed in the commune of Romena. They pleaded that unless granted governmental clemency they would feel "gravely deceived." Thus, to keep their newborn allies who had turned against their former lords, the Florentines reduced the community's *estimo* by 8 *lire* 10s. Although this petition was filed in 1374, during the plague, no mention of it or demographic decline entered these vassals' final (and probably sanitized) arguments. Instead, as was characteristic of the pre-1402 demands and pleas, it was a matter of politics – defense, treaties, and Florentine territorial expansion.[30]

After 1402, peasants' efforts to change fundamentally their tax obligations by lowering their *estimo* assessments increased over fourfold.[31] Moreover, in these cases the stated causes for the villagers' appeals did not turn so often as before on Florentine defense. In 1402, for instance, Borgo San Lorenzo – in the heartland of the Mugello and not near the northern mountain passes – appealed for lower wine and meat gabelles, simply because of difficulties in paying its taxes and because the

---

[28] *Ibid.*, 44, 74v–5r, 1356.ii.22.   [29] *Ibid.*, 49, 32r–v, 1361.x.8.   [30] *Ibid.*, 62, 61v–2r, 1374.vi.16.
[31] Before 1402 the councils honored twenty-three readjustments in fifty-five years; afterwards, forty-six in thirty-three years.

commune had lost trade in these commodities since the last gabelle
rates had been set. As a result, their wine gabelle was reduced from
1,000 to 600 *lire* and the meat gabelle from 170 to 100 florins.[32] In the
same year Montelupo, just west of Florence and not in an area threatened by the Milanese war, with similar arguments won adjustments to
its gabelles, a reduction of its meat and retail wine gabelles by one-
third.[33]

Such adjustments in yearly gabelle rates increased in number for communities across the *contado* and district from 1404 on.[34] While for
Scarperia, Cortona, and Empoli they meant savings of thousands of *lire*,
after 1402 Florence also gave equal attention to smaller places such as
the commune of San Godenzo near Romagna, whose savings may well
have meant that its *contadini* could remain on their farms but hardly mattered to Florentine finances: in 1418 its meat gabelle was chopped from
an annual payment of 15 to 9 florins.[35]

In addition to gabelle rates, Florence also placated disgruntled and
impoverished peasants by reducing and reapportioning their *estimi* after
1402. Here, more than with any other form of governmental clemency,
the politics of demography were clearly spelled out in every case. For
instance, with the close of Florence's war with Siena in the opening years
of the fifteenth century the councils awarded reductions to the badly
damaged southern Chianti commune of Staggia of 400 to 300 *lire* in its
retail wine gabelle and of 25 to 10 florins in its meat gabelle. But the government's more important concession came with its reduction of its
estimo assessment on which numerous other taxes were based and some
like the extraordinary tax at multiples as high as six times the assessed
"lira." To gain this concession, Staggia argued that its population had
been reduced since the last *estimo* survey of 1401 from a hundred to now
only twenty men. While these figures show a disastrous demographic
decline, none of the previous plagues of the fourteenth century – not
even the Black Death of 1348 – had occasioned a readjustment of any
community's tax base, even though this tax base was calculated on the
number of able-bodied men between fourteen and seventy. But, as a
consequence of Staggia's post-1402 demographic crisis, Florence

[32] *Ibid.*, 91, 6r–7r, 1402.iv.18.   [33] *Ibid.*, 32r–v, 1402.iv.26.
[34] *Ibid.*, 93, 149v–50v, 1404.xii.9; 152v–3r, 1404.xii.9; 229r–31r, 1404.ii.21; 95, 6r–7r, 1406.iv.22; 96,
176v–7r, 1407.xii.17; 101, 252v–3r, 1412.xi.23; 291r–v, 1412.xii.2; 104, 102r–4r, 1414.ii.22; 106,
127r–8v, 1416.viii.26; 108, 99r–100v, 1418.vi.16; 193r–4r, 1418.xii.22; 116, 171v–3r, 1426.ix.20; 119,
261r–2r, 1428.x.21; 120, 506r–7r, 1429.ii.23; 122, 359v–60v, 1431.ii.19.
[35] *Ibid.*, 108, 193r–4r, 1418.xii.22.

lowered its *estimo* from a base of 125 to 20 *lire* without waiting for the next *contado*-wide survey.[36]

Other communes after 1402 similarly framed their requests around demographic arguments, claiming losses almost as extraordinary as those of Staggia. In answering the Alpi Fiorentine's pleas for tax concessions, the government stated its motives bluntly – to conserve the population of the region.[37] It then reduced their *estimo* from a base rate of 600 to 480 *lire*. Corniolo in the Romagna obtained an adjustment of its household tax, the *gabelle fumantium*, by claiming in 1407 that only nineteen families had survived because of the war, and of these eighteen were in "maximum poverty."[38]

In 1410, Santo Stefano de Gabbiola in the *pieve* of San Giovanni in Sugana (Soava) won the prerogative to redraft a new *estimo* for this village alone. Even though the village was charged a mere 6 *lire* and 11 *soldi* (the amount a single prosperous peasant household might be assessed), the villagers argued that the sum was excessive and that many families had left because of the high rates, leaving behind only the most destitute, who possessed no property at all but worked lands owned by Florentine citizens. If their rates were not adjusted, they claimed that that onus alone would bring the parish's destruction (*qui solus hic onus sufficiens foret ad destructionem populi predicti*) and force the remaining families to flee. In addition to redrafting its *estimo*, Florence absolved the villagers of paying their 1408 extraordinary *estimo* charged at half a florin on the *lira*.[39] In 1420, the parishes of San Lorenzo a Montalbino and Santa Maria [sic] a Mensola[40] obtained a revision of their *estimo* from the paltry sum of 5 *lire* 6s 7d, claiming that the lion's share, 3 *lire* 6s 7d, pertained to households whose families had left since the last *estimo* because of excessive taxation and the debts they had incurred.[41] The petition then named the five remaining household heads with their assessments.

Still other communes used demographic arguments to seek reductions in their salt taxes. Even more than the *estimo*, these taxes (based on the census taken from *estimi*) centered on population figures, where the unit of assessment was the number of mouths (*bocche*) and not households. Such demographic arguments, however, rarely led to changes in the salt tax before 1402, not even after the first four waves of plague in

---

[36] *Ibid.*, 96, 176v–7r, 1407.xii.17.
[37] *Ibid.*, 93, 149v–50v, 1404.xii.9: "Et volentes ipsis gratiam facere et ipsos homines et personas conservare." [38] *Ibid.*, 95, 321v–2r, 1406.ii.25. [39] *Ibid.*, 99, 101v–2v, 1410.viii.26.
[40] A San Martino a Mensola was coupled with San Lorenzo a Montalbino but not a Santa Maria.
[41] Provv. reg., 110, 146r–8v, 1420.x.24: "Et quantum extramitate oneris pertinebat se absentavit."

1348, 1363, 1375, and 1383. Before 1402 the salt tax was a sacred cow of the Florentine Commune. Even in pacts of submission, it was one of the few taxes not to be exempted in the opening years of a village's adjustment to Florentine domination. In the first wars with Milan, between 1351 and 1356, a number of communes in the Mugello, where fighting was the heaviest, won three-year exemptions from the *estimo* and most other taxes because of their defense of the realm and their losses in property and population. For these exemptions, Florence's first condition was that they should continue to be liable to pay half the salt tax during these three years; afterwards, payments would resume at their prewar quotas, even though these communes' populations had been decimated.[42]

Between 1353 and 1402 the government made only one exemption (even in part) from or revision to the salt tax – to the people of Civitella in 1398 following its return to Florentine sovereignty. The one other possible exception proves the rule. In April 1394, the league of the Chianti pleaded that they had been oppressed and devastated by fire and robbery during the recent war. The villages had then failed to pay their salt tax (*canonam salis*), believing they had been exempted from it along with their other exemptions. Because of their great losses of population, they added that they now found it impossible to pay at the rates levied before the war. But, despite their cries, Florence listened with sympathy to only half their pleas. They granted an exemption retrospectively for the unpaid salt taxes during the war but refused to adjust them afterwards, thus bringing them in line with the villages' current population.[43]

Instead, the first petition that centered on the salt tax and succeeded in winning an adjustment did not come until 1403, when "the many communes in the Valdinievole" – Buggiano, Montecatini, Montevettolini, and others – argued that their population and property values had slumped since their salt tax had been last established in 1380. As a consequence, they claimed now to be paying two to three times what they should. The councils first absolved these communes from half their salt taxes in arrears, which stood at 1,302 gold florins, and then reduced their yearly consumption of salt from 640 to 240 *staria*.[44] In the following year other communes such as Tirli in the Alpi Fiorentine did even better, gaining a four-year total exemption from the Florentine salt monopoly.[45]

At the same time, the government cracked down on those who tried to

[42] *Ibid.*, 39, 92r–v, 1351.ii.10; 131v, 1352.iv.17; 147v–9v, 1352.v.5; 40, 20r–v, 1352.xi.15; 37v–8r, 1352.xii.17.   [43] *Ibid.*, 83, 37v–9r, 1394.iv.27.   [44] *Ibid.*, 92, 182v–3v, 1403.xi.27.
[45] *Ibid.*, 93, 46v–7v, 1404.vi.9.

evade the salt tax[46] and in 1415 systematically attempted to extend salt taxes throughout their dominion including newly incorporated frontier outposts that heretofore had not been subject to the Florentine monopoly, among them communes in the Florentine Romagna,[47] Piancaldoli along the border with Bologna,[48] and Valiano near Montepulciano.[49] In the following year, the list of communes forced to accept the Florentine salt gabelles and to take censuses of their populations for these purposes extended to the former districts of Pistoia, Volterra, the Valdinievole, and Arezzo.[50] Even in the 1420s, areas such as Bientina in the marshes of Pisa seemed to have slipped through the net.[51] Yet the government responded favorably to community arguments about changes in population and continued to grant exemptions[52] and adjust consumption quotas for small parishes such as San Jacobo a Stigliano near Monterappoli[53] as well as for large consumers such as the city and commune of Pistoia in 1422, 1423, and 1432,[54] and for Cortona in 1432.[55] While Florence was centralizing and standardizing its tax burdens across its territory, its fiscal policy became more flexible with a keener eye to the sudden shifts in the demographic fortunes of its subjects.

These cases and others from the post-1402 petitions need to be juxtaposed to the government's silence in the face of violent falls in population due to the Trecento plagues, none of which gave rise to a single successful bid by a peasant commune or town for revising its taxes. It was, moreover, this post-1402 sensitivity to territorial changes in population that underlay Florence's decisions to draw up new tax surveys in the early fifteenth century. Thus the demographic change occasioned by the plague of 1412, hardly known to historians and much less virulent than the Trecento epidemics, was the impetus in that year for launching a new *estimo*.[56]

Even more than downsizing local *Podestà* or revising taxes, government renewals of tax immunities distinguish the post-1402 period from the

---

[46] See, for instance, the law "Contra salis gabellam fraudantes," 110, 99r, 1420.ix.28.

[47] *Ibid.*, 104, 123v–4v, 1414.ii.25; and 105, 280r–v, 1415.xii.28.

[48] *Ibid.*, 105, 168r–v, 1415.x.22; 116, 281r–2v, 1426.ii.19; 123, 329v–30r, 1432.xii.16.

[49] *Ibid.*, 105, 168r–v, 1415.x.22.

[50] See the long lists of communes ordered in 1416 "to accept" the salt gabelle and make surveys of their populations; *ibid*, 105, 297r–8r, 1415.ii.17.   [51] *Ibid.*, 115, 305v–6v, 1425.ii.26.

[52] *Ibid.*, 105, 328r–v, 1415.ii.20; 108, 110v–11r, 1418.vi.28; 109, 113v–14v, 1419.viii.14.

[53] *Ibid.*, 124, 195r–6v, 1433.viii.29.

[54] *Ibid.*, 112, 57v–9r, 1422.v.30; 277v–8r, 1422.ii.20; 122, 395r–v, 1431.iii.17.

[55] *Ibid.*, 123, 230v–1v, 1432.ix.30.

[56] *Ibid.*, 101, 13r–15v, 1412.iii.27: "Considerato maxime quod elapsi ab aliis multi sunt anni et in hoc medio tempore fuerunt guerra, pestis, et caritudo et sic multa sunt variata."

past. To be sure, the Florentine Commune had offered peasant villages and towns exemptions as part of their "submission" pacts from the birth of the guild Republic.[57] But almost two-thirds of the immunities found in petitions from 1347 to 1434 were granted in roughly the last third of this period, after the 1402 waves of peasant insurrections.[58] The most sweeping of these came immediately after revolts in 1403 and again in 1426, when rebellious communes along with some of their neigbors who remained "devoted" to Florence received exemptions from all taxes and gabelles, often including even the jealously guarded gabelle on contracts.

In addition, before 1402 only 5 percent of the immunities previously granted were renewed, and of these almost all were extensions to a community's original pact of submission and not to a previous petition. Florence seldom took kindly to such renewals. Terminations to exemptions were demanded even in the face of petitions that claimed that at the end of the exemptions' specified time-periods the peasants had almost nothing worth taxing.[59] Before the plague of 1363, Florence even passed decrees that disallowed communities from asking for renewals no matter what the future might bring.[60] By contrast, renewals of immunities trebled after 1402, which meant that their yearly number increased by almost nine times. Certain impoverished and war-torn communities had their five- or three-year immunities renewed continually from the early 1400s to the return of the Medici and beyond.

A comparison between the histories of pre- and post-1402 immunities in the commune of Foiano highlights the turn of the century as the critical divide in the Florentine government's attitude and clemency toward its hinterland. With its submission to Florence in 1383, Foiano was given extensive immunities for ten years.[61] In 1394, it pleaded that invading troops from Milan and Siena had burnt and devastated the town (*castrum*), reducing them to "such misery that they could no longer live and bring up their families." Their numbers fell from 500 to 250 and "nearly all who remained had been reduced to maximum poverty." Further, they were in arrears on a 500-florin loan, and "the major part" of their fortifications had been reduced to ruins. Yet, despite these demographic, economic, and even military pressures, Foiano failed to win a renewal of its immunities given with its submission. Instead, the

---

[57] See *I Capitoli*, I.   [58] Seventy-one in the first period, 104 in the second.
[59] See the 1353 petition from the communes of the Valdinievole, Provv. reg., 40, 156v–7r, 1353.x.16: "iam dicti comunis quasi nullas habuerunt vel substinuerunt expensas."
[60] *Ibid.*, 40, 156v–7r, 1353.x.16; 50, 28v, 1362.x.13; 38r–v, 1362.x.24; and 118v–19r, 1362.iii.7.
[61] *Ibid.*, 72, 183r–5r, 1383.xi.24.

government granted the commune the lesser privilege of not being obliged to accept the Florentine *Podestà* with his bevy of one notary, three soldiers, and one horse for a period of five years, allowing the less advantageous savings of 120 *lire* a semester. Even this grant was conditional on the commune paying off its 200 *lire* of debts to the *Podestà*.[62]

In August 1398, the Foianesi again appealed for aid, pleading that the present war had "multiplied the damage to their village and their oppression, that day and night they had to be vigilant in defending their town [and as a result] could not cultivate their fields." Again, they threatened "to leave for other countries." Yet the privileges of three years earlier now up for renewal were refused. Instead, the villagers won other less remunerative immunities for three years and were told that their salt tax would remain unchanged despite their diminished numbers. Florence turned a deaf ear as well to their pleas that guard duty and the munitioning of their own fortifications required their "constant vigilance" and insisted that Foiano continue to provision the citadel of Arezzo on pain of heavy penalties.[63]

In 1400, Foiano's "ambaxiatores" again traveled to Florence, pleading that the damages suffered during the past years of war "were clear to every Florentine citizen." This time they won a five-year reduction in the salary of their *Podestà*, but these savings could not be used to offset their debts as they had hoped; instead, in the old style these tax credits were to be used for mending their fortifications.[64]

From 1403 to the end of my survey, the petitions the Foianesi brought to Florence show a marked change in what they could expect from their rulers, especially in regard to the renewal of exemptions. Rather than denials or watered-down privileges, they succeeded in winning renewals verbatim and usually for the same periods of time. Thus, in 1403 the three-year tax immunities first granted in 1401[65] were renewed for another three years and again for the same length of time in 1406, 1409, and 1413.[66] At the end of 1404, the five-year reductions in the *Podestà*'s salary were renewed for another five years, and then another six times until the end of my survey: in 1409, 1413, 1417, 1422, 1427, and 1432.[67] Finally, in 1433, because of the damages of war and the Foianesi's inabil-

---

[62] *Ibid.*, 83, 267v–8v, 1394.i.25.   [63] *Ibid.*, 87, 205v–6r, 1398.viii.21.

[64] *Ibid.*, 89, 62v–3v, 1400.iv.26.   [65] *Ibid.*, 90, 302r–3r, 1401.xi.23.

[66] *Ibid.*, 92, 227v–8r, 1403.xii.18; 95, 164v, 1406.viii.23; 98, 128v–9v, 1409.xii.23; 102, 62r–3r, 1413.ii.19.

[67] *Ibid.*, 93, 140v–1r, 1404.xi.27; 98, 128v–9v, 1409.xii.23; 102, 62r–3r, 1413.ii.19; 107, 313v–15r, 1417.xi.25; 112, 136v–7v, 1422.x.13; 117, 311r–13r, 1427.viii.16; 123, 207v–8v, 1432.viii.28.

ity to harvest their grain during the past two years of fighting, the councils added to the exemptions of the *Podestà*'s salary a further 108-florin deduction.[68]

The petition of 1404 shows another change: unlike the pre-1402 petitions, Foiano's "ambassadors" did not necessarily have to put forward new wars, new plagues, or new disasters to justify their renewals of past exemptions; rather it was enough to claim that the war and plague suffered earlier (in this case, the plague of 1400) still gave rise to their present suffering and need for clemency. Foiano's post-1402 success was not exceptional; the numerous pleas and renewals of immunities for the Montagna Fiorentina, the Podere Fiorentino, the Romagna Fiorentina, and the Isle of Giglio trace similar outcomes that stretched through the first third of the century and probably beyond.[69] Once again 1402 marked a new era in peasant petitions and government clemency.

The most significance change in the appeals from the territory regards the reduction or cancellation of public debts on past taxes, fines, and fees. Such solutions to peasant misery and their threats to emigrate comprised over 40 percent of these petitions after 1402, while earlier they accounted for only 8 percent.[70] The most drastic change came with the peasant revolts themselves in 1403, when Florence answered peasant demands by absolving public debts in twenty-four separate petitions, followed by twenty-two the next year, and seventeen in the third. Moreover, these remissions were made to large areas that comprised numerous villages such as the Alpi Fiorentine with twenty-one parishes (in 1403), the Podere with fourteen, Romena with eight, the Florentine province of Romagna with as many as thirty, and large *pievi* in the Chianti such as San Marcellino with fifteen parishes.[71] Thus, in these three years alone several hundred parishes and communes across the territorial state had their debts wiped off their books or significantly reduced. But these three years alone do not account for the post-1402 difference. Before 1402, in only two years did the communities of peasants or subject townsmen receive five or more grants that reduced their public debts (in 1393, six; and in 1401, five). Afterwards, in fourteen of the thirty-three years

---

[68] *Ibid.*, 124, 108v–9r, 1433.vi.27.

[69] For Giglio, see the following petitions: *ibid.*, 106, 246v–7r, 1416.xii.17; 111, 6v–8r, 1421.iv.2; 116, 203v–4v, 1426.xi.14; 124, 266r–7v, 1433.iii.18. Exemptions were renewed in 1406 and 1411 as is made clear in subsequent *provvisioni* but do not appear in these registers.

[70] Forty in the first period, 176 in the second.

[71] See, for instance, the *provvisione* "Plurium populorum plebatus Sancti Marcellini et plebatus Sancti Poli de partibus chiantis," Provv. reg., 93, 218v–22r, 1404.ii.21.

concerned Florence absolved or reduced public debts in five or more petitions per annum.[72] The per annum count had increased eightfold.

A more detailed comparison of Florence's reduction of debts before and after 1402 reveals qualitative as well as quantitative changes. Before 1402, when the government gave its "gratia" to debt-burdened peasant communes, its clemency usually treated the debts as inviolate and often allowed no more than ten days to pay them off. Its pardons extended no further than canceling the heavy fines on unpaid *estimi*, gabelles, or other fees in arrears. While such resolutions to peasant fines had ranked at the top of governmental forms of clemency before 1402, afterwards this less generous form of relief accounted for only thirteen, or 3 percent, of the favorable resolutions.

Earlier, when the government went further in its generosity, the canceled debts usually included no more than a single sum for a few back taxes. By 1403 the accumulated debts itemized in peasant petitions show matters had changed. Instead of several missed payments of the *estimo* or debts accruing from one or two gabelles, the petitions of 1403 itemized debts that cut through most of their obligations – *estimo* payments, both the ordinary and extraordinary, taxes on roads and bridges, the salt taxes (the *canone salis* and the *pagis salis et saline*), gabelles on wine, both retail and in bulk, the meat gabelle, the salaries of the *Podestà* and other officials, taxes for fortifications, various fines and condemnations, and occasionally failure to present the honorific silk *palium* or wax on San Giovanni Day.

A glance at the long lists of debts that suddenly appear with great frequency in 1403 show, in effect, that a silent tax revolt – a refusal to pay taxes – had been brewing within the war-torn zones of Florence's mountain periphery for several years before these communities, assisted by Florence's enemies, decided to risk armed struggle. Some of these post-1402 debt lists filled several folios of large *provvisione* parchment as did those from the Chianti *pieve* of San Marcellino in 1404[73] and went as far back as 1392, as seen in the commune of Tasso's successful bid to reduce its past tax burdens in 1403.[74] But most of the debts itemized in the 1403 petitions start with 1399, when the "extraordinary tax" reached its peak of 1.5 florins, sextupling the *lira*'s base charges at the beginning of the decade.

The second qualitative change that transformed peasant petitions

---

[72] For 1403 (twenty-four), 1404 (twenty-two), 1405 (seventeen), 1406 (five), 1408 (five), 1413 (seven), 1414 (five), 1415 (seven), 1418 (five), 1419 (seven), 1422 (five), 1427 (twelve), 1429 (nine), and 1433 (seven).   [73] Provv. reg., 93, 218v–22r, 1404.ii.21.   [74] *Ibid.*, 92, 105v–6r, 1403.viii.14.

after 1402 was the intervention of the *Monte del Comune* (Florence's "mountain" of funded debts) to assist Florence's subject communities. The first use of the *Monte* to aid those from the countryside appears in 1372, when the parishes of San Bartolomeo Gavena and San Leonardo Gonfienti argued that because of the war, their proximity to the enemy's borders, and other adversities, they were reduced to begging and, as a consequence, their public debts had mounted to 500 *lire*. Florence relieved the peasants of their fines for late payments by passing their debts on to the "Old Monte."[75] Such transfers to the *Monte*, however, did not become a usual practice during the Trecento. The next case did not occur until 1390, when the government allowed Pontorme to convert 1,000 *lire* of its debts into *Monte* credits.[76]

The take-off in *Monte* appearances instead came in 1403; in that year alone seven peasant petitions representing numerous villages had their public debts absorbed by Florence's mountain of rising debt. After 1402, the number of petitions in which Florence transferred communities' public debts to the *Monte* increased eightfold per annum.[77] Its appearance became even more marked as the century progressed. In the peasant petitions of 1403 less than a third of canceled or reduced public debts were transferred to the *Monte* (seven of twenty-four petitions); in 1413 the *Monte* assumed peasant public debts in six of seven petitions.

Such a solution to indebtedness of the hinterland strengthened the sense in which these communities were incorporated into the city of Florence's fiscal universe. Increasingly, Florence addressed the cries of its subjects by transferring part or even all of their public debts to the *Monte*. On occasion, the *Monte* absorbed the debt in its entirety, canceling a community's charge completely. More often, it assumed the principal but charged the community interest on it at the low rate of 5 percent, much under that demanded by private bankers and money lenders.

This incorporation reversed the territory's (and primarily the *contado*'s) place within Florence's universe of finances. Since the *Monte*'s foundation in 1345, it had been the *contado*'s direct taxes combined with payments from the gabelles which offset Florence's ever-growing mountain of debts and had made possible the redemption of its shares from time to time to Florence's privileged urban elite at handsome rates of

---

[75] *Ibid.*, 59, 19r–v, 1371.iii.12: "ad quod comune Florentie tenetur suis creditoribus . . . montevec-chio." [76] *Ibid.*, 79, 241v–3r, 1390.x.25.
[77] Fourteen, or one every four years (over fifty-five years), came before 1402; afterwards, they increased to sixty-six, or slightly over two per annum (over thirty-two years).

interest.[78] After 1402 peasants were no longer exclusively on the *Monte*'s paying side; with petitions, protests, and threats to abandon the Florentine state they now also swung around to the receiving line as the *Monte* stepped in to relieve them of their debts and fiscal misery. If not in title then in effect *contadini* had become shareholders in the *Monte*, with a new stake in the solvency of the Florentine state.

Once again, 1402 and the successful peasant revolts on Florence's mountainous frontiers had been the dividing line in Florence's attempt to incorporate its hinterland into a new sense of a regional state or "territorium" as humanist legists began to call it at the turn of the century. In addition to equalizing and lowering taxes in the *contado* during the early fifteenth century, Florence looked on a wide range of peasant problems with greater sympathy and generosity. Such a change in governmental attitudes paralleled a shift in geographical distribution of villages that won tax remissions after the first wave of peasant revolts. From the military hot spots on or near the borders of Florence's *contado*, successful village petitions spread more evenly across Florence's territory, into its agricultural heartland to parishes often of little fiscal or military importance (see maps 3, 4, and 5).

After 1403, the government's approved petitions tell new stories about peasant life, certainly lived earlier, but previously unreflected in these documents. Unlike the petitions to lower the massive debts of Empoli or readjust the *estimo* base for the entire vicariate of the Alpi Fiorentine with its nineteen to twenty-two parishes, these pleas concern the everyday horrors of survival in small rural villages that hardly affected the city's efforts to balance its books. For instance, the tiny village of Pulicciano, 10 kilometers south of Arezzo in the Val di Chiana, petitioned Florence for tax relief in 1406. Its syndics described how on one Saturday morning in August, when all the men were off to market in Arezzo, their houses had burnt to the ground. Here, it was not the usual story of enemy invasion, violence, and plunder. Instead, according to the plea, the women, "as was usual on Saturday mornings," were left behind to bake the bread for the village. While one woman was returning to the communal oven with her uncooked dough, a sudden burst of wind swept hot coals from her pan through the parish, setting the village ablaze. For this tragedy that in no way threatened Florentine security or its economy, the government nonetheless paid it the time and money of its highest

---

[78] On the social composition of *Monte* shareholders, see Herlihy and Klapisch-Zuber, *Les Toscans*, pp. 250–5.

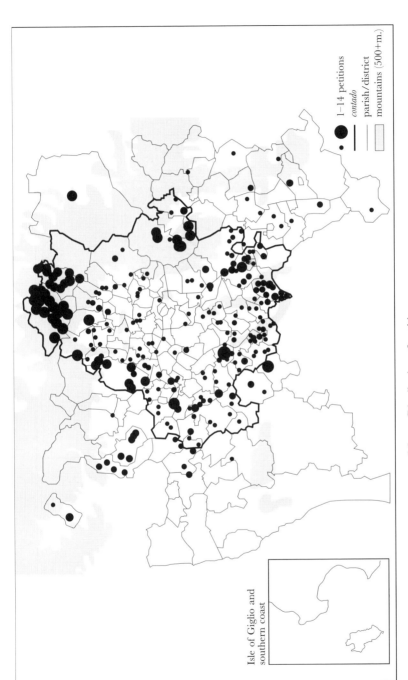

Map 3 Distribution of petitions, 1347–1402

Isle of Giglio and
southern coast

● 1–14 petitions
contado
── parish/district
▨ mountains (500+m.)

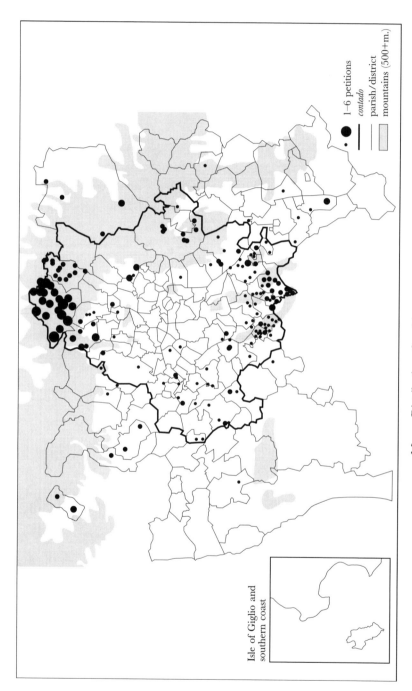

Map 4 Distribution of petitions, 1403–1405

Isle of Giglio and
southern coast

● 1–6 petitions
contado
— parish/district
mountains (500+m.)

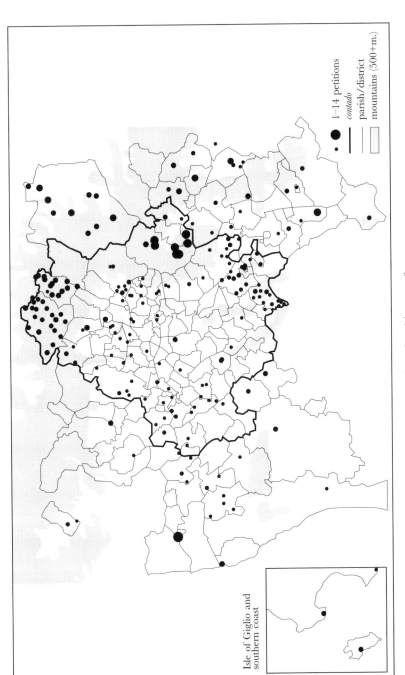

Map 5 Distribution of petitions, 1406–1434

Isle of Giglio and
southern coast

1–14 petitions
contado
parish/district
mountains (500+m.)

councils' deliberations, vetting, and voting. The villagers won a four-year leave to skip annually their fourth payment of the *estimo*, a yearly saving of 50 *lire*.[79]

Similarly, other almost deserted parishes of little or no economic or military importance to the Florentine state lodged petitions that were able to tap governmental sympathies in the early fifteenth century and that, given the absence of such cases earlier, suggest a change in government attitudes as well as in the mechanisms, formal and informal, that brought such cases to the Florentine councils. In 1415, in the midst of Florence's remarkable decade of peace, the parish of Sant' Andrea a Sveglia outside Fiesole appealed to the councils for financial relief. It reported that only four families remained in the village, all of whom were "in maximum poverty," and that without governmental assistance these "unfortunate families" would either have to leave or go to prison. The government reduced their unpaid taxes, some of which extended back to 1400, from 86 to 50 *lire*.[80] A successful petition from another small parish of the center, Sant' Alessandro a Signano in the *pieve* of Vaglia (Mugello), comprised in 1429 only six households, and turned on the fate of a single man, the only property holder left in the village, who earlier had been made insolvent by paying his son's ransom during Florence's war with the King of Naples.[81]

With the plagues and escalating warfare of the latter half of the Trecento, communities of similar size and relative unimportance to Florence's defenses would no doubt have been just as desperate if not more so, but the Florentine ruling class must have calculated that it was cheaper (at least in the short run) to allow such villages to be reduced to ruin rather than waste Florentine bureaucratic time on their revival. After all, the time and money involved in adjudicating such cases, sending out two or more citizens to survey the damages, checking the books of the *Camera del Commune* to ascertain the community's exact debts, hearing the case argued before the *Tre Maggiori*, perhaps calling in special committees, marking the votes in the *Libri fabarum*, and having Florence's foremost notary, the notary of the *Riformagioni*, inscribe in duplicate the case with all its richly wrought Latin formulae in the final registers of the *provvisione*'s large sheets of parchment probably cost the Commune more than the 50 *lire* or less that was at stake in granting these villages remission.

---

[79] Provv. reg., 95, 159r–v, 1406.viii.8.   [80] *Ibid.*, 105, 117v–18v, 1416.viii.21.
[81] *Ibid.*, 120, 382r–3r, 1429.x.26.

This change in the sympathies of Florence's ruling elite reflected in the statistics taken from the *provvisioni* and the stories that underlay them also finds expression, even if belatedly, in the debates of Florence's ruling class. Such were the thoughts of Michele Castellani, who in May 1413 openly condemned Florence's exploitation of its territory, describing it "as a wasteland populated by subjects who had been robbed of their pastures, their rights, and their property by rapacious officials."[82]

Within these two large historical blocks – pre- and post-1402 – other shifts in Florence's policy towards its hinterland might be detected, such as the change in labor legislation after the 1363 plague, when the carrot replaced the stick. Yet neither 1363, 1364, nor the plague and famines of 1373–6 are distinguished as turning-points when placed in the context of other legislative acts or changes in the government's clemency toward its hinterland: these years or the ones immediately thereafter register no sudden jump in the numbers of approved petitions or qualitative changes in what the government considered worthy of approval and the concessions it was willing to make (see figures 8.1–8.3).

As for the post-1402 period, one might see within it a further shift in Florence's policies and attitudes toward its region with its major fiscal innovation of the republican period, the *catasto* of 1427. Although historians have recently disputed its long-term fiscal significance, they have nonetheless marked it as a major shift toward a more repressive Florentine rule over its territory.[83] But did Florence's post-1427 acts of clemency mark a decline in its generosity toward its hinterland? As we have seen, in the last years of our analysis, particularly by 1430, the councils sought to mollify villagers' burdens incurred from war, pestilence, and indebtedness by a sharp increase in grants that lowered administrative costs for localities. Such cost-cutting was often not as generous as tax exemptions and revisions, or the absolution of debts; nor were they always welcomed by the communities which petitioned for financial relief. Rural and town communities alike relied on the services of these Florentine judges and police not only for personal security but also to attract outsiders to trade freely in their local markets. From 1347 to 1402 such administrative cost-cutting comprised a mere 3 percent of the government's acts of clemency;

---

[82] Brucker, *The Civic World*, pp. 217–18.
[83] Petralia, "Imposizione diretta," p. 639; and "Fiscality, politics and dominion."

from 1402 to 1428, they doubled to 6 percent, but in the remaining years of my analysis they shot up to over a quarter.[84]

In addition, these cost-cutting measures changed after 1427. Before, with few exceptions, the councils restructured communities' law enforcement agencies for five-year periods or even as a permanent change; afterwards, these cuts became more limited, lasting on average only a year and a half.[85] In some cases, they were granted for only a single semester of a *Podestà*'s term[86] or for only as long as a war threatened the villages under question, with a month or two added on for extra financial cushioning.[87]

But were these post-1427 acts of clemency harbingers of a new, more coercive, period of Florentine territorial domination? If the number of successful petitions from the countryside is a guide, the answer is no. First, 1427 scored more acts of clemency toward communities within the territory than any other year except 1403. Nor was this year of renewed rural insurrections an exception. From 1428 to 1434 the number of approved petitions increased rather than declined, exceeding in these seven years any other seven-year period found across my eighty-seven-year survey with the exception of 1402 to 1407. On the one hand, it might be argued that such an increase only reflects the dire conditions into which the Florentine countryside had fallen, as the wars with Milan and then Lucca coupled to produce Florence's most monumental indebtedness.[88]

Yet, unlike the cost-cutting grants of *Podestà*'s salaries and the like, other governmental grants of clemency in these last seven years do not suggest a decline in generosity. The most sought-after and generous of Florence's awards, outright exemptions from gabelles or direct imposts, continued to increase from 1.3 a year before 1402 to almost three a year from 1402 to 1427 and then to 3.9 in the remaining years. If the pleas of 1427 are included, the number of tax immunities won in these last eight years more than doubled those from 1402 to 1426, soaring to almost ten grants per annum. Moreover, unlike the measures to cut police forces and their expenses for local communities, the number of years for tax

---

[84] In the period 1347 to 1401, the councils offered clemency through reduced administrative costs in 15 of 471 petitions (3.2 percent) or 0.27 per annum. From 1402 to 1427, these grants rose to 20 of 349 (5.7 percent) or 0.74 per annum, and in 1428 to 1433, to 23 of 84 (27.4 percent) or 3.83 per annum.

[85] Twenty-two observations, the mean is 1.58 years; the median, one per annum.

[86] Provv. reg., 122, 245r–v, 1431.x.29; 278r–v, 1431.xi.17; 124, 108v–9r, 1433.vi.27; 135r–v, 1433.vii.7.

[87] *Ibid.*, 123, 103v–4v, 1432.v.27; 151r–2v, 1432.vii.15; 152r–v, sd.

[88] See Molho, *Florentine Public Finances*, pp. 153–82.

exemptions did not decline but remained the same, averaging around five.[89]

Nor, as we have argued, do cardinal dates in the constitutional history of Florence effectively divide this eighty-seven-year history in Florentine attitudes towards the countryside. Neither the rise of the Ciompi, the government of the Minor Guilds in 1378, the restoration of the oligarchy in 1382, the consolidation of power in the hands of the Albizzi and their elitist reforms in 1393, nor the constitutional transformation of 1410–11 and the formation of the Council of Two Hundred account for the quantitative or qualitative changes in what peasants and subject townsmen could expect from their government. Rather the opening years of the century constituted a shift in politics blind to particular changes of regime or the social composition of the ruling elite. Whether these changes set in motion by the events of 1402 continued after the political reforms of Cosimo de' Medici must await further study of the *provvisioni*, but the trends in taxation of the countryside, rural wealth, and demographic growth, particularly in the *contado*, suggest that they did.

---

[89] In order to include perpetual grants of tax immunity I have calculated the median instead of the mean. The means varied from five and a half to seven years, when perpetual grants were put at the highest finite number of years granted in these petitions (fifteen years).

Conclusion

The Florentine oligarchy was slow in reckoning the demographic consequences of the Black Death and peasant flight for the political fate of its territorial state. The mid and late Trecento plagues passed without legislative intervention or welfare measures to soften the blows of illness, death, and increased taxation. The first inklings of change came with Florence's transformation of its policies toward agricultural labor. In 1364, Florence replaced the whip of labor restrictions with the carrot of tax incentives to entice Florence's own agricultural laborers to return from foreign lands and to attract new foreign laborers to work its lands.

Although the Florentine councils repeated such measures with increasing incentives through the Trecento, it was as though Florence's policy toward its rural subjects was governed by one hand taking from what the other gave. The city hammered its rural subjects with ever-increasing levies which exacted ever-increasing proportions of the peasants' surplus, even as the countryside was increasingly torched by warfare and disembodied by disease. Further, these fiscal policies created economic differences between the lowlands near the city and the distant mountains of the Florentine periphery. New Florentine wars against Milan and the elitist politics of the Albizzi regime in the closing years of the fourteenth century accelerated still further Florentine demands on the countryside and fiscal inequalities between lowlanders and highlanders. By the 1390s communities in the Florentine highlands were taxed as much as twenty-nine times more than peasants near Florence's city walls. Some mountain communes were asked to hand over as much as 44 percent of their wealth annually in direct taxes alone. The economic consequences of this Florentine fiscal policy were striking as can be seen in the fiscal returns themselves as well as in the notarized dowries exchanged between peasants. In a generation (1371 to 1402), the wealth of Florence's mountain peasants was halved, while that in the plains maintained a steady keel.

These fiscal policies forced independent peasant proprietors in the mountains to flee their homesteads, but they did not migrate downward as historians have assumed and perhaps as members of the Florentine oligarchy, hungry for labor on their lowland farms, may have wished. Instead, they left the Florentine realm altogether, migrating to even higher places in the Apennine villages of Pistoia, Modena, Bologna, and elsewhere.

Following this silent revolt of peasant flight, waves of peasant insurgency in 1401 to 1404 spread across the mountainous perimeter of the Florentine state from the Pistoiese to the Chianti. Although contemporary chronicles and memoirs, even by those stationed in the very zones where these revolts flared, shrouded these revolts in an "ideology of silence," the events nonetheless proved to have long-lasting political consequences. The clearest of these was the restructuring of Florentine taxation, leading progressively to lower tax rates in Florence's *contado* and, even more importantly, to a narrowing of the flagrant inequalities of rural taxation. The year 1402 was here a watershed leading to the *catasto* reforms of 1427 and the abolition once and for all of the medieval mosaic of rural fiscal inequalities.

In addition, the decrees and petitions approved by Florence's highest councils show 1402 as the divide in the government's welfare measures toward its hinterland. Before the peasant insurrections, clemency for Florence's rural subjects revolved around military strategy and fortifications. Afterwards, concern for the defense of its realm widened to embrace the politics of demography: through compromises and negotiations Florence sought to placate its peasantry and thereby reverse the drastic depletion of its regional population. Beyond the devastation of war, Florence began to intervene with tax exemptions and other forms of fiscal relief to alleviate the damages from scourges that Florence's oligarchy had previously met with scant concern. Only after 1402 did the government begin to consider plagues, floods, crop failures, and hailstorms, in isolation from war, as justifications for rural assistance.

The year 1402 marked a divide in the government's largesse toward its *contado* and district. Not only did successful petitions increase in number; the government granted more extensive exemptions and showed greater concern for its rural subjects' indebtedness, absolving or reducing long lists of debts which on occasion reached back a decade or more. By contrast, before 1402 the Florentine councils had been reluctant to do more than absolve the penalties for late payments while keeping the principal inviolate. Most indicative of Florence's post-1402 change in attitude was the role of its funded debt. From being a resource that poured profits on privileged citizens, the *Monte* and its ever-spiraling deficit finance came to aid and not solely to milk peasants from the *contado*. Increasingly after 1402, the *Monte* assumed peasant debts and thereby cushioned the blows of war, disease, and other adversities.

While this process of territorial incorporation broke the mosaic of community inequalities, blurred the lines between *contado* and *districtus*, and standardized justice and jurisprudence through large swathes of the territory,[1] it also had a repressive side. As seen in the debates of the *Consulte e Pratiche* and prosecutions in the criminal acts of the new vicariates of Pisa, the Valdarno Superiore, Anghiari, and other places in the hills and mountains of Arezzo, incorporation was accompanied by Florence's zeal to bring these communities under its sense of law, devotion, and "buon costume."[2] As the criminal records of the new vicariate courts of the early fifteenth century make clear, these "good customs" often concerned sexual practice.

Increasingly, the Florentine police entered the bedrooms of mountain dwellers, using force, torture, and mutilation to repress practices and relationships it found "contra naturam."[3] By 1416, local statutes partially imposed on mountain communes even required the election of "secret guards" (*guardie segrete*) to fine those "who cursed and blasphemed the Lord or saints."[4] This desire to force Florence's rural subjects into behavioral conformity was intensified in 1429 with the creation of a new centralized tribunal, the *Conservatori delle leggi*, which passed new laws prosecuting crimes of blasphemy, gambling, card games, luxury consumption, and "crimes of the night."[5] Thus, while Florence insisted that every newly incorporated community make its own laws, it also approached Leonardo Bruni's dream that all people subject to Florence

[1] At the turn of the century Florence standardized justice in the territory by reorganizing old *Podesterie* into new vicariates and by replacing foreign judges (*Podestà* and *Capitani*) with Florentine citizens. These changes took place both in the new frontier areas of the Pisano and Aretino and within the traditional *contado* of Florence; see Chittolini, "Ricerche sull'ordinamento," p. 299, and 305–6; Zorzi, *L'Amministrazione*, pp. 34 and 45; and "Giusdicenti," p. 520.
[2] *Le "Consulte" e "Pratiche" (1401)* pp. 213–14; *Le Consulte e pratiche (1404)*, p. 25; and Chittolini, "Civic Religion."
[3] See Cohn, *Women in the Streets*, ch. 6. Also, Zorzi, *L'Amministrazione*, p. 55, notes a rise in the percentage of prosecutions against crimes of morality with the formation of the new vicariates. Similarly, Comba, "'Apetitus libidinis coherceatur': Strutture demografiche, reati sessuali e disciplina dei comportamenti nel Piemonte tardomedievale," *Studi Storici*, 27, no. 3 (1986), p. 550, finds a "new vigilance" in the prosecution of crimes of adultery in the countryside of Piedmont in the first decade of the fifteenth century.
[4] Statuti 420 (Mangona), c. 50, 30r–v: "Della electione delle guardie segrete."
[5] Zorzi, *L'Amministrazione*, p. 62; "I fiorentini," pp. 746–7.

live under the same laws (although, it must be added, not with the same resources and advantages).[6]

This stamp of unity can be seen symbolically as well in Florence's early-fifteenth-century campaign to plaster or paint its emblem of the *Marzocco* in the square of every major village and town within its territory.[7] While the archival records do not cite a single incident of attacks against this symbol of Florentine pride in the insurrections of 1401 to 1404, with the next wave of peasant revolts, that spread through the Casentino mountains in 1426, these symbols had become the first objects of insurrectionary violence.[8]

On the other hand, the change in Florentine clemency toward the peasantry, particularly those within the traditional *contado*, shows that the peasant revolts of 1402 had a lasting impact on the mentality and policy of the Florentine elites. By 1403 Florence's city fathers had reconsidered their territorial politics, now seeing their own welfare as being more intertwined with that of their peasantry. They now perceived the *contado* as more than a reservoir for tax revenues and a buffer against foreign invasion, or, at the very least, they now sought to achieve these goals through negotiation, protection, and support of their peasant subjects in hard times, no matter whether these adversities had been brought on by war, plague, or hailstorms.

Despite the repressive side of incorporation, it was not by force alone that Florence consolidated and controlled its territory more successfully and thoroughly than any other state in fifteenth-century Italy.[9] Nor did the formation of this regional state with its more standardized taxation, laws, and morality, its increasing centralization and bureaucratization lead inexorably to the impoverishment and decline of the peasantry as some historians of Florence have assumed and social and political

[6] See Jane Black, "Communal Statutes and the Florentine Territorial State: The Contribution of the Jurists." In *Florentine Tuscany*.
[7] Géraldine Johnson, "The Lion in the Piazza: Patrician Politics and Public Statuary in Central Florence," in *Secular Sculpture, 1350–1550*, ed. by Thomas Frangenberg and Phillip Lindley (Stanford, 1999); and Cohn, *Women in the Streets*, p. 207.
[8] Cohn, *Women in the Streets*, pp. 124–5.
[9] For this assessment, see Chittolini, "Ricerche sull'ordinamento," p. 326. For a comparison between Florence and Milan, see Martines, *Lawyers and Statecraft in Renaissance Florence*; between Florence and Venice, James Grubb, *First Born of Venice: Vicenza in the Early Renaissance State* (Baltimore, 1988); and for relations between Venice and its hinterland, Law, "'Super differentiis'." Recently, Petralia, ("Fiscalità") and Epstein ("Cities, Regions") have argued that Florence's political success in subduing its territorial subjects had negative economic outcomes for fiscality (Petralia) and for commerce and industry (Epstein). Nonetheless, they have not disputed Florence's political success in the control and centralization of its state during the fifteenth century, even if it failed to establish a universal fiscal regime throughout its dominion in 1427.

scientists have generalized as the inevitable consequences of state building in early-modern Europe. Instead, Florence's new zeal to unify, consolidate, and expand its territory stemmed the tide of its peasants' flight
from the *contado* and contributed to their prosperity, especially in the
highlands. Against Braudelian notions of mountain backwardness,
poverty, and flight to supposedly greener valleys down the slopes, the statistics from the Florentine tax registers show a mountain population
whose material well-being increased sevenfold from the Florentine wars
against the Duke of Milan in 1400 to the time of Cosimo de' Medici's
death in 1464. By the early years of the fifteenth century, the Florentine
oligarchy had begun to learn a lesson later enshrined in Machiavelli's
advice to princes: "the best kind of fortress is not to be hated by the
people."[10] Their first teacher, however, was neither a humanist nor a
political philosopher but thousands of mountain peasants on the out-
skirts of the Florentine state.

---

[10] Te Brake, *Shaping History*, p. 168, also notes this passage.

Regression models

I THE DETERMINANTS OF WEALTH IN 1393

Taxable wealth (est) was regressed against the following independent variables: whether residence was in the mountains (moun), whether a family's structure was complex (e.g. more than nuclear [cmpx]), whether the head was aged (e.g. older than sixty [senex]), handicapped (hcap), or female, and whether the village was in the district of Prato. The city of Prato was excluded; there were 1,230 observations; adjusted R-squared $= 0.0596$; $P=$probability.

est	Coef.	Std. Err.	t	$P>|t|$
moun	12.73094	7.333233	1.736	0.083
cmpx	61.83488	8.040802	7.690	0.000
senex	16.35392	7.31832	2.235	0.026
female	−14.42621	15.25286	−0.946	0.344
Prato	−8.422644	11.28644	−0.746	0.456
hcap	−40.1256	12.88301	−3.115	0.002
constant	35.66669	6.329763	5.635	0.000

II PROBIT ANALYSIS OF OUT-MIGRATION, 1393

Out-migration was regressed against distance of the village from Florence (squared) (dist1), the village tax rate (inrat), average family size (inct), average wealth (inest), whether the village was in the mountains, hills, or plains, and whether the village was in the district of Prato; number of observations = 1,685; $\chi^2(8)$ = 106.42; Prob χ^2 = 0.0000; Log likelihood = -848.71186; Pseudo R-squared = 0.0590.

out	Coef.	Std. Err.	z	$P>|z|$
dist1	1−0.0033885	0.002326	−1.457	0.145
inrat	−10.41573	1.081044	−9.635	0.000
inct	1−0.0508827	0.0187473	−2.714	0.007
inest	1−0.0001064	0.0000809	−1.315	0.189
moun	1−0.0691562	0.202201	−0.342	0.732
plain	1−0.4965324	0.1505923	−3.297	0.001
hills	1−0.3000103	0.170879	−1.756	0.079
Prato	1−0.1396218	0.1090379	−1.280	0.200
constant	1 −1.145803	0.1699143	−6.743	0.000

III TAX RATES IN 1393/4

Individual tax rates were regressed against residence in the mountains, hills, or plains, wealth (est), family size (ct), distance of village from Florence (dist1), whether a family's structure was complex (e.g. more than nuclear [cmpx]), whether the head was aged (e.g. older than sixty [senex]), handicapped (hcap), or female, and whether the village was in the district of Prato. The city of Prato was not included; number of observations = 627; Prob > F = 0.0000; R-squared = 0.2439; Adjusted R-squared = 0.2316.

ratio2	Coef.	Std. Err.	t	$P>|t|$
moun	−0.0500451	0.0047858	−10.457	0.000
hills	−0.0061166	0.0038649	−1.583	0.114
plain	−(dropped)			
est	−0.0000689	8.38e-06	−8.218	0.000
ct	−0.0016797	0.0005716	−2.939	0.003
dist1	−0.000597	0.0000605	−9.864	0.000
cmpx	−0.0012385	0.0030049	−0.412	0.680
senex	−0.0005874	0.0026426	−0.222	0.824
hcap	−0.0053784	0.006317	−0.851	0.395
female	−0.0004165	0.0057744	−0.072	0.943
Prato	−0.0063538	0.0047521	−1.337	0.182
constant	−0.0208154	0.0038457	−5.413	0.000

IV TAXES ON THE PROPERTYLESS

The tax base (lira2) was regressed against the variables listed below (for their abbreviations, see III). The city of Prato was excluded; number of observations = 590; Prob > F = 0.0034; R-squared = 0.0414; adjusted R-squared = 0.0265.

lira2	Coef.	Std. Err.	t	$P>|t|$
moun	−34.84879	20.06812	−1.737	0.083
hills	−7.930156	14.98847	−0.529	0.597
ct	−7.188645	2.723396	−2.640	0.009
dist1	−0.6758483	0.3217036	−2.101	0.036
cmpx	−18.53127	12.90431	−1.436	0.152
senex	−5.614011	10.68898	−0.525	0.600
hcap	−3.004111	15.3334	−0.196	0.845
female	−16.65229	22.43276	−0.742	0.458
Prato	−25.02008	14.3087	−1.749	0.081
constant	−75.21263	14.20298	−5.296	0.000

V DETERMINANTS OF TAXES (THE *LIRA*), 1394

Number of observations = 1,367; Prob > F = 0.0000; R-squared = 0.5232; adjusted R-squared = 0.5194.

lira2	Coef.	Std. Err.	t	$P>|t|$
moun	−156.3465	33.84438	−4.620	0.000
hills	−18.08082	30.24758	−0.598	0.550
plain	−55.57236	27.38242	−2.029	0.043
est	−0.7270161	0.0253376	−28.693	0.000
ct	−24.35326	2.863814	−8.504	0.000
dist1	−2.797656	0.3354595	−8.340	0.000
cmpx	−34.7143	14.4696	−2.399	0.017
senex	−19.8541	12.52006	−1.586	0.113
hcap	−58.95612	19.91628	−2.960	0.003
female	−7.912242	26.76364	−0.296	0.768
Prato	−71.29451	20.30999	−3.510	0.000
constant	−98.11203	31.01886	−3.163	0.002

Tax coefficients, 1350–1423 (P = Provvisioni registri; C = Camera del Comune).

Year	Peditum (*soldi*)	Mercatum	Ponti et vie	Ordinaria	Straordinaria	Source
1350	20					P
1352	10					P
1353	10					P
1354	10					P
1355	10					P
1356	10					P
1359	10	2				P
1362	10					P
1363	10	2	2			P
1364	25	2	2			P
1365	30	2	2			P
1366	20					P
1367	10					P
1368	40					P
1369	20	2	2			P
1370	40					P
1371				12		P
1372				12		P
1375				24		P
1376						P
1377			14			P
1378						P
1379				10		P
1380				10		P
1381				10+		P
1382		2	2	12		P
1384				10+		P&C
1385				10+		C
1386				10+		C
1387				20		P
1392				20		P
1394				20	80	P
1395				20	80	P&C

Year	Peditum (*soldi*)	Mercatum	Ponti et vie	Ordinaria	Straordinaria	Source
1396					80	C
1397					80	P&C
1398					120	C
1399				20	120	P&C
1400				20	120	P&C
1401				20	120/80	P&C
1402				20	80	P&C
1403					80	P&C
1404					80	P
1405					80	C
1406					48	P&C
1407					40/48	P&C
1408					40	C
1412					40	P
1414					100	P
1416					100	C
1418					80	C
1419					80	C
1420					80	C
1423[a]					80	C

Note: [a] I was unable to find any coefficients after this date.

Bibliography

ARCHIVAL SOURCES

ARCHIVIO ARCIVESCOVILE DI FIRENZE
Visite pastorali, 1383, 1422

ARCHIVIO DI STATO DI FIRENZE
Arte dei Giudici e notai
Atti del Podestà (AP)
Camera del Comune:
    Entrata e Uscita
    Provveditori e Massai
Capitano del Popolo (CP)
Carte Strozziane
    Falcucci Paliano di Falco, *Ricordanze*, 1382–1406
    Ricordanze di Niccholo del Buono di Bese Busini
Catasto
Consulte e Pratiche
Deliberazioni dei conservatori del contado
Dieci di Balìa:
    Deliberazioni, Condotte e stanziamenti
    Missive Legazioni e commissarie
Diplomatico: Archivio generale
Esecutore degli ordinamenti di Giustizia
Estimo
Giudice degli appelli e nullità (Giudice)
Libri Fabarum (LF)
Notarile antecosimiano (Not. antecos.)
Otto di Guardia
Prestanze
Provvisioni Registri (Provv. reg.)
Signori: Responsive originali

Signori carteggio: Rapporti e relazioni di oratori
Signori e Collegi, Deliberazioni: fatte in forza di ordinaria autorità
Signori e Collegi, Deliberazioni: fatte in speciale autorità
Statuti della comunità autonome e soggette (Statuti)
Ufficiali della Grascia, I Libri di Morti

ARCHIVIO DELL OPERA DEL DUOMO

Registro delle fedi di battesimo, I (1450–1)

BIBLIOTECA NAZIONALE DI FIRENZE

Panciatichi, 158, *Croniche di Firenze tratte da" Villani e da altri Autori*

PRINTED SOURCES

Albizzi, Rinaldo degli. *Commissioni di Rinaldo degli Albizzi per il comune di Firenze dal MCCCXCIX al MCCCCXXXIII.* Ed. by Cesare Guasti. 3 vols. Florence, 1867–73.
Ammirato, Scipione. *Istorie fiorentine.* Ed. by Luciano Scarabelli. Turin, 1853.
Ammirato, Scipione. *Istorie fiorentine con l'aggiunte di Scipione il Giovane.* Florence, 1848.
Bartolommeo Cederni and his Friends: Letters to an Obscure Florentine. Ed. by F. W. Kent and Gino Corti. Florence, 1991.
Bartolomeo del Corazza, *Diario fiorentino (1405–1439).* Ed. by Roberta Gentile. Rome, 1991.
Boccaccio, Giovanni. *Decameron.* Ed. by Vittore Branca. Milan, 1976.
Bracciolini, Poggio. *Facezie di Poggio Fiorentino,* 2nd edn. Rome, 1885.
  Historiarum Florentini Populi. Ed. by Riccardo Fubini. Turin, 1966.
Bruni, Leonardo. *Historiarum Florentini Populi: Libri XII.* Ed. by Emilio Santini. *Rerum Italicarum Scriptores* [hereafter *RIS*], XIX, part 3. Città di Castello, 1914–26.
  Rerum suo tempore gestarum commentarius [aa. 1378–1440]. Ed. by Carmine di Pierro. In *RIS*, XIX, part 3. Città di Castello, 1914–26, pp. 403–69.
Buoninsegni, Domenico. *Historia Fiorentina.* Florence, 1580.
Cambi, Giovanni. *Istorie di Giovanni Cambi.* In *Delizie* XX–XXIII (1785).
I Capitoli del Comune di Firenze. Ed. by Cesare Guasti. 2 vols. Florence, 1866.
Capponi, Gino. *Monumenta Historica de Rebus Florentinorum . . . ab anno 1378 usque ad annum 1419 cum continuatione Nerii illius filii usque ad annum 1456.* Ed. by Lodovico Muratori. In *RIS* [original series], XVIII. Milan, 1731, pp. 1097–220.
Carta della Toscana. Ed. by Italo Moretti and Pietro Ruschi and taken from Fedor Schneider, *L'ordinamento pubblico nella Toscana medievale.* Florence, 1975 [Rome, 1914].
Cavalcanti, Giovanni. *Istorie fiorentine.* Ed. by F.-L. Polidori. Florence, 1838.

Le "Consulte" e "Pratiche" della repubblica fiorentina nel Quattrocento, I *(1401)* *(Cancellierato di Coluccio Salutati)*. Ed. by Elio Conti. Pisa, 1981.

Le Consulte e pratiche della repubblica fiorentina (1404). Ed. by Renzo Nenci. Fonti per la storia d'italia. Rome, 1991.

Il Contratto di mezzadria nella Toscana medievale, I: *Il contado di Siena, Secolo XIII-1348*. Ed. by Giuliano Pinto and Paolo Pirillo. Florence, 1987.

Il Contratto di mezzadria nella Toscana medievale, II: *Il Contado di Firenze, Secolo XIII*. Ed. by Oretta Muzzi and Maria Nenci. Florence, 1988.

Il Contratto di mezzadria nella Toscana medievale, III: *Il Contado di Siena, 1349–1518*. Ed. by Gabriella Piccinni. Florence, 1992.

Corpus Chronicorum Bononiensium. Ed. by Albano Sorbelli. In *RIS*, XVIII part 1. Città di Castello, 1905.

La Cronica di Bologna. Ed. by Muratori. In *RIS* [original series], XVIII [*Memoriale di Matteo Griffoni*, XVIII part 2].

Dati, Gregorio. *L'Istoria di Firenze di Gregorio Dati dal 1380 al 1405*. Ed. by Luigi Pratesi. Norcia, 1902.

Dei, Benedetto. *La Cronica dall'anno 1400 all'anno 1500*. Ed. by Roberto Barducci. Florence, 1984.

Delayto, Jacobo. *Annales estenses Jacobi de Delayto . . . ab anno MCCCXCIII usque ad MCCCCIX*. Ed. by Muratori. In *RIS* [original series], XVIII, pp. 905–1096.

Delizie degli: Eruditi Toscani. Ed. by Fr. Ildefonso di San Luigi. 24 vols. Florence, 1770–89.

Diario d'Anonimo fiorentino dall'anno 1358 al 1389. Ed. by Alessandro Gherardi. In *Cronache dei secoli XIII e XIV: Documenti di storia italiana*, VI. Florence, 1876, pp. 207–588.

Guicciardini, Francesco. *Opere inedite di Francesco Guicciardini: Storia Fiorentina*. Ed. by Piero and Luigi Guicciardini. Florence, 1859.

Karmin, Otto. *La Legge del Catasto Fiorentino del 1427*. Florence, 1906.

Machiavelli, Bernardo. *Libro di ricordi*. Ed. by Cesare Olschki. Florence, 1954.

Machiavelli, Niccolò. *Istorie fiorentine*. Ed. by Franco Gaeta. Milan, 1962.

   The Prince and other Political Writings. Ed. and transl. by Steven Milner. London, 1995.

Mercanti Scrittori. Ricordi nella Firenze tra medioevo e rinascimento. Ed. by Vittore Branca. Milan, 1986.

Minerbetti. *Cronica volgare di Anonimo Fiorentino dall'anno 1385 al 1409 già attribuita a Piero di Giovanni Minerbetti*. Ed. by Elina Bellondi. In *RIS*, XXVII, part 2. Città di Castello, 1915–18.

Montaigne, Michel. *Journal de voyage*. Ed. by Louis Lautrey. Paris, 1906.

Morelli, Giovanni di Iacopo. *Ricordi fatti in Firenze (1385–1437)*. In *Delizie*, XX (1785), pp. 1–164.

Morelli, Giovanni di Pagolo. *Ricordi*. Ed. by Vittore Branca. Florence, 1956.

Naddo da Montecatini. *Memorie storiche cavate da un libro di ricordi scritto da Naddo di ser Nepo di Ser Fallo da Montecatini, dall'anno 1374 all'anno 1398*. In *Delizie*, XVIII (1784), pp. 1–174.

Nardi, Iacopo. *Istorie della città di Firenze*. Ed. by Lelio Arbib. Florence, 1842.

Niccolini, Lapo di Giovanni. *Il libro degli affari proprii di casa de Lapo di Giovanni Niccolini de' Sirigatti*. Ed. by Christian Bec. Paris, 1969.

Petrarca, Francesco. *Rerum Familiarum libri I-VIII*. Transl. by Aldo Bernardo. Albany, N.Y., 1975.

Piattoli, Renato, ed. *Regesta chartarum Italiae: Le Carte del Monastero di S. Maria di Montepiano (1000–1200)*. Rome, 1942.

Pitti, Buonaccorso. *Ricordi*. In *Mercanti Scrittori*, pp. 341–503.

Poliziano, Angelo. *Angelo Polizanos Tagebuch (1477–1479)*. Ed. by Albert Wesselski. Jena, 1929.

Pucci, Antonio. "Proprietà di Mercato Vecchio." In *Poeti Minori del Trecento*. Ed. by Natalino Sapegno. Milan, 1952, pp. 403–10.

Rinuccini, Filippo di Cino. *Ricordi storici di Filippo di Cino Rinuccini dal 1280 al 1460*. Ed. by G. Aiazzi. Florence, 1840.

Rucellai, Giovanni. *Giovanni Rucellai ed il suo Zibaldone*, I: *Il Zibaldone quaresimale. Pagine scelte*. Ed. by Alessandro Perosa. London, 1960.

Sacchetti, Franco. *Il libro delle rime*. Ed. by Franca Ageno. Florence, 1990.

Il Trecentonovelle. Ed. by Antonio Lanza. Florence, 1984.

Salviati, Iacopo. *Cronica, o memorie di Iacopo Salviati dall'anno 1398 al 1411*. In *Delizie*, XVIII (1784), pp. 175–381.

Segni, Bernardo. *Storie fiorentine dall'anno MDXXVII al MDLV*. Florence, 1835.

Sercambi, Giovanni. *Le Cronache di Giovanni Sercambi*. Ed. by Salvatore Bongi. 3 vols. Lucca, 1892.

Ser Luca Dominici. *Cronache di Ser Luca Dominici*. I: *Cronica della venuta dei Bianchi e della moria 1399–1400*; II: *Cronica seconda*. Ed. by Giovan Carlo Gigliotti. Pistoia, 1933.

Sermini, Gentile. *Le Novelle di Gentile Sermini da Siena*. Ed. by F. Vigo. Livorno, 1874.

Sozomeni pistoriensis Specimen historiae, Ed. by Muratori. In *RIS* [original series], XVI. Milan, 1730.

Statuta Populi Communis Florentiae (1415). 3 vols. Freiburg, 1778–83.

Statuti della repubblica fiorentina, I: *Statuti del Capitano del Popolo degli anni 1322–25*, II: *Statuti del Podestà dell'anno 1325*. Ed. by Romolo Caggese. Florence, 1910–21.

Stefani. *Cronaca fiorentina di Marchionne di Coppo Stefani*. Ed. by N. Rodolico. In *RIS*, XXX, part 1. Città di Castello, 1903.

Traversari, Ambrogio. *Hodoeporicon*. Ed. by Vittorio Tamburini. Florence, 1985.

Varchi, Benedetto. *Storia fiorentina*. Ed. by Lelio Arbib. Florence, 1843.

Villani, Giovanni. *Nuova Cronica*, Ed. by Giuseppe Porta. 3 vols. Parma, 1990.

Villani, Matteo. *Cronica di Matteo Villani*. Ed. by Ignazio Moutier. 5 vols. Florence, 1825.

SECONDARY SOURCES

Abate, Maria. "Classi di imposta del contado fiorentino secondo l'estimo del 1357." Tesi di laurea, Università degli Studi di Firenze, Facoltà di Magistero. Relatore Prof. Elio Conti, 1969–70.

Anderson, Perry. *Lineages of the Absolutist State*. London, 1974.

Annuario Generale dei comuni e delle frazione d'Italia: Edizione 1980/1985 [*AG*]. Milan, 1980.

Anzilotti, Antonio. "Il tramonto dello stato cittadino," *Archivio Storico Italiano* [*ASI*], 82 (1924): 72–105.

Barbadoro, Bernardino. *Le finanze della repubblica fiorentina: Imposte diretta e debito pubblico fino alla istituzione del Monte*. Florence, 1929.

Barbieri, Giuseppe. "Il Mugello. Studio di geografia umana," *Rivista Geografica Italiana*, 60 (1953): 89–133 and 296–378.

Barbolani di Montauto, Fabrizio. "Sopravvivenza di Signorie feudali: la accomandigie al Comune di Firenze." In *I Ceti dirigenti nella Toscana tardo comunale: atti del III convegno, Firenze 5–7 decembre 1980*. Florence, 1983, pp. 47–55.

Baron, Hans. *The Crisis of the Early Renaissance*, 2 vols. Princeton, 1955; revised edn., 1966.

"Leonardo Bruni: 'Professional Rhetorician' or 'Civic Humanist'?" *Past and Present*, 36 (1967): 21–37.

Bec, Christian. *Cultura e società a Firenze nell'età della rinascenza*. Rome, 1981.

Les marchands écrivains: affaires et humanisme à Florence 1375–1434. Paris, 1967.

"La paysan dans la nouvelle toscane (1350–1530)." In *Civiltà ed economia agricola*, pp. 29–52.

Becker, Marvin. "Economic Change and the Emerging Florentine Territorial State," *Studies in the Renaissance*, 13 (1966): 7–39.

Florence in Transition, I: *The Decline of the Commune*; II: *Studies in the Rise of the Territorial State*. Baltimore, 1967–8.

"The Florentine Territorial State and Civic Humanism in the Early Renaissance." In *Florentine Studies*, pp. 109–39.

"Problemi della finanza pubblica fiorentina della seconda metà del Trecento e dei primi anni del Quattrocento," *ASI*, 123 (1965): 433–66.

Berengo, Marino. "Il Cinquecento." In *La storiografia italiana negli ultimi vent'anni*. Milan, 1970, pp. 485–518.

Berkner, Lutz. "The Stem Family and the Developmental Cycle of the Peasant Household: An Eighteenth-Century Austrian Example," *American Historical Review*, 77 (1972): 398–418.

Biscaro, G. "Gli estimi del Comune di Milano nel secolo XIII," *Archivio di Stato di Lombardia* (1928): 343–495.

Bizzocchi, Roberto. *Chiesa e potere nella Toscana del Quattrocento*. Bologna, 1987.

Black, Jane. "Communal Statutes and the Florentine Territorial State: The Contribution of the Jurists." In *Florentine Tuscany*.

Black, Robert. "Arezzo and the Florentine Territorial State, 1384–1515." In *Florentine Tuscany*.

Bocchi, Francesca. "Le imposte dirette a Bologna nei secoli XII e XIII," *Nuova Rivista Storica*, 57 (1973): 273–312.

Bois, Guy. *Crise du féodalisme: Economie rurale et démographie en Normandie orientale du début du 14e siècle au milieu du 16e siècle*. Paris, 1976.

Bortolami, Sante. "Lotta e protesta contadina nel Veneto dal Medioevo all prima età moderna: un bilancio." In *Protesta e rivolta contadina*, pp. 45–64.

Bouwsma, William. *Venice and the Defense of Republican Liberty*. Berkeley, Calif., 1968.

Branca, Vittore. "Introduzione" to *Mercanti Scrittori*, pp. ix–lxxxviii.

Braudel, Fernand. *Écrits sur l'histoire*. Paris, 1969.

"History and the Social Sciences, The Long Term." In *Society and Economy: Articles from Annales*. Ed. by Peter Burke. New York, 1972, pp. 11–40.

The Mediterranean and the Mediterranean World in the Age of Philip II. Transl. by Sîan Reynolds. 2 vols. New York, 1966 [Paris, 1949].

Bridbury, A. R. "The Black Death," *Economic Historical Review*, 2nd ser. 26, no. 4 (1973): 584–92.

Brown, Alison. "Lorenzo, the *Monte*, and the Seventeen Reformers." In *The Medici in Florence: The Exercise and Language of Power*. Florence, 1992, pp. 151–83.

Brown, Judith. *In the Shadow of Florence. Provincial Society in Renaissance Pescia*. Oxford, 1982.

Brown, Peter. *Power and Persuasion in Late Antiquity: Towards a Christian Empire*. Madison, 1992.

Brucker, Gene A. *The Civic World of Early Renaissance Florence*. Princeton, 1977.

"The Economic Foundations of Laurentian Florence." In *Lorenzo il Magnifico e il suo mondo. Convegno Internazionale di studi (Firenze, 9–13 giugno 1992)*. Ed. by Gian Carlo Garfagnini. Florence, 1994, pp. 3–15.

Florentine Politics and Society, 1343–1378. Princeton, 1962.

"Humanism, Politics and the Social Order in Early Renaissance Florence." In *Florence and Venice: Comparisons and Relations*, I: *Quattrocento*. Ed. by Sergio Bertelli, Nicolai Rubinstein, and Craig Hugh Smyth. Florence, 1979, pp. 3–11.

Bueno de Mesquita, D. M. *Giangaleazzo Visconti, Duke of Milan (1351–1402): A Study in the Political Career of an Italian Despot*. Cambridge, 1941.

Burke, Peter. "Mediterranean Europe 1500–1800: Notes and Comparisons." In *Religion and Rural Revolt: Papers Presented to the Fourth Interdisciplinary Workshop on Peasant Studies, University of British Columbia, 1982*. Ed. by Janos M. Bak and Gerhard Benecke. Manchester, 1984, pp. 75–85.

Caferro, William. *Mercenary Companies and the Decline of Siena*. Baltimore, 1998.

Caggese, Romolo. *Classi e comuni rurali nel Medio Evo italiano*. 2 vols. Florence, 1908.

Roberto d'Angio e i suoi tempi. Florence, 1921.

Calindri, Serafino. *Dizionario, corografico, georgico, orittologico, storico*. 5 vols. Bologna, 1781–5; reprinted 1978.

Campbell, Bruce. "Population-Pressure, Inheritance and the Land Market in a Fourteenth-Century Peasant Community." In *Land, Kinship and Life-Cycle*. Ed. by Richard M. Smith. Cambridge, 1984, pp. 87–135.

Capponi, Gino. *Storia della Repubblica*. 3 vols. Florence, 1876, reprinted, 1976.

Carmichael, Ann. *Plague and the Poor in Renaissance Florence*. Cambridge, 1986.

Casini, Stefano. *Dizionario biografico geografico, storico del Comune di Firenzuola*. 3 vols. Florence, 1914.

Cassuto, Umberto. *Gli ebrei a Firenze nell'età del rinascimento*. Florence, 1918.

Chayanov, A. V. *The Theory of the Peasant Economy.* Ed. by D. Thorner, D. Kerblay, and R. Smith. Homewood, Ill., 1966 [1925].

Cherubini, Giovanni. "Appunti sul brigantaggio in Italia alla fine del medioevo." In *Studi di storia medievale e moderna per Enesto Sestan,* I: *Medioevo.* Florence, 1980, pp. 103–33.

"La 'civiltà' del castagno in Italia alla fine del Medioevo," *Archeologia Medievale,* 8 (1981): 247–80.

Una comunità dell'Appennino dal XIII al XV secolo: Montecoronaro dalla signoria dell'abbazia del Trivio al Dominio di Firenze. Florence, 1972.

"Conclusioni." In *Strutture familiari,* pp. 535–42.

"Paesaggio agrario, insediamenti e attività silo–pastorali sulla montagna tosco-romagnola alla fine del medioevo." In Cherubini, *Fra Tevere, Arno e Appennino. Valli, communità, signori.* Florence, 1992, pp. 39–69.

"Qualche considerazione sulle campagne dell'Italia centro-settentrionale tra l'XI e il XV secolo." In *Signori, contadini, borghesi: Ricerche sulla società italiana del basso medioevo.* Florence, 1974, pp. 51–119.

"Risorse, paesaggio ed utilizzazione agricola del territorio della Toscana sud-occidentale nei secoli XIV–XV." In *Civiltà ed economia agricola,* pp. 91–115.

"San Godenzo nei suoi statuti quattrocenteschi." In *Fra Tevere, Arno e Appennino,* pp. 145–65.

"La società dell'Appennino settentrionale (secoli XIII-XV)." In *Signori, contadini, borghesi,* pp. 130–1.

Chiffoleau, Jacques. *La Comptabilité de l'au-delà: Les hommes, la mort et la religion dans la région d'Avignon à la fin du Moyen Age (vers 1320–vers 1480).* Rome, 1980.

Chittolini, Giorgio. "Civic Religion and the Countryside in Late Medieval Italy." In *City and Countryside,* pp. 69–91.

"The Italian City-State and its Territory." In *City States in Classical Antiquity and Medieval Italy: Athens and Rome, Florence and Venice.* Stuttgart, 1991, pp. 589–602.

"Ricerche sull'ordinamento territoriale del dominio fiorentino agli inizi del secolo XV." In *La formazione dello stato regionale e le istituzioni del contado: secoli XIV e XV.* Turin, 1978, pp. 292–352.

Ciappelli, Giovanni. "Il cittadino fiorentino e il fisco alla fine del Trecento e nel corso del Quattrocento: uno studio di due casi," *Società e Storia,* no. 46 (1989): 823–72.

City and Countryside in Late Medieval and Renaissance Italy: Essays presented to Philip Jones. Ed. by Trevor Dean and Chris Wickham. London, 1990.

Civiltà ed economia agricola in Toscana nei secc. XIII–XV: Problemi della vita delle campagne nel tardo medioevo (Pistoia, 21–24 aprile 1977). Pistoia, 1981.

Clarke, Paula. *The Soderini and the Medici: Power and Patronage in Fifteenth-Century Florence.* Oxford, 1991.

Cochrane, Eric. *Historians and Historiography in the Italian Renaissance.* Chicago, 1981.

Cognasso, Francesco. "Il Ducato Visconteo da Gian Galeazzo a Filippo Maria." In *Storia di Milano,* VI: *Il Ducato Visconteo e la repubblica Ambrosiana (1392–1450).* Milan, 1955, pp. 30–67.

Cohn, Jr., Samuel K. *The Cult of Remembrance: Six Renaissance Cities in Central Italy.* Baltimore, 1992.

Death and Property in Siena: Strategies for the Afterlife. Baltimore, 1988.
"Fiscal Policy and Demography in the Florentine Contado, 1355–1487." In *Florentine Tuscany.*
"Insurrezioni contadine e demografia: il mito della povertà nelle montagne toscane (1348–1460)," *Studi Storici,* 36, no. 4 (1995): 1023–49.
"Inventing Braudel's Mountains. The Florentine Alps after the Black Death." In *Portraits of Medieval and Renaissance Living. Essays in Honor of David Herlihy.* Ed. by Cohn and Steven A. Epstein. Ann Arbor, 1996, pp. 383–416.
The Laboring Classes in Renaissance Florence. New York, 1980.
"Marriage in the Mountains: The Florentine Territorial State, 1348–1500." In *Marriage in Italy, 1300–1650.* Ed. by Trevor Dean and K. J. P. Lowe. Cambridge, 1997, pp. 174–96.
"Piété et commande d'oeuvres d'art après la peste noire," *Annales, HSS,* 51 (1996): 553–71.
Women in the Streets: Essays on Sex and Power in the Italian Renaissance. Baltimore, 1996.
Comba, Rinaldo. "'Apetitus libidinis coherceatur': Strutture demografiche, reati sessuali e disciplina dei comportamenti nel Piemonte tardomedievale," *Studi Storici,* 27, no. 3 (1986): 529–77.
"Emigrare nel Medioevo: Aspetti economico-sociali della mobilità geografica nei secoli XI–XVI." In *Strutture familiari,* pp. 45–74.
"Il problema della mobilità geografica delle popolazioni montane alla fine del medioevo attraverso un sondaggio sulle Alpi Marittime." In *Medioevo rurale.* Ed. by V. Fumagalli and G. Rossetti. Bologna, 1980, pp. 299–318.
"Rivolte e ribellioni fra Tre e Quattrocento." In *La storia: I grandi problemi dal Medioevo all'Età Contemporanea. Il Medioevo,* II: *Popoli e strutture politiche.* Ed. by Nicola Tranfaglia and Massimo Firpo. Turin, 1993, pp. 673–91.
Connell, William J. "Changing Patterns of Medicean Patronage: The Florentine Dominion during the Fifteenth Century." In *Lorenzo il Magnifico e il suo mondo.* Ed. by G. C. Garfagnini. Florence, 1994, pp. 87–107.
City of Sorrows: Clientage and Faction in the Republican State (forthcoming).
"Clientelismo e Stato territoriale. Il Potere fiorentino a Pistoia nel XV secolo," *Società e Storia,* no. 53 (1991): 523–43.
Conti, Elio. *I Catasti agrari della repubblica fiorentina e il Catasto particellare toscano (secoli XIV–XIX).* Rome, 1966.
La formazione della struttura agraria moderna nel contado fiorentino, I: *Le campagne nell'età comunale*; II, part 2: *Monografie e Tavole Statistiche (secoli XV–XIX).* Rome, 1965.
L'imposta diretta a Firenze nel Quattrocento (1427–1494). Rome, 1984.
Ricordi fiscali di Matteo Palmieri (1427–1474). Rome, 1983.
Cortonosi, Alfio. "Demografia e popolamento nel contado di Siena: la terra montalcinese nei secoli XIII–XV." In *Strutture familiari,* pp. 153–81.
Cristiani, Emilio. "Città e campagna nell'età comunale in alcune pubblicazioni dell'ultimo decennio," *Rivista Storica Italiana,* 75 (1963): 829–45.
Dameron, George. *Episcopal Power and Florentine Society 1000–1320.* Cambridge, Mass., 1991.

"Patrimony and Clientage in the Florentine Countryside: The Formation of the Estate of the Cathedral Chapter, 950–1200." In *Portraits of Medieval and Renaissance Living. Essays in Honor of David Herlihy.* Ed. by S. K. Cohn Jr. and S. A. Epstein. Ann Arbor, 1996, pp. 259–81.

Daniell, Christopher. *Death and Burial in Medieval England 1066–1550.* London, 1997.

Dean, Trevor. "Marriage and Mutilation: Vendetta in Late Medieval Italy," *Past and Present,* 157 (1997): 3–36.

Deregnaucourt, Jean-Pierre. "Autour de la mort à Douai: Attitudes, pratiques et croyances, 1250/1500." 2 vols. Thèse de troisième cycle, Université Charles de Gaulle, Lille, 1993.

"L'élection de sépulture d'après les testaments douaisiens (1295–1500), *Revue du Nord,* 65 (1983): 343–52.

Di Simplicio, Oscar. *Le rivolte contadine in Europa: I grandi movimenti che scuotono le campagne nell'epoca moderna.* Rome, 1985.

Du Cange, Carolo Dufresne. *Glossarium ad Scriptores mediae et infimae Latinitatis.* 6 vols. Paris, 1733–6.

Eckstein, Nicholas. *The District of the Green Dragon. Neighbourhood Life and Social Change in Renaissance Florence.* Florence, 1995.

Elam, Caroline and Ernst Gombrich. "Lorenzo de' Medici and a Frustrated Villa Project at Vallombrosa." In *Florence and Italy. Renaissance Studies in Honour of Nicolai Rubinstein.* Ed. by Peter Denley and Elam. London, 1988, pp. 481–92.

The English Rising of 1381. Ed. by R. H. Hilton and T. H. Aston. Cambridge, 1984.

Epstein, Stephan R. "Cities, Regions and the Late Medieval Crisis: Sicily and Tuscany Compared," *Past and Present,* 130 (1991): 3–50.

An Island for Itself. Economic Development and Social Change in Late Medieval Sicily. Cambridge, 1993.

"Regional Fairs, Institutional Innovation and Economic Growth in Late Medieval Europe," *Economic History Review,* 2nd ser. 47 (1994): 459–82.

Ertman, Thomas. *Birth of the Leviathan: Building States and Regimes in Medieval and Early Modern Europe.* Cambridge, 1997.

Fabbri, Lorenzo. "La sottomissione di Volterra allo stato fiorentino. Controllo istituzionale e strategie di governo (1361–1435)." Ph.D. diss. Università degli Studi di Firenze, 1994.

Fasano Guarini, Elena. "Centro e periferia, accentramento particolarismi: dicotomia o sostanza degli Stati in età moderna?" In *Origini dello Stato: Processi di formazione statale in Italia fra medioevo ed età moderna.* Ed. by Giorgio Chittolini, Anthony Molho, and Pierangelo Schiera. Bologna, 1994, pp. 147–76.

"Gli Stati dell'Italia centro-settentrionale tra Quattro e Cinquecento: continuità e trasformazioni," *Società e Storia,* no. 21 (1983): 617–39.

Fioravanti, Iacopo Maria. *Memorie storiche della città di Pistoja.* Lucca, 1758.

Fiorini, Vittorio. *Istorie Fiorentine di Niccolò Machiavelli.* Florence, 1894.

Fiumi, Enrico. *Demografia, movimento urbanistico e classi sociali in Prato dall'età comunale ai tempi moderni.* Florence, 1968.

"Fioritura e decadenza dell'economia fiorentina," part 1, *ASI*, 115 (1957): 385–439; part 2, 116 (1958): 443–510; part 3, 117 (1959): 427–502.

Storia economica e sociale di San Gimignano. Florence, 1961.

"Sui rapporti economici tra città e contado nell'età comunale," *ASI*, 114 (1956): 18–68.

Florentine Studies: Politics and Society in Renaissance Florence. Ed. by Nicolai Rubinstein. London, 1968.

Florentine Tuscany: Structures and Practices of Power. Ed. by William Connell and Andrea Zorzi. Cambridge, forthcoming.

Fourquin, Guy. *Les soulèvements populaires au Moyen Age.* Paris, 1972.

Franceschi, Franco. *Oltre il "Tumulto": I fiorentini dell'Arte della Lana fra Tre e Quattrocento.* Florence, 1993.

Francovich, Riccardo. *I Castelli del contado fiorentino nei secoli XII e XIII.* Florence, 1976.

Friedman, David. *Florentine New Towns: Urban Design in the Late Middle Ages.* Cambridge, 1988.

Fubini, Riccardo. "Dalla rappresentanza sociale alla rappresentanza politica. Sviluppi politico-costituzionali in Firenze dal Tre al Cinquecento." In *Italia Quattrocentesca. Politica e diplomazia nell'età di Lorenzo il Magnifico.* Milan, 1994, pp. 41–61.

"Diplomazia e governo in Firenze all'avvento dei reggimenti oligarchici." In *Quattrocento fiorentino. Politica, diplomazia, cultura.* Pisa, 1996, pp. 11–98.

"Le edizioni dei 'Libri fabarum'." In *I Consigli della repubblica fiorentina. Libri fabarum XVII (1338–1340).* Ed. by Francesca Klein. Rome, 1995, pp. xi–xxi.

"From Social to Political Representation in Renaissance Florence." In *City States in Classical Antiquity and Medieval Italy.* Ed. by A. Molho, K. Raaflaub, and J. Emlen. Stuttgart, 1991, pp. 223–39.

"Italia quattrocentesca: un'introduzione." In *Italia Quattrocentesca*, pp. 19–39.

"Prestito ebraico e Monte di Pietà a Firenze (1471–1473)." In *Quattrocento fiorentino*, pp. 159–216.

"Il regime di Cosimo de' Medici al suo avvento al potere." In *Italia Quattrocentesca*, pp. 62–86.

"Renaissance Historian: The Career of Hans Baron," *Journal of Modern History*, 64 (1992): 541–74.

"La rivendicazione di Firenze della sovranità e il contributo delle 'Historiae' di Leonardo Bruni." In *Leonardo Bruni cancelliere della repubblica di Firenze (Convegno di studi [Firenze, 27–29 ottobre 1987]).* Ed. by Paolo Viti. Florence, 1990, pp. 29–62.

Gigliotti, Giovan Carlo. "Introduzione." In *Cronache di Ser Luca Dominici*.

Gilbert, Felix. *Machiavelli and Guicciardini: Politics and History in Sixteenth-Century Florence.* Princeton, 1965.

Goldthwaite, Richard. "I prezzi del grano a Firenze dal XIV al XVI secolo," *Quaderni Storici*, 10 (1975): 5–36.

Private Wealth in Renaissance Florence: A Study of Four Families. Princeton, 1968.

Gonon, Marguerite. *Les Institutions et la société en Forez au XIVe siècle d'après les testaments.* Mâcon, 1960.

Grohmann, Alberto. *L'imposizione diretta nei comuni dell'Italia centrale nel XIII secolo: La libra di Perugia del 1285.* Rome, 1986.

Grubb, James. *First Born of Venice: Vicenza in the Early Renaissance State.* Baltimore, 1988.

Guidi, Guidubaldo. *Il Governo della città-repubblica di Firenze del primo Quattrocento,* I: *Politica e diritto pubblico*; II: *Gli istituti "di dentro" che componevano il governo di Firenze nel 1415.* Florence, 1981.

Gutkind, Kurt S. *Cosimo de' Medici, il Vecchio.* Florence, 1940.

Hanagan, Michael, Leslie Moch, and Te Brake, eds. *Challenging Authority. The Historical Study of Contentious Politics.* Minneapolis, 1998.

Hankins, James. "The 'Baron Thesis' after Forty Years and Some Recent Studies of Leonardo Bruni," *Journal of the History of Ideas,* 56 (1995): 309–38.

Hatcher, John. "England in the Aftermath of the Black Death," *Past and Present,* 144 (1994): 3–35.

Plague, Population and the English Economy 1348–1530. London, 1977.

Henderson, John. *Piety and Charity in Late Medieval Florence.* Oxford, 1994.

Herlihy, David. *The Black Death and the Transformation of the West.* Ed. by Cohn. Cambridge, Mass., 1997.

"Direct and Indirect Taxation in Tuscan Urban Finances, ca. 1200–1400." In *Finances et comptabilité urbaines du XIIIe au XIVe siècle.* Brussels, 1964, pp. 385–405.

"The Josephine Waters Bennett Lecture: Tuscan Names, 1200–1530," *Renaissance Quarterly* 41, no. 4 (1988): 561–83.

Medieval and Renaissance Pistoia. The Social History of an Italian Town, 1200–1430. New Haven, 1967.

"The Problem of the 'Return to the Land' in Tuscan Economic History of the Fourteenth and Fifteenth Centuries." In *Civiltà ed economia,* pp. 401–21.

"The Rulers of Florence, 1282–1530." In *City States in Classical Antiquity and Medieval Italy.* Ed. by A. Molho, K. Raaflaub, and J. Emlen. Stuttgart, 1991, pp. 197–221.

"Santa Maria Impruneta: A Rural Commune in the Late Middle Ages." In *Florentine Studies,* pp. 242–76.

"Veillir à Florence au Quattrocento," *Annales, E.S.C.,* 24 (1969): 1338–52.

Herlihy, David and Christiane Klapisch-Zuber. *Les Toscans et leurs familles. Une étude du Catasto florentin de 1427.* Paris, 1978.

Higounet, Charles. "Les 'terre nuove' florentines du XIV siècle." In *Studi in onore di Ammintore Fanfani,* III. Milan, 1962, pp. 3–17.

Hilton, R. H. *Bondsmen Made Free. Medieval Peasant Movements and the English Rising of 1381.* London, 1973.

Hintze, Otto. "Military Organization and the Organization of the State." In *The Historical Essays of Otto Hintze.* Ed. by Felix Gilbert. New York, 1975, pp. 178–215.

Household and Family in Past Time. Ed. by Peter Laslett and Richard Wall. Cambridge, 1972.

Ianzitti, Gary. "A Humanist Historian and his Documents: Giovanni Simonetta, Secretary to the Sforzas," *Renaissance Quarterly*, 34 (1981): 491–516.

Humanist Historiography under the Sforzas. Politics and Propaganda in Fifteenth-Century Milan. Oxford, 1988.

Johnson, Géraldine. "The Lion in the Piazza: Patrician Politics and Public Statuary in Central Florence." In *Secular Sculpture, 1350–1550*. Ed. by Thomas Frangenberg and Phillip Lindley. Stanford, 1999.

Jones, Philip J. "Commune and Despots: The City-State in Late-Medieval Italy," *Transactions of the Royal Historical Society*. 5th ser. 15 (1965): 71–96.

The Italian City-State: From Commune to Signoria. Oxford, 1997.

"Italy." In *The Cambridge Economic History of Europe*, I. Ed. by M. M. Postan. Cambridge, 1966, pp. 340–431.

"Review of Baron," *History*, 53, no. 179 (Oct., 1968): 410–13.

Kent, D. V. "Dinamica del potere e patronato nella Firenze del Medici." In *Ceti dirigenti nella Toscana del Quattrocento*. Florence, 1987.

The Rise of the Medici: Faction in Florence 1426–1434. Oxford, 1978.

Kent, D. V. and F. W. Kent. *Neighbours and Neighbourhood in Renaissance Florence. The District of the Red Lion in the Fifteenth Century*. Locust Valley, N.Y., 1982.

Kent, F. W. *Household and Lineage in Renaissance Florence: The Family Life of the Capponi, Ginori, and Rucellai*. Princeton, 1977.

Klapisch-Zuber, Christiane. "Mezzadria e insediamenti rurali alla fine del medio evo." In *Civiltà ed economia*, pp. 149–64.

"Women Servants in Florence during the Fourteenth and Fifteenth Centuries." In *Women and Work in Preindustrial Europe*. Ed. by Barbara A. Hanawalt. Bloomington, 1986, pp. 56–80.

Klapisch-Zuber, Christiane and Michel Demonet, "A Correspondence Analysis of a XVth Century Census: the Florentine Catasto of 1427," *Journal of European Economic History*, 4 (1975): 415–28.

"'A uno pane e uno vino': La famille rurale toscane au début du XVe siècle," *Annales, E.S.C.*, 27 (1972): 873–901.

Kotel'nikova, L. A. *Mondo contadino e città in Italia dal XI al XIV secolo dalle fonti dell'Italia centrale e settentrionale*. Bologna, 1975 [Moscow, 1967].

Kuehn, Thomas. "'Cum Consensu Mundualdi': Legal Guardianship of Women in Quattrocento Florence," *Viator* 13 (1982): 309–33.

La Letteratura italiana, XXXI, part 1. *Storici e politici fiorentini del Cinquecento*. Ed. by Angelo Baiocchi. Naples, 1994.

La Letteratura italiana: Gli Autori, Dizionario bio-bibliografico e Indici. 2 vols. Ed. by Giorgio Inglese. Turin, 1991.

Lamberini, Daniela. *Calenzano e la Val di Marina: storia di un territorio fiorentino*. 2 vols. Bologna, 1987.

Lanza, Antonio. *Firenze contro Milano: Gli intellettuali fiorentini nelle guerre con i Visconti (1390–1440)*. Rome, 1991.

Larner, John. "Crossing the Romagnol Appennines in the Renaissance." In *City and Countryside*, pp. 147–70.

The Lords of Romagna: Romagnol Society and the Origins of the Signorie. New York, 1965.

la Roncière, Charles M. de. "Aspects de la religiosité populaire en Toscane: le contado florentine des années 1300." In *La Toscana nel secolo XV: Caratteri di una civiltà regionale.* Ed. by S. Gensini. Pisa, 1988, pp. 337–84.

Un changeur florentin du Trecento: Lippo di Fede del Sega (1285 env. – 1363 env.). Paris, 1973.

"Les confrèries à Florence et dans son contado aux XIV–XVe siècles." In *Le mouvement confraternal au Moyen Age: France, Italie, Suisse: Actes de la table ronde organisée par l'Université de Lausanne, 9–11 mai 1985.* Rome, 1987, pp. 297–339.

"Dans la campagne florentine au XIVe siècle: les communautés chrétiennes et leurs curés." In *Histoire vécue du peuple chrétien.* Ed. by Jean Delumeau. Toulouse, 1976, pp. 281–314.

"Fidélités, patronages, clientèles dans le contado florentin au XIVe siècle," *Ricerche Storiche* 15, no. 1 (1985): 35–60.

"Indirect Taxes or 'Gabelles' at Florence in the Fourteenth Century: The Evolution of Tariffs and Problems of Collection." In *Florentine Studies*, pp. 140–92.

"L'influence des franciscains dans la campagne de Florence au XIVe siècle (1280–1360)," *Mélanges de l'Ecole française de Rome: Moyen âge-Temps moderns*, 87, no. 1 (1975): 27–103.

"A Monastic Clientele? The Abbey of Settimo, its Neighbours and its Tenants (Tuscany, 1280–1340)." In *City and Countryside*, pp. 55–67.

"Orientations pastorales du clergé, fin du XIIIe–XIVe siècle: le témoignage de l'onomastism toscane." In *Académie des Inscriptions et Belles-lettres. Comptes-rendus des séances de l'année, 1983 janvier–mars.* Paris, 1983, pp. 43–65.

Prix et salaires à Florence au XIVe siècle (1280–1380). Rome, 1987.

Lauwers, Michel. *La mémoire des ancêtres, le souci des morts. Morts, rites et société au moyen age.* Paris, 1997.

Law, John E. " 'Super differentiis agitatis Venetiis inter districtuales et civitatem' – Venezia, Verona e il contado nell' 400," *Archivio Veneto*, 116 (1981): 5–32.

Le Roy Ladurie, Emmanuel. "Chaunu, Lebrun, Vovelle. The New History of Death." In *The Territory of the Historian.* Paris, 1973; Chicago, 1979, pp. 273–84.

"The 'Event' and the 'Long Term' in Social History: The Case of the Chouan Uprising." In *The Territory of the Historian*, pp. 111–32.

"L'histoire immobile," *Annales, E.S.C.*, 29 (1974): 673–92.

Les paysans de Languedoc, 2 vols. Paris, 1966.

Leverotti, Franca. "La crisi demografica nella Toscana del trecento: l'esempio delle Sei Miglia lucchesi." In *La Toscana nel secolo XIV. Caratteri di una civiltà regionale.* Pisa, 1988, pp. 67–150.

Popolazione, famiglie, insedimento: Le Sei Miglia lucchesi nel XIV e XV secolo. Pisa, 1992.

Lillie, Amanda. "Lorenzo de' Medici's Rural Investments and Territorial Expansion," *Rinascimento*, 36 (1993): 53–67.

Litchfield, R. Burr. *Emergence of a Bureaucracy: The Florentine Patricians 1530–1790.* Princeton, 1986.

Luzzato, Gino. "L'inurbamento delle popolazioni rurali in Italia nei secoli XII e XIII." In *Studi di storia e diritto in onore di Enrico Besta,* II. Milan, 1939, pp. 183–203.

McNeill, J. R. *The Mountains of the Mediterranean World: An Environmental History.* Cambridge, 1992.

Magna, Laura. "Gli Ubaldini del Mugello: Una signoria feudale nel contado fiorentino." In *I ceti dirigenti dell'età comunale nei secoli XII e XIII. Atti del II Convegno, Firenze, 14–15 dicembre 1979.* Pisa, 1982, pp. 13–66.

Maire Vigueur, Jean-Claude. "Per una periodizzazione delle lotte contadine nell'Italia medievale." In *Protesta e rivolta,* pp. 261–8.

"Les rapports ville-campagne dans l'Italie communale: pour une révision des problèmes." In *La ville, la bourgeoisie et la genèse de l'état moderne (XIIe–XVIIIe siècles).* Ed. by Neithard Bulst and J.-Ph. Genet. Bielefeld, 1985, pp. 21–34.

Maitland, Frederic William. *Domesday Book and Beyond: Three Essays in the Early History of England.* Cambridge, 1987.

Mallet, Michael. *The Florentine Galleys in the Fifteenth Century.* Oxford, 1967.

"Pisa and Florence in the Fifteenth Century: Aspects of the Period of the First Florentine Domination." In *Florentine Studies,* pp. 403–41.

Martines, Lauro. "Forced Loans: Political and Social Strain in Quattrocento Florence," *Journal of Modern History,* 60, no. 2 (1988): 300–11.

Lawyers and Statecraft in Renaissance Florence. Princeton, 1968.

Marzi, Demetrio. *La Cancelleria della Repubblica Fiorentina.* Rocca San Casciano, 1910.

Mazzi, Maria Serena and Sergio Raveggi. *"Gli uomini e le cose" nelle campagne fiorentine del Quattrocento.* Florence, 1983.

Melis, Federigo. *Aspetti della vita economica medievale. Studi nell'archivio Datini di Prato.* Siena, 1962.

"Momenti dell'economia del Casentino nei secoli XIV e XV". In Melis, *Industria e commercio nella Toscana medievale.* Ed. by Bruno Dini. Florence, 1989, pp. 192–211.

Miliband, Ralph. *The State in Capitalist Society.* London, 1969.

Molho, Anthony. "Buoninsegni, Domenico." In *Dizionario biografico degli Italiani,* XV. Rome, 1972, pp. 251–2.

"Cosimo de' Medici: 'Pater Patriae' or 'Padrino'?" *Stanford Italian Review,* 1 (1979): 5–33.

"Domenico di Leonardo Buoninsegni, *Istoria Fiorentina,*" *Renaissance Quarterly,* 23 (1970): 256–66.

"Fisco ed economia a Firenze alla viglia del Concilio," *ASI,* 148 (1990): 807–44.

"Fisco e società a Firenze nel Quattrocento (a proposito di una ricerca di Elio Conti)," *Società e Storia,* no. 30 (1985): 929–36.

"The Florentine Oligarchy and the *Balìa* of the Late Trecento," *Speculum,* 43 (1968): 23–51.

Florentine Public Finances in the Early Renaissance, 1400–1433. Cambridge, Mass., 1971.
"Investimenti nel Monte delle Doti di Firenze: Un analisi sociale e geografica," *Quaderni Storici*, 61 (1986): 147–70.
Marriage Alliance in Late Medieval Florence. Cambridge, Mass., 1994.
"A Note on Jewish Moneylenders in Tuscany in the Late Trecento and Early Quattrocento." In *Renaissance Studies in Honor of Hans Baron.* Ed. by Molho and John Tedeschi. Florence, 1971, pp. 97–117.
Politics and the Ruling Class in Early Renaissance Florence," *Nuova Rivista Storica*, 52 (1968): 401–20.
"Lo stato e la finanza pubblica. Un'ipotesi basata sulla storia tardomedioevale di Firenze." In *Origini dello Stato: Processi di formazione statale in Italia fra medioevo ed età moderna.* Ed. by G. Chittolini, A. Molho, and Pierangelo Schiera. Bologna, 1994, pp. 225–80.
Mollat, Michael and Philippe Wolff. *Popular Revolutions of the Late Middle Ages.* Transl. by A. L. Lytton-Sells. London, 1973.
Monti, Alessandro and Franek Sznura. *"Riparo della città", Il Castello di Campi nel Trecento: Un caso di ristrutturazione urbanistica.* Signa, 1997.
Moon, David. "Reassessing Russian Serfdom," *European History Quarterly*, 26, no. 4 (1996): 481–526.
Mucciarelli, Roberta and Gabriella Piccinni. "Un'Italia senza rivolte? Il conflitto sociale nelle aree mezzadrili." In *Protesta e rivolta*, pp. 173–205.
Muzzi, Oretta. "Aspetti dell'evoluzione demografica della Valdelsa fiorentina nel tardo medioevo (1350–1427)." In *Strutture familiari*, pp. 135–52.
Najemy, John. *Corporatism and Consensus in Florentine Electoral Politics, 1280–1400.* Chapel Hill, N.C., 1982.
"The Dialogue of Power in Florentine Politics." In *City States in Classical Antiquity and Medieval Italy.* Ed. by A. Molho, K. Raaflaub, and J. Emlen. Stuttgart, 1991, pp. 269–88.
"Guild Republicanism in Trecento Florence: The Successes and Ultimate Failure of Corporate Politics," *American Historical Review*, 84 (1979): 53–71.
Oman, Sir Charles W. C. *The Great Revolt of 1381.* Oxford, 1906.
Ottaviani, Maria Grazia Nico. "Sistemi cittadini e comunità rurali nell'Umbria del Due-Trecento." In *Protesta e rivolta*, pp. 83–113.
Ottokar, Nicola. *Il comune di Firenze alla fine del dugento.* Florence, 1926.
Paganini dal Ventura, Giovanni Francesco. *Della Decima e di varie altre gravezze imposte dal comune di Firenze.* 4 vols. Lisbon, 1765–6.
Palmieri, Arturo. *La montagna bolognese del Medio Evo.* Bologna, 1929.
Pandimiglio, Leonida. "Giovanni di Pagolo Morelli e la ragion di famiglia." In *Studi sul Medioevo cristiano offerti a Raffaello Morghen*, II. Rome, 1974, pp. 553–608.
Panero, Francesco. "Popolamento e movimenti migratori nel contado vercellese, nel Biellese e nella Valsesia (secoli X–XIII)." In *Strutture familiari*, pp. 329–54.
Pasqui, Ubaldo. "Una congiura per liberare Arezzo dalla dipendenza dei Fiorentini (1431)," *ASI*, ser. 5 55 (1890): 3–19.

Patronage, Art and Society in Renaissance Italy. Ed. by F. W. Kent and Patricia Simons. Oxford, 1987.

Percorsi e valichi dell'Appennino fra storia e leggenda. Futa, Osteria Bruciata, Giogo. Manifestazione espositiva itinerante. Florence, 1985.

Perrens, François Tommy. *Histoire de Florence depuis la domination des Médicis jusqu'à la chute de la république (1434–1531).* 3 vols. Paris, 1888–90.

Petralia, Giuseppe. " 'Crisi' ed emigrazione dei ceti eminenti a Pisa durante il primo dominio fiorentino: L'orizzonte cittadino e la ricerca di spazi esterni." In *I ceti dirigenti nella Toscana del Quattrocento.* Florence, 1987, pp. 291–352.

"Fiscality, Politics and Dominion in Florentine Tuscany at the End of the Middle Ages." In *Florentine Tuscany.*

"Imposizione diretta e dominio territoriale nella repubblica fiorentina del Quattrocento." In *Società, istituzioni, spiritualità: Studi in onore di Cinzio Violante,* II. Spoleto, 1994, pp. 639–52.

Pezzarossa, Fulvio. "La tradizione fiorentina della memorialistica." In *La "Memoria" dei mercatores: Tendenze ideologiche, ricordanze, artigianato in versi nella Firenze del Quattrocento.* Ed. by G. M. Anselmi, F. Pezzarossa and L. Avellini. Bologna, 1980, pp. 41–149.

Pini, Antonio Ivan. "Un aspetto dei rapporti tra città e territorio nel Medioevo: la politica demografica 'ad elastico' di Bologna fra il XII e il XIV secolo." In *Studi in Memoria di Federigo Melis,* I. Naples, 1978, pp. 365–408.

Pinto, Giuliano. *Città e spazi economici nell'Italia comunale.* Bologna, 1996.

"Controllo politico e ordine pubblico nei primi vicariati fiorentini: Gli atti criminali degli ufficiali forensi," *Quaderni Storici,* 49 (1982): 226–41.

La Toscana nel tardo medio evo: Ambiente, economia rurale, società. Florence, 1982.

Pirillo, Paolo "Uno caso di pianificazione territoriale nel contado di Firenze (secc. XIII–XIV)." In *Studi e Ricerche: Istituto di Storia* I. Florence, 1981, pp. 179–200.

Plesner, Johan. *L'émigration de la campagne à la ville libre de Florence au 13e siècle.* Copenhagen, 1934.

Una rivoluzione stradale del dugento. Copenhagen, 1938.

Pocock, J. G. A. *The Machiavellian Moment.* Princeton, 1975.

Pounds, N. J. G. *An Historical Geography of Europe.* Cambridge, 1990.

Prato: Storia di una città, I, part 2: *Ascesa e declino del centro medievale (dal Mille al 1494).* Ed. by Giovanni Cherubini. Prato, 1991.

Procacci, Ugo. *Studio sul catasto fiorentino.* Florence, 1996.

"Sulla cronologia delle opere di Masaccio e di Masolino tra il 1425 e il 1428," *Rivista d'Arte* (1953), xxviii, 3a ser.-vol. III (Florence, 1954): 3–55.

"L'uso dei documenti negli studi di Storia dell'Arte e le vicende politiche ed economiche in Firenze durante il primo Quattrocento nei loro rapporti con gli artisti." In *Donatello e il suo tempo. Atti dell'VIII convegno internazionale di Studi sul Rinascimento Firenze-Padova 1966.* Florence, 1968, pp. 11–39.

Protesta e rivolta contadina nell'Italia medievale. Ed. by Giovanni Cherubini. In *Annali dell'Istituto "Alcide Cervi",* no. 16 (1994).

Putnam, B. H. *The Enforcement of the Statutes of Labourers during the First Decade After the Black Death.* New York, 1908.

Rado, Antonio. *Dalla Repubblica fiorentina alla Signoria medicea. Maso degli Albizi, e il partitio oligarchico in Firenze dal 1382 al 1393.* Florence, 1926.

Raggio, Osvaldo. *Faide e parentelle: Lo stato genovese visto dalla Fontanabuona.* Turin, 1990.

Rambaldi, Susanna Peyrouel. "Podestà e inquisitori nella montagna modenese: Riorganizzazione inquisitoriale e resistenze locali (1570–1590)," *Società e Storia*, no. 52 (1991): 297–328.

Raveggi, Sergio. "La condizione di vita." In *Prato: Storia di una città*, I, part 2, pp. 479–528.

Regni, Claudio. "Fiscalità cittadina e comunità rurali: Perugia, secoli XIV e XV." In *Protesta e rivolta*, pp. 139–55.

Repetti, Emmanuele. *Dizionario storico della Toscana.* 6 vols. Florence, 1833–45.

Ridolfi, Roberto. *Vita di Niccolò Machiavelli*, 2nd edn. Rome, 1954.

Rodolico, Niccolò. *La democrazia fiorentina nel suo tramonto, 1378–82.* Bologna, 1905.

Rokkan, Stein. "Dimensions of State Formation and Nation-Building: A Possible Paradigm for Research on Variations within Europe." In *The Formation of National States in Western Europe.* Ed. by C. Tilly. Princeton, 1975, pp. 562–600.

Rombai, Leonardo. "Per una storia della viabilità provinciale di Firenze: La 'rivoluzione stradale' dell'età comunale, gli interventi dei governi granducali, la gestione provinciale." In *Le Strade provinciali di Firenze: Geografia, storia e toponomastica*, I. Florence, 1992, pp. 83–115.

——. "Prefazione: Strade e politica in Toscana tra medioevo ed età moderna." In *Il Libro Vecchio di Strade della Repubblica fiorentina.* Ed. by Gabriele Ciampi. Florence, 1987, pp. 5–29.

Rombai, Leonardo and Marco Sorelli. "La viabilità del Mugello occidentale intorno alla metà del Settecento. Dall'assetto *ancien régime* alla 'rivoluzione stradale' lorenese." In *Percorsi e valichi*, pp. 35–49.

Rosenwein, Barbara. *To be the Neighbor of Saint Peter: The Social Meaning of Cluny's Property.* Ithaca, N.Y., 1989.

Rubinstein, Nicolai. "Cosimo optimus civis." In *Cosimo "il Vecchio" de' Medici, 1389–1464. Essays in Commemoration of the 600th Anniversary of Cosimo de' Medici's birth.* Ed. by Francis Ames-Lewis. Oxford, 1992, pp. 5–20.

——. *The Government of Florence under the Medici (1434 to 1494).* Oxford, 1966.

Salvadori, Patrizia. "Rapporti personali, rapporti di potere nella corrispondenza di Lorenzo de' Medici." In *Lorenzo il Magnifico e il suo tempo.* Ed. by G. C. Garfagnini. Florence, 1992, pp. 125–46.

Salvi, Michelangelo. *Historie di Pistoia e Fazioni d'Italia.* 3 vols. Rome, Pistoia, and Venice, 1656–62.

Sapori, Armando. *La crisi delle campagnie mercantile dei Bardi e dei Peruzzi.* Florence, 1926.

Seigal, Jerold. "'Civic Humanism' or Ciceronian Rhetoric? The Culture of Petrarch and Bruni," *Past and Present*, 34 (1966): 3–48.

Philosophy and Rhetoric in the Italian Renaissance. Princeton, 1966.

Shaw, Brent. "Bandit Highlands and Lowland Peace: The Mountains of Isauria-Cilicia," *Journal of the Social and Economic History of the Orient,* 33 (1990): 199–233 and 237–70.

Silva, Pietro. *Pisa sotto Firenze dal 1406 al 1433.* Pisa, 1910.

Skinner, Quentin. *The Foundations of Modern Political Thought.* 2 vols. Cambridge, 1978.

Skocpol, Theda. "Bringing the State Back In: Strategies of Analysis in Current Research." In *Bringing the State Back In.* Ed. by Peter Evans, Dietrich Rueschemeyer, and Skocpol. Cambridge, 1994, pp. 72–95.

Slicher Van Bath, B. H. *The Agricultural History of Western Europe, 500–1850.* Transl. by O. Ordish. London, 1963.

Stella, Alessandro. *La révolte des Ciompi: Les hommes, les lieux, le travail.* Paris, 1993.

Sterpos, Daniele. "Evoluzione delle comunicazioni transappenniniche attraverso tre passi del Mugello." In *Percorsi e valichi,* pp. 7–22.

Storia della letteratura italiana, II: *Il Trecento.* Ed. by Enrico Malato. Rome, 1995.

Strutture familiari, epidemie, migrazioni nell'Italia medievale. Ed. by Rinaldo Comba, Gabriella Piccinni, and Giuliano Pinto. Naples, 1984.

Szabó, Thomas. *Comuni e politica stradale in Toscana e in Italia nel medioevo.* Bologna, 1992.

Sznura, Franek. "Edilizia privata e urbanistica in tempo di crisi." In *Prato: Storia di una città,* I, part 2, pp. 301–58.

Te Brake, Wayne. *Shaping History: Ordinary People in European Politics, 1500–1700.* Berkeley, 1998.

Thomson, J. A. F. *The Transformation of Medieval England, 1370–1529.* London, 1983.

Tilly, Charles. *Coercion, Capital, and European States, AD 990–1992.* Cambridge, Mass., 1990.

"Entanglements of European Cities and States." In *Cities and the Rise of States in Europe, A.D. 1000 to 1800.* Ed. by Tilly and Wim Blockmans. Boulder, Colo., 1994, pp. 1–27.

"Reflections on the History of European State-Making." In *The Formation of National States in Western Europe.* Princeton, 1975, pp. 3–83.

Todd, Emmanuel. "Mobilité géographique et cycle de vie en Artois et en Toscane au XVIIIe siècle," *Annales, E.S.C.,* 30 (1974): 726–44.

Twigg, Graham. *The Black Death: A Biological Reappraisal.* London, 1984.

Valeri, Nino. *L'Italia nell'età dei principati,* 2nd edn. *Storia d'Italia,* IV. Milan, 1969.

Viazzo, Pier Paolo. *Upland Communities: Environment, Population and Social Structure in the Alps since the Sixteenth Century.* Cambridge, 1989.

Vitolo, Giovanni. "Rivolte contadine e brigantaggi nel Mezzogiorno angioino." In *Protesta e rivolta,* pp. 207–25.

Wallace, William. *Michelangelo at San Lorenzo. The Genius as Entrepreneur.* Cambridge, 1994.

Wallerstein, Immanuel. *The Modern World-System: Capitalist Agriculture and the Origins of the European World-Economy in the Sixteenth Century.* New York, 1974.

Weinstein, Donald. "The Myth of Florence." In *Florentine Studies*, pp. 15–44.

Weissman, Ronald. *Ritual Brotherhood in Renaissance Florence*. New York, 1982.

White, Stephen D. *Custom, Kinship, and Gifts to Saints. The Laudatio Parentum in Western France, 1050–1150*. Chapel Hill, N. C., 1988.

Wickham, Chris. "Economic and Social Institutions in Northern Tuscany in the Eighth Century." In *Istituzioni ecclesiastiche della Toscana medievale*. Ed. by Wickham, M. Ronzani, Y. Milo, and A. Spicciani. Galatina, 1980, pp. 7–34.

The Mountains and the City: The Tuscan Appennines in the Early Middle Ages. Oxford, 1988.

Wills, Christopher. *Plagues: Their Origin, History and Future*. London, 1996.

Witt, Ronald. "The Crisis after Forty Years," *American Historical Review*, 101, no. 1 (1996): 110–18.

Zangheri, Renato. *Catasti e storia della proprietà terriera*. Turin, 1980.

Zorzi, Andrea. *L'Amministrazione della giustizia penale nella Repubblica fiorentina: Aspetti e problemi*. Florence, 1988.

"I fiorentini e gli uffici pubblici nel primo Quattrocento: Concorrenza, abusi, illegalità," *Quaderni Storici*, 66, no. 3 (1987): 725–51.

"Giusdicenti e operatori di giustizia nello stato territoriale fiorentino del XV secolo," *Ricerche storiche*, 19, no. 3 (1989): 517–52.

"Lo Stato territoriale fiorentino (secoli XIV–XV): aspetti giurisdizionali," *Società e Storia*, no. 50 (1990): 799–825.

Index